Hengeworld

Mike Pitts, the only living archaeologist to have directed excavations at both Stonehenge and Avebury, studied at the Institute of Archaeology (University College London) before moving to Wiltshire for a stint as Curator of the Alexander Keiller Museum. He has written extensively for academic journals, as well as for radio, newspapers and popular magazines and his first book *Fairweather Eden* was published in 1997 to critical acclaim.

Also by Mike Pitts

Fairweather Eden

Hengeworld

Substantially revised, including the latest
on the newly discovered Stonehenge skeleton.

Mike Pitts

ARROW

Published by Arrow Books in 2001

1 3 5 7 9 10 8 6 4 2

First published in the United Kingdom in 2000 by Century

Arrow Books Limited
The Random House Group Limited
20 Vauxhall Bridge Road, London SW1V 2SA

Random House Australia (Pty) Limited
20 Alfred Street, Milsons Point, Sydney,
New South Wales 2061, Australia

Random House New Zealand Limited
18 Poland Road, Glenfield,
Auckland 10, New Zealand

Random House South Africa (Pty) Limited
Endulini, 5a Jubilee Road, Parktown 2193, South Africa

The Random House Group Limited Reg. No. 954009

www.randomhouse.co.uk

A CIP catalogue record for this book
is available from the British Library

Papers used by Random House UK Limited are natural, recyclable products made from wood
grown in sustainable forests. The manufacturing processes conform to the environmental
regulations of the country of origin.

ISBN 0 09 9278758

Typeset by MATS, Southend-on-Sea, Essex
Printed and bound in Great Britain by
Cox & Wyman Ltd, Reading, Berkshire

For my Mum and Dad

For new story developments, feedback, tourist information etc.
visit: www.hengeworld.co.uk

'The web at its best: useful, usable information, presented with
an irresistible twinkle of glee.' *Sunday Times Doors*

Hallowed Ground

On entering from the south-west by the car park
    observe in the field
to your left these geometric chalk-etched figures
    cognate in their symmetry
less to white horses than corn circles.

    Note too at the east
and west extremities (a solar orientation?)
    pairs of post-holes, empty,
which suggest poles may have been removed
    to be replanted annually
for a seasonal ritual. (Just when you think
    you've got the story
straight somebody always moves the goalposts.)

– from 'A Day at the Earth-house', in Philip Gross,
A Cast of Stones (Avebury: Digging Deeper 1996)

Contents

Plate captions

1 The sarsens of the huge outer circle at Avebury are all undressed, and betray the roughly hexagonal slab shapes of the original rocks. © Mike Pitts.

2 Modern Druidic ceremonies at Stonehenge are the contemporary manifestation of a continuing tradition of reinvention and rediscovery at the monument that reaches back to the very erection of the original megaliths 4000 years ago. © Mike Pitts

3 The first magnetometer survey at Stanton Drew (Sept 1997) revealed an astonishing array of concentric circles inside the great stone circle (white squares are standing stone positions) and a wider ring outside suggesting a filled ditch.

4 The subsequent caesium gradiometer survey (Oct 1997) showed the rings to consist of individual anomalies, most likely large numbers of huge post holes. Both images © Ancient Monuments Laboratory, English Heritage.

5 William Hawley (with moustache, seated right) with his men in 1920. Straightening of stone 7 has begun behind the iron fence. The men sit on the two pieces of stone 9, perhaps one of the first to have fallen, before 3600 years ago. © Stonehenge Archive Wessex Archaeology.

6 The straightening of stones 6 and 7 (here the lintel is being removed) in 1919–20 initiated the largest excavation project ever conducted at Stonehenge, directed by Hawley 1919–26. © Stonehenge Archive Wessex Archaeology.

7 Straightening trilithon 53/54 in 1964. The small standing stone in front of the metal frame is bluestone 37 (spotted dolerite). The larger fallen stone is sarsen 14. © Stonehenge Archive Wessex Archaeology.

8 There were originally four Station Stones on the periphery of Stonehenge (two survive). Their small, undressed shapes contrast with the massive architecture of the inner monument. © Mike Pitts.

9 Late afternoon every day, if the sun shines, the tooling on the side of sarsen 16 shows strongly, looking like adzework on timber. © Mike Pitts.

10 Bluestone 36 after excavation by Richard Atkinson, and before reburial, in 1954. The finely worked sockets on this stone (spotted dolerite) suggest it performed as a lintel in an unidentified structure before its incorporation in the bluestone circle. The standing stone behind is sarsen 11, a uniquely small stone in the outer circle. © Stonehenge Archive Wessex Archaeology.

11 The skeleton of the man killed by arrows excavated at Stonehenge in 1978 was extremely well preserved. These digital images show his skull and three views of the face fitted by Robin Richards. © Mike Pitts.

12 The most informative excavations at Avebury stone circle were conducted by Harold St George Gray 1908–22. Here his men pose in one of the deep ditch sections, with ladders made specially by the village carpenter. Photo H. Gray, © Alexander Keiller Museum.

13 William Stukeley drew the stone circles at the Sanctuary in 1723. The inner circle had just been removed, and the outer was about to go.

14 The site was rediscovered and excavated by Ben and Maud Cunnington in 1930. As well as the stone circles, they found concentric rings of post holes. Here their nephew Robert Cunnington (with notebook) stands in a stone pit, while the men either side of him stand in deeper post holes. Photo W. Young, © Alexander Keiller Museum.

15 At the author's Sanctuary excavation in 1999, considerable light was thrown on the earlier dig of 1930. © Mike Pitts.

16 The technology used in the 1930s by Alexander Keiller to re-erect megaliths at Avebury (here on the West Kennet Avenue) was not that far removed from what must have existed 4000 years before. Photo A. Keiller, © Alexander Keiller Museum.

17 Mark Brennand (in pit, right) assists in the removal of a 3000-year-old wooden post from Seahenge in 1999. © Mike Pitts.

18 A buried megalith discovered in 1999 at Avebury, part of the lost Beckhampton Avenue. Behind stand Andy Payne and Louise Martin (Ancient Monuments Laboratory geophysics survey), and Josh Pollard, one of the dig's directors. © Mike Pitts.

Preface to Paperback Edition

On 7 April 2000, a group of 'authorised volunteers' assembled around a boulder from the Preseli hills in south Wales. The goal was to move it to Stonehenge using timber, ropes and human muscle (the plan to wear 'appropriate clothing' of skins and furs had to be abandoned for safety reasons). It was no easy task. First unsuccessful attempts proved only that the size of the gang required to move it had been grossly misjudged. Under way, the stone reached only a third of the expected speed. The wooden sledge was appropriated by rivals. Original team members began to tire and drift away. At the nearby coast, the stone was roped between two hide-covered boats (narrowly avoiding the destruction of one) and floated out to sea. As the wind got up, the stone slipped its cradle and fell to the bottom.

There may have been eighty or ninety similar stones, weighing a total of about 300 tons, taken to Stonehenge over 4000 years ago.[1] The people who did this were not primitive, but modern humans like you and me. However, unlike the gang that lost their stone beneath the Pembrokeshire waves, their efforts were not monitored by the Health and Safety Executive and the local police. They could not advertise for more volunteers over the internet. If things went wrong, they could not hire a crane to right the stone, or seek assistance from professional, rubber-suited divers. They did not benefit from a generous Heritage Lottery Fund grant. Neither, I suppose, if asked why they were doing it, would they have replied they were 'having fun – the prehistoric way!' The original millennium goal was to reach Stonehenge at the autumn solstice in September. It is now approaching midsummer 2001. Perhaps it's all been abandoned: the website is still and the press releases have dried up.

The people involved may not see it this way, but for me the

modern project was a success. This was only the latest and most ambitious of many efforts at 'showing how it was done in the stone age'. As these experiments are often conducted for television, they are typically scheduled over a few days, and one way or another are brought to technical conclusion. The stone is moved and stood up or the bridge built. By failing to achieve their stated goal, the Welsh team proved a crucial point. We know, 4000 years ago, people could do it: Stonehenge was built. If today we can put a village into orbit, we can surely move a small rock a few hundred kilometres. But engineering is not just about ropes and poles. It is about people, about method and motivation. The achievement of the ancient Stonehenge is not just the monument, but the vision and the organisation behind it. Even as they searched the sea mud for their lost stone, Menter Preseli (the rural development group responsible) were demonstrating the superior skills of their Neolithic forebears in managing large projects. Huge numbers of people had to be mustered, fed and sheltered. The materials – massive timbers, ropes, hand tools and the stones themselves – had to be in the right place at the right time. Everyone from the child fetching water to the engineers, surveyors and skilled masons had to know their role and perform as part of a team. It was this that made the difference between farce, and Stonehenge.

Meanwhile, archaeologists have been having fun too. In just the few months since the first edition of *Hengeworld* went to press there have been developments affecting our understanding of both Stonehenge and Avebury. Excavations at Beckhampton continue. It looks as if Stukeley's suggestion that a 'cove' of three enormous megaliths once stood there is correct (page 206). Provisional radiocarbon dates for the ditched enclosure and the avenue suggest both are broadly contemporary with the Avebury rings, albeit this remains a tantalisingly vague statement (page 12). In the continuing wet weather, an old excavation shaft from the top of Silbury Hill collapsed, providing a unique opportunity to examine the mound interior. Exactly how this be done without endangering life is at this moment still under discussion.

Since I first wrote about human skeletons in Boles Barrow and the possible implications for the history of Stonehenge, I realised that the bones still survived for examination. I also considered a new dig at the barrow, as described in chapter 22. The bottom line for me is that the sheer size of the 'Boles stone' makes suggestions that it was found by William Cunnington in the barrow in 1801 patently absurd (judge for yourself by visiting Salisbury Museum's new Stonehenge gallery). I now find that archaeologist Arthur ApSimon came to the same conclusion ten years ago.[2] If this sounds too mysterious, all should be clear when you read chapter 22.

At Stonehenge itself the story of the remains of people buried there continues. In the first edition, I had had to write of an extraordinary lost skeleton that I had located: 'I am then in the interesting position of not knowing something you do, for when you read this the new date will have been published'. Well the new date was published, and I could hardly claim to have correctly predicted the result. I have substantially rewritten the last chapter, referring not only to the dating, but discussing the historical context and other scientific work that has been done, as well as explaining how the mystery of the unidentified Welsh dentist was solved.

I was able to lay to rest another unsolved problem about human remains with the discovery of a letter in the Public Record Office. We knew that four bags of bones had been re-buried at Stonehenge in 1935, but there was some uncertainty as to whether these were human or animal (chapter 13 and footnote 202). In the new letter Robert Newall had written to the Office of Works asking permission to bury 'all the [human] cremations found during the excavations at Stonehenge. I can see no use in keeping them. At present I have the bones in my loft . . .'

Today we can see great use in these bones. They are almost the only evidence we have for a major episode in the history of Stonehenge (chapter 15), and when, one day, the pit containing them is re-excavated the interest will be enormous (not least for the chance of dating the cremation cemetery, with a new radiocarbon technique for burnt bone).

If you are unfamiliar with Stonehenge archaeology, it will probably come as a surprise that something as apparently fundamental as the cremated remains of fifty Stonehenge people could have been stored in someone's roof-space, reburied and temporarily 'lost'. But this is in essence the story of Stonehenge in the twentieth century, and the legacy has yet to be righted. With the imminent construction of a substantial visitor reception area on the edge of the World Heritage Site, and the attendant improvements in facilities and environment, we have an opportunity to show due respect for our remote ancestors. I believe strongly that now is the time to build a proper museum for Stonehenge, at Stonehenge.

This is not a new idea. In 1927, when most of the finds from Stonehenge digs were still available to research, marmalade playboy Alexander Keiller offered to build a museum at his own expense, 'out of sight of but in close vicinity to the circle'. If this had happened, archaeology, and all of us, would be immeasurably the richer. But after much soul searching, the Office of Works declined Keiller's offer and instead bought 100 army sandbags at 3 1/4d each for the disposal of what was left. The major reason it never happened was public objection, and, astonishingly, the bulk of this came from archaeologists, in particular the Wiltshire Archaeological Society. A prominent member at the time claimed that there were 'not more than half a dozen objects . . . of any importance whatever' (Newall had catalogued 4577 objects in his home, and amongst stuff still stored in an old hut at Stonehenge were 86 stone hammers used to carve the megaliths and 70 antler 'picks' used to dig out the holes).[3]

Most of these stone and antler tools are now in Salisbury Museum. So if Stonehenge's finds are lost or well looked after in Salisbury, what would be the point of another museum?

The fact is, everything is not in Salisbury. Surviving finds and records, the physical archive for the entire history of Stonehenge, are scattered across at least sixteen institutional and private addresses. The major archive, created by the admirable English Heritage project that made this book possible, still has no permanent home. Curating documents, in particular, is essential if future generations are to continue investigating and re-thinking Stonehenge's story. The place to have the museum is where the people are, where museum and 'visitor facilities', academic and public, can interact. In the new visitor complex, this could be a concept that benefited from the best in museum technology and design, and in contemporary architecture. Does Stonehenge deserve anything less?

A new Stonehenge museum would:

1 curate all documents (excavation surveys, photos etc) relating to a defined curation area (eg the 2000 hectares of the World Heritage Site), including items held elsewhere (by 'curate', I mean facilitate the proper conservation, storage, recording, publication and arrangement of public access to artefacts or documents; by itself, it does not imply that things have to be stored in the new museum)

2 curate all artefacts as above

3 curate and hold everything from the curation area from date of museum establishment

4 maintain regularly updated permanent Stonehenge display

5 run programme of temporary exhibitions

6 publish catalogues of exhibitions and of holdings, and souvenir guides

7 deal with specialist and general enquiries about archaeology of Stonehenge and its landscape

8 act as communications centre for new Stonehenge research

9 consider conducting or commissioning original research

10 assist training of custodial staff in knowledge of Stonehenge and its landscape

11 build and maintain a comprehensive Stonehenge library

12 maintain an up to date Stonehenge web site

13 make all holdings available for bona fide researchers

Existing museums share responsibility for a few of these roles as far as what is in their own buildings. But the majority are completely unattended to. No archaeologist or historian, with special knowledge of Stonehenge, works in any existing museum with a Stonehenge collection. There is no organisation, public or private, whose major, let alone sole, concern is looking after Stonehenge. The results of this neglect are clear. A rock at the bottom of a Welsh harbour is not only the failure of a millennium game: it is an apt symbol for the way Stonehenge was treated by the twentieth century.

But it's not too late. In their ground-breaking plan for the Stonehenge World Heritage Site, prepared for English Heritage, Chris Blandford Associates wrote that the results of research:

> should be disseminated in a manner that is comprehensible and usable by both academic and popular audiences. The new visitor centre will have a particularly important role to play in this respect.[4]

We can, now, show we care.

---

[1] Though the opposing view has been well publicised, I believe it unreasonable to doubt, on current evidence, that the bluestones were taken to Stonehenge by people. In chapter 23 I refer to three

ancient plank-built boats from Yorkshire as indication that the marine technology was probably available at the time. When I wrote that, we thought the boats were 1000 years younger than Stonehenge. As this book goes to press, exciting confirmation of my case has appeared. New dates (which make laboratory allowance for the old preservatives used on the wood) have been announced, suggesting the boats are much closer to the age of Stonehenge. The original dates quoted in the text (page 210; footnote 454; Appendices 2–3: Ferriby boats 1–3) should now be ignored. The new dates are 1880–1680 cal BC (Ferriby 1), 1940–1720 cal BC (Ferriby 2) and 2030–1780 cal BC (Ferriby 3, 'likely to date to the earlier end of the range'). Information from Alex Bayliss and English Heritage Press Release 21 March 2001.

[2]   ApSimon, A. 1990. 'The Heytesbury Bluestone, Bowls Barrow or Stonehenge?' Unpublished typescript in Salisbury Museum.

[3]   Cremations: December 9 1934, Newall to Raby PRO WORK 14/2463. Wiltshire Archaeological Society: April 12 1929, B. H. Cunnington reported in Office of Works memo Raby to Earle PRO WORK 14/489.

[4]   Chris Blandford Associates 2000. *Stonehenge World Heritage Site Management Plan* (English Heritage: London), para 4.7.8.

Antiquaries (next to the Royal Academy in London), was a tea and biscuits affair, without a journalist in sight. But what a momentous occasion! For the first time, the information from all the digs at Stonehenge was made available.[5]

Meanwhile, the past forty-five years have seen some extraordinary discoveries in the landscape around Stonehenge and further afield. Academic debate on the meaning of these has been intense. Radiocarbon dating, newly developed when Atkinson wrote his book, is now a sophisticated science. As part of their Stonehenge study, English Heritage sponsored a large dating programme.

Of course, if none of this had changed our understanding of Stonehenge, if Atkinson and all those sampling his tunes were proved right, there would be no problem. But everything has changed. One of the world's most famous ancient ruins needs to be totally reinvented. That's what this book is about.

References to published works

You cannot measure Stonehenge and close the book. There will always be new things to learn, new ways of looking at the past: archaeologists know there can never be a 'standard study' (anything claiming to be this, or, as one recent title put it, to have 'finally solved the riddle', has by definition misunderstood Stonehenge and the nature of archaeology). It was no surprise to me that in the course of writing *Hengeworld* I made some significant new discoveries, reported on now for the first time. So for both the professional and the amateur with an interest to match my own, I have provided notes with full documentation. Short items are fully referenced in the notes. More substantial pieces are collected in the bibliography, and indexed in the notes using the Harvard reference system: 'Atkinson 1979', for example, refers to 'Atkinson, R. 1979. *Stonehenge* (3rd edn.). Harmondsworth: Penguin' in the bibliography.

Radiocarbon dating

Radiocarbon dating has been around for fifty years, but the process and the thinking behind its application are constantly developing. Stonehenge has benefited from a remarkable and pioneering new dating study. Our understanding of Hengeworld is due to change

Acknowledgements

You cannot write intelligently about Stonehenge or Avebury without drawing deeply on the work of archaeologists, and although not all of them would agree with all I say, I would first acknowledge the research and thoughts of others without which this book would have been impossible, not least those of the late Richard Atkinson. In the writing of *Hengeworld* I would particularly like to thank Alex Bayliss (English Heritage), Ros Cleal (Alexander Keiller Museum), Andrew David (English Heritage), Jackie McKinley (Wessex Archaeology), Josh Pollard (University of Wales, Newport) and Dave Wheatley (Southampton University) for continuing help and inspiration.

Thanks also to: Mike Allen (Wessex Archaeology), Richard Bradley (University of Reading), Mark Brennand (Norfolk Archaeological Trust), Chris Bronk Ramsey (ORAU, Oxford University), Don Brothwell (York University), Paul Bryan (English Heritage), Nick Burton (English Heritage), Roy Canham (Wilts County Council), Amanda Chadburn (English Heritage), Peter Clark (Canterbury Archaeological Trust), Mick Clowes (English Heritage), Pamela Coleman (Wiltshire Archaeological Society), Clare Conybeare (formerly Alexander Keiller Museum), Andrew Deathe (Salisbury and South Wilts Museum), Peter Drewett (Institute of Archaeology, London), Jeremy Dronfield, Margaret Ehrenburg, John Evans (University of Wales, Cardiff), Dave Field (RCHM, English Heritage), Kate Fielden, Mike Fulford (Reading University), Julie Gardiner (Wessex Archaeology), Alex Gibson (English Heritage), Mark Gillings (University of Leicester), Chris Gingell (National Trust), Chris Green (Royal Holloway University of London), Nick Griffiths, Phil Harding (Wessex Archaeology), Lorna Haycock (Wiltshire Archaeological Society), Frances Healy (Newcastle University), Claire Jackson (Royal College of Surgeons), Tony King (King Alfred's College, Winchester), Rob Kruszynski (Natural History

Museum), Andy Lawson (Wessex Archaeology), Paul Linford (English Heritage), George McDonic, Louise Martin (English Heritage), David Miles (English Heritage), Stuart Needham (British Museum), Terry O'Connor (York University), Simon Parfitt (Natural History Museum), Mike Parker Pearson (Sheffield University), Andy Payne (English Heritage), Francis Pryor (Fenland Archaeological Trust), Colin Richards (Glasgow University), Julian Richards, Robin Richards (University College Hospital, London), Paul Robinson (Wiltshire Archaeological Society), Clive Ruggles (Leicester University), Dale Serjeantson (Southampton University), Colin Shell (Cambridge University), Isobel Smith, Maisie Taylor (Fenland Archaeological Trust), Julian Thomas (Southampton University), Pete Topping (English Heritage), Geoff Wainwright (formerly English Heritage), Alan Wakefield (RAF Museum Hendon), Karen Walker (Wessex Archaeology), Alasdair Whittle (University of Wales, Cardiff), Andy Young (Avon Archaeological Unit).

I am grateful for Barbara West's instantly provided help with completing illustrations. Tom Blagg and Judy Medrington have again aided my London visits, for which much thanks, and not forgetting Zoë, who would be first, and Amanda who knows not the meaning of last.

The Channel 4 film 'Murder at Stonehenge' was both a personal pleasure and an opportunity to advance Stonehenge research. For making it work I would like to thank Pauline Duffy, Jeremy Freeston and Mark McMullen (YAP), Dave Batchelor, Suzanne Bode, Clews Everard, Elspeth Henderson, David Miles and all the Stonehenge staff (English Heritage), Paul Budd and Janet Montgomery (Archaeotrace), Mike Fulford (Reading University), Malin Holst and Sarah King (York University), Chris Knüsel (Bradford University), Andy Reynolds (Institute of Archaeology, UCL), Sarah Semple (Oxford University), Chris Stringer (Natural History Museum) and, not least, Ceri and Penrhyn Peach.

Finally, I should thank my editor, Mark Booth, and Random House (Century/Arrow) for not only publishing my lengthy footnotes, tables and bibliography, but also making it possible for me to update a book less than a year after it first went to press. In academic publishing such things are becoming unpopular: in a trade title like this it is little short of astonishing.

1

New Posts

On a shelf behind me are two or three dozen books about Stonehenge, at least half of them published in the last twenty years – and this is but a selection from those written in English. FASTSearch has just selected 55,978 web sites where I can read about Stonehenge, which even allowing for the legion of plumbers, double glaziers and insurance brokers who appear to have been named after a stone circle is a lot of Stonehenge reading. Stonehenge itself has changed little for at least five centuries. What more can there possibly be to say?

The writers of all this stuff rely, directly or indirectly, on a single title, Richard Atkinson's *Stonehenge*, for almost everything they confidently claim to know about the monument (none of them has actually dug there, and very few are archaeologists). Atkinson's book is forty-five years old, and is undoubtedly a classic, but it is grossly out of date and its arguments are frequently unsupported by evidence. For someone wishing to understand Stonehenge today, it is, frankly, irrelevant.[1]

We are interested in our past. In little more than a century the science of archaeology has risen from nothing to become one of the most popular degree topics at university, a big audience-puller on television (one evening in March 1999 a repeat archaeology film on BBC2 had more viewers than Channel 4's exclusive Monica Lewinsky interview), and the recipient of considerable grants and funds. Archaeology is now an arena where people from a huge variety of scientific and creative backgrounds get together and consider some of the most fascinating issues that concern us as an intelligent species.

But only a generation or so back, there were so few archaeologists that study of the entire sweep of human history in Britain – something we now know to encompass at least half a million years – had to be parcelled out between less than a dozen men. There were others, women amongst them, but there was a clear sense that

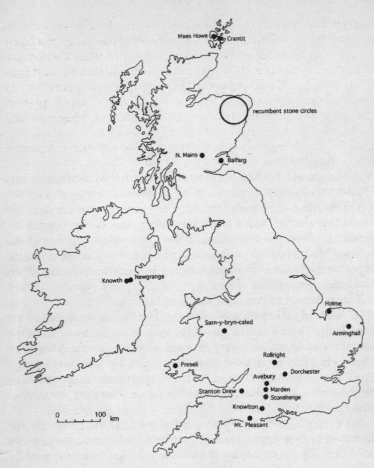

Figure 1. Some important locations mentioned in the text.

the grand picture of prehistory was being assembled by a male elite. And it so happened that Stonehenge fell to one of them, a shy, modest, conscientious objecter to war, one Richard John Copland Atkinson.

Atkinson first dug at Stonehenge in 1950, and continued on and off into the Sixties. In 1978, when a younger archaeologist was re-excavating one of Atkinson's trenches to gain some new insight into Stonehenge, the man himself was pottering about in the background, digging yet more holes in search of a solution to another tricky problem. And yet over all those years Atkinson analysed and published but a bare fraction of what he dug up. When you excavate a 4000-year-old deposit you destroy it. It is as if you have an old manuscript, of which only one copy survives. As you read the pages, you rip them up. If you don't quickly pass on the story, your memory becomes the only record. Then you find another manuscript, read and rip up; and another, and another, until the plot of one mixes with the argument of the next. You lose it.

What's more, Atkinson made it difficult for students to access records of excavations in the 1920s by William Hawley, also not fully published, that were far larger and more important than his own. This is why you will find so few recent books written by archaeologists about Stonehenge. We knew that too much of the information needed to understand the site was in Atkinson's head; in archives of earlier digs acquired and hoarded by him; and in his own unpublished and carefully guarded records (some of which only came to light after his death in 1994).

Rural archaeology doesn't get a lot more complex than Stonehenge. Without the modern array of specialists, scientific gadgets and processes, the many minds ready to consider each little issue, people like Hawley and Atkinson were struggling. Their public wanted a full and interesting story; their sponsors wanted the job done quickly with no fuss. Only archaeologists knew the truth of how difficult it really was.[2] So when, in 1995, English Heritage finally presented a detailed study of all the Stonehenge digs, it was no surprise that it had taken a large team. We learnt the astonishing and sobering fact that there were excavations at Stonehenge in over one year out of every three in the twentieth century. The Avenue, an important earthwork that runs for 2.75km from the stones, had a typical history. It had been dug into at various places on twenty different occasions since 1919, yet from only two of those projects had a full record survived.[3] The book had seventeen authors (eight of them women, including lead author Ros Cleal) and the project came under three different managers. The number of researchers involved was almost countless.

The appearance of *Stonehenge in its Landscape*, as this massive report was named, was a milestone.[4] Its launch, in the appropriately antique, creaking rooms of the Society of

Antiquaries (next to the Royal Academy in London), was a tea and biscuits affair, without a journalist in sight. But what a momentous occasion! For the first time, the information from all the digs at Stonehenge was made available.[5]

Meanwhile, the past forty-five years have seen some extraordinary discoveries in the landscape around Stonehenge and further afield. Academic debate on the meaning of these has been intense. Radiocarbon dating, newly developed when Atkinson wrote his book, is now a sophisticated science. As part of their Stonehenge study, English Heritage sponsored a large dating programme.

Of course, if none of this had changed our understanding of Stonehenge, if Atkinson and all those sampling his tunes were proved right, there would be no problem. But everything has changed. One of the world's most famous ancient ruins needs to be totally reinvented. That's what this book is about.

References to published works

You cannot measure Stonehenge and close the book. There will always be new things to learn, new ways of looking at the past: archaeologists know there can never be a 'standard study' (anything claiming to be this, or, as one recent title put it, to have 'finally solved the riddle', has by definition misunderstood Stonehenge and the nature of archaeology). It was no surprise to me that in the course of writing *Hengeworld* I made some significant new discoveries, reported on now for the first time. So for both the professional and the amateur with an interest to match my own, I have provided notes with full documentation. Short items are fully referenced in the notes. More substantial pieces are collected in the bibliography, and indexed in the notes using the Harvard reference system: 'Atkinson 1979', for example, refers to 'Atkinson, R. 1979. *Stonehenge* (3rd edn.). Harmondsworth: Penguin' in the bibliography.

Radiocarbon dating

Radiocarbon dating has been around for fifty years, but the process and the thinking behind its application are constantly developing. Stonehenge has benefited from a remarkable and pioneering new dating study. Our understanding of Hengeworld is due to change radically as more sites and objects are dated with new precision and accuracy.[6] Dating is discussed extensively in the text (for example, in chapter 13). There are internationally agreed conventions for quoting radiocarbon dates, yet few writers heed these, resulting in enormous confusion. For this reason it is necessary to make a clear statement on the use of radiocarbon dating in this book.

All the individual determinations ('dates') referred to in the text are gathered together in appendices, where they are listed with documentation: where the samples came from, what they consisted of, their laboratory numbers, the radiocarbon ages and the calibrated date ranges.[7] When quoted in the text, dates are referenced by their lab numbers, through which they can be checked against their appendix entries.

Radiocarbon dating by itself does not, and never will, produce a single specific date such as a year. Rather, the result is given as a probability range. For example, a piece of red deer antler from a pit in which one of the biggest megaliths at Stonehenge still stands, perhaps used in excavating the pit, produced a date of 3860±40 BP (OxA-4839). The ± (plus or minus) 40 is a normal error term quoted by the laboratory (in this case the Oxford Radiocarbon Accelerator Unit, of whose data base this is sample no. 4839) at one standard deviation. 'BP' stands for 'before present', which by convention is taken to be AD 1950. Before we can 'use' this date, it has to be calibrated by reference to known variations in the atmospheric source of radiocarbon. This is not an option: it is a necessity.

The result is an older date (at least for the time of Hengeworld) and a wider estimated range, now, again by convention, quoted in years BC. But in this case, the range is not simply a normal bell curve, where the central quoted number is statistically the most likely. The calibrated curve can be very flat or can have more than one peak, so that use of a standard error term would be inappropriate. Instead, an actual range is quoted: in the case of our example, 3860±40 BP becomes 2465-2200 cal BC (i.e. calibrated BC) at 95 per cent confidence (i.e. there is only a one in twenty chance that the 'real' date lies outside this range) (figure 2).

Even for archaeologists now getting used to this concept (very few of us, after all, are statisticians), comparing different phases from several different sites with a pile of date ranges can be mind-boggling; it has to be said that some of the outcomes are equally extraordinary. For this reason, I have listed central figures for these

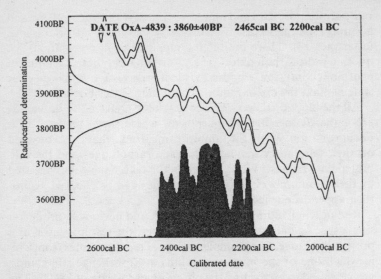

Figure 2. Graph for radiocarbon sample OxA-4839 (antler from Stonehenge trilithon pit) produced by the calibration program OxCal. The raw date is the bell curve on the left side (3860±40). The wobbly lines from top left to bottom right constitute the 'calibration curve', reflecting measured variations in global concentrations of atmospheric radioactive carbon. Combining the two produced the histogram at the bottom. This illustrates well the problem of using a central date derived from the calibrated result. There are five peaks here, at approximately 4440, 4390, 4320, 4215 and 4245 years ago (i.e. before 2000). Statistically, one of these is the most likely 'real' date (giving us a range of over two centuries between the extremes). But the central date is 4335 years ago.

ranges in the date appendices, and sometimes use these in the text. Thus 2465-2200 becomes 'around 4335 years ago', or perhaps 'about 4300 years ago'. It is important to realise that this 'about' figure is not necessarily any more likely as a 'correct' date than one near either end of the given range. Still more important is that these figures should not be used outside the context of this book. Do use the tables (as I write, they are the most complete listing of calibrated radiocarbon dates available for the period of Hengeworld). Do not use the single computed 'years ago' figure. Enough.[8]

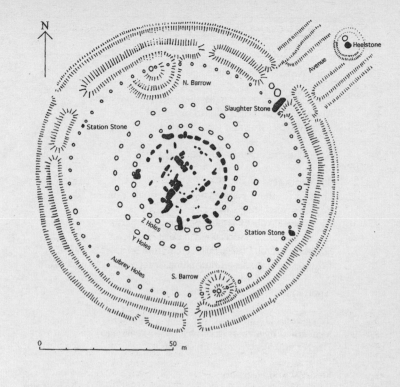

Figure 3. Stonehenge. The earthworks (inner circular bank, outer ditch and slight outer bank, North and South 'Barrows' – neither actually containing a burial – and Avenue banks and ditches) and megaliths (black shapes) are as can be seen today. The white shapes (the Aubrey Holes, the Y and Z Holes, beside the Heelstone and Slaughter Stone, and in the centre of each 'barrow') are prehistoric pits that have been excavated by archaeologists and refilled. The Aubrey Holes alone are marked by white discs in the turf. *After Cleal et al.*

Figure 4. Phases at Stonehenge.

Phase	Features
1:	Approximately 5000 years ago
1	Ditch and main inner bank dug, ditch primary filling
1	Ancient animal bones placed on ditch bottom
1	Aubrey Holes dug and used for posts
2:	Approximately 5000–4400 years ago
1 or 2	Smaller outer bank
2	Posts in southern passage and centre of monument
2	Posts on north-east causeway
2	First use of Aubrey Holes for cremation burial
2a	Secondary ditch filling, more cremation burials
2b	Features cut into secondary filling, some with Grooved Ware
3:	Approximately 4550–3600 years ago
3	Stone holes D and E
3	Man killed by arrows in ditch (*c.* 4300 years ago)
3	Dagger and axe carvings on sarsens
3a	Stone 97 and Heelstone
3b	Stone 97 removed, Heelstone ditch dug (bluestone near bottom)
3b	Station Stones and 'Barrows'
3c	Avenue ditches and banks dug (*c.* 4500–4000 years ago)
3i	Q and R Holes
3ii	Sarsen Circle and Trilithons (*c.* 4300 years ago)
3iii	Poorly understood features pre-dating 3iv
3iv	Bluestone Oval and Circle (*c.* 4100 years ago)
3v	Stones removed from Oval to leave Bluestone Horseshoe
3vi	Y and Z Holes (*c.* 3600 years ago)

After Cleal et al. 1995. The relationships between Phase 2 and those marked 2a–b, and between Phase 3 and those marked 3a–c and 3i–vi are not known.

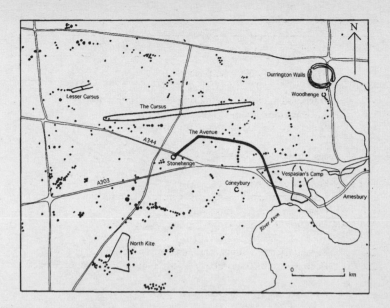

Figure 5. Stonehenge lies in the midst of a rich archaeological landscape that contains major earthworks contemporary with parts of its history (such as the Cursus and Durrington Walls) as well as the North Kite (early Bronze Age) and Vespasian's Camp (an Iron Age fort). The black spots are all burial mounds. *After Cleal et al.*

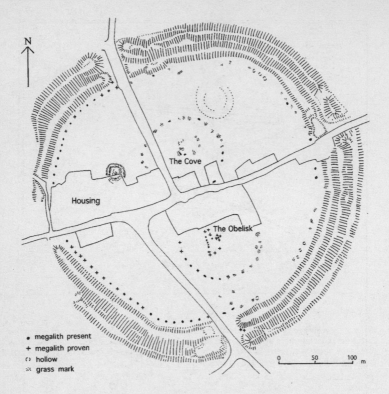

N

The Cove

Housing

The Obelisk

- • megalith present
- + megalith proven
- ⌒ hollow
- ⸜ grass mark

0   50   100 m

Figure 6. Compared to Stonehenge, there has been very little excavation inside Avebury. Even the great outer stone circle is known mostly from evidence visible on the surface. On the west side, Alexander Keiller re-erected megaliths or, when they were missing, placed concrete posts. To the east the former presence of stones is indicated by hollows, where stones were burnt and broken in the seventeenth and eighteenth centuries, or parch marks in the grass visible in drought, probably indicating complete buried megaliths. The two rings north-east of the Cove stone circle were revealed by geophysics, and may be the site of a timber henge. West of this circle concentric parch marks may represent a flattened burial mound. *After Bewley et al. and Ucko et al.*

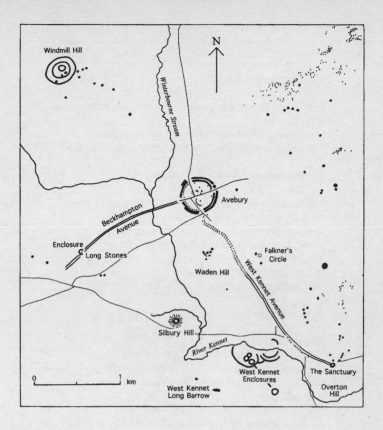

Figure 7. Avebury is notable for the two stone avenues, parallel rows of standing megaliths (the Beckhampton Avenue, almost completely gone, was proved to exist in 1999). The small spots to the east constitute the western edge of the natural sarsen 'fields' of the Marlborough Downs. Larger spots are barrows. *After Smith*.

Figure 8. Events at Avebury compared to Stonehenge.

Phase	Features
1:	Approximately 6000–5000 years ago
	Long barrows, including Beckhampton, South Street and West Kennet
	Enclosures on Windmill Hill (*c.* 5500 years ago)
	Activity of unknown nature at Avebury and other sites
2:	Approximately 5000–4500 years ago
	Beckhampton enclosure (4700–4300 years ago?)
	Avebury henge (*c.* 5000 years ago?)
	Avebury stone circles (4700–4300 years ago?)
	Beckhampton and West Kennet stone avenues?
	The Sanctuary?
	Silbury Hill (*c.* 4600 years ago?)
	West Kennet Enclosures (*c.* 4600–4200 years ago)
3:	Approximately 4500–3500 years ago
	Enlargement of Avebury henge?
	Avebury stone circles (4700–4300 years ago?)
	Beckhampton enclosure (4700–4300 years ago?)
	Beckhampton and West Kennet stone avenues?
	The Sanctuary?
	West Kennet Enclosures (*c.* 4600–4200 years ago)
	Burial of woman in Avebury ditch (*c.* 4100 years ago)
	Burials beside stones
	Hemp Knoll round barrow (*c.* 3900 years ago)

Most of the features in 2 and 3 are undated.

PART I:

From Woodhenge to Superhenge

2

A Very British Habit

On the evening of Monday 1 September 1997, Andrew David was at home with his family in London, when the phone rang.[9] It was his colleague Mark Cole, who was in Somerset with Tim Horsley, a student from the Department of Archaeological Sciences at Bradford University. Mark and Tim were ahead of Andrew, who was to join them the next day, starting a project at a large yet strangely overlooked stone circle on the edge of a little village known as Stanton Drew.

'I can't believe what we've found,' said Mark.

Andrew David is the head of English Heritage's Archaeometry Branch, a section of the internationally respected Ancient Monuments Laboratory (AML). Stanton Drew was one of those places he'd hoped to work on for years. In an old meadow stands the second largest stone circle in Britain. You can see twenty-seven megaliths today, in varying states of decay and collapse: originally there might have been thirty, in a ring about 110m across. Close by to the east is a small ring of eight stones, and a third to the south that perhaps once consisted of twelve stones. To the west, through the farm buildings and equidistant from the church and the pub, are two large stones known as the Cove. An obvious focus for research, you might think (figure 9). Actually there has never been an excavation here that anyone can remember. Nor any useful geophysical study till that September day.[10] There's not even a modern map of the stones.

So when, after much discussion in London, poring over plans, scheduling time and staff, Project Time Number 20019 was entered into the diary, Andrew David had every reason to be pleased. At such a large and unknown site, anything might turn up. And if it didn't, well, it was worth the try.

'We gridded out the site,' Mark was saying, 'took out the machines and started the survey. It was so quiet we thought nothing was being detected.'

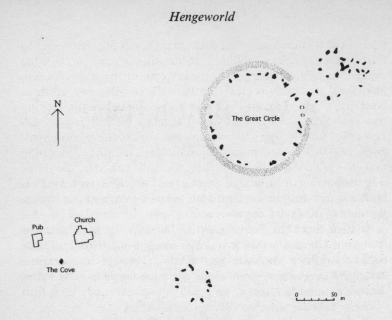

Figure 9. The ditch around the Great Circle at Stanton Drew (stippled) was first revealed by geophysics in 1997. The rings of post holes (not mapped) are inside the stones. There has been no excavation, but probing has revealed at least two buried stones (broken rings). In addition to two smaller stone circles and short avenue-like arrangements at the eastern two, two large stones stand alone behind the pub. *After Grinsell and AML.*

Quiet: meaning that the needles and numbers showed little reaction. It was like the scene at Stonehenge, which they'd surveyed three years before. There the magnetic response was weak, and in places badly disturbed by modern interference. At Stanton Drew, however, there shouldn't have been much disturbance to worry about.

'But when we plotted all the data on the computer this evening, we can see these circles. I don't understand it. I can't believe it.'

Andrew discussed the call with his partner. Obviously Tim and Mark had found something exciting, even if he couldn't make much sense of it over the phone. He'd find out tomorrow, when his colleagues would have had a little more time to consider their results. But as he went to bed, Andrew David had absolutely no idea just how extraordinary this new discovery was.

The way we see Stonehenge today has changed radically since

Richard Atkinson wrote of the monument nearly fifty years ago. In Part II of this book we will look at Stonehenge itself through the experiences of archaeologists in the last century, on which English Heritage's new study is based. In Part III we will move north to Avebury, which in recent years has attracted much of the exciting new research and ideas. Drawing it together we will find a fresh vision that while young and incomplete is also, I believe, more sympathetic to the past and more rewarding for us today than anything that has come before. But first we will consider the huge 'superhenges' and the timber structures of which Stanton Drew is but the latest discovery. These finds have transformed our understanding of the Stonehenge world.

In 1946, the Oxfordshire County Surveyor (a keen amateur archaeologist) had sent a civil engineering journal to Professor Richard Atkinson. As Atkinson was leafing through the magazine, he came across a piece about site exploration for dams. The writer described 'resistivity surveying', with equipment made by a firm called Evershed and Vignoles.

Atkinson's imagination was fired. He contacted the manufacturers, explained his position, and the next thing was that Evershed and Vignoles were conducting, almost for free, the very first archaeological geophysics survey. On the ground near Dorchester in Oxfordshire were ditch circles discovered from the air, and soon to be destroyed by gravel quarrying. The new gadgets, cumbersome and slow to use as they were, enabled Atkinson precisely to locate what he was looking for, and to begin a series of excavations at a major Neolithic complex of religious and ritual monuments. Within weeks, he had hired some lighter machinery and begun to experiment in ways of improving the efficiency of the work. 'This', he wrote, 'is how it all began.'[11]

In a resistivity survey, varying ground moisture (affected by disturbances such as filled ditches) is examined by measuring the resistance of the soil to an electric current. For a decade, this was the only process used by archaeologists to detect things beneath the ground without excavation. Then as experiments continued, led by Tony Clark and others, anything and everything was tried. Clark was an enthusiast for invention, and with tiny budgets and no computers his surveys could have the appearance of something genuinely English and eccentric, employing nylon thread, string and a 'liberal use of rubber bands'. 'In those days,' he wrote, looking back, 'the Megger Earth Tester was built in the venerable tradition of mahogany and brass. It was powered by a hand-driven generator producing a high enough voltage to make handlers of uninsulated probes jump.' Lack of volts could be an issue, too. This was overcome on one occasion by warming a battery with candles borrowed from a local pub.

In the 1960s, a colleague, Martin Aitken, devised an 'instant grid' made from plastic-coated clothes line. The idea was that instead of measuring a grid out across the field every time you wanted to make a survey, you could just unroll this wide-spaced net and start work at once. It was, noted Clark, very effective – until it became entangled in bushes, or eaten by sheep, 'by whom it was regarded as a rare delicacy'.

And then there were the long cables by which readings were sometimes taken during magnetometer surveys. In one experiment in 1973 Clark had trouble with a bent and corroded wire, which overnight spiders had found a convenient anchor for their webs. Sheep did not eat wire, but cows might walk through it, dragging the whole assembly round the field. 'It was therefore quite soon abandoned', he wrote, 'in favour of a sealed rotary potentiometer linked by meccano gears from the nearest toy shop.'

With the development of electronics and computers, things have changed dramatically. In the late 1950s, Irwin Scollar, a pioneer in the computer processing of resistivity data, would set out for a Roman wall from the Rheinisches Landesmuseum, Bonn, Germany, with his data-logging system bursting through the windows of his VW minibus. Today, quantities of data then unimaginable are stored electronically in equipment that can be carried across a field at a fast walking pace. The data are then downloaded onto a laptop, and can be subjected to sophisticated analysis there and then.

Commercial software and equipment are mostly designed for big mineral and civil engineering jobs, or environmental searches for toxic substances. Archaeology is uniquely concerned with the very shallow and with fine detail. Building on Tony Clark's achievements, English Heritage's AML continues to be one of the world leaders in archaeological geophysics. Stanton Drew was not about to damage their reputation.

Mark and Tim continued the survey on Tuesday, and in the evening Andrew David came down from London.

Sitting on the sofa in the lounge of their bed and breakfast, they got out the laptop – a familiar scene for this roving band of surveyors. As the data scanned down the screen, Andrew could immediately recognise the plan of the Great Circle. The megaliths showed up as black and white squares, where survey data could not be collected.

'Christ,' he thought. 'It's true.'

Somehow on the phone the day before he hadn't quite caught on that they'd found concentric rings, and that these were actually inside the great stone circle. Well there was no doubt now. The little screen looked like a grey and white dartboard, a shimmering map of halos, like one of those ridged rubber mats you put under a teapot. Andrew pressed his finger to the screen, and counted nine rings. His eyes couldn't take in the information fast enough. What could these rings be? Ditches? Shallow gullies for fences? There was a thicker ring *outside* the stone circle. This was ridiculous! That had to be a ditch – with a clear gap, an entrance on the north-east side (plate 3).

Stanton Drew was transformed. The ditch added a completely new dimension to the site. And if that fat ring was a ditch, then the thin ones were probably lines of post holes. There are a few ancient ditch rings enclosing concentric circles of post pits elsewhere in Britain – very famous amongst archaeologists – but none even half the size of this. Then he noticed that one of the smaller stone circles had got into the survey up on the top right. There were four huge blobs in the middle suggesting massive post pits . . .

The next day, they were back outside with fluxgate magneto-meters. They decided to extend the survey by taking in rectangles to the north of the stone circle and east towards the little River Chew, where the two stone circles appeared to have 'avenues', short parallel rows of once standing stones.

'By then,' remembers Andrew, not one normally to be flustered, 'my imagination was almost boundless.' He walked the floodplain without recording data, just looking at the dial – 'scanning'. Perhaps there was a superhenge, a vast array of giant earthworks now flattened and visible only to the white plastic-boxed machine under his arm. In any case, they knew they had something that would catch the public imagination, and six weeks later Andrew David was back at Stanton Drew.

At a shop price of £20,000 the Canadian-made Scintrex caesium gradiometer was four times the cost of the fluxgate version. The technique was not new. Caesium gradiometers were first used in aeroplanes for global surveys (handy for locating iron tanks in a war zone), but miniaturised systems had been commercially available only for two or three years. English Heritage had been renting a Scintrex for their project. It was then the only one in Britain. Like the fluxgate, the Scintrex looks for very subtle variations in the local magnetic field. But it works much faster and can take many more readings: up to ten a second, so that on a 30m traverse some 250 readings are recorded on its CD (the fluxgate can cope with a cassette tape). It has ten to twenty times the sensitivity of the fluxgate.

What they hoped to establish was whether the narrow rings were continuous, in which case they were probably gullies, or discrete pits. It took four days to complete the survey, a rectangle some 90 by 75m that covered about two thirds of the area inside the great stone circle.[12] On Monday 10 November, exactly ten weeks after the first day when Tim and Mark began the Stanton Drew survey, English Heritage marshalled a press conference in London. They faced a conundrum: on the one hand they clearly had a find of international significance; on the other there was really very little that could be said about it.

Andrew described the plots. The caesium survey showed that the rings consisted of hundreds of discrete spots about 1m across at intervals of around 2.5m (plate 4). If these were post holes, they must have held 400 or 500 huge timbers. No one was quite sure what exactly made these pits so visible, but one interesting theory was that 'magnetotactic' bacteria that would have fed off the rotting wood 5000 years ago were still, ever so subtly, affecting the magnetic field.[13]

Geoffrey Wainwright, then Chief Archaeologist at English Heritage, was over the moon. He'd begun his career with institutional British archaeology by discovering what was then the only example of one of these vast and mysterious wooden structures excavated in modern times. He'd long since given up digging. Now he could relive the excitement of his days in the field. It was, he said, 'the most significant discovery in British prehistoric archaeology in thirty years' (his dig at Durrington Walls, Wiltshire, where he made the great find of his career, was thirty years before). 'We have about three thousand stone circles in Britain, but previously had only seven timber temples.'[14]

The then Chairman of English Heritage, Sir Jocelyn Stevens, was equally ecstatic. He said that Britain was apparently the only place in the ancient world where these extraordinary temples were built. 'They were expressing their power by building these great rings, just as we are celebrating the Millennium by building a huge dome. This is clearly a very British habit, and it is five thousand years old.' These structures were 'symbols of power . . . believed by the people . . . to control the supernatural'. It is thought that Stevens was still referring to Stanton Drew.

But without excavation, all this excited talk of timber temples, forests of carved posts erected in 3000 BC and sophisticated prehistoric peoples was sheer guesswork. Some archaeologists, a little uneasy about the strong media interest, wondered about alternative explanations for the rings. Perhaps they were looking at a lost medieval maze? Could it be, suggested someone who had spent a large part of his career thinking about Neolithic timber rings, that at some time in the past the site had been ploughed in concentric rings inside the stone circle? The fact that even the most informed archaeologist could come up with little better than this left intact the possibility of a huge prehistoric temple of some kind. So where did this idea come from?

As Wainwright said, there were a few known instances of large circular wooden structures of approximately the same date as the Stanton Drew stone circle (itself undated, but likely by analogy to be around 4000–5000 years old). Most of these were on the chalk of Wessex, not far from Somerset. No one was quite sure what they were, but, though it was thought the rings of posts held massive thatched roofs, everyone was agreed that they weren't simply big houses. In some loose way they were related to Stonehenge, some 55km south-east of Stanton Drew.

Journalists naturally wanted a reconstruction drawing. In the time available, no one at English Heritage had been able to produce one. While the other sites were all thought to be thatched, and this is how the drawings showed them, at around 100m across there was no way the Stanton Drew site could have supported a continuous roof. Fortunately, English Heritage had on file a fine watercolour by Peter Dunn that showed half-naked men struggling with a mass of carved wooden posts – and no roof in sight. It was actually an imaginative view of Durrington Walls, before the roof was put on, but it did the trick.

So what were all these strange wooden constructions? How were they built, and what did they really look like? What ceremonies took place in them? What do these things have to do with Stonehenge, if anything? What actually is a henge? What did it all *mean*? It is questions like these that this book is about. Beyond a doubt, the geophysics team had found something astonishing at Stanton Drew, but this was only the latest in a series of remarkable discoveries. The big wooden temples – if that's what they were – are so extraordinary, and so little heard of, that we will look quite closely at some of the best-preserved. We will even do a little excavation at one of them ourselves.

Welcome to Hengeworld.

3

A Way of Life

In 1973, Danish archaeologist Erik Brinch Petersen did something that archaeologists of the outdoor variety frequently do. He dug up some human skeletons. On a slight rise in the ground near the village of Dragsholm in Zealand were two graves, 2m apart. There was nothing to mark the graves: no stones or posts, no mounds, just a couple of pits, each slightly longer and wider than a human form. In one pit were the remains of two women, in the other those of a man. A few Stone Age-looking objects – animal teeth, flint arrowheads, an old pot – indicated the great age of the burials. Radiocarbon dates confirmed they were around 5000 years old.

When we look closer at these burials, a remarkable thing emerges. They are not precisely the same age. In fact the radiocarbon dates are about three centuries apart, and the older burial pit – the two women – contains artefacts that are subtly but significantly different from those in the younger. The pot, the flint axe, the carved stone 'battle axe' and the arrowheads the man took with him mark him as a Neolithic farmer. A couple of paces away, perhaps unknown to the man and his mourners, the women had previously been buried with a decorated bone knife, a bone awl, and red deer and boar teeth whose arrangement suggests the fringe of a leather jacket. These two ladies were not Neolithic at all.

Richard Bradley, Professor of Archaeology at Reading University, has vividly described the powerful symbolism of Petersen's find.[15] On the one hand were two people whose lives revolved around the wild woods and shores, hunting, gathering and fishing (chemical analysis of their bones indicated seafood in their diet). There was no reason to think that, in broad terms, their values, their way of life, did not cover most of Europe and go back for thousands of years till the time when the last great ice sheets were shrinking away into the highest mountains. Indeed, the red ochre in the grave connects with ochre found on human remains that date from *within* the Ice Age; the time of the great cave paintings and wild animals long extinct.

On the other hand was a man who knew the labour of sowing and reaping. He died near the beginning of a long era of Stone Age farming, when at different times and in different parts of Europe there were many different ways of gaining food, of building houses and of burying the dead. His world was almost as remote from that of his two neighbours in state as is ours.

Although it used to be thought that farming rushed across Europe on a tidal wave of wheat-planting immigrants sweeping away the forest on which the native hunters relied, many archaeologists today dispute this vision. This is partly a simple matter of chronology. When the 'Neolithic Revolution' was first posited by archaeologist Gordon Childe in 1935, the shift from hunting to farming seemed to have taken place almost overnight.[16] Over half a century later, with the aid of radiocarbon dating, we can see that this transformation was varied and erratic: we are talking millennia, not decades.

The Neolithic way of life in Europe – the new foods, the new ideas – began in the south-east around 9000 years ago, reached the west Mediterranean a millennium later, central Europe in 1500 years and the north-west in 3000. By 4000–5000 years ago things were moving on in northern Europe, with the new use of metals and new more intensive systems of producing food.[17] The era of Stone Age farming in Britain lasted about twenty centuries, from 6000 to 4000 years ago, the same span of time that we now celebrate in our millennial calendar.

But it's not just a matter of dates. There is also a significant change in the way archaeologists think about the whole phenomenon of a farming lifestyle. First, it is now believed that most, perhaps all north European farmers were descended from hunting and fishing forebears. People – some of them – were growing crops and rearing animals, some of which (like sheep and wheat) ultimately came from the Near East, but they were doing this in lands they knew well from generations of familiarity. The decisions that would turn their backs on millennia of tradition were not whimsical. If they had added cultivated cereals to their traditional range of wild plant foods, this was not because they had seen wheat and taken to it like a child to a new toy. Or if they had stopped hunting deer and boar and fish and birds, this was not the result of swallowing one mouthful of lamb and seeing the light.

In some places, particularly in central Europe, farming was adopted wholesale quite rapidly. In others, such as Scandinavia, northern France and perhaps Britain, bits and pieces of a farming lifestyle were melded with a successful economy that depended mostly on wild foods. Only later, over several centuries and many generations, might things have changed to the point when we could say, yes, those people were farmers. If it suited them, they changed some of their ways; if it didn't, they could ignore alien foods and technologies that had little to offer.

But it was not just a question of new foods. In this Neolithic era in different parts of Europe, people lived in huge, long timber houses; they lived in small square huts; they lived, all too frequently, in something that left little trace for archaeologists to dig up. Sometimes they built hilltop enclosures, throwing up banks and erecting wooden palisades. They buried their dead (or some of them) in great long mounds that echoed the long houses. Sometimes these mounds had chambers of large stones that you could repeatedly enter, to revisit your ancestral bones. Some had wooden rooms that rotted and collapsed. Some mounds had no burials in at all.

All this is very different from earlier, hunting times. The most we normally expect to find as evidence that hunters and fishers interfered with the earth are their simple grave pits – and these were only dug in limited parts of Europe. A number of archaeologists, like Richard Bradley, are now taking the view that the changes in values, in ideology, in the way people thought about themselves and the world around them were as important, even perhaps more so, than the organisational shift from wild to domesticated foods. Former Cambridge Professor of Archaeology Ian Hodder gave one of his books a title that stresses that it was not just the pigs that were being domesticated: it was Europe.[18]

In the old times, says Bradley, people made no big distinction in their lives between themselves and nature. The women in Petersen's grave were festooned with animal teeth, and other graves contain shed deer antlers. The forests with their plants and animals were places of birth and life. 'Any simple division', he writes, 'between culture and nature might have been meaningless.'[19]

For the farmers, things could hardly have been more different. Their world was one of control over nature, where that boundary between wild and tame was readily drawn. While Petersen's women were returned to the earth with uncarved boar teeth, his man cradled a pot – clay physically transformed through control of fire. Domestication and rearing of animals, clearing land for fields and gardens and, especially, moving wood, earth and stone to shape huge monuments: all these were aspects of domination. 'The new idiom', says Bradley, 'was concerned with power.'[20]

And if power was the idiom, rarely was that vernacular more explicit than in Britain at the end of the Neolithic era, around 4000–5000 years ago.

It used to be thought that Stonehenge was Bronze Age, the era that followed the Neolithic. Richard Atkinson associated the great megaliths at the site with the many round burial mounds close by. Some of these mounds were known to contain, amongst other things, copper and bronze daggers and other early, small decorative metal objects.[21] On one of the biggest stones, Atkinson himself discovered a carving of a dagger, which he confidently identified with the world of Agamemnon in Mycenaean Greece, then dated to 3500–3600 years ago (figure 10).[22]

Then in 1995 along came an English Heritage team armed with the latest in science and logic, to prove conclusively with radiocarbon dating that Stonehenge was older than this by some centuries. The empty site was selected and first worked on around 5000 years ago, and the last stones dropped into their pits about a millennium later. By the mid Nineties, this re-dating was actually not much of a surprise to archaeologists: at least now Stonehenge, like the many henges to which it gave its name, was seen to be Neolithic. That left just one problem: Stonehenge is not a henge.

This bizarre contribution by the archaeological profession to the English language was first used by a British Museum Keeper, Thomas Kendrick, in 1932.[23] It was taken up by other archaeologists as they discovered new additions to the few monuments originally identified. Grahame Clark, Disney Professor of Archaeology at Cambridge, listed around twenty known sites a few years later.[24] In 1951, Richard Atkinson's expanded catalogue contained about forty.[25] The most recent lists reach well over 300 – and that was over a decade ago.[26]

So what *is* a henge? Archaeologists have avoided this simple question by compiling yet more surveys, lists and catalogues. What they were for, what they meant, is something we will explore in Part III. What they look like now – the majority have not been excavated, so can be assessed only from their current surface

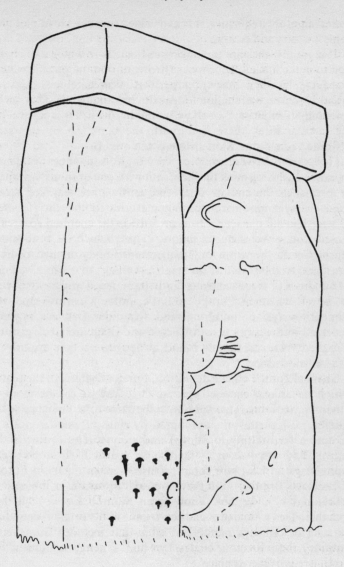

Figure 10. The famous dagger carving at Stonehenge is on the front of stone 53, surrounded by a group of axe carvings. The contrast between sarsen stone 53 (very finely shaped from a particularly tough rock) and adjacent 54 (betraying the nature of the original slab) is typical of the trilithons. The overlying lintel is also very well carved. *Carvings after Newall.*

appearance or, frequently, marks visible from the air in ploughed fields – is easy to describe.

Technically, they are earthwork enclosures in which a ditch was dug to make a bank, which was thrown up on the outside edge of the ditch. To the military-minded, this immediately excludes any practical, defensive function for the ditches and banks. This is what rules out Stonehenge: though we would hardly call this place a fort, the circular ditch there is outwith the bank, so by this strict definition of a henge, Stonehenge is not one.

Henges can be very small or very large, sometimes with more than one enclosing bank or ditch, and with one or more 'entrances' or breaks in the circuit. They frequently have standing stones somewhere in or around them. When excavated, they are often seen to have had large erect posts in or outside the enclosed space. But most of all, every henge is unique. These may have been sacred places, but they were not built to a common blueprint like medieval churches. And it is one of the strangest things that while we know of hundreds of these enclosures in Britain, few if any have yet been found elsewhere in Europe. What's more, a curious and very distinctive style of pottery found from the Orkneys in north Scotland to the south coast of England, which archaeologists call Grooved Ware, commonly found at henges, appears exclusive to Britain and Ireland.

So much for the official definition. I prefer to think of them more simply as circular enclosed spaces. That way we can bring all the other strange sacred structures into the same fold. So, circular – or roughly so – earthworks are joined by rings of wooden posts (at around a further fifty locations) and stone circles (a further 900 sites). These often occur by themselves (particularly stone circles; stone rings, at least, are common elsewhere in northern Europe, particularly Brittany). But they also exist in various combinations, sometimes – as we now know from Stanton Drew – all three together. This was what Kendrick meant in his original definition: he only described a handful of sites that included Stonehenge, Avebury and a few stone circles. For him, a 'henge monument' was just a circular 'sacred place'.[27]

Just as in the technical literature, one place can appear in dismembered parts in several lists (an earthwork henge here, a stone circle there, a group of timber rings somewhere else), so the same problem occurs when we think about time. The construction of henges and stone circles – the wholesale delineation of circular

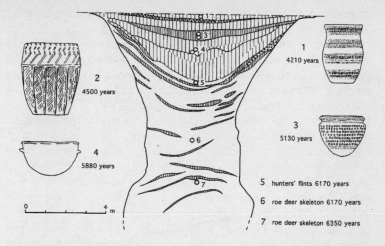

Figure 11. Part of a section dug by Martin Green through a natural sink hole in the chalk at his farm in Dorset. The deep stratigraphy ranging from mesolithic to Late Neolithic is unique in Britain, and provides an extraordinary opportunity to study environmental change at a single spot. I have selected a few key radiocarbon dates for this diagram of the Fir Tree Farm sink hole (see Appendix 2 for details). The lower layers are mostly chalk, in which were found the remains of two deer that had fallen into the open shaft (7–6). The first human activity is represented by the small flint components of a hunting spear lost some 6170 years ago (5). Above this, animal bones and artefacts indicate the appearance of a farmed landscape. Three of the four major categories of neolithic pottery were found, with dates typical of the rest of Britain: Early Neolithic Bowl (4), Peterborough (3) and Beaker (1). Grooved Ware (2), although present on settlement close to the shaft, was not found in it. *After Green and Allen.*

sacred spaces – took place over a time that archaeologists still conventionally refer to as the Late Neolithic and subsequent Early Bronze Age. Specialists tend to study the Neolithic or the Bronze Age, rarely both. So we get more dismemberment, for many places were active at 'both' these times.

We wish to confront real people in real worlds, the inhabitants of what I call Hengeworld. I chose this term to avoid explicit reference to date, people, place, pottery styles or anything else with which archaeologists might choose to partition the past. It refers to that time and place when people were digging out the ditches and banks, cutting the trees for the massive circular timber circles and, on occasion, dragging huge stones into place, at the end of the Neolithic and the very beginning of the Bronze Age. Strictly, it is the world of the earthworks with their banks outside and ditches inside, and the distinctive Grooved Ware ceramics (figures 11 and

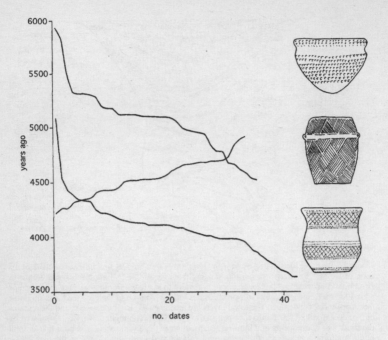

Figure 12. There are three major types of later Neolithic pottery in Britain (from the top, Peterborough Ware, Grooved Ware and Beaker), each showing considerable variety. In this graph over 100 radiocarbon-dated samples are arranged in age order (Grooved Ware young to old, others old to young). It is clear that, broadly, Peterborough came before Grooved Ware, which was succeeded by Beaker. How far the ceramic traditions overlapped is a topic of much academic discussion (dates in years before 2000, as described in chapter 1). *Dates after Gibson and Kinnes, Garwood, Kinnes and Gibson, and Needham. Full details at www.hengeworld.co.uk.*

12). But sometimes we will extend it further back into the past, and sometimes nearer the present.

Above all, Hengeworld is the people themselves, their homes, their lives and their thoughts, 4000–5000 years ago. When we look them in the face, what we see is unnerving, and moving, even occasionally shocking.

From the seat of a Sopwith Snipe flying at 2000 feet, it might be pretty terrifying too. But fortunately for us, Squadron Leader Gilbert Insall was of stern stuff. Our story begins with what he found, in a ploughed field, one day shortly before Christmas 1925.

4

The Discovery of Woodhenge

After everything, it was the shock of a burglary that nearly got him. They took all sorts of stuff, including his VC and MC, and he collapsed of a heart attack. His medals were recovered in a few months, but he survived only another two years, dying in February 1972, in Bawtry, a small blur from the A1M south of Doncaster, Yorkshire. *The Times* honoured Gilbert Insall with a 10cm summary of his military career.[28] There are biographical notes describing his adventures in the First World War, chasing the enemy in a biplane, surviving against all odds.[29] The Wiltshire Archaeological Society marked his death with four lines in their journal.[30] Military historians would remain unaware of his passion for archaeology; archaeologists would not know about his life in the Air Force.

Perhaps Insall would be pleased. In 1952, seven years into his retirement, he was sought out in his rented apartments at Newstead Abbey by an enterprising journalist on the *Nottingham Evening News*. The retired Group Captain, the only one of the first five Air Force VCs to survive the First World War, did his duty with stories of military japes in the Arabian desert. But we learn little about a real life. The French, he said, have a phrase for it (he was fathered in Paris by an English dental professor in 1894, and went to Paris University). '*Vivons heureux, vivons cachés*' – Live secretly, live happy.[31]

Insall had a successful RAF career. He also made many archaeological discoveries, in and outside Britain, working with some of the most prominent archaeologists of his time. In particular, he found the first and still one of the greatest timber structures of Hengeworld. It was a stunning coup whose significance, even now, remains to be appreciated by all but a few academics and determined tourists. Yet the archaeology would not have happened without the fighter pilot. It is time to put the record straight. We may not get much nearer the man, but we can at least consider his achievements.

His First World War exploits today sound like something from a comic book – as befits a time when the true horrors of modern warfare were rarely recorded. Aged twenty, he volunteered to join up in 1914, and the following year was back in France with Number 11 Squadron, the first air unit formed (at Netheravon in Wiltshire, 8km north-east of Stonehenge) specifically to go out and hunt other aircraft. Perched between two canvas wings in a cross between a bath-tub and an early two-seater sports car sans wheels (a terrifying-looking contraption known as a Vickers FB5), Insall flew on various photo reconnaissance missions. He entered fully into the spirit of things by chasing German planes about the sky whenever he saw them, while his observer fired a fat Lewis machine gun between the beautifully polished wooden blades of the propeller.

It was on one such occasion that Insall's plane was hit by ground fire, encouraging him to land just outside the German lines to do some overnight DIY. He and his observer-mechanic, T. H. Donald, had earlier forced a two-man German Aviatik to land in a ploughed field. Insall took the FB5 down to 500 feet (150m) so that Donald could shoot at the fleeing crew and lob a little bomb over the side onto the stranded plane. Thus Insall's VC and Donald's DCM. Before he could receive the VC, however, Insall was wounded in the air and had to land. He was captured, hospitalised and held prisoner. After two unsuccessful attempts – by which time the war was nearly over – he finally escaped and earned an MC. He stayed with the RAF for the rest of his working life, moving from one base to another – Germany, Iraq and, mostly, England – training pilots, leading squadrons and commanding stations. Meanwhile, archaeologists were becoming increasingly excited about the opportunities that aeroplanes offered for making new discoveries.

Appropriately enough, the first aerial photographs of an archaeological site are thought to be two of Stonehenge, taken from an army balloon by Lieutenant P. H. Sharpe of the Royal Engineers and exhibited in London in 1906.[32] With the arrival en masse on Salisbury Plain of the military at the outbreak of the Great War, there was no shortage of craft overhead to spy on the old stones. There was even a Stonehenge aerodrome just to the west.[33] But it was from Netheravon, where in a few quick weeks Gilbert Insall first learnt to fly, that he took off on 12 December 1925, and flew over Stonehenge at 2000 feet (600m) in his single-seater Sopwith

Snipe. As he headed back to his aerodrome, following the Marlborough road and the River Avon, he spotted something in a field, just 3km from Stonehenge. A couple of years later, when he was stationed at Basra, Iraq, commanding 70 Squadron, he wrote to Osbert Crawford describing what he had seen.

If Sir Mortimer Wheeler laid the foundations for the way in which archaeologists today excavate, Crawford was, in between the two world wars, the practical thinker.[34] He founded the journal *Antiquity*, still the leading cross-specialist archaeological magazine; he first brought archaeology into the Ordnance Survey, the outstanding British mapping organisation; he helped several young men who later became prominent professional archaeologists; and he enthusiastically promoted the value of aerial photography to archaeology.[35]

The delighted Crawford published the letter in full in his very first issue of *Antiquity*.[36] In the same copy, a Wiltshire archaeologist called Maud Cunnington described what she had found halfway through digging up this new addition to the Stonehenge landscape. 'It is', she wrote, 'the most sensational archaeological discovery made by means of photography from the air.'[37]

Crawford had been an observer on the Western Front, where he had realised the value of aerial photography not only for military intelligence but also for tracking down the past. The archaeologist as spy could gain a huge amount of potential information at relatively little outlay and at great speed, discovering ancient remains that were unrecorded and in a single shot from the camera outdo weeks of surveying on the ground.[38] Immediately after the war Crawford tried unsuccessfully to access the RAF's collection of air photos. In 1923, with the Ordnance Survey behind him, he pulled it off, and toured Air Force stations in southern England. One of the photos that caught his eye, taken in a dry summer in 1921, revealed for the first time a massive extension to the Avenue, the approach way flanked by parallel ditches and banks that leads to Stonehenge.[39] Although the earthwork was long ploughed flat, the ditches showed as clear white lines of chalk in the dark earth of the fields.

The following year he teamed up with the marmalade heir Alexander Keiller to hire a plane over Wessex from which they took some 300 photos[40] with a captured German Ica equipped with a 4.5 Zeiss Tessar lens, both bought from the War Disposals Board. They had a vision to photograph the whole of the British Isles.

Some ten years later, Keiller flew to New York on the *Hindenburg* with the Zeppelin's designer, Hugo Eckener. This was even better than an airplane. 'It's so slow and so large', he told a colleague, 'that you could plot sites straight on to six-inch maps – and it's even got a *bar!*'[41]

In retirement, flying and taking photos in Nottinghamshire for the Ministry of Works, Insall himself mused similarly about helicopters: 'They would have been ideal for air surveys'.[42] But grand schemes to blanket-photo the British Isles were never the answer. The great discoveries have come from carefully planned missions in aeroplanes. Insall's find near Stonehenge in 1925 was one of the first, and a classic of its kind.

The Snipe was a businesslike biplane that evolved from the Sopwith Camel, a highly successful fighter brought into action towards the end of the war.[43] Like the FB5, it had an open cockpit. From a distance, Insall would have been able to see something light in the corner of a field. Closer to, he could make out a large circle with rings of white spots in the centre. The photos he took over the coming months, however, would have required more than a gentle fly-by.

Unlike the FB5, where Insall was accompanied by a gunner-observer, in the Snipe he was alone. Thanks to clever mechanics, he could fire his bullets between his propeller blades, but he needed a clear view for his camera. The lower wing on the Snipe is raked back, but it is still fair and square below the cockpit. With his joystick in one hand and camera in the other, he would have had to put his plane into a sharp turn, with one wing down for the view, the wind in his face at 160kph, concentrating more than anything on avoiding a stall. The Camel and the Snipe were both famous for their strong torque and unforgiving behaviour in the hands of an inexperienced pilot. Early aerial archaeology required a cool head.[44]

Insall looked the site up in the *Wiltshire Archaeological Magazine*, and discovered it was already known – as a round burial mound that had been all but ploughed flat. But he could see that this was no barrow, and he kept up the observation. What would happen when crops grew in the field? By July 1926, when the corn was in full growth, there was no doubt. There were 'five or six or perhaps even seven' rings of spots, which again Insall photographed. Back on the ground, he motored over to the site and clambered up a hayrick. 'Although a few dark patches could be seen in the standing wheat, no pattern was visible, and they would have passed unnoticed.'

Insall showed his photos to Maud Cunnington, who visited the site early in August. She could see 'taller deeper coloured growth of the wheat forming a continuous band along the course of [a] ditch, and tufts over . . . pits, . . . but without the advantage of a bird's eye view it was not possible to see on what plan they were arranged.' Cunnington talked to farm workers, who told her they had long known of corn so thick in patches that it got beaten down by the wind and rain, and became difficult to reap, but they had never worked out the pattern that these patches made.

By the end of the month, Mrs Cunnington was digging the site up. It was a bit of a family do, with her husband Benjamin assisting and their nephew Lieutenant Colonel Robert Cunnington (Royal Engineers) taking care of the survey. In all they spent fifteen weeks there over the next three years, in 1928 moving to some other cropmark sites just to the south. When they had finished digging, Maud and Ben bought the land, tidied it up for visitors and, in 1929, privately published a book about what they had found.[45] It seems that, if you had the money, life then as an archaeologist could be quite simple.

Wheat over soil-filled deep pits and ditches had grown profusely compared to plants on the water- and nourishment-starved chalk. From the air, the effect was exactly like a plan of the site after excavation. It seemed that all Cunnington had to do was to open up the pits to see what was in them. She only had to do this once to realise they had something big. In the photos, the site looked like nothing less than Stonehenge in plan: concentric rings of pits (at Stonehenge, of course, most still holding standing stones) with a ditch around them. The ditch even had a break that, like Stonehenge's, opened to the north-east. The finds showed the site to be prehistoric. But more than this, the potsherds were of a type that were not contemporary with the Bronze Age Stonehenge (as then thought), but older. The artefacts in the pits under the dark spots were Neolithic.

They assumed at first that the holes had held stones, but the evidence soon convinced them that they had in fact held huge wooden posts. They excavated every single pit in the ground they could find. By the end, the tally came to 168 post holes – all but a few arranged in six concentric oval rings, which Cunnington named rings A to F, from the outside in. Enclosing all this was a ditch 4 or

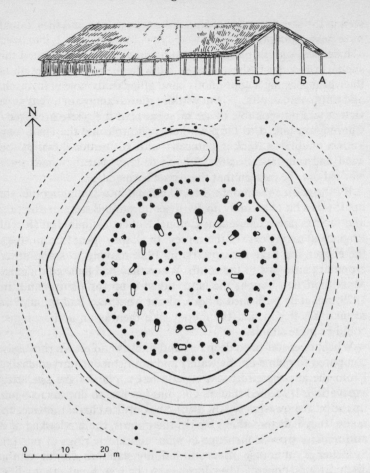

Figure 13. The six concentric rings of post holes at Woodhenge (labelled A–F from the outside in) were excavated in 1926–7. Holes in rings B and C have post erection ramps (white); a small megalith stood in each of these rings at the south. The lone pit in the centre held the remains of an infant. The whole was enclosed by a deep ditch, and beyond this a bank (now denuded). In 1940 Stuart Piggott imagined the site as a roofed building with an open centre court, an interpretation less favoured today. *After Cunnington and Piggott.*

5m wide and some 2m deep. So the bank, the rubble from the ditch piled up beyond its outer edge, must have been considerably higher than its present levelled smear of 15cm of chalk (figure 13).

Some of the pits were massive. The sixteen biggest, in the fourth ring from the centre (ring C), were typically more than 1.75m deep; the deepest was 2m. That they had held wooden posts was clear. Much of each pit had been backfilled with chalk rubble, but in the centre was a soft, dark core that fell cleanly away from the surrounding packing. When they dug out the core first, they were left with a cylindrical hole, sometimes with flecks of charcoal around the sides, as if the post that had once stood there and later rotted had been slightly burnt before erection. Sadly, the excavators recorded the details of very few of these 'circular pipe-like cavities', now familiar to archaeologists from many sites as 'post pipes'. If the packing that goes back into the pit around the post holds its shape well (chalk does; sand does not), as the post slowly rots in place the space is perfectly filled with fine earth. The opportunity is there to learn a great deal about the size and shape of posts, and thus aid considerably any reconstruction of the original appearance of the site above ground. Cunnington did no more than list the diameters of twenty of the post pipes from all 168 post pits. The largest (in ring C) were 85cm across; the smallest (ring E) 23cm.

The bigger pits had been provided with underground ramps on one side. Cunnington compared these to the ramps she had seen being dug for telegraph poles. Iron bars were sometimes placed at the back of the pit, against which the butt of the tall pine pole would slide as it was hauled up from the ramp. The ancient pits commonly showed where the huge posts (which charcoal suggested to be oak) had crushed the chalk as they were being raised against the pit side opposite the ramp.

Maud Cunnington calculated the possible size of one of the largest posts, once standing in pit C14 (at 1.5m deep, the smallest in ring C). Taking into account the slope of the ramp and the height of the impact blow on the back of the pit, she estimated a post that was at least 9m long (or six times the depth of the pit), standing nearly 7.5m above the ground. An oak bole like that would have to have been the trunk of a tree from a closed forest, where growth would be tall and straight. It would have weighed nearly five and a half tons[46] – about three-quarters the weight of a sarsen lintel at Stonehenge.

There were also a few pits that did not hold posts. Placed neatly between a pair of posts in each of rings B and C were oblong pits that had no post pipes. One of these (the outer) contained the distinctive crushed chalk of a pit that had once held a megalith. Perhaps they were both stone holes. In the upper fill of these two pits were quantities of burnt sarsen fragments, suggesting that at some unknown time a sarsen stone (the same hard sandstone as most of the stones at Stonehenge), or stones, had been fired and broken up.

In the centre, at the back of the oval layout, was a lone pit in which a young child had been buried. The archaeologists found its skull in two pieces. 'There must be two skeletons', they exclaimed when what looked like two skulls were first exposed.[47] But they turned out to be the two halves of one skull, side by side. The skull must have been deliberately split, said Maud, before burial. Writers since have made much of this, describing the sacrifice of a young girl with her head cleft by a stone axe.[48] The reality is that first, we do not know if it was a boy or a girl, and second, the skull had probably separated along a natural 'suture'. The young calvarium or brain-case consists of a few large plates that grow at their edges to accommodate the expanding brain. These sutures remain open until a person stops growing. Because this and hundreds of other ancient skeletons were destroyed when the London Royal College of Surgeons was bombed in the last war, we do not have the opportunity to re-examine this skull, so we can never be sure. At least, so it had been believed since 1941. While writing this book, I was to make a discovery that changed all that, as we shall see.

The two megaliths and the burial hinted that there was more to Woodhenge than a sort of large village hall: it was impossible not to think of the great stone circles a few minutes' walk to the south. As excavation proceeded, the original comparison with Stonehenge became yet more relevant. By superimposing plans of the two sites, Maud Cunnington showed how similar they were: the long axes of the four inner rings at Woodhenge are very similar in size to the two stone circles and two horse-shoe arrangements at Stonehenge; the fifth ring at Woodhenge is similar in size to a ring of pits just outside the Stonehenge stones; and the outer Woodhenge ring is exactly half the diameter of the wide circle of Aubrey Holes at Stonehenge. Both sites are orientated approximately on the midsummer sunrise.[49] It was no wonder that, within a week or two of the first excavation season, they were calling the new site Woodhenge.[50]

The word 'Stonehenge' is about as ancient as writing in Britain, being an Old English combination of 'stone' and, it has been suggested, a word that in modern English would mean either a hinge (referring to the arrangement of connecting stones) or a gallows.[51] Gallows seems singularly appropriate, catching both the iconic shape of two verticals and a horizontal, and the bleak, roadside location. When Maud Cunnington published their nickname for the wooden rings, she had these gallows in mind. Woodhenge looked like Stonehenge not just in plan, she imagined, but also in its arrangements of rings of posts linked with wooden horizontals. She was careful to qualify this interpretation. 'It has been suggested', she wrote, that ring C consisted of lintelled posts (this ring of very large holes is not far from the same size as the big ring of lintelled sarsens at Stonehenge). 'This seems not improbable, but there is of course no direct evidence for or against it.'[52]

Stonehenge, with its carved megaliths, its ring of horizontal stones high in the air, is unique. As a wooden version of Stonehenge, Woodhenge had no parallel. But neither Insall nor the Cunningtons had finished. There were more extraordinary discoveries to be made.

5

Raising the Roof

In 1929, Gilbert Insall, by then Wing Commander, made his second contribution to the ancient landscape of Hengeworld. It was not as dramatic as Woodhenge. But then Woodhenge, surrounded by burial mounds and sacred earthworks, and just up the road from Stonehenge itself, was not exactly in a place where such a discovery caused total surprise. This second wood henge, spotted and photographed from 2000 feet (600m), was on the edge of a large town in Norfolk, where nothing remotely similar was known before. It had survived almost miraculously between the London and North East Railways line (actually shown running *through* the site on the first edition Ordnance Survey map), a small gravel pit, a country road and some vegetable plots. By the time archaeologists came to dig, the Central Electricity Board had plonked the four feet of a pylon between the two circular ditches of the monument. Sometimes the romance of archaeology demands imagination from its practitioners.[53]

A week after the discovery, Insall and O. G. S. Crawford went to have a look. One large dark blob turned out to be a clump of stinging nettles growing on a drain outflow, but they could see the rest of the site – two concentric circles enclosing eight dark patches arranged in a ring – very clearly in the short grass. At Arminghall Insall had, wrote Crawford, found the Norwich Woodhenge.[54] In 1935, Grahame Clark, then a lecturer in archaeology at the University of Cambridge and on his way to becoming one of the key archaeologists of his time, explored the site below ground. Sections through the dark rings showed them to be ditches, the outer 1.5m deep and the inner 2.3m; they had once had a bank standing between them. The eight dark blobs were large post holes. Each had a ramp, like the largest pits at Woodhenge, and the two that Clark fully excavated had clear post pipes nearly 1m across (figure 14).[55]

This was a much simpler monument than Woodhenge, but the

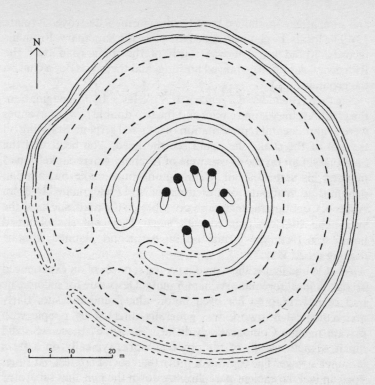

Figure 14. A much simpler timber henge than Woodhenge was discovered at Arminghall in Norfolk, again from the air by Wing Commander Insall. Eight massive post holes, each with its own ramp, were enclosed by two ditches, between which a bank probably stood. *After Clark*.

links were strong: large ramped post holes arranged in a ring, enclosed by circular ditches and bank with a single entrance, the whole thing of no obvious domestic or military use. And both were large places: the outer ditch at Arminghall is over 75m from side to side, comparable to the longer axis of the oval ditch at Woodhenge.

Meanwhile Maud Cunnington had been doing some more exploring in Wiltshire. She had finished digging in the Woodhenge area in 1928, and published the report the following year, just as Insall was making his aerial discovery in Norfolk. In 1930 she set out to find a missing stone circle in the north of the county, close to Avebury. Her best guide was Stukeley, a brilliant eighteenth-century antiquary who had sketched the fallen stones of the circle and soon after complained bitterly when farmers destroyed it (plate 13). The locals, he claimed, called the place the Sanctuary. From his records, Maud knew it was south of the main road over the Ridgeway. Air photos showed nothing, and there was not a clue on the ground.

She then remembered a remark of Stukeley's. In his imagination, the great Avebury stone circles and the two double rows or avenues were a monumental representation of a sacred serpent. Standing on the tail of the snake, he could see the head. The head was the Sanctuary. Out on the downs west of Avebury where Stukeley had mapped his serpent's tail, Cunnington could make out a small distant triangular patch in the corner of Mill Field, named by John Aubrey. Counting the telegraph poles beside the road, she fixed the spot. The site was planted with sugar beet, but she obtained permission from the farmer on 26 April and planned to start digging on 20 May.[56]

As at Woodhenge, she would have the services of an experienced archaeological foreman, William Young. Desperate for income, he had been writing to her even before she found the site. Early archaeological fieldwork was generally directed by people with private means. Comparatively little is heard of those who did much, sometimes all, of the physical work, typically on a farm labourer's wage. The topic is of more than social interest. At times you can feel the ancient past slipping down the gulf that separated director from foreman, and foreman from labourer. In the case of the Sanctuary, there was a further twist: the foreman was acting, perhaps unconsciously, as spy for a second wealthy, but absent, archaeologist.[57]

Young had a strong interest in archaeology, but he needed to be paid. 'After ten years' experience in archaeological work', he wrote a year after the Sanctuary dig, 'I have come to the conclusion that it is very well for those who can afford to spend their whole time at it, but rather hopeless for anyone like myself. In the past six months my earnings have not averaged one pound a week!! My letters and other writing have to be done often when I am dead tired after a day's work in the field or garden (It is nearly midnight as I write this entry).' The next day's journal begins: 'Weather very dull with drizzling rain. Cold S.W. wind. Went hoeing mangolds.'[58]

Young left the Sanctuary slightly before the dig was over, to fulfil a contract on another excavation in Somerset. In September he was at a third site, this time of a Bronze Age barrow. He directed this almost entirely by himself, yet the published report appeared under the name of the man who paid him, Father Ethelbert Horne (notwithstanding that they were good friends). His employer at the Sanctuary, Maud Cunnington, was married to the great great grandson of the father of William Cunnington, wool merchant, who in the early nineteenth century had excavated many richly endowed prehistoric barrows around Stonehenge with his patron Sir Richard Colt Hoare.[59] When Ben and Maud had finished at the Sanctuary, they bought the field on behalf of the Wiltshire Archaeological Society, as they had done at Woodhenge.[60] But Maud, prompted by her husband, who engaged the diggers, was not going to have Young on her payroll until it was absolutely necessary.

'We are definitely beginning to trench the area on Tuesday May 20th', she wrote to him on the 10th. 'Directly we know what to expect we will send you a wire. We shall have a couple of tents on the ground, so if you preferred [to staying with the Cunningtons in a private hotel in Avebury], you could sleep in one of them.'

Young made his own arrangements.

The Cunningtons began by trenching across the area, looking for the ditch that Aubrey had described. They never found this, but on the third day they came across the first two holes that had held the missing stones. On Friday evening, Maud wired Young asking him to join them on Monday. Young wrote to Alexander Keiller. He and Keiller had worked together about five years before, when Keiller had hired him as foreman to Harold St George Gray to begin his excavations on Windmill Hill, an older, Early Neolithic enclosure just north-west of Avebury stone circle. Keiller had arrived in Wiltshire from Scotland with energy, fast cars, not entirely concealed curious sexual interests, and plenty of money of his own (in 1934, somewhat outdoing the magnanimity of the local archaeologists in their purchase of the Sanctuary, he bought Avebury).[61] He cared little for conventions, and in his passion for the archaeology of the Avebury district saw the Cunningtons as nothing but an impediment. The feeling was quite mutual.

Progress at the Sanctuary was rapid. When Young arrived on Monday, they had already completely excavated a ring of thirty-two post holes they had found inside the wide ring of stone pits. By the time he left on 16 June, eighteen days later (they took Sundays off, but not what was then a public holiday on Whit Monday), they had cleared out a total of fifty-eight stone holes (plus a further eight stone

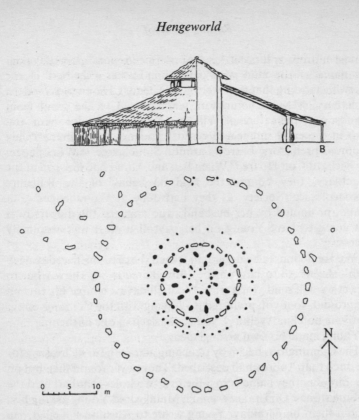

Figure 15. At the Sanctuary in 1930, two stone circles (rings A and C) were found to be combined with six post circles (B–G). At Woodhenge Piggott brought all the posts into a single building. Here he separated them into three successive structures, of which the last (top) contained the inner stone ring (C) under its roof. *After Cunnington and Piggott.*

pits at this southern end of the West Kennet Avenue) and nearly all of the ninety-three post holes that were eventually revealed (figure 15, plate 14). The Sanctuary is not as big as Woodhenge, but compared to the ten weeks over two years the Cunningtons spent excavating that site, this was pretty fast moving. It is no surprise to find the records of this unique place not all one would want.

In the understandable desire to keep down costs, Ben Cunnington did what he could to economise on labour. There was, for example, little time to run about with wheelbarrows, so spoil from an excavation was shovelled immediately into the nearest space that had been previously dug out. 'It meant', wrote Robert Cunnington, looking back some twenty years later, 'that the site looked untidy, and indeed meaningless except to a trained eye.' And this was from the man who conducted the survey.[62]

In fact, the whole event sounds decidedly curious to a modern archaeologist. Maud was shy of publicity, and when a group from her own Wiltshire Archaeological Society came to visit she concealed from them the discovery of a human burial, for fear they might get carried away with sensational thoughts. At Woodhenge, muttering 'Oh lor' under her breath, she had gone so far as hurriedly to rebury a skeleton when threatened with approaching strangers.[63]

She and her husband worked together efficiently. Ben started the proceedings by lightly digging over the site, marking holes as he went (at Woodhenge, where the post holes contained a lot of animal bones, he scattered the place with neat little heaps of bones). Maud then decided what to dig out, and they sent in the workmen. If something special turned up, Young took over with his trowel. The Cunningtons themselves rarely actually dug.[64] This is what happened at the Sanctuary burial. E. Hambridge, one of the four workmen on site, found some skull fragments on the Tuesday, which he showed to Young, who continued the work enough to reveal a crouched skeleton and a crushed pot; on Wednesday, Maud and her friend Mr Pugh completed the excavation.

Keiller was less than impressed. 'I think she is a very unpleasant old woman, Young,' he wrote on 5 June from his London residence – she was then aged sixty-one – 'but then I always have thought so . . . It is very depressing and damned hard lines on you.' Young did not commit his thoughts to paper, merely recording dutifully the details of everything he dug up, and doing what was required by 'her whose work we mutually abhor and mistrust', as Keiller put it.

Keiller, of course, thought he should be digging the site himself. And, in so many words, wrote so to Cunnington. Maud replied by politely declining his offer to come down and do the survey for her,[65] as her nephew Robert – trained in the Royal Engineers – was perfectly capable. A fortnight later, Keiller heard that Robert was in the museum he had installed on the ground floor of his London house. He rushed down to greet him. No amount of talk about Keiller's shining new theodolite and his Elder's Field Co-ordinator could persuade the man to let him in on the site. To Keiller, this just confirmed his opinion of 'this member of that unfortunate family . . . [who was] harmless but lamentably ignorant'.[66]

Notwithstanding local animosities, Maud, as was her style, fast published the results of the dig. If she had not gone to the trouble of writing this report, it could have been that we would know almost nothing about what she found, for she left no field records. On the other hand, if some other archaeologists of the time had excavated the site we would know a great deal more than we do.[67] Understanding the past sometimes has echoes of communication between a seat of power in nineteenth-century Europe and a military commander in a remote part of a distant empire: it's not so much the content that strikes you, it's the fact that the message gets through at all.

At Woodhenge Maud had uncovered six concentric oval rings of post holes inside a deep ditch, with a central grave and one or two standing stones. The finds from the holes at the Sanctuary were very similar, indicating that this new site was about the same age as Woodhenge. Here there were six rings of post holes, one of which also had stone pits between the posts. Where the surrounding bank might have been as at Woodhenge, there was a second, larger ring of stones. All these rings were circular. Like Woodhenge, the Sanctuary had a single grave. In this case, an adolescent was buried at the foot of one of the stones in the inner circle. Her published report, out the following year, contained very little at all on what she thought the Sanctuary looked like, other than her conclusion that it was probably not roofed.[68] She was more forthcoming in a public lecture given a few weeks after the dig finished. She thought the stone circles had been put up to replace the earlier wooden rings, which were erected for 'ceremonial purposes'. 'It is not necessary to picture these timbers as merely bare posts', she said. 'They could have been coloured and adorned in many ways, perhaps even carved into various forms.'[69]

These days, the Sanctuary and Woodhenge, and several other related sites that have since come to light, are usually portrayed as vast roofed buildings.[70] So what happened to Maud Cunnington's idea that they looked like Stonehenge, with no roofs? The distinction is really quite important, for it has obvious implications for what might have been happening at these strange places.

The change began with an article by her own nephew, Robert Cunnington, published soon after the Sanctuary dig was over.[71] He placed a single roof over the whole site. But it was Stuart Piggott, in a paper that came out after the start of the Second World War, who turned opinion round. Fresh from the excavation of an Iron Age village, where he had worked on the uncovering of a massive post-built round house, he looked at the Sanctuary with new eyes. Instead of a confusion of standing posts, he saw three successive roofed buildings, each of the final two larger than the one that came before. The third building contained the inner stone circle within its walls (figure 15).[72]

All the posts at Woodhenge, he thought, were standing together in just one building, but the site was so large, it could not have been spanned with a single conical roof. Instead he imagined an open centre court, with a roof sloping in from an oval ridge – reminiscent of an Elizabethan theatre (figure 13).[73] Piggott was a prominent national archaeologist, and he accompanied his argument with attractive drawings of his proposed buildings. His was an unassailable case.

After that, things quietened down on the wood henge front. Nothing really comparable was found anywhere else, and it began to look as if these two sites – Woodhenge close to Stonehenge, and the Sanctuary connected to Avebury by the West Kennet Avenue – were unique and complex timber structures peculiarly associated with the two grandest stone circles in Europe. Then in 1966, everything changed.

Some years before, a Welsh archaeology student had attended a lecture by the famous Kathleen Kenyon, discoverer of ancient Jericho. I'd like to be an archaeologist, he said. Are there any jobs? 'No chance at all', she boomed. 'You need a private income.'[74] That was a red rag to a bull for this miner's son. He continued his university education and soon found himself working for the government doing what he most enjoyed: digging. He felt little need to consult older archaeologists. Where tradition said you worked with a trowel, this man brought in armies of mechanical excavators and dumper trucks. They tried to stop him, but he moved so fast that it was not until he was done that anyone had the proper time to consider what was happening. By then Geoffrey Wainwright had conducted the largest and most dramatic excavation seen in Britain.

British archaeology would never be the same again. And neither would Hengeworld.

6

The Consensus of Learned Opinion Is against You

'The customs were cruel, useless and a savage reminder that the prehistoric world was not ours.'[75] These are the words of archaeologist Aubrey Burl. Guidebook writers can be even more brutal in their judgement, portraying murder, sacrifice and naked maidens stretched screaming over prostrate stones.[76] Yet sometimes we forget the violence that occurs in our own time.

Between 1982 and early 1999 there were fifteen road fatalities within a 1.5km radius of Stonehenge.[77] The most poignant incident occurred a bit further out, north-west of Woodhenge. Here five people, representing three generations of a single family, were simultaneously killed in a three-car pile-up. It was, said the *Salisbury Journal* of 18 May 1967, the worst road crash in the district for years.

But not the first. In September 1967, work began on a major road-straightening project between Amesbury and Durrington, 3km east of Stonehenge and close to Woodhenge. 'The improvement was designed', said General George Fanshawe, chairman of the Wiltshire County Council Roads Committee, 'to eliminate a particular black spot at the cross-roads adjoining Stonehenge Inn, Durrington, which had one of the worst accident records in the county.'[78]

I can't help wondering if they were also thinking of the luckless A. E. Ledger Hill (OBE), who seemed to have suffered more than his fair share of motoring mishaps. 'For the third time now, in recent years,' he wrote to Durrington Parish Council in 1964, 'a stolen car presumably driven by drunks has crashed through my chestnut fencing and privet hedge ... I find this extremely annoying.'[79]

What may have been a blow struck for road safety, however, was seen as nothing less than wanton destruction by some archaeologists. The fact was, this shining new road was driven right through a huge prehistoric site that, when Stonehenge was new, might have been the scene of as many as a dozen wooden henges, all enclosed by a vast encircling ditch and bank. You don't do that without upsetting somebody.

'It was unfortunate', wrote Glyn Daniel, successor to O. G. S. Crawford as editor of *Antiquity*, 'that a main road is being built through the centre of this complex of pagan temples.' 'Durrington Walls', as this vast enclosure is known, 'ought to have been preserved'. It was not the fault of government archaeologists, however. Daniel blamed 'the Ministers responsible and the British public who are sufficiently unaware of their ancient heritage to permit this vandalism to take place without wide public protest'.[80]

Mr Ledger Hill was one member of the British public who perhaps had things other than ancient heritage on his mind when he wrote again to the council on 11 June 1965: 'Unfortunately last weekend another Army jeep coming towards Bulford ploughed up a long length of hedge and ended up in the river.'

Denis Grant King, teacher, artist, socialist, amateur archaeologist, was less polite to the highway authorities. He saw no place for a road inside an ancient monument. 'The first initiative came from you,' he hammered at the road committee, 'and there was still time for you, as responsible, cultured men, to have withdrawn your order . . . It is quite impossible for you to hide under the umbrellas of the Ministry's impotence. The consensus of learned opinion throughout the world is against you.'[81]

The local press did not record this expression of international angst, but Grant King's protests were well covered. He was supported by Hugh Shortt, then Curator of Salisbury Museum. Shortt bewailed 'the tremendous haste with which this went through'[82] and felt 'it was deplorable that the County Council could take such action before anyone knew anything about it'.[83]

Grant King saw conspiracy. Influential members of the Wiltshire Archaeological Society had too many friends in the County Council. Protests had been suppressed. 'The ramification of these pressures appears to penetrate deeply into the Army and the high-ups of the County Council . . . This same Major General Fanshawe . . . is striking blow after blow at Scheduled Buildings in Wiltshire towns . . . Salisbury is being assailed on a large scale.' But his particular concern, expressed in a PRIVATE and CONFIDENTIAL letter, was that Glyn Daniel, as *Antiquity*'s editor, might be tainted by association with him and his fight against corrupt bureaucracy.[84]

Daniel grandly proclaimed his independence – 'The Editor of ANTIQUITY must always say what he thinks is right to say on any issue.' 'I certainly have no fear', he continued, 'that my own name will be injured by reason of any association with yourself.'[85]

All this righteous debate was more than understandable. The trouble was, it was a bit late. The road had already been built.

'I remember standing in the pub', Geoffrey Wainwright recalls. 'I was deeply hung over, I had a broken toe, and I was surrounded by thrusting young things. It was time to change.'

By coincidence I am writing this in the week that English Heritage's Chief Archaeologist retires. Excavator for the Ministry of Works, twenty years ago he decided to forsake digging to move to a London office. He then transformed the way archaeological fieldwork is conducted in England, and by influence, in the rest of Britain. 'I've not lost the fire for fieldwork', he says. Wainwright's weathered face lights up as he stresses this point. 'Especially digging. But I'm realistic. 1980 was a good time to move on.'[86]

Forty years ago, when C. P. Snow spoke of the 'two cultures' of art and science, there were two cultures in archaeology. There were diggers and thinkers. Outdoors were explorers in quest of physical solutions about the past, attracted no less by the smell of damp earth, and the team companionship of the digging circuit as it repeated itself from one season to the next. In universities were the theorists, polemicists who might dip into diggers' writings, but less often themselves would venture outside. Sometimes it seemed they were not just different cultures, but separate species. Yet each depended on the other.

By his own admission, Geoff Wainwright is no intellectual.[87] But in fifteen years of excavations, mostly in southern England, through his discoveries and the example of his style, he did more than any normal digger or philosopher would dream of achieving. His discoveries, and his example, have changed our understanding of the past in Britain. It began a few hundred metres from Woodhenge. If Wainwright had not confronted the challenge of Durrington Walls, the archaeologists would never have known that they had something to protest about when that road was built. And to achieve that, not only did he have to hold up the roadworks, he had to take on the archaeologists too.

Durrington or Long Walls was recognised as something ancient at least 200 years ago, when according to Sir Richard Colt Hoare it had already 'been for many years in tillage, its form ... much mutilated'.[88] This was the problem for antiquarians and archaeologists. The only obviously visible structure was a low bank describing a wide, circular enclosure, but it was plainly a shadow of its former self, and there was no indication of its age or purpose. With no standing stones, no great mounds and no dramatic finds, the Walls did not enter tourist folklore, like Stonehenge or the Sanctuary, or Avebury itself.

'The pretty little village of Abury,' wrote John Lubbock (later Lord Avebury) in 1865, 'like some beautiful parasite, has grown up at the expense, and in the midst, of the ancient temple.'[89] The same thing was happening to the south at Durrington Walls, if less romantically, as military accommodation and roads approached from all sides.

In 1917 the first opportunity to penetrate the mystery arose when a drain for Army huts was dug through the bank. A skull came up on a workman's pick, and a local amateur archaeologist was summoned. He found some prehistoric pottery, and concluded that the site was contemporary with Stonehenge. The trouble was that he thought Stonehenge was built by Druids and that Durrington Walls was the site of a college for Druidic priests.[90] Even in 1917, everyone who took the trouble to find out[91] knew that Stonehenge was centuries older than the Druids and had nothing to do with them. So not a lot of notice was taken of his report.

Later O. G. S. Crawford used air photos to examine the Durrington circuit in detail, emphasising for the first time that the all but vanished ditch was inside the bank (and holding his nose against 'the reeking dump of refuse' flooding from the Larkhill houses). This, he said, linked the site to Avebury and other ceremonial monuments.[92] But it was the evidence revealed in 1951 by a water mains trench beside the old road through the site that finally clinched the case. Struggling through a wet winter and in a flooded cutting, archaeologists found quantities of the same distinctive pottery that the Cunningtons had dug up at Woodhenge.[93] Durrington Walls was a huge henge. It may have looked less impressive than Avebury, but its bank ring was bigger: 525m across at its widest point, some 100m more than Avebury. That made it the largest henge of them all.

So when in 1966 the Ancient Monuments Division of the

Ministry of Public Buildings and Works was formally told by the County Council that they were moving the A345 Amesbury–Marlborough road, archaeologists knew full well what Durrington Walls was. But it was ploughed flat. It may have been that farming had already destroyed evidence for ancient activity inside the enclosure. The Ancient Monuments Board (an advisory committee of archaeologists) learnt that the council had considered passing the road outside the monument, but local geology demanded that it go through it. The Walls were 'scheduled', given legal protection as an ancient monument, when O. G. S. Crawford got out the air photos in 1928. But that's all right, said the Board (without, as we have seen, consulting local archaeologists): you can build your road. As long as you let us organise an archaeological dig before you do it.

Geoff Wainwright's first job had been university lecturer in environmental archaeology in India. Tired of this, he had returned to Britain to find the government's Inspectorate of Ancient Monuments (which later became English Heritage) advertising some new posts. What had struck Wainwright and his friend Ian Stead, a Yorkshireman who later became a Keeper at the British Museum, was that the Inspectorate were asking for people to take control, to go out and dig. The two men seized the opportunity. Wainwright took the prehistoric sites, Stead the late Iron Age and Roman.

These men, and others who followed, had the chance to work in a very different way from their older colleagues. In the 1950s the Ministry of Works had recognised that much archaeological destruction was taking place, as postwar development and intensification of farming got under way. They recognised the problem, and could be seen to be doing something about it. Archaeologists were contracted to excavate and record known sites before they were destroyed – or, as was commonly the case, after they had already been all but obliterated. But the heart wasn't in it. Reading the many reports of this work, one can hear the ghost of William Young complaining about the lack of money before he had to go out and hoe mangolds. The archaeologists were paid to dig, but not to publish the results.[94]

Salisbury Plain, and the area around Stonehenge, was a typical scene of Ministry excavation. There is a huge concentration of Early Bronze Age burial mounds around Stonehenge. Many of these barrows, these silent monuments to forgotten rituals, oh so many, have now gone, bulldozed, ploughed away, bombed, carved up by tanks or swept aside by roadworks. Archaeologists found one barrow at Shrewton, 4km north-west of Stonehenge, stuffed with 200 tins of corned beef.[95]

Several of these were excavated, or 'rescued' as the euphemism had it, in the late 1950s and early Sixties. Most of the diggers depended on the work for income. Typical were Faith and Lance Vatcher. Faith had aspirations to be an influential archaeologist, known for her great discoveries and brilliant interpretations, but it never happened. She barely published any of her work. When you look at her schedule, you can see why. Between August and November 1961, for example, she and her husband were paid to excavate eleven barrows within 6km of Stonehenge.[96] There was barely time to take photos, let alone to think. And as soon as the digging stopped, so did the money. Sometimes they weren't even allowed to dig as much as they thought necessary.[97] As long as the attempt was being made, it seems, that was enough.

Well, times had changed. The Ministry of Transport agreed to delay the roadworks at Durrington Walls by eleven months, to start in September 1967. Wainwright knew what he wanted to do. He didn't want to dig a few small trenches and let the road take most of it away without record. He didn't want to spend weeks in the field, and have no time to research and publish the results. Although he had no idea what they might or might not find, he wanted total excavation of the route of the road through the Walls. Was he frightened of committing all that money and finding nothing? 'No, no, no', he says now. 'It was a case of suck it and see. You see, I never lacked self-confidence.'

He wrote to John Hamilton, then in charge of government rescue archaeology, and told him they had to dig everything that was threatened at Durrington Walls, and how much it would cost. The next day, the file came back: I approve (figure 16).[98]

There had really never been anything like it in British archaeology. The Cunningtons dug Woodhenge with 'rarely less than four men'[99] (and no wheelbarrow). The Ministry burial mound diggers used unemployed people from the local agencies, or hired labourers (typically from R. Butcher and Son at Warminster); but they did much of the work themselves, not least all the recording (such as it was) and the tricky bits like human skeletons. True, at Stonehenge, Richard Atkinson, cigarette in long holder, had to work around gangs of men and massive machinery

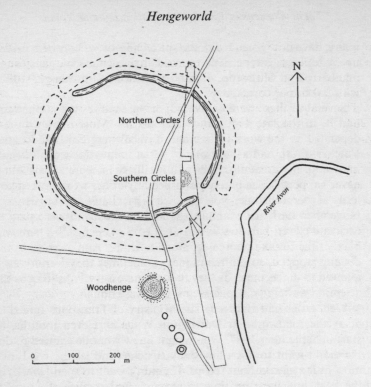

Figure 16. The huge enclosure at Durrington Walls, with its characteristic ditch inside the bank, was paid little attention until a road was driven through it in the 1960s. The remains of enormous timber structures were found in the trench excavated along the path of the road. *After Wainwright.*

as the Ministry repositioned unsafe megaliths. But the excavations themselves were small, delicate affairs.

Durrington Walls was different.[100] Wainwright had to clear an area over 760m long and up to 40m wide, as well as an extension to cover the proposed slip road to Woodhenge,[101] an area totalling nearly 3 hectares, and in only a few months. He appointed three archaeology graduates to supervise the workers, another to look after the finds, five more to help them, and his wife to deal with 'the physical welfare of the volunteer labour force'.[102] The team was completed with men from the local labour exchange.

It was the equipment that upset the applecart. It wasn't just the two axes, fifteen benches, thirty hand brushes and shovels, fifty buckets or 200 wooden pegs. It wasn't the four elsan closets or the five huts, the white marquee or the site telephone, or even the 1400 metres of electric fencing. Such things, if in more modest quantities, were the stuff of field archaeology. It was the diesel-powered JCBs, trucks and conveyor belts.

The Walls surround a small but deep valley, and over the centuries ploughing inside has caused soil to wash down into the bottom. To get to the prehistoric levels, Wainwright had to go deep: up to 1.5m deep and, when it came to emptying the ditch, nearly 6m. No problem. He hired four bright yellow JCBs with back-actors, and a fleet of a dozen dumper trucks. As this vast area of chalk downland crawled with belching machines and hordes of dusty labourers, the older archaeologists in the area saw something little better than the roadworks to come. The Vatchers were horrified. This wasn't how things were done.

Stuart Piggott dropped by, off for a weekend at the Glamorgan-shire home of the other famous Stonehenge excavator Richard Atkinson. He was fresh from a social evening with the Vatchers. He wrote to Faith to thank her 'for all that splendid hospitality and all that Wessex archaeological dirt'. There was dirt, however, and there was dirt. En route to Wales, he reported: 'I went to Wainwright's horribly scruffy dig at Durrington Walls . . .'[103]

'Atkinson', remembers Wainwright, 'thought it absolutely dreadful.' The Ministry barrow diggers ganged up against him.[104] They asked Arnold Taylor, the Chief Inspector of Ancient Monuments, to take him off the job. 'It was a bit of a gentleman's club in Wessex', says Wainwright. Taylor, advised by John Hamilton, told Atkinson 'to bugger off'. Or, as Peter Drewett, one of Wainwright's site supervisors, remembers it, Taylor took Atkinson for a chat at his club, the Athenaeum. But the club scene was changing.[105]

Even if they had found nothing, they had their hands full. And it must have seemed, at times, that all that money (a uniquely large budget for those days) was being employed to clean chalk. In the huge area south of the bank and ditch, close to Woodhenge where much might have been expected, they uncovered a few scattered post holes. More spectacular was the trench they dug across the fields to the north, where they emptied a section of the henge ditch that bottomed at over 5m down. There were a few hearths in the ditch fill, but not a lot else. Was this what it was all for?

In that 1966 autumn they had to keep outside the enclosure; the private owner wouldn't let them in, and they waited until the

County Council had acquired the land for the road. In June 1967 they were back. Tony Clark came down from the Ancient Monuments Lab with his canes and red carpet tape to see if resistivity could map the course of the buried ditch. Combined with aerial photos taken by Crawford, his data contributed to the first detailed survey of the earthwork. Then they moved the machines in.

The vast scale of the earthwork was emphasised when they cleared out a 34m-long stretch of ditch beside the south entrance, nearly 20m wide at the top. This was a big hole, even for JCBs and dumper trucks. Right on the bottom, scattered over an area of chalk rock 4 or 5m across, were some of the tools used to carve out the ditch in the first place: fifty-seven pieces of red deer antler that had been held in the hand like a small pick, now looking puny in the cavernous excavation. Something pretty powerful had motivated those first builders.

But it was inside the enclosure, underneath the protective silt, that all hopes were directed. The instruction from Geoff Wainwright was to take the dirt off down to the clean chalk. There would probably be evidence for medieval and Roman farming in this deep soil – and possibly later prehistoric too – perhaps even the occasional sign of settlement. But it had to go; no time for that. This is how it had worked at other digs: one minute you were in ploughsoil, the next you hit hard chalk and you could see the dark tops of pits and ditches against the white. At one stage ten JCBs were working away together, shovelling and dumping, their heavy rubber tyres churning the earth.

Then in the southern end of the strip, near the ditch, they hit something they weren't expecting. The solid chalk hadn't yet appeared, the machines were pushing down, yet all of a sudden blocks of chalk and lumps of dark soil started coming up in the buckets. The first signs of something that would evoke old memories of the Cunningtons' Woodhenge dig, that would rescue henges from academic obscurity and make the subject sexy again, that turned the entire project from a controversial and expensive hole in the ground into a glorious and value-for-money triumph, were shovelled into the oil-spitting dumper trucks. The Wainwright vision was on the march.

Peter Drewett was supervisor for this site. Now a lecturer at the University of London, this has to have been Drewett's moment. He had just finished his anthropology degree. The JCBs were dismissed. They got out the shovels and brooms and cleared off the disturbed ground, then moved on to the more sensitive tools: pointing trowels, hand brushes, buckets and hand shovels. They found the whole area pitted with deep holes, like a free-for-all gold quarry. It was what Geoff had hoped for all along: a massive prehistoric structure made from close-set wooden posts, whose pits now remained in the ground, their fill showing clear post pipes as the Cunningtons had found on the hill above at Woodhenge.

They'd started with twelve supervisors; now they were down to four. Only one had any prior experience of this sort of thing, and now he worked with Drewett. Pete Donaldson was in some ways a latterday William Young, a man who lived on digging, whose accumulated experience people like Wainwright came increasingly to trust and rely on. At Durrington Walls, if any one person was responsible for the organisation, it was Pete. He and Drewett spent hours puzzling over the post holes.

First they saw lines. The machines worked across the site in strips, and in each strip were more postholes. This gave the impression that the pits were arranged in rows. Geoff wanted them to resolve into huge long houses, the places where the worshippers at Woodhenge had lived, inside the big enclosure. But once they'd got it all cleared, they started to see rings instead. Now Donaldson's and Drewett's early evenings were taken up with predicting circles, laying out tapes on the ground. As they cleaned off the last few square metres, it became clear they had a huge circular structure, perhaps getting on for 200 post holes, all so close together that it was extremely confusing to look at.

Volunteers with trowels covered the ground, scraping away to clean the chalk, looking for every little pit and stake hole. They were aware from fairly early on that there were at least two phases, for some of the pits seemed to have been dug through other holes that had already been backfilled. What was so special about the huge post holes was their preservation. At Woodhenge and the Sanctuary recent ploughing had removed all the surface layers, so that all that survived were features actually below the chalk. But here the old surface had become buried under millennia of ploughwash that had accumulated at the base of the little combe. That's why they'd hit archaeology with the machines before they reached the chalk rock. Large blocks of chalk had been packed into the bigger post holes to grip the tall posts, and some of them still poked up above the original chalk. Further north, near the northern edge of the enclosure and up the hill, was a second timber structure with rings of posts, but here there was no protective ploughwash, and the chalk had been ploughed away so that little remained. The southern site was a unique opportunity to examine one of these Neolithic timber henges in detail.

Drewett and Donaldson imagined they were excavating a place thick with free-standing posts, like a timber Stonehenge – as Maud Cunnington had originally conceived Woodhenge. If there had been a roof, there would have been vast amounts of water running off in rain storms; but there was no evidence at all for any erosion gullies where the eaves might have been. Geoff, on the other hand, wanted a roofed building.

It was only when they planned all the pits that they could begin to make sense of it. The post holes seemed to resolve into two successive circular structures, a part of each lying outside the strip for the road embankment, and thus remaining unexcavated. In the first phase there were five rings of slight but often quite deeply set posts, shielded from the nearby gap in the ditch circuit by a fence or façade. These were replaced by six further rings, the widest nearly 40m across, the largest posts 1m or more thick, set in pits that were sometimes well over 2.5m deep (figure 17). Wainwright's favoured interpretation of this, elaborated by Chris Musson, an architect turned archaeologist, was a vast roofed rotunda, with an open centre, similar to Stuart Piggott's idea of Woodhenge (figure 18).[106]

Besides these extraordinary timber structures, they recovered a unique collection of finds. The post holes at Woodhenge contained a fair bit of some rather odd pottery, covered in abstract plastic designs, pinched, scratched and moulded into the walls of the vessels, most of which had flat bases: Neolithic pottery generally consisted of round-bottomed bowls. At Durrington Walls they found huge amounts of this stuff, now known as Grooved Ware. So much, in fact, that Ian Longworth, a gentle, dapper man from Yorkshire with a penchant for cream-coloured suits, came down from his office in the British Museum to look at the pottery even as it was emerging from the ground and piling up in the sheds. Well over 2000 sherds were found in the post holes of the large timber rings, and a further 1300 from a chalk platform just outside the structure. Longworth's study of these broken pots took up well over a third of the entire book describing the dig.

Wainwright's excavation suddenly made Grooved Ware a highly

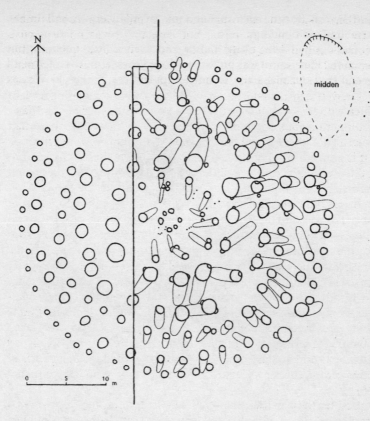

N

midden

0   5   10
              m

Figure 17. The Southern Circles at Durrington Walls present a confused mass of post holes, the bigger ones with large erection ramps. The western third of this site remains unexcavated (here completed with a mirror image). *After Wainwright.*

fashionable thing to study.[107] But it wasn't just pots. There was an enormous amount of broken flint tools, weapons and manufacturing debris, 8500 animal bones, and 316 red deer antlers. Over 100 of these antlers, which as we saw were used as picks for excavating the chalk, came from just five post holes. For the museum in Salisbury that had to find space for all these finds, and then sort and catalogue them, Durrington Walls made its own special impact: the bones and antlers alone came in 103 tea chests and boxes. Sorting the antlers took over an entire hall in the rambling old buildings.

The dig had been noisy, messy and even a little uncouth, but when the long report was published three years later, complete with grand fold-out plans and technical appendices,[108] the old Wessex

Figure 18. The excavator separated posts of the Southern Circles at Durrington Walls into two phases. He imagined each was a roofed building similar to Woodhenge, as seen here in the larger second phase, with an entrance facing the southern causeway across the ditch. *After Wainwright/Musson.*

archaeologists had to admit it had been worth it. Wainwright felt fully vindicated. And now he had a bee buzzing in him. Durrington Walls was just the beginning.

7

Shelling Peas

In between excavating further large sites for the Ministry, Geoff Wainwright sat back and thought about what had happened at Durrington Walls.[109] Both the scale of the work and the extraordinary finds had caused no little controversy within the profession. Government-paid archaeologists were used to thinking small, with even smaller budgets, and targeting their work on big, visible monuments. It was true that in the 1920s and Thirties the Cunningtons had totally excavated the timber rings at Woodhenge and the Sanctuary, and that at neither site was there anything to see above ground. But this was exceptional. More usual were excavations at burial mounds or other upstanding structures like Stonehenge (the latter an ongoing, if utterly directionless, project since 1901).

The great stone circles at Avebury present a typical scene of monument digging. Since 1908 there had been archaeologists at work in the area in thirty-one of the fifty-nine years to 1967. They had been on Windmill Hill emptying Early Neolithic ditches, inside the great henge re-erecting megaliths and looking deep into the encircling ditch, replacing more megaliths on the West Kennet Avenue, having a superficial look at the huge mound of Silbury Hill, opening burial chambers in the West Kennet long barrow (like the Windmill Hill ditches, dating from an era long before that of the standing stones) and, in the previous fifteen years, excavating other barrows with grants from the Ministry of Works. And yet in all this time, no one had looked inside the Avebury henge to see if there was anything there apart from megaliths. If they had (and it still hasn't happened), perhaps Wainwright's discoveries of huge wooden structures at Durrington would have come as less of a surprise.

Avebury was well protected from roadworks or building, under permanent pasture, but Wainwright knew there was a small handful of other big henges, as little understood as Durrington Walls had been a few years before, when the situation was less happy. By now he was well entrenched in his position as a senior excavator in the Ministry, one who could be trusted to organise a large project to completion, with a loyal band of experienced staff. The Ministry's goal was to rescue what sites they could as they disappeared beneath roads and ploughs and urban expansion. But there was never any illusion that everything could be saved. Difficult decisions had to be taken, and in 1968 Geoff Wainwright had a suggestion. Over the next three years, he would see what was happening at the two large Wessex henges that, unlike Avebury, were actually under plough and disappearing fast. Perhaps he would find some more timber circles. If, that is, the sites did actually turn out to be henges.

So in the summer of 1969 the team were back together at the Hatfield enclosure, an all but ploughed flat and little-known earthwork near the village of Marden, about halfway between Durrington Walls and Avebury. It was not the sort of place that normally attracted the modern archaeologist.[110]

The situation at Marden was not unlike that at Durrington Walls before the recent excavations. Connections had been made with Avebury, but there was no evidence to confirm this. The strongest hint came in the first recorded reference to the site, in a letter written by John Mayo, a local vicar, to the Society of Antiquaries in London in 1769, exactly 200 years before Wainwright's dig.[111]

Mayo made explicit comparison to the Avebury earthwork, describing two entrances through a circular ditch that enclosed about 30 acres (12ha). He noted that when the farmer had levelled part of the bank in the previous year, 'a great many Staggs Horns were digged up' (a human skeleton was found, too, which Mayo reckoned to be a person 'about 6 ft 2 or 3 inches high' – 1.9m). This reference to deer antlers was suggestive, for as we have seen, Wainwright found quantities of antlers at the Walls, where they had been used as digging tools.

But there was more. Within the enclosure Mayo saw two large mounds. Reports of the larger, known as the Hatfield Barrow, attracted Sir William Colt Hoare in 1807 (just a few months before he went to see Durrington Walls). This mound was said to be the largest in the area, after Silbury, 150m in diameter and 7m high. Hoare's friend and foreman, William Cunnington, employed eight men on his behalf to open a huge hole in the centre. After ten days' digging they found signs of burning, but not the hoped-for human burial. More memorable was the workmen's lucky escape. Barely had Cunnington taken them away from the excavation on some errand than the deep trench collapsed, filling the hole with tons of earth. Ten years later, perhaps encouraged by the recent disturbance, the farmer had completely levelled this 'Giant of Marden'.

The second, smaller mound was close to the River Avon, which flows immediately to the south of the enclosure. Cunnington's description of this was even more tantalising. In fact, this was not so much a barrow as another enclosure, 60m in diameter. 'Its vallum [or bank] is slightly raised', Cunnington reported back to Hoare, 'and the interior rises gradually to a low apex. On digging within the area, we found a few bits of old pottery, and a little charred wood but no marks of any interment.'

Cunnington and Hoare had also seen the low earthwork at what would later become known as Woodhenge, and thought it was a large barrow that had been flattened. The description of the Marden enclosure rising 'gradually to a low apex' further recalls Woodhenge. It was this feature that earned Woodhenge its earlier nickname of the Dough Cover. Could there be another wood henge inside the Marden enclosure? At 60m across, this would be a little smaller than Woodhenge, but considerably larger than the Sanctuary.

At Durrington Walls, the size and positioning of his trenches were determined by the roadworks. At Marden, Wainwright could choose where he wanted to dig.[112] Tony Clark's geophysical survey was no help, as the wet sandy subsoil yielded no clues. So Wainwright decided to dig at the one entrance that was accessible, that to the north. At the Walls, the large southern circles were close to the southern entrance, and the end of the ditch there had been particularly rich in pottery and other finds. And, lo and behold, in their relatively small trench just inside the entrance they found the post holes of a simple, circular structure, and in the ditch a human skeleton, red deer antlers and quantities of Grooved Ware exactly like that found at Durrington Walls.

The interior enclosure that was so reminiscent of Woodhenge has never been examined. Arrangements were made to put the whole site down to permanent pasture, and Wainwright prepared for the third big putative henge: Mount Pleasant in Dorset. This time, things would turn out to be a little more dramatic.

Once again, there was an all but obliterated earthwork enclosure that no one was quite sure about. It was not until the newly wed

Stuart Piggott and (as she later became) Peggy Guido went exploring in Dorset in 1936 and 1937 that anyone considered the possibility that Mount Pleasant was a henge.[113] As before, it was the vestiges of a ditch that was on the inside of the bank that pointed this way. The Piggotts also noticed what looked like an Early Bronze Age round barrow built on top: the bank would then have to be older than the barrow. But that was all Wainwright had to go on.

Like Durrington Walls, Mount Pleasant was on chalk, a subsoil where geophysical survey had proved effective. Wainwright called on Tony Clark again, and in October 1969 he was out with his equipment on this low hill to the east of Dorchester. By taking readings with a resistivity meter at 1m intervals along twenty-six traverses, Clark easily found the enclosure ditch and identified three entrances. He also followed up the faint suggestion in an old air photo of a smaller circular ditch within the larger enclosure. Here, with the help of a proton magnetometer, he located this ring ditch precisely on the ground. And, unexpectedly, he found traces of a line running inside and parallel to the larger enclosure ditch.[114]

The following year found Geoff Wainwright with his team of staff and volunteers in Dorset, the now well-established Ministry of Works itinerant tent community strung out along two sides of a field in another hot summer.[115] Thanks to the geophysics they knew where to dig: at the west entrance through the large ditch (in the search for rubbish deposits), at a nearby stretch of the mysterious linear feature, and at the ring ditch. It was almost as if they had been there before (figure 19).[116] The outer ditch was a bit of a disappointment. It *was* a big ditch, and it was a henge. But Wainwright knew that anyway: as he said, he never lacked confidence. The problem was that the ditch fill consisted of little more than chalk and soil. There was no sign of the heaps of Neolithic artefacts and bones he was used to finding.

There were, however, compensations. The ring picked up in the air photo and the magnetometer survey turned out to be a circular ditch some 45m in diameter with a single break. The space inside was completely filled with arcs of post holes, arranged in five rough circles with four separating corridors. In some of the spaces between the groups of post holes were pits that appeared to have held small standing stones. The outer holes were so close to the ditch edge that the bank thrown up when the ditch was dug (now completely ploughed away) had to have been without. Wainwright

65

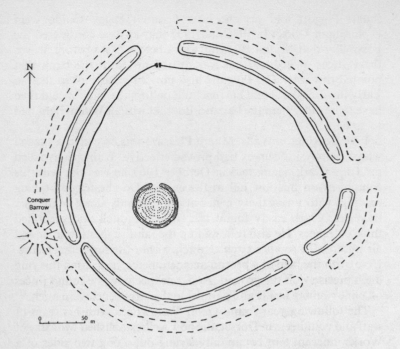

Figure 19. At Mount Pleasant in Dorset, Wainwright found a similar earthwork to that at Durrington Walls. Here there was a timber henge enclosed by its own ditch, and close to the large enclosure ditch, a deep palisade trench with two small gateways. *After Wainwright.*

had found what he was looking for: another wooden henge that, like the Sanctuary, displayed a combination of posts and stones (figure 20). It was, he says, 'like shelling peas out of a pod'.[117]

The rationale behind the henge project, having ascertained that these two big enclosures were henges like Durrington Walls and Avebury, was to see how well they were surviving under plough. This newly discovered timber henge gave a simple answer: they weren't. Buried under ploughwash at the bottom of a small valley, the post holes at Durrington Walls survived intact, the largest being nearly 3m deep and over 2m in diameter. All that survived at Mount Pleasant were the stubs of the holes, barely 30cm deep. Once, when the chalk had been scraped clean for photography, a light shower of rain passed over. As the sun came out, thin grooves

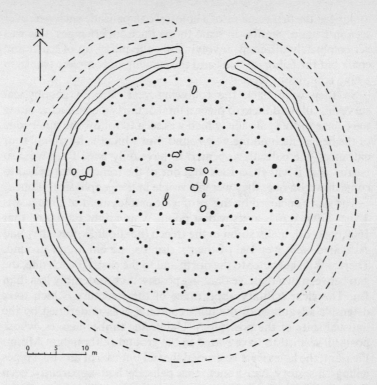

Figure 20. Some small pits among the post holes of the Mount Pleasant wood henge seem to have held standing stones in a square arrangement with three outliers. The outer ring of posts is so close to the ditch that the bank must have been on the outside, but it was completely ploughed away. *After Wainwright.*

could be seen crossing the site. You could actually see the destructive scrape of the last ploughing.

The real surprise, though, and the cause for great excitement, was the line picked up by the geophysics just inside the big ditch. This was yet another ditch, but of very different character from those they were used to excavating. It ran in from one end of the 33m-long archaeological trench and out the other side without a break. It was only about 1.25m wide, but the sides went straight down for well over 2m. Every 50cm there was a huge post pipe. At the south end of the cutting the tops of the pipes were just a mass of ash and charcoal: the posts had gone up in flames. If this deep, vertical-sided trench continued right around the hill, they were looking at the first remains of a colossal oak palisade enclosure ever seen in Britain. Similar in scale to the huge superhenges, this was yet completely different, involving not the piling up of earth and chalk but the felling of trees and the massing of complete trunks in a high continuous fence.

So they were back the following year. Precise geophysical surveying allowed them to place a total of thirty-one trenches along the course of this palisade, which was seen to follow the inner edge of the henge ditch all the way round. But while the ditch had four entrances, the palisade appeared to have only two. They were so narrow that it was sheer luck that one of the trenches happened to come down on one: they weren't visible in the geophysical plots.

The space enclosed by this profligate employment of timber was 4.5ha, 270m across at its widest point. Wainwright estimated that 1600 posts originally stood in the trench (he should know, they had excavated well over 100 of them), rising some 6m above ground. There was an entrance to the north and to the east. At each one, the gap between two massive flanking posts was considerably less than 1m. The clear military appearance of the structure, which took defensive advantage of the hill's contours, was underlined by the unusual state of the post pipes. Unlike the timber henges, whose posts all seemed to have rotted in the ground (although at Mount Pleasant, the holes were so eroded that all but two of any post pipes telling this story had gone), this palisade had apparently been deliberately destroyed. This was a completely new addition to the architecture of Hengeworld.

In the same season, they had another go at the large henge ditch, this time at the north entrance. Although there was still not the concentration of debris found at Durrington Walls and Marden in similar locations, they did find Grooved Ware on the ditch bottom – confirming the usual association of this ceramic with the henges – flint tools and the skeletons of two infants. Radiocarbon dates explained why the entrance they explored in 1970 was different. Antler from the west entrance was around 500 years younger than charcoal from primary silts at the north entrance.[118] The ditch they had excavated in 1970 was not part of the original henge. Rather, it was an extension added centuries later to bridge the gap across the old west entrance. This appeared to have happened at the same time as the palisade was constructed; at this point, the timber defence ran straight past the old break in the earthwork without a gateway.

The dig at Durrington Walls began in autumn 1966. Exactly nine years later, Wainwright finished his last report for publication on the work at Mount Pleasant.[119] In less than a decade, at the same time as he was excavating at other places around England and Wales, he had transformed archaeologists' perception of Hengeworld. He had brought three huge earthwork enclosures, two in Wiltshire (Marden and Durrington Walls) and one in Dorset (Mount Pleasant), into the fold. Before, only Avebury was known for certain to be prehistoric, and was then unique in its scale (the evidence was there for the ancient age of Durrington Walls, but no one had really taken on board what this meant). He had discovered and excavated four circular timber structures, at least one of which (at Mount Pleasant), with its integral ring ditch and megaliths, was precisely analogous to the famous sites of the Sanctuary and Woodhenge. And he had brought to life a previously unseen construction that looked more military than spiritual (again at Mount Pleasant). And all this on government budgets, with senior staff paid £1.75 a day or less, and teams of volunteers on beer money (technically known as subsistence) (figure 21).[120]

The whole project inspired many younger archaeologists to think about henges, the artefacts and bones found at them, and what they all meant. At the same time a new generation of researchers was starting to tackle some big unanswered questions about stone circles. How much was there in old claims for a standard unit of measurement and sophisticated surveying? What was the evidence for astronomy?

Meanwhile, excavation proceeded unabated throughout Britain, as the rich ancient tapestry of our towns and countryside continued to be destroyed. While nothing quite like the massive timber henges at Durrington Walls or Mount Pleasant came to light, several smaller or less well preserved sites were discovered. These mysterious wooden structures were not unique to Wessex, or even southern England. I will give just a few examples.

Amongst those most comparable to Woodhenge, Mount Pleasant and Arminghall, where timber rings were surrounded by a ditch, is Balfarg in Fife, Scotland. Excavation by Roger Mercer in 1977 and 1978 exposed a roughly circular ditch some 70m across, with evidence that the lost bank stood outside, surrounding a ring of fifteen or sixteen large post pits. The evidence isn't that clear, but surviving pits that appear to have held megaliths (two stones are actually still standing) indicate that two stone circles, or perhaps a

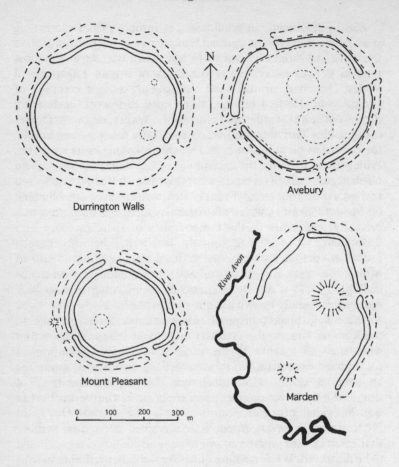

N

Durrington Walls

Avebury

River Avon

Mount Pleasant

Marden

0   100   200   300 m

Figure 21. The four Wessex superhenges. *After Wainwright.*

single oval of stones, stood between the post ring and the ditch. As at similar sites in the south of England, Grooved Ware pottery was found in some of the post holes.[121]

North Mains, Perthshire, is another comparable Scottish site, excavated by Gordon Barclay. A ring of twenty-four large posts once stood quite close to the inner edge of a ditch 40 or 50m in diameter. Inside this ring, slightly to one side, was an oval of perhaps twenty smaller pits. There is no evidence as to whether these two timber structures stood together, or if one followed the other.[122]

Alex Gibson, an archaeologist then with the Clwyd-Powys Archaeological Trust in central Wales, over the winter of 1990–1 excavated a circle of twenty post holes (each with very clear post pipes) 20m across at Sarn-y-bryn-caled. With echoes of Durrington Walls, a relief road was due to sweep through a complex of neolithic ritual monuments identified from air photos (upstanding earthworks had long been ploughed away). There were few artefacts, but radiocarbon dating showed this site was another relic from Hengeworld. In the centre of the ring had stood six posts. After these had rotted away, a scoop was dug through the infilled post pits for the insertion of a couple of human cremations. Close by was an oblong pit with a post pipe at each end that suggested the two split halves of a tree trunk had been placed opposite each other, rising into the air.[123]

This discovery inspired its finder. They held an open day for the public at the site, with new timbers in the post holes, in a sort of wake before the road was built. Alex then took the opportunity to assemble evidence for all timber rings then known in Britain.[124] There were, he wrote, forty or so timber circles scattered throughout Britain and Ireland. They varied considerably, in size, numbers of rings, and associated features like standing stones or ditches, or other wooden constructions. But none of them looked as if it had been a circular building used for domestic business like sleeping, cooking or group meetings. The largest excavated post ring is still the outer oval at Woodhenge (at 72m); the smallest in Alex's list are 7m across (sites in Wales and Scotland). Our main focus, however, will be on the Wessex region, where there is more than enough to keep us occupied.[125]

While there has still been no excavation inside the great circle at Avebury, there has been considerable fieldwork in the area. Most dramatically, Alasdair Whittle, over three summers between 1989 and 1992, established the existence of two timber enclosures comparable in size and construction to that found by Geoff Wainwright at Mount Pleasant.

The monumental West Kennet palisade enclosures lie in the Kennet valley just south of the megalithic avenue, without the additional protection of the older earthwork seen at Mount Pleasant. Partial excavation has revealed three smaller circular timber rings inside one of the palisades.[126] Parts of another palisade enclosure, which might be as much as 380m across, have been found not far from Mount Pleasant in Dorchester, at Greyhound

Yard. Truly massive pits 3m deep were dug out for posts thought to have been 12m long.

Meanwhile, on Cranbourne Chase in Dorset, Martin Green, a farmer with a passion for archaeology that he indulges with regular excavations and the maintenance of his own museum, has been uncovering places where the people of Hengeworld actually seem to have lived. His evidence so far points to small groups of circular huts, perhaps no more than a few families living together: a very different scale from the superhenges and the structures they enclose.

And then there is Stonehenge.

In 1980, Julian Richards began a seven-year field project in the landscape around Stonehenge, depressingly, but all too necessarily, exploring the extent to which anything survived of ancient settlement in the area at all. In fact, although so much of his evidence was garnered from the ploughsoil, it turned out to be a very productive exercise. His very first dig was on a low hill south-east of Stonehenge known as Coneybury, at what was once thought to be a ploughed-out barrow but in air photos looked more like a henge. Julian went to investigate.

The oval ditch, 45m across at its longest diameter, had a single gap. Like that at Woodhenge and Stonehenge, it faced into the north-east arc. About 5m in from the ditch edge was a line of small post holes marked at a point opposite the gap in the ditch by a pair of large pits. There were about a dozen pits near the centre, some of which might have been post holes, but which made no obvious pattern. The whole of the interior area was more or less covered with small, circular stake holes. They 'box-sectioned' some of these, carving square holes out of the chalk, one side of which cut down through the centre of the stake holes. From these they could see the sharp ends of the holes, shaped by a hard stick of pointed timber. With its deep ditch and external bank, its north-easterly orientation and its ring of post holes, Coneybury was like Woodhenge. But while Woodhenge was full of massive post pits, Coneybury sported a delicate outer ring of posts and hundreds of tiny wooden stakes. It seemed to be part of the timber henge tradition, but it added a new dimension.[127]

When in 1925 Gilbert Insall photographed what later became known as Woodhenge, this site was unique. The connection with Stonehenge was inescapable, and much discussion took place as to which was imitating which. Many felt Woodhenge to be a poor copy of its grander stone neighbour; Woodhenge was almost an appendage to Stonehenge, a bit like a shed round the back of a cathedral.

Thirty years later, Richard Atkinson and Stuart Piggott were so struck by the contrast between Stonehenge and other places like Woodhenge that they were convinced its designer must have come from outside northern Europe altogether. 'Stonehenge is unique,' wrote Piggott, 'the individual creation of an architect whose capabilities in design and proportion were far beyond those of barbarian north-west Europe at the time . . .'[128] 'For all their evident power and wealth,' echoed Atkinson, 'these men [Wessex chieftains] were essentially barbarians.'

You can sense the imperceptible flick of his cigarette holder as he continues: 'As such, can they have encompassed unaided a monument which uniquely transcends all other comparable prehistoric buildings in Britain . . .? It seems to me that to account for these exotic and unparalleled features one *must* assume the existence of influence from the only contemporary European cultures in which *architecture*, as distinct from mere construction, was already a living tradition.' In short, in Greece.[129]

It seems to me we've come a long way since then. Wood henges and the huge superhenge earthworks are now firm, powerful and distinctive features of the ritual landscape of Hengeworld. This is a transformation that has taken place since 1966, and it is very big news. We don't need to embark on detailed reconstructions of what may have stood in the post holes of some of these sites to imagine some pretty clever building work, and to see Stonehenge not as exotic or unparalleled, but as indigenous: wood turned to stone, soft to hard, the decaying to the imperishable. The epithet 'mere construction' can only be read with incredulity today.

Seeing it like this gives us a completely new perspective. This point of view permeates the rest of the book. It is a perspective that allowed me and some of my colleagues to feel great excitement at the news of the enormous, bragging timber henge at Stanton Drew, but no great surprise. And it is with this in mind that we finally come to enter the circular ditch and bank that surround what is probably the most written-about heap of broken stones anywhere in the world: Stonehenge.

PART II:

Peopling Stonehenge

8

A Darn' Nuisance

'We found some bones in the section. When John was taking his soil samples.' It was Jenny Price phoning from Salisbury.

'What, my section? The ditch section?'

'Yes. There were leg bones sticking out.'

Margaret Ehrenburg, a research student at Cardiff University, was in London. Every spring the Prehistoric Society, the leading independent forum in Britain for archaeologists with interests in prehistory, has held a weekend conference. In 1978 the theme was metalworking in prehistoric Europe. Margaret's thesis went deep into Bronze Age axe heads. She couldn't miss this conference. She left the little excavation at Stonehenge before they had quite finished. Well, they *had* finished, really, as far as she was concerned. The archaeology was done. All that was left was some scientific sampling; that wasn't her department. Jenny, an old friend, was then Keeper at Salisbury Museum, and had been helping out at the dig.

In fact, they weren't really looking for archaeology at all. And when they found it, John Evans, project director, was not amused – 'It was a darn' nuisance – messed up the stratigraphy of the thing.'[130]

Evans, now Professor, was then Lecturer in Archaeology at University College, Cardiff. He had written his doctorate at the Institute of Archaeology in London, on the use of land snails in reconstructing past environments. He had worked with Geoff Wainwright in the henge project. He had also sampled the Avebury henge, in an excavation by Faith Vatcher (and later he would have another opportunity at one of mine).[131] There wasn't a lot John didn't know about snails, and they proved particularly enlightening as environmental indicators at these henge sites.

It was snails that had brought him, with some Cardiff students, to Stonehenge in 1978. He had written to the Chief Inspector of Ancient Monuments for permission to dig at Stonehenge. No problem. 'It was', he reflects now, 'all very casual in those days.' It had helped that, at least inside Stonehenge itself, his plan had been only to re-excavate two trenches dug in 1954 by Richard Atkinson. He also dug some new trenches away from the monument, down the hill to the north, to look at the ditches beside the Avenue.

His student research had shown that many of the wide variety of snail species found in Britain are extremely fussy about their habitat. Certain snails live only in environments that are damp, or dry, or shaded, or open, and so on. Snail shells are essentially calcium, and survive very well on the chalk. The types of snail that lived at these sites 4000–5000 years ago, as shown by the shells buried in the ground, were indicative of the vegetation then prevalent.

John had collected samples from the ditches at Mount Pleasant and Woodhenge, and from the soils buried when the henge banks at Marden, Durrington Walls, Mount Pleasant and Avebury were thrown up (such soils 'die', and can preserve a great deal of information about land use and the environment at the time they were buried). First in a London lab and later in Cardiff he had identified and counted thousands of microscopic snail shells from amongst the soil and chalk of his samples. The different assemblages at different points in the sequences, for example the changing ratios between 'grassland' and 'woodland' species, allowed him to reconstruct a Neolithic vegetation, which, it was clear, was not a static thing that could be taken for granted.

He summarised the results of this research in the Mount Pleasant excavation report.[132] The snails told a story of forest spreading over the open landscape at the end of the Ice Age some 10,000 years ago. Hunters and fishers (as well as natural occurrences such as windthrow and fires) maintained openings in this forest, although at Avebury the evidence suggested particularly dense woodland. With the arrival of Neolithic farming, the forest began to break up. By 4000 years ago the big henges were being built in an environment, at least locally, of mature grassland. These tiny fossil molluscs had helped dispel the myth that the open turf of chalk downland is a 'natural' vegetation: it is an artefact of farmers and their grazing animals.

John liked to take his samples from archaeologists' sections, the carefully cleaned vertical walls cut through thick deposits to reveal the different layers of earth, rubble and silt that accumulate over weeks or centuries. He would typically arrive towards the end of a dig, like a doctor at a dying patient, peg out his strings and tapes, and dig little square holes in columns into the section faces. By the time he had finished, the archaeologists' sections would, in their eyes, be an embarrassing mess.[133] Margaret Ehrenburg did the business at Stonehenge. The real work would start when she had finished.

There was little to think about once she had surveyed in the edges of the trench, for they had deliberately sited it over the older excavation of twenty-three years before. Margaret took out Atkinson's backfill, gently cleaned back his section a centimetre or two in readiness for the sampling, and on Friday set up her drawing kit. Then she saw something that bothered her.

'John,' she said, indicating some subtle changes in colour and texture on the section face, 'there's a cut here. Don't know what it's doing.' She could see signs that a pit, or perhaps another ditch, had been dug into the partially refilled Neolithic ditch, so that they were now looking at the fill not just of the original ditch, but, about halfway up from the bottom on the right-hand side, of another prehistoric feature too. Richard Atkinson hadn't recorded this. John couldn't see it. He didn't need it. He wanted a nice clean, simple sequence of ditch fill for his samples. They bickered about it. Margaret put the 'cut' on her section drawing. The next day, when she was in London, John took his samples from the other side of the ditch.

And then the section fell in, exposing some human bones. Margaret had been right: there was a pit dug into the ditch. It was a grave.

9

No Fooling About

Archaeologists are sometimes accused of being less than forth-coming in their explanations of Stonehenge. Nonetheless, one of the clearest statements on its function was made by an archaeologist, one William Flinders Petrie. The theory was presented, on behalf of Petrie and three other men (not archaeologists), in a writ at High Court in March 1904. Stone-henge, the court was informed, was 'an ancient building and place of assembly for public worship, the burial of the dead [and] deliberation on public affairs or other public purposes'. It followed (and this was the desire of the writ) that the public could walk through Stonehenge as and when they chose. The defence countered with an alternative hypothesis on prehistoric life, that Stonehenge had always been in private hands, 'from time immemorial and in fact at all times'.[134]

The defence won.

What I find particularly interesting about this legal exchange is that in 1904 no one could have had the slightest idea why Stonehenge was built. They could guess. They could compare it to other large buildings they knew well, such as medieval cathedrals or ancient Egyptian pyramids. But they had no local, contemporary context for the stones. They had no idea what history of construction lay behind the present ruins, and only a hint of when the work took place. There were no other stone circles or similar remains elsewhere that they could claim, with supporting evidence, to have been built by the same people. It was all a complete mystery.

A century later, things are very different. A dig in 1901 produced the first indication of Stonehenge's real age. Larger-scale work directed by William Hawley between 1919 and 1926 saw half the monument stripped bare, revealing the complexity of its story. Smaller excavations throughout the rest of the century, especially by Richard Atkinson and colleagues in the 1950s but also by several other teams in subsequent years, added detail to the emerging picture.

Until the recent English Heritage project, the results of most of this work were inaccessible, even to archaeologists. Not any more. In this part of the book I will attempt to tell the story of Stonehenge as we now understand it. We cannot dissociate this from the way it was dug up: archaeologists have achieved much, but to do this they have also destroyed much, not always with good justification, and not always with proper record. We need to know how this happened if we are properly to understand what they found.

In these days when the question of who has rights of access to Stonehenge – who 'owns' Stonehenge – is frequently and sometimes bitterly aired, it is easy to be unaware that the arguments are not new. As the 1904 High Court writ reveals, they did not begin with police attacking a travellers' convoy at the Battle of the Beanfield in 1985. They were not born of a confrontation between a Conservative government of oppressive law and order (represented at Stonehenge by the police, the National Trust and English Heritage) and fringe communities defending basic human rights.[135]

Neither is the present squalor that is the visitor experience, politely characterised by the Public Accounts Committee of the House of Commons as a 'national disgrace', anything new.[136] Consider these two comments. Can you say which was made in 1997, and which very nearly a century before?

> Have we really fallen so low, are we so devoid of a sense of history, is political will and leadership so far decayed that we cannot even maintain, still less feel a sense of pride in, our foremost ancient monument without having to call in a leisure company to shore up the enterprise?

> STONEHENGE FOR SALE. In any other country, so grotesque looking an announcement as the above would hardly come within the scope of practical possibilities.

(The phrase 'leisure company' gives it away: the first is 1997, the second 1899.)[137]

In fact, in several respects things are better at Stonehenge today than they have been for a long time.[138] Megaliths are not propped up by a motley collection of wooden poles (as some were between

1881 and 1920), neither, now encased in concrete footings, are they likely to fall over (as two did in the twentieth century). It is no longer possible to drive through the stones, as it was until 1901, or across the earthwork around them: a road used to pass right across bank, ditch and prehistoric pits (accounting for heaps of horse dung and straw in pre-combustion engine days). There is not now a sprawling mass of hangars, outbuildings and runways (not to mention soldiers and airmen) threatening to engulf Stonehenge, as there was in the First World War. Neither are there custodians' cottages and huts prominent on the near horizon, or even, on wheels, actually amongst the megaliths. The visitor's peace is not disturbed by the din of others hammering away at stones for souvenirs (as a *Times* letter complained in 1871). The centre of the monument has not been packed with people like a subway carriage, standing in a sea of mud or a whirl of scouring dry dust, since the stones were fenced off in 1978.

There is absolutely no denying that Stonehenge today is an embarrassing, abominable, inexcusable mess. But, incredible though it may seem, it has been worse. From a purely archaeological perspective, however, matters seem to have been much better a hundred years ago. To unravel all this, we need to go back to the beginning.

What we might call the first excavations at Stonehenge by archaeologists were conducted by that great Wiltshire team, William Cunnington and Richard Colt Hoare. A famous friendship developed between baronet-landowner-banker Sir Richard and trader Cunnington, who pooled their talents and resources to conduct a sumptuously published campaign of excavation and fieldwork in Wiltshire between 1801 and 1810, focusing especially on barrows near Stonehenge.[139]

Two small jobs at Stonehenge constitute their first and last recorded digs. In 1798, shortly before the two met, Cunnington poked about under the stones of the northern trilithon, which had fallen the previous year, and found pottery, animal bones and a piece of glass. In 1810 the men were there together when they dug under the Slaughter Stone to ascertain whether or not it once stood up (they decided it had).[140]

These were modest little affairs that produced useful results with little damage. In 1824, Stonehenge came into the ownership of the Antrobus family, with whom it stayed until its sale in 1915.[141] As much through a determination to maintain their personal authority over private property as through any concern about conservation, the Antrobuses saw to it that throughout this near-century there were only two significant excavations, one of which (in 1839 by Captain Beamish in front of the Altar Stone) was in an area even then probably already fully dug over.[142] All hell might break loose above ground, but below the turf little happened that was outside the control of rabbits, insects and worms.

Things would have been different if archaeologists had had their way. The Wiltshire Archaeological Society, John Lubbock (later Lord Avebury), John Evans and Lane Fox (later General Augustus Pitt-Rivers), and Flinders Petrie were all refused permission to dig.[143] Charles Darwin got away with it, digging around fallen stones, investigating the cumulative power of the individually tiny efforts of earthworms (his book on the subject included a chapter on 'The part which worms have played in the burial of ancient buildings').[144] Henry Cunnington (Maud's father-in-law), on the other hand, plainly one of the less successful practitioners in that archaeological dynasty, agreed in 1881 to publish a written apology for presuming to remove some turf.[145]

Then, on the last day of December 1900, the real end of the century, a stone fell, throwing its lintel to the ground, where it broke in two.[146] Sir Edmund Antrobus, fearful of an accident, fenced off Stonehenge and charged an admission fee. Meanwhile Petrie had heard the news in Egypt, and had written to *The Times*, instructing how the excavation should be managed.[147] The advice was sound ('There must be no fooling about driving up each day from an hotel in Salisbury to find that workmen have wiped out historical evidences before breakfast') if dry ('no festive luncheons and notabilities must be allowed to distract the recorder for a moment').

Antrobus ignored almost all counsel (as plentiful then as it is now). The one concession he made was to approve the straightening of stone 56, the largest megalith still standing on the site, which looked set to follow the recent precedent and crash to the ground. The plan was to winch the stone to a vertical position, excavate around the base, fill the hole with concrete – and while they were at it, to do something about the archaeology.

The man chosen for this job was William Gowland, Associate (later Professor) of the Royal School of Mines at South Kensington. There is no record of his having dug another site before or since. 'Perhaps', notes that pithy observer of other archaeologists, Christopher Chippindale, 'that explains why his work was so good.'[148] And astonishingly good it was.[149] His small trenches have every right to be judged, by the changing standards of the times in which they were all dug, the best archaeology of any done at Stonehenge.

The work took place over twenty-nine days in August and September 1901. With the aid of specially constructed measuring frame and rod, while the huge leaning megalith was boxed in wooden frame, supported on larch poles sunk into the ground, and slowly edged upright with thick cables and blocks, Gowland excavated an area of about 17 square metres around the base, recovering all finds down to ⅛ inch (3mm) across.[150] Under what must have been difficult working conditions, he drew numerous sections showing the subsoil, the stone pit and the base of the stone itself.[151]

On 19 December the same year (exactly four months after the dig began) he presented his full report to the Society of Antiquaries, sixty-nine pages of immaculate description and faultless interpretation. His text was accompanied by some powerful photos of the work (taken from the 'excellent series of photographs of Stonehenge . . . [by] Miss Clarisse Miles'), and copious diagrams and illustrations of artefacts. Not only that, but he was able to find a geologist, Professor J. W. Judd of the Royal College of Science, who prepared a detailed study of the rock fragments from his excavation, in time to incorporate the results into his own paper.[152]

So what was he able to tell his audience in the rooms in Burlington Gardens?

'Immediately beneath the turf and intermingled with its roots,' he said, 'chips and fragments of flint were very abundant.' He also found heaps of 'clay-pipe stems, pieces of broken crockery, bottles and glasses, together with pins, buttons, and other rubbish'. All of this clearly had nothing to do with the people who actually built Stonehenge, for as he went deeper it disappeared. Instead, he found numerous 'chippings and pieces of all the rocks of which the stones consist'. Fragments of sarsen (as seen in the large megaliths of local sandstone) and bluestone (as in smaller megaliths of rocks from further afield, mostly igneous) 'occurred together down to the chalk rock', which he found at about 1m below the surface.[153]

The pit in which the stone stood was some 2m deep. Here he found a piece of deer antler 'embedded in a lump of chalk'. 'This', he said, was 'of considerable importance as evidence of the use of deer's horn picks for excavating.'[154] Other finds included over 100 stone implements, mostly 'hammerstones', oval or sphere-like lumps of flint and sarsen that had been worn down by intensive pounding in the dressing of megaliths. Stonehenge is thought to be the only stone circle in Britain where megaliths were carved: it is one of the features that gives it its unique appearance. Gowland called the largest hammers 'mauls'. All these were of a type of very hard sarsen; they weighed up to a massive 26.5kg.[155]

But more than anything, everywhere he dug, he found pieces of rock. 'The chippings and pieces of stone are those which had been detached from the stones and the tools during the operations of shaping and dressing. They were found in very large quantities.'[156] In fact, if nothing was left but the pits in the ground, and the debris that Gowland found in their fill, it would be possible for an archaeologist to say that something like Stonehenge had once stood there, just from the subterranean evidence. Even below the turf, Stonehenge is unique.

The tall sarsen had been erected from inside the circle, and the much smaller bluestone beneath it had been added later. Judd noted that bluestone fragments were far more numerous than sarsen, the opposite of the ratio between the two rock types above ground. This meant, he thought, that the sarsens had been roughly dressed at their distant quarry, and finished on site; while the smaller bluestones had been brought to Stonehenge in an undressed state, and worked on after their arrival.[157]

These finds pointed to a date in the Neolithic 'or, it may be . . . the Early Bronze Age'. Stonehenge was built not by some missionising megalithic race from abroad, but by our own 'rude forefathers'. It was not a burial ground, as many had suggested, 'but a place of sanctity dedicated to the observation or adoration of the sun'.[158]

It would be difficult to come up with a more accurate description of the general state of affairs at Stonehenge below the ground, even after the passage of a century and the excavation of a further 500 trenches. Neither, after a major radiocarbon dating programme conducted in the past few years, can we argue with his broad assessment of the date. We agree with him that Stonehenge was built by native peoples, that it was not primarily a cemetery (at least for most of the time), and that the sun did have some role to play in its web of meanings.

There was really only one thing he got seriously wrong. 'The monument as a whole', he wrote, 'is of one date. Its parts do not belong to different ages.'[159] At that point, Gowland could not have known how mistaken he was. The huge excavations that shattered the superficial appearance of a timeless, unchanging monument were yet to take place. And today, archaeologists are still arguing about how the complex sequence should be interpreted. In fact, some of the disputes have been so bitter that the chief uncoverer of the evidence has been branded a villain, a mindless destroyer of Stonehenge who, without reason or record, dug away half the underground deposits.

What pleasure, then, to be able to reveal that in this case, reality is happier than archaeological folktale. Gowland found a worthy successor in Lieutenant Colonel William Hawley. It is time the full story was told of the largest excavation programme ever conducted at Stonehenge.

10

Why Didn't You See that Pit?

John Evans had started by taking nineteen bags full of soil and chalk from the vertical section that Margaret Ehrenburg had prepared for him through the ditch silts. The samples were arranged in a column, designed to study the different layers that could be seen clearly in the section, curving in from the sides. Each bag was carefully labelled, ready for analysis back in Cardiff, where John would examine the tiny fossil snail shells that would help him build up a picture of changing vegetation at Stonehenge as the ditch filled. The ditch itself was nearly 2m deep, with a wide flat bottom.

So far so good. Older excavations at Stonehenge had shown that snails were well preserved there, and John had every reason to expect positive results from his work in the lab. There was one problem. When was the ditch dug? He and other workers had constructed quite a detailed picture of the ancient environment around Stonehenge, but to fit Stonehenge itself into the picture he would need to be able to say what was contemporary with what. Which is why he had started to think about deer antlers.

We have seen that shed red deer antlers were a favoured tool for digging the chalk at this time, and that they were commonly thrown into the excavations when they were done. Antler is a good material for radiocarbon dating. At his own excavation at Woodhenge, John and Geoff Wainwright had recovered a pile of ten antler picks on the ditch floor. One of these had recently been crunched up at the British Museum lab in exchange for a date of around 4200 years ago.[160] Perhaps, he'd thought, there was an antler in the Stonehenge ditch, just behind the wall of fill in front of him. One would be enough. So he'd crouched down, got out his trowel and begun to hack into the chalk rubble near the ditch bottom. Anything he found would have got there at or very soon after the time the ditch was dug.

He didn't find any antler. But the section above him fell down. And sticking out into the new space was the end of a human tibia. Whoops.

It didn't take long to realise that someone had been buried there, in a pit dug into the ditch after it had partially filled up. The orientation of the tibia – a lower leg bone – indicated that the body had been laid out roughly parallel to the ditch sides. It was the foot end that was exposed, so presumably the rest of the skeleton was still in the ground. They had no option but to dig it out. This was not what John Evans had come to Stonehenge to do, and it didn't help that Margaret was in London at a conference, and virtually all the staff had gone.

They carefully removed loose soil from around the bones, and found themselves looking down on a severely scrambled specimen of human anatomy. The jaw was still in place below the skull, but one shoulder blade was up against the nose, back bones were scattered all over the place, and some of the ribs were wrapped around the legs. The explanation seemed prosaic. Animal burrows were visible in the ditch section, and they'd found a polecat skull. In the burial pit itself were two pieces of chalk with scratches that looked as if they had been made by a badger. If badgers had made a sett here, it was remarkable that the bones had survived at all. That they were prehistoric, there was no doubt. The condition alone suggested that. They were extremely well preserved, but fragile – typical of ancient bone found on the chalk. And there were further clues.

Still close to the body – mixed up with the bones – were three beautiful little flint arrowheads and a thin stone object shaped a bit like a finger biscuit with a small circular hole at each end. Both the arrowheads and the 'bracer', as the finger biscuit is known (such items are thought to have been used by archers as wrist protectors), are distinctive of burials frequently accompanied by a particular type of pot technically known by archaeologists as a 'Beaker'. Beakers, often very finely made, are covered with small-toothed comb impressions. The pots are found over much of Europe. They and other items such as arrowheads are so distinctive that in the past archaeologists spoke of a 'Beaker People', who swept across Europe with their fine pots, loosing arrows into the air.

This is a controversial topic in archaeology, but it would be true to say that though Beaker People can still be found in books or heard about in guided tours, for the past twenty years or so few practising archaeologists have believed in them. Instead, the fine pots and other artefacts are thought to be a still visible manifestation of some lost fashion, ritual practice or social phenomenon that spread from one community to another, subtly changing as it passed.

Fragments of Beakers are commonly found at other sites contemporary with graves that contain complete pots. The Cunningtons found Beaker sherds at Woodhenge and the Sanctuary, and Wainwright found them in his henge excavations (the skeleton against the stone at the Sanctuary actually had a complete Beaker with it). Whenever it's possible to tell, the Beaker sherds are in deposits that are slightly more recent than those containing Grooved Ware. By the time Beaker pottery was being used, it seems, people had more or less given up making Grooved Ware (see figures 11 and 12).

Although there was no pottery in the Stonehenge grave, because of the arrowheads and the bracer they started to call it the 'Beaker burial'. A classic Beaker grave contains the remains of a man or a woman (occasionally a child), lying on their side in a crouched position, with knees bent and a few objects around them. These would most obviously be the Beaker (often lying on its side rather than standing) and a handful of the distinctive tanged flint arrowheads, sometimes arranged in such a way that they seem to indicate a vanished quiver of arrows. Other, rarer items include copper objects such as daggers and rings, jet or bone belt rings, jet buttons and the stone bracers. The burials are not uncommon. The largest modern British study of Beakers, completed in 1969, came up with 1235 removed by archaeologists from graves, and many have been found since.[161]

Short-staffed and with little time, John and his team were not able to prepare the normal detailed technical drawing of the burial in the ground. But Dick Spicer, like Margaret a Cardiff student, took some high-quality near-vertical photographs that could later be used to augment their sketches. The bones were boxed up, the arrowhead and bracer handled like antique jewellery, and it all went back to Cardiff with the soil samples (figure 22).

Richard Atkinson was excited by the burial find, and helped John prepare a quick note to announce it in the November issue of the nearest thing archaeologists then had to a news magazine, *Antiquity*. A burial of 'Beaker age' had been found in the ditch at Stonehenge, they wrote, and the body was accompanied by some very nice grave-goods.[162] This was the only human skeleton to have been found at Stonehenge in modern times. Indeed, it was the only one that most archaeologists even knew about, as the very few

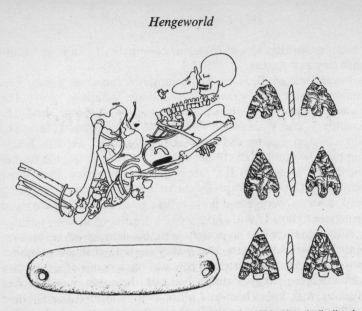

Figure 22. The skeleton found in the ditch around Stonehenge in 1978 had been badly disturbed by burrowing animals, but the man's bowstring wrist guard was still lying beside his lower left arm. Three flint arrowheads of barbed and tanged type were in the region of his chest. The tip of the largest (bottom right) was found in one of his ribs; the tip of a fourth was in his breast bone. *After Evans.*

others from the site had not been fully published and the bones were lost. The arrows and the wrist guard said he was an archer. Someone buried at Stonehenge when it was new, still being altered, had to have been an important, significant person.

It was a surprise to have found this burial. It was a nuisance for John, because it had distracted him from his sampling – although he later realised it actually had a lot to say about the way the ditch had filled up, which was important to his study. Margaret was not pleased to have missed it. Before she went up to London she had tried to persuade John that she could see a pit in the side of the ditch, but he hadn't believed her. No, he said, it's just animal disturbance. Now he teased her about it. Why didn't you see that pit, Margaret?

Yes, it was a surprise, but no one yet knew what was to turn up when they looked more carefully at the bones. That was not to be a surprise. It would be a shock. They didn't yet know it, but they had chanced on one of the most extraordinary things ever dug up at Stonehenge.

Whoops.

11

I Do Not the Least Mind
the Loneliness

Lieutenant Colonel William Hawley, a balding man with jutting jaw and moustache of independent existence, reached up in his thick tweed outdoor suit and dropped some small pieces of mud-covered flint into a metal tray. There were three trays, labelled 1, 2 and 3 with three pieces of white card. As he turned his back, an old lady, towering over Hawley, who had his boots planted at the bottom of a trench in the shadow of the Stonehenge stones, poked him with her umbrella.

'I think I'll have one of the tuppenny ones, please Sir.'[163]

Well, sadly for the lady, these flints were not for sale. And sadly for us, they are now probably buried back in the ground not far from where they were first excavated in the early 1920s. One of the stranger Stonehenge facts is that most of the things dug up then at this remarkable site (which means most of the things dug up there, ever) were poured back into holes in the ground. They are, as far as we know, still there. We even know where, approximately, the holes are. Stone tools by the hundred, chips and flakes by the barrowload, animal and human bones, old nails, bits of teacup, who knows what. In one pit are, so we suppose, the remains of most of the fifty-odd human cremations (though we don't know exactly how many). If they were each in a paper bag when they were reburied, then skilled excavation could, in theory, recover the cremations one by one as separate entities, even though the paper would have rotted away. The possibilities for future understanding of Stonehenge if this was the case are truly exciting. If they were just poured in like so much path cinder, then very little will be left to learn at all.[164]

For the visitor, the dreamer, the advertising agency, Stonehenge is extraordinary, the perfect combination of deep human mystery, isolation and visual icon. For the archaeologist, it is more. It is an opening into a lost but real world, rich in information and symbol.

But they see something else that most people don't, and it isn't simply because the archaeologist knows more about the ancient history of the place.

I earlier commented (chapter 9) that for nearly a century the private owners of Stonehenge did their best to prevent anyone from digging it up. Controversy raged about what to do with the monument that everyone could see, but below ground little moved except the animal life in a soil that had been developing for 4000 years. Something very different happened this century.

Stonehenge found its way into public hands in 1918. At the 1915 sale it was bought by a local man, Cecil Chubb, but three years later he gave it to the nation. The very first Commissioner of Works, on behalf of the government, accepted the deeds in a ceremony amongst the stones attended by Druids and important archaeologists (it's a shame they didn't have video cameras then).[165] Passed down through the Office of Works, the Ministry of Works, the Department of the Environment and now English Heritage, we still own it (along with all those finds buried in the ground).

Our new guardians were responsibly concerned about the danger of more megaliths falling, and used their expertise in what was presumably the first time experienced structural engineers had considered the monument in its entirety since it was designed and built around 4500 years before. Their approach was sensitive, in this respect reflecting Flinders Petrie's recommendations, who had written that 'to trim up the place, by re-erecting every stone that has fallen, would be no benefit either to its appearance or to archaeology'.[166] The goal was to make it entirely safe, yet to change as little as possible of its outward face.[167] And like Edmund Antrobus in 1901, they wanted to see that any disturbance to the ground was properly examined by an archaeologist. This time, the Society of Antiquaries put up experienced excavator William Hawley for the job. His programme lasted eight years. But things didn't stop there. Other archaeologists picked up the torch, in total opening over 500 cuttings.[168]

So now there are two monuments at Stonehenge. The first is the familiar lichen-spattered political football and mysterious icon. The other is more ethereal, more informative and, in some respects, more captivating. Unknown to most of those who would 'save' Stonehenge, it is at least as precious as the above-ground remains. This is the world the archaeologist knows, Stonehenge underground. It is a world of pits and ditches, graves, hidden megaliths and strange artefacts. It is also a world of archaeological endeavour, of people pitting themselves against the odds to understand Stonehenge, to rescue what morsels of contact they can with our remote ancestors who were there 4000–5000 years ago. And it is the finds and records that survive from this work, scattered across museums, libraries, private houses and ageing memories.

And without a doubt, in this century that saw the creation of the underground Stonehenge, the most important time was that eight-year period when Lieutenant Colonel William Hawley and his assistants laid bare nearly half the site (plates 5–6). It is a story that even few archaeologists know.[169]

Seeming 'to forget his years at Stonehenge',[170] the fifty-eight-year-old Hawley put both his imagination and his back into the job. Not being local, and his budget not reaching to a hotel room, he moved into a hut on the site. At other times he lived in an old mill at Figheldean[171] in the Avon valley, not many miles away, reaching his room by an outside ladder. Sometimes he dined with a lady who lived at the bottom of the hill.[172] The whole operation was a remarkable achievement, pursued with determination over nearly a decade, at a location that was really quite remote, in weather that was frequently appalling and, particularly in later years, in an atmosphere where it must have seemed that his efforts were little appreciated by the archaeologists 'in town', up in London.

In the first twelve months, Stonehenge was a hive of activity. There were several men engaged in operating the machinery used for straightening the megaliths, with whom Hawley seemed to be on good terms. He commented that the labourers 'get very interested in "old time" work',[173] and he posed for a photograph with them, sitting on a fallen stone looking (almost) one of the lads.[174]

A skilled Office of Works draughtsman and surveyor, Mr Wright, came down every so often to plan the trenches and record the megaliths. Hawley was interviewed by a Mr Darwin from *The Times*, proudly answering all the questions he could.[175] There was hardly an archaeologist or an archaeological society that didn't come to see what was going on. He had the personal assistance of Robert Newall, who found a bottle of port under one of the stones,[176] which they believed had been left for them (though sadly it was undrinkable) over a century before by William Cunnington and Sir Richard Colt Hoare. He was a happy man.

The job of restoring megaliths was soon over, however, and Hawley was on his own. The visitors dropped away, and the interest of members of the Society of Antiquaries in London seemed to diminish each time he gave a new talk. At first, Hawley's passion for the site was enough to sustain him. 'The Office of Works', he wrote to Gowland in 1921, 'are not doing anything here for the next 2 years so I am all alone and am doing the work myself without labour but shall have a man later for filling in. I do not the least mind the loneliness and am perfectly happy with the work and a comfortable little compartment in a hut.'[177]

But the site began to take its toll. In 1921, he wrote that rheumatism in his left arm was slowing him down.[178] He was also distressed by the difficulty he had compiling his seasonal report, 'owing to the confusion of so many things going on at a time last year'.[179] His diary entries become shorter, and less enthusiastic. In November 1921, he complained of 'a long interval owing to waiting for instructions [from London], . . . and also the man having left without giving notice and the late bad weather . . .'[180]

The weather at Stonehenge is always capable of extremes, but in 1922 it was terrible: if his trenches weren't flooded, the whole place was cut off for days by snow, or Hawley himself was boiled in the heat.[181] In 1923 he wrote that the 'work has been far from interesting lately'.[182] And instead of chummy references to workmen, we get asides that 'the man' did this, 'the man' did that. In 1926, the last season, he didn't start until July, 'from the wish of the Society of Antiquaries that it should be a short season owing to want of funds'.[183] It started with great excitement and achievement, but fizzled out with failing interest and diminishing returns.

After his death, Hawley was deeply criticised by Richard Atkinson. Normally the most polite and gentle of men, Atkinson was moved to call Hawley's Stonehenge work 'melancholy . . . mechanical . . . inadequate . . . destructive [and] lamentable', an opinion, he claimed, that had 'long been expressed by archaeologists, with even greater vehemence, in private'.[184] This was all the more strange because Hawley was himself 'the most modest and self-effacing of men, generous to a fault and greatly appreciative of competence in others, being himself skilled in all manner of ways'.[185]

The popular view today – like so much of Stonehenge folklore, based on what Atkinson wrote in 1955 – is that while Atkinson's work was the epitome of good archaeology, Hawley's much bigger excavations were nothing short of a disaster.[186] At Hawley's annual lectures to the Society of Antiquaries, speakers from the floor at first politely praised him for his determination to stick to the facts. Before long, however, he was being harangued for doing just that. The city archaeologists, bored with descriptions of holes in the ground, wanted answers to big questions. Who built Stonehenge, and why? One suspects that some of them imagined there would be dramatic finds of gold treasure, perhaps even inscriptions – the sort of thing they were used to seeing plundered (as some of us would now say) from the Near East. Even Hawley admitted that the broken bones and stones were tediously repetitive.

But answers to such sweeping questions do not come directly out of the ground. You can't hope to say why Stonehenge exists until you have at least some idea of what it looked like, how it was built, what went on amongst the stones and when all this happened. At this more prosaic level, Hawley was ever inquisitive, and framed – and sometimes answered – many of the questions that still concern us today.

A committee with stronger leadership would undoubtedly have ended the excavations sooner, for it was clear from early on that their expectations were not being met. But they were too embarrassed to admit this, and instead quietly left Hawley to it. We have Hawley and Newall to thank for the detailed records they continued to keep to the end, and the Office of Works survey department for the superb plans and drawings. The archive for Hawley's work is far better than that for any of Maud Cunnington's excavations (there are no field records for Woodhenge at all), to say nothing of Atkinson's. For future generations, it is always that archive – publications, diaries, notes, correspondence, photographs, drawings – that is the most critical thing.

So what do we learn? The work began late in 1919, at stones 6 and 7. These two sarsens of the main stone circle had long been propped up by wooden poles, and had leaned away from each other so that the lintel above was near to being thrown to the ground. This stone, weighing 6 or 7 tons, was winched into the air. The uprights were cased in timbers, and gently edged back into place with steel ropes and jacks, while Hawley dug out the foundations, recording finds with a measuring frame in direct imitation of his predecessor, William Gowland.

Hawley must have been extremely grateful for Newall's assistance, a competent excavator in his own right. Although his
contribution has never been seen like this, Newall should I believe
be recognised as Hawley's assistant director at these important
excavations.[187] Only a few months after they had started, Newall
suggested they look for pits which John Aubrey had apparently
seen in the seventeenth century on the perimeter of the site, close to
the encircling ditch. They couldn't see a thing on the surface now,
but with the aid of a steel bar,[188] thudding the ground for a hollow
sound, they found first one, then another, until, by the end of 1920,
they had excavated altogether twenty-three (twenty-one personally
by Newall). They were evenly spaced, which allowed a precise
estimate of fifty-six pits to be made for the entire circuit. At first
they called these the X Holes; later, the Aubrey Holes (figure 3).[189]

As time passed, Hawley and Newall unearthed one unsuspected
hole after another. By the time they had finished, these added up to
a substantial addition to what then seemed a very incomplete
picture presented by the megaliths alone. There were, for example,
two rings of pits closer to the megaliths than the Aubrey Holes;
these still retain their original names, the Y and Z Holes. There was
an incomprehensible jumble of stone pits and post holes within the
area defined by the large sarsen ring. There was a rash of wooden
post holes between the stones and the ditch to the south of the
stones, and again across the north-east causeway in the ditch.
There were further stone and post pits between the Avenue ditches
and the Heelstone. There were numerous human cremations, and
unburnt human bone all over the place.

As if this wasn't enough, Hawley excavated a stretch of the
Avenue, half of a circular ditch around the Heelstone, and about
half of the entire circuit of the main ditch enclosure; and he
'trenched' the whole area between the ditch and the stones on the
east side. All this, of course, threw up quantities of animal bones,
bits of stone and other ancient finds (not forgetting all the glass,
cartridge cases and boot nails). All in all, quite a haul.

When Flinders Petrie described the detailed survey that he and
his father made of the monument (his numbering scheme for the
megaliths is still in use), he drew attention to the circular
earthwork, proposing that it was of an earlier age than the stones it
encloses.[190] Hawley was able to prove this theory. The key was
what he called 'the Stonehenge Layer', a near continuous blanket
of debris not far beneath the turf which contained numerous chips

of stone from the megaliths. He believed that the chips came from the dressing of stones before they were erected. It followed that any features covered by this layer had to be older than the megaliths.

He wrote to William Gowland in 1921, encouraging him to come and visit the dig, and explained his idea: 'I think there were two distinct periods here, for the Ditch appears to have been completely silted up, before the rubble with objects of the Stonehenge building period were [*sic*] deposited over it. The silting, especially the upper part, must have taken a long time to complete.'[191] It is a convincing argument, and the beginning of a hugely important insight that archaeology has brought to Stonehenge: it was not built in a day.

Hawley developed his idea as the excavations progressed, and soon came to believe in three main periods. The ditch and bank came first. Following popular opinion of the time, he looked for clues that the ditch was actually lived in by the people who dug it out; but the evidence wasn't there. Instead, he imagined them safe and snug in the centre of the enclosed space: 'the original use of the site was as a defensive dwelling'. The holes scattered all over the wide causeway through the ditch held posts 'to impede collective attack through the gateway'. Pits at the ditch ends were 'dwelling-pits . . . for guards on the flanks'.[192]

His second period consisted of a wide stone circle, now gone, that stood in the Aubrey Holes, just inside the old defensive ditch. The evidence that the Aubrey Holes were not dug until the ditch had nearly silted up consisted, thought Hawley, in a thin layer of chalk near the top of the ditch fill. He interpreted this as the spread of debris excavated from the ring of pits.[193]

All the stones in the centre, which Hawley referred to simply as 'Stonehenge', constituted the third period. These two stone phases, in contradistinction to the first domestic use, were 'of sentimental or sacred significance'.[194]

This three-phase history of Stonehenge, buried in one of Hawley's seasonal reports, was soon forgotten about. In the discussion following Hawley's 1924 London talk, archaeologist George Engleheart, always ready with a serious put-down, commented, somewhat missing the point, 'that it was necessary to be on guard against fashionable theories, such as the division of Stonehenge into two periods'.[195] Thirty years later, Richard Atkinson elaborated a three-phase history of Stonehenge (which became the standard Stonehenge story, as if engraved on a tablet handed down from the sky), without the least acknowledgement to Hawley.[196]

It is true that Atkinson's phasing differed in many significant details from Hawley's (and the idea of an earlier defended settlement never caught on, and now seems silly). But without the evidence so painstakingly collected and recorded by Newall and Hawley, Atkinson would have had difficulty getting started – and so would we.

12

The Clean Museum

He – this nuisance, this unexpected male stiff under the ground at Stonehenge – sits on a long wide table in the high-ceilinged white Elizabethan panelled room with the sun streaming through the windows, in two cardboard boxes. In the education room at Salisbury Museum, across the grass from the high, ornate front of the cathedral, Jackie McKinley is about to show me the bones.

When the Stonehenge archer reached Cardiff in 1978, he was examined by a research student (now Professor of Archaeological Science at the Department of Archaeology, University of York), Terry O'Connor. He looked at the mammal bones too, for really they were his expertise, but he produced an excellent study of the human skeleton. In fact it was so good that, aided by technical language ('Two other notable traits in the skull are the presence of bilateral parietal foramina, and the distinctly spatulate form of the maxillary incisors, with small accessory tubercles being present on the lingual surfaces'), he managed to squeeze a complete description into little more than a page of printed text.[197]

Unfortunately, I can hardly understand a word of it, so I have asked Jackie, a specialist in human remains who had recently examined what little she had been able to find of the burials from the other Stonehenge excavations,[198] to explain it all for me.[199] There is an additional interest. The previous year (1998) she unpacked the archer's bones for a BBC television crew.[200] The poor man only made it onto the screen as an extra in the background, but Jackie noticed something she hadn't expected to see. A year later, she couldn't remember what it was. Well now we would find out.

As she lays the pieces out on the table in their approximate anatomical positions, she talks to them.

'He's got a really masculine square jaw.'

The smaller box contains the skull, wrapped in white tissue

paper. Although it is lighter in weight and more fragile than modern bone (it is, after all, radiocarbon dated to well over 4000 years old[201]), every little bump and splinter seem perfectly preserved.

The head alone speaks to Jackie of a strong, muscular male. In his report, Terry had commented on the 'large mastoid processes', rounded projections on either side of the head just behind the jaw. Jackie turns the skull upside-down to show these lumps (you can feel them by rubbing your fingers against your head between the bottom of your ears and the back of your jaw), and a heavy ridge at the back – the 'external occipital protuberance' – which is very large. These are muscle attachments, and tend to be bigger in men than in women. On this head they are particularly well developed, as is the brow, or 'supra-orbital', ridge, a swelling in the bone above the eyes. If you are female you are unlikely to have much of a ridge there, but if you are a man you will be able to feel a significant bulge. If you have a heavily muscled face you will feel ridges similar to those on the Stonehenge archer, and if your neck is very strong you will have an occipital ridge to match.

Terry also commented on the pelvis, which – as you might expect – shows differences between the sexes related to the fact that a woman's hips are specially adapted for childbirth. The ancient pelvis, he wrote, is clearly male.

And so it goes on. As Jackie lifts the large box, it rattles as if full of plastic toys. She lays out the neck.

'They're all big bones.'

She fits together the top two of the seven 'cervical vertebrae', and demonstrates how they work as a rotating joint that allows the head to turn. They also act as part of a protective tube for the vital supply cables to the brain – blood and nerves – and anchors for muscles that help hold the head up.

'Bone is a living tissue', she continues. 'It's constantly changing, constantly forming. Because it's the one thing that remains after death, people think of it as a dead tissue. But in a living person it's alive.'

Jackie is looking for signs of life. She finds them in the next twelve bones down the back, the 'thoracic vertebrae'. These bones have 'costo-vertebral joints', little wings where the ribs attach. The joints are lipped, showing new bone growth. The lower four of these thoracic vertebrae have facets on the central body, and slight pitting.

'All this is due to wear and tear', says Jackie. 'It's caused by strain on the chest – the rib cage. This man's been doing a lot of lifting.'

The lower thoracic vertebrae and, continuing down, the 'lumbar vertebrae' have roughened surfaces where the bones came into contact with the discs that once separated them. These are known as 'Schmorl's nodes', and are the result of disc damage caused by back strain.

'This is the area of greatest spinal curvature,' says Jackie, 'where there is most pressure. The damage is only in its early stages – not very pronounced. But he's been working hard.'

The fifth lumbar vertebra is not properly fused – it's not grown as it should have, and there's a heavy wear facet on the left side. This was most likely caused by a trauma when the man was young, perhaps a fall. Lower down, at the base of the spine where the vertebrae grow together to make a chunky bone known as the coccyx, the joint surfaces are lipped and roughened, again on the left side. At the time of the incident that caused this, he would have felt some pain, and was probably left with a continuing awareness that something was not quite right.

'He would have had a slight stiffness, but at this stage of life it would not have been a major problem.'

And what stage of life would that have been? Terry noted four things about the skeleton that pointed to the man's age. His teeth are in extremely good nick, with no decay and very little wear ('dental attrition is slight, there being exposure of the dentine at only a few points'). The 'basi-sphenoid synchondrosis', a plate of soft cartilage bridging the gap between two immature bones of the skull, is fused, a process typically completed in the early twenties. All the 'appendicular epiphyses' are also fused; these are areas of cartilage separating the articular ends (the knobby bits) of long bones from the shafts that start to ossify (turn into solid bone) around twelve years, and typically are fully hardened by twenty-five years. The sacrum and coccyx, the vertebrae at the base of the spine that fuse together, indicate to Terry a confused picture, as strictly they combine the characteristics of youth (sacral bodies not fully fused) with age (the first coccygeal vertebra is fused to the bottom of the sacrum). But all such changes are only averages, and vary considerably from person to person. All in all, Terry is happy to write that this man died at around twenty-five to thirty years old, fit and in the prime of life – prompting the question, why did he die?

Jackie comments on the quality of the teeth. In fact, she says, for this ancient era they are remarkably lightly worn for someone over twenty-five. Before the days of modern processing, food needed more chewing and carried varying amounts of erosive grit from dirt. The archer's teeth are so good, it may be that he benefited from a special diet. On the other hand, Jackie finds tiny little holes in the top of the eye orbits (known as 'cribra orbitalia'). These indicate slight anaemia – an iron deficiency, perhaps caused by a diet that was not very high in protein.

'But his teeth are good. Maybe it was just an absorption problem – he ate the protein, but his body didn't quite take it in. He wouldn't have known about it.'

But there are some things he would have known about. Like his missing tooth. He lost his upper incisor on the right side of his face at least several months before his death, in time for the healthy bone to grow over the gap.

'Bearing in mind the rest of his teeth are absolutely perfect,' says Jackie, 'he's received a blow, or fallen over. He probably got a tooth infection, and it fell out. The bone closes up naturally. He met with an accident, or had a bit of a punch-up.'

She is holding up the archer's sternum, the bone a bit like a mysterious slug-like fossil from the deep ocean, that connects the ribs at the front of the chest. She has remembered what it was that she noticed the last time she unpacked these boxes.

13

Oh My God, We've Got Our Dates Wrong

Stonehenge Phase 1: Approximately 4950–4900 years ago

> Ditch and main inner bank dug, ditch primary filling
> Ancient animal bones placed on ditch bottom
> Aubrey Holes dug and used for posts

28 January 1935 witnessed one of the strangest ceremonies to occur at Stonehenge. Six days before, Robert Newall had called on William Young at the museum in Avebury, with four hessian sandbags. The bags contained 'surplus bones' from Stonehenge. They were all that had been saved of prehistoric human cremations that Newall and Hawley had recovered in their digs. Permission had now been obtained from the Office of Works and the Society of Antiquaries to rebury them, in Aubrey Hole number 7. Newall had wanted Young to do the job.

Young delighted in the operation, taking care to lift the turf in four unequal portions, so he could fit them back again in precisely the same locations, posing for a photo for his diary as he crouched in the hole with his pointing trowel, and cleaning out the pit to the bottom. Newall arrived with the bones after lunch. The bags were laid down with a lead plaque bearing 'an inscription recording at length all the circumstances which led to their being deposited here, and the date'. Young then refilled the hole, relaid the turf and put down a fresh circle of white chalk to mark the Aubrey Hole. No one would be the wiser.[202]

You might like to remember this undistinguished mass burial of the remains of some fifty of our ancestors next time you visit Stonehenge. It lies under the fourth white disc counting north from the small stone by the ditch on the south-east side (no. 91).

Suppose there was no lead plate in the pit, no diary entry. A century from now, an archaeologist excavates Aubrey Hole 7 and finds some human bones at the bottom. Radiocarbon dating shows them to be, say, 4500 years old. What would that tell the archaeologist? Does it say when the Aubrey Hole was made? No, because we know from Hawley's excavations that the Hole had been dug, used and refilled before any cremations were buried. Does it say when the bones were put into the pit? Obviously not. Aubrey Hole 7 did originally have cremated bone in it, so it's possible that some of the bone in the four sandbags had been returned to its source, but that is a coincidence; the bone as it is found by our future archaeologist had only been put into the pit a century and a half before. Only the inscription would have told them that, but we hid it. So what *does* the date say? No more, nor less, than that the people whose bones lay in a heap 1m down, died, on average, about 4500 years ago.

If one pit can be so confusing, imagine what unravelling the whole of Stonehenge is like. There are hundreds of holes, pits and trenches that were dug out and refilled, or, in the case of a few, left holding upright megaliths, over a period of well over 1000 years. But in 1993 English Heritage were determined to get a good chronology, a serious financial as well as intellectual commitment. And it worked. Two years later, they had dated Stonehenge.

The programme is unusual because of the large number of dated samples from a single site (forty-three from Stonehenge itself, and a further eleven from associated monuments), and the thoughtful way in which it was conducted.[203] The 'Aubrey Hole 7 principle' was savagely applied. If there were reasons for doubting the connection between a sample and the event it was hoped to date (a bone, for example, and the digging of the pit in which it was found) the sample was rejected. Six of the sixteen dates obtained before 1993 were binned. And when they got the dates, they applied some pioneering statistics to help understand them.

Christopher Bronk Ramsey, senior physicist and statistician at the Oxford Radiocarbon Accelerator Unit, wrote OxCal, the software that turned the Stonehenge 'radiocarbon ages' into calendar estimates, typically 500–600 years older than the uncalibrated determinations. But OxCal can do more than that, with statistics introduced by an English priest in 1763.

OxCal began when the Oxford lab were dating the 'iceman', the well preserved Neolithic body found in the Ötztal Alps in Italy. Samples from his skin gave slightly different dates from his bone, yet of course skin and bone died on the same day. The Reverend Thomas Bayes was able to help out.[204] Bayes' theorem, boosted by the power of modern computers, deals with adjusting probabilities to take account of existing and new information as it accumulates. The moment we begin the new story of Stonehenge, we can see how.

Radiocarbon proved Hawley right: the ditch around the stones is indeed the oldest part of the monument.[205] The one date obtained before the new programme had suggested the ditch was 4100 years old.[206] The new work uses not only nine dated antler picks from the ditch bottom, but also (courtesy of Bayes' theorem) bones from higher up the ditch fill. The bones come from articulated animal skeletons, which means they must be younger than the digging of the ditch: tendons connecting the bones would only have survived a short time after death, and if the bones had been disturbed from deeper in the ditch, they would no longer be together. The result is an estimate, with 95 per cent confidence, that the ditch was dug between 5015 and 4935 years ago, a millennium older than the original estimate (figure 23).[207]

This was the beginning of the dating that forced a complete rethink about what Stonehenge meant and why it was built. Every recent book about Stonehenge written before English Heritage's study says it is Bronze Age. It's not: it's Neolithic. It's as if we picked up Europe's most daring Gothic cathedral and dropped it into the Dark Ages.

But this is only half the story about the ditch. Although there is no evidence in the form of post holes or ditches that anything happened on the site before 5000 years ago, precise radiocarbon dating held a further surprise. Animal bones had been placed on the bottom of the ditch that were already anything between 70 and 420 years old when it was dug.

This was a shock to the team, for at first sight it looked as if the new radiocarbon dates were making no sense at all. Objects which on the face of it were contemporary, all found in the primary silts on the ditch bottom, produced a huge range of dates. As Alex Bayliss said to me, remembering the initial reaction to the laboratory results: 'We thought, Oh my God, we've got our dates wrong.'[208]

But there was an unexpected solution. The ditch, about half the circuit, produced well over 100 red deer antlers. Thirty-four of these were on the ditch bottom. Natural, seasonally discarded antlers were used throughout Europe in the Neolithic as digging

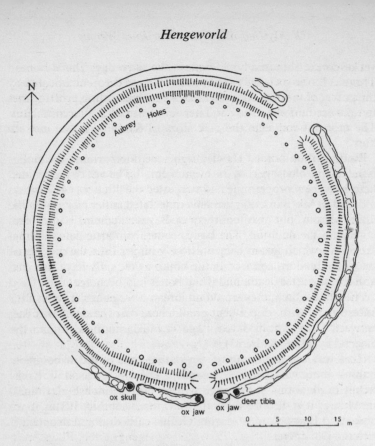

Figure 23. Stonehenge Phase 1: circular bank and ditch with two entrances, and fifty-six Aubrey Holes, probably holding tall posts. Near the south entrance were some animal bones which radiocarbon dating showed to be considerably older than the digging of the ditch around 5000 years ago (see Appendix 1 for dates). *After Cleal et al.*

tools, held by the beam in bare hands, with the larger of the protruding tines doing the earth and rock breaking. Hawley saved a lump of chalk that actually had the tip of an antler tine embedded in it, where it had broken off when a stone pit was being dug all those years ago.[209] It is logical to assume that any antler digging tools found on the bottom of the ditch were used to dig that ditch. We have already noticed a propensity of work gangs to throw their tools into pits and ditches when they had finished.[210] It turned out that the nine dated antlers from the ditch had very similar dates; the older dates came from bones. None of these bones could have been used as tools to dig the ditch. So what were they doing there?

These were not just any old bones. They were special, old bones: an ox skull, two ox jaws and a bone from a red deer – not an antler, but a tibia, a leg bone. Both jaws had lost some teeth, suggesting the bones were buried some time after the death of the animals. But they were in good condition, so had apparently been well looked after.[211]

Radiocarbon dating told of a structure, a ceremony, a ritual – *something* – that was older even than the oldest part of the Stonehenge monument, for which we today have no further evidence at all. But the ancient memory of this *something* was so powerful that bones had been 'curated', as archaeologists say, for more than a generation, perhaps considerably more, before being buried at the bottom of the new circular ditch. Radiocarbon alone has revived the existence of that memory. What it told of, for the moment at least, is a complete mystery.

Five thousand years ago, what became Stonehenge may not, quite, have been unique. We know of a handful of sites with similar circular ditches. The most recently excavated is to the south, partly underlying Thomas Hardy's Dorchester house at Max Gate. Archaeological investigation before roadworks at the demolished Flagstones House revealed a completely unsuspected circular enclosure consisting of unevenly spaced pits (the Stonehenge ditch was dug as a series of pits, but they mostly connect better than those at Flagstones). It is similar in scale to the Stonehenge enclosure (diameter 100m). Like the Stonehenge ditch, Flagstones had some stuff deliberately placed on the bottom. In this case, the remains were human: a heap of cremated adult bones under a large sarsen, a two- or three-year-old child beneath a slab of sandstone and a six- to twelve-month-old child crushed up in the corner of a ditch segment. The ditch and burials are dated to around 5000 years ago.[212]

Further afield, there is a circular enclosure (diameter 70m), like Stonehenge, with a bank inside the ditch, at Llandegai, north Wales. There was a setting of pits outside the single western entrance containing human cremations around 5200 years old.[213] In Somerset, at Priddy, not far from Stanton Drew whose own ditch, as yet known only from the geophysical survey, is also similar, are four circular enclosures, set in a row. They have ditches outside the banks, ranging from 150 to 170m in diameter. Two of these have entrances facing north-north-east. Little more is known about them.[214]

So while it looks as if the Stonehenge ditch may itself be part of a tradition that archaeologists would describe as being Middle Neolithic, the few other identified sites are no better understood. Two of them have human burials, but mortuary ritual would not seem to be the prime purpose. There is a considerable quantity of human material from Stonehenge, but none definitely associated with the excavation of the ditch.

But Stonehenge does have something these other sites don't have: the Aubrey Holes. Despite the most detailed and modern consideration of the evidence,[215] these fifty-six pits remain an enigma. We can't even be sure when they were dug. They are about 5m inside the bank, and the circles share the same centre point. Like the ditch, the Aubrey Holes contain no chips from any megaliths except at the very top of their fills. But these are only suggestions that Aubrey Holes and ditch are contemporary. Nothing suitable for new radiocarbon dating survives. The one date we do have, the very first analysed for Stonehenge, tells us only that charcoal from the pit was somewhere between 4920 and 3470 years old – a range of nearly 1500 years! – and that was with a cremation that was buried at some unknown time after the pit was dug.[216]

Here is a clear need for new excavation (twenty-one Aubrey Holes apparently remain completely undisturbed since the time of Hengeworld). Even then we might dig out a couple of pits and still find nothing dateable. But I'd take that risk. Meanwhile, neither can we agree on why they were dug. The original excavators at first thought they had held small megaliths. Then Maud Cunnington dug up Woodhenge, and Hawley and Newall were convinced that the Aubrey Holes were post pits. As Stuart Piggott said in a BBC radio talk in 1946: they 'almost certainly held . . . posts; possibly they were painted or even carved like Indian totem-poles, and at all events they formed an open, circular sanctuary'.[217]

This is the current view. But curiously, between 1950 and 1995, when so many ideas involving computers and astronomy were promoted about these fifty-six pits, it was believed that they had held nothing at all. Richard Atkinson and his colleagues excavated two Aubrey Holes, and decided they had not contained posts: the very act of digging the pits was the ritual.[218] But now we expect large rings of posts when we dig into Hengeworld, and we see no problem in envisaging this vast timber circle.

New radiocarbon dating has had a huge impact on our

understanding of Stonehenge, by moving it from the Bronze Age to the Neolithic. So this reinterpretation of the Aubrey Holes as post holes, rather than pits that were left open or packed with chalk, forces a radical reappraisal. The many ideas put forward over the past thirty years to explain them, from eclipse predictors, solar calendars and lunar calendars to high tide predictors, have been inspired by the fact that nothing was thought to have stood in the pits.[219] Now, apart from the precise number of posts – and the challenge in turning the pits into predictors lay in computing formulae that eventually produced that magic fifty-six – there is nothing to distinguish that one ring of posts from many others that have never been thus theoretically appropriated.

So we might imagine these widely spaced poles, standing 4m high in pits 1m deep, enclosed by a gleaming white chalk bank and ditch, reaching up from the turf in a spectacle unlike anything else seen locally at the time. Something comparable can be experienced today at the Ring of Brogar, all the way north in the Orkneys. A circular ditch similar to Stonehenge's (diameter 104m) encloses a striking ring of sixty megaliths, the tallest of which is 4.2m high. There is no date for this site, although a nearby stone circle and henge is apparently nearly 5000 years old.[220]

In the landscape around the wood and chalk Stonehenge, most of the things now familiar to us were yet to come: no roads, of course, but also no Woodhenge or Durrington Walls, none of the round burial mounds that rise all around wherever we walk, indeed not a lot else that we know of. The site was already grazed turf, but a great deal of old woodland probably still existed in the area. There is evidence, in the form of broken pottery in ploughed fields, for some form of activity, probably small scattered houses tied to areas of garden fields and grazing or browsing.

It is unfortunate that, once again, we do not have satisfactory radiocarbon dates for two remarkable earthworks north of Stonehenge, the Stonehenge Cursus and the Lesser Cursus. It's possible they were built two or three centuries before Stonehenge, by whose construction they became grown over and inconspicuous; or they may have still been new and, in the case of the Stonehenge Cursus, a massive visual component of the landscape (figure 5).

These strange features are of a class found throughout Middle Neolithic Britain, their number being continually augmented by aerial photography. The largest is in Dorset, two parallel banks and quarry ditches that run for 10km. They are often associated with other religious-looking monuments, particularly long communal burial mounds, but there is really very little to indicate what happened at them.

The Stonehenge Cursus (the odd Latin name was given by William Stukeley in the eighteenth century: he fancied it to be a Druidic race course) is 100m wide and nearly 3km long. It runs in a roughly east–west direction about 1km north of Stonehenge, connecting the two north–south ridges that frame the small Stonehenge plateau. The Lesser Cursus is a slighter thing to the north-west.[221] These two linear earthworks speak of a clear religious or ritual aspect to this patch of downland that, like the bones found buried at the bottom of the Stonehenge ditch, reaches back generations before the first Stonehenge was built. Cursus monuments are not rare, but you don't find them on every little hill. So from the start, Stonehenge was built in a place of spiritual and emotional power. That all that is as mysterious to us as Stonehenge itself was to everyone a century ago is our current misfortune.

Some of what was soon to come at Stonehenge is also a bit of mystery. But some was not. In the second phase, many people left their mark in the most personal way possible, in the form of their immortal remains. Stonehenge's unique and eternal fire was lit at last.

14

Traumatic Pathology Is Manifest

'Traumatic pathology', wrote Terry O'Connor in his report, 'is manifest throughout the thorax. A small fragment of flint, apparently the tip of a projectile point, is embedded in the posterior surface of the first segment of the mesosternum.'[222] This tiny chip of flint behind the breast bone of the body from the ditch had been noticed when the skeleton was being cleaned fresh from the dig. Terry had the help of Len Wilkinson, a human anatomy specialist then Reader in the Department of Anatomy at Cardiff University. He was interested in the body, and useful to have around. Terry would hold up a rib. Which rib is this? And Len would lay it on the table in the right place.

They looked at the flint in the bone, and thought if this is an arrow tip, it had to have entered the body somewhere. Perhaps the arrow left another trace. The flint was angled to the left, so they looked with special care at ribs on the left side. They found two damaged bones. One had a small, deep groove on the edge. There seemed little doubt that this was where the sharp edge of a flint arrowhead had nicked the rib as it penetrated the lower chest. Len and Terry discussed the two possibilities. Was this the arrow that hit the breast bone, or was it a second arrow? They took the simpler option, Occam's razor. An arrow had struck the man in the back on the left side, hit the rib, been deflected up towards the heart, changing its trajectory again as it sliced through the heart muscle, until it stuck into the sternum. One arrow, one dead man.

But there was more than one arrow. The other damaged left rib, higher up in the chest than the first, had a further splinter of flint wedged in a thin hole. When this tiny triangle, the tip of a second arrowhead, fell out of the bone, they found it fitted perfectly onto the broken point of one of the arrowheads recovered from the grave. This was getting interesting. All three of the flint arrowheads

111

from the ditch had their tips missing. But it hadn't occurred to the archaeologists that they were anything other than the remains of three arrows that had been buried with the man, along with the stone wrist protector, as the natural accoutrements of an archer. The Stonehenge archer. Except now it seemed he wasn't the archer. He was the target.

They found yet another damaged rib on the opposite side of the body. A third arrow had entered the chest from the right. Three arrowheads with missing points, four wounds, two arrow tips: how many arrows had it taken to fell this man? If two of the arrowheads had indeed been part of the man's possessions (only one could be directly linked to the body, through its lost tip), then he had still been hit by at least three arrows when he died. All the bone is completely unhealed, so none of the wounds could relate to an earlier event (figure 22).

But if he had taken all three of the excavated flint arrowheads in a concerted attack, he could have fallen with at least five arrows in his body: three represented by the wounds and a further two by arrowheads that can't be linked directly to the damaged bones. Or, thought Jackie McKinley, holding the mesosternum in the light of the Elizabethan stone window at Salisbury Museum, six arrows.

That was it, that was what she had noticed when she had got the skeleton out for the BBC. The flint tip in the breast bone, still firmly embedded, was so clearly angled straight to the left that it seemed impossible for it to be the same arrow that had scarred the lower rib. Terry and Len had rightly been cautious when they first examined the patient. No one had really seen anything quite like this before, and it was a bit of a shock. But it seemed to Jackie, nearly twenty years later, that perhaps they had been too cautious. He might have had at least four arrows in him, or as many as six – or even more, for there was no reason why every missile that hit him had to leave an indelible mark in his bones, or had stuck fast to be buried with the corpse.

This couldn't be explained by imagining that he'd been on a hunting expedition and had somehow got in the way, perhaps falling in a shower of arrows intended for a deer. Arrows had hit him from left and from right. And because none of the wounds indicated a falling arc, an arrow dropping from the sky, he had been pretty close to the assailants – surely more than one bow was involved here.

So what on earth had been going on? Was this murder? A

sacrifice? A battle victim, or even some bizarre accident? Is this what the flint arrows filling collectors' mantelpieces and museum cases had been made for – killing people? Or was the bow and arrow normally a hunting weapon? This is, after all, Stonehenge, where we might expect to find the unusual, the atypical. Why was this man buried there, anyway, just the one? Half Stonehenge has been excavated: they might have missed a lot of fine detail in the early digs, but you don't mistake a complete stiff, laid out with highly desirable flint arrowheads. What was so special about this lone man – strong, fit, in the prime of life – that he should end his days 1m under and stuffed with arrows, at the entrance to one of the grandest religious monuments of the ancient world?

We know more about arrowheads than bows, but the few remains we do have indicate a well-established bow technology. Parts of five prehistoric bows have been found in Britain, all radiocarbon-dated. They range from around 5300 years old to 3500, placing the death of the Stonehenge man (at about 4300 years ago[223]) well within the era of prehistoric longbow use.[224] They are all self bows, that is, expertly made from single staves of wood. All but one (from Scotland, made in oak) are of yew wood, a material still favoured at the height of longbow use in medieval European warfare.[225]

Experimental archaeologists have suggested that these yew bows would have been made from wood taken from the border between sapwood and heartwood. This would have had the incidental effect of giving the bows a distinctive appearance (sapwood is white, heartwood reddy-orange). But there is a functional explanation. Sapwood has the tough, elastic properties required of the 'back' (the side facing the quarry), while heartwood has compressive strength for the hollow 'belly' facing the archer. The ancient bow from Meare Heath was actually considered to be a better weapon than the medieval longbow, its design more closely reflecting modern understanding of the requirements of a bow with long limbs.[226]

The power of these long, slender objects should not be underestimated. Neither should it be thought that a Stone Age technology compromised the efficiency of the weapon. There is a story of early Spanish explorers in Florida, USA, who had seized a local man. Asked to demonstrate his bow from 150 paces in return for his freedom, he deftly shot a reed arrow with a stone tip through two suits of chain mail.[227] Metal cannot compete with the lethal feathered edge of freshly knapped flint.

Figure 24. At Hillingdon, west London, the skeleton of an aurochs (now extinct wild cattle) was found in a deep pit with six flint arrowheads of the same type as those in the Stonehenge man. The evidence suggested the entire animal might have been buried, rather than eaten. The bows in this imagined scene are based on one found in the Somerset Levels. *After Museum of London.*

Neolithic archery does not seem to have been about hunting small game. The great majority of animal bones found at Neolithic sites are from domestic breeds. Rare finds of flint arrows buried with their quarry suggest that something else was going on, perhaps demonstrations of bravery, perhaps warfare, perhaps ritual killings. Intimations of battle are clearest in the Early Neolithic, centuries before Hengeworld, when arrowheads were frail, leaf-shaped things. At Carn Brae in Cornwall, excavation on a hilltop enclosure uncovered an astonishing total of over 750 arrowheads.[228] At Crickley Hill in Gloucestershire, the pattern of arrowhead loss on the ground is even more suggestive. The points lie exactly where arrows would have been fired in an attack, against the rampart and in floods through the gates.[229] Inside the West Kennet long barrow at Avebury was a skeleton with an arrowhead amongst the throat bones.[230]

As we will see later (chapter 26), some of the distinctive arrowheads found at Durrington Walls were fired at domestic swine as part of what were almost certainly major ceremonial events. At Hillingdon, west London, an extraordinary pit was found containing the butchered remains of an aurochs, large and dangerous wild cattle still around in Hengeworld. Six flint arrowheads like those found with the Stonehenge body lay amongst the bones, confirming the impression from the burial that the animal was buried with flesh on. This was no hunting spoil for the pot (figure 24).[231]

Barbed and tanged arrowheads, probably mounted on arrows, are common in graves, suggesting they had symbolic meaning. The confirmed association of these flints with the death of a man is currently unique to Stonehenge,[232] but archery and its associated equipment often transcended the mundane. The bow was a male prerogative: arrows are found with male skeletons,[233] and longbow use demands great strength. The action was perhaps associated with passages in life, with demonstrations of skill and allegiance. The route was terminal for the man in the Stonehenge ditch. His death seems far from chance, and the story of his passing may have given his grave peculiar prominence. For though his remains were special, he was far from alone.

15

Badly Broken in Transit

Stonehenge Phase 2: Approximately 4900–4400 years ago

1 or 2	Smaller outer bank
2	Posts in southern passage and centre of monument
	Posts on north-east causeway
	First use of Aubrey Holes for cremation burial
2a	Secondary ditch filling, more cremation burials
2b	Features cut into secondary filling, some with Grooved Ware

You'd think it would be obvious, but in fact we do not know how many people were buried at Stonehenge. If anything serious was lost as a result of Hawley's excavations, this was it: the chronicle of people who died on Salisbury Plain and were buried at Stonehenge, before many if not all of the megaliths had been erected. You don't often hear about these people, and most of what we now know came from the recent English Heritage project. It's a story that needs to be told (figure 25).

Hawley kept all finds as he dug, sorted them, noted them down in the diary, and then threw most back into the ground. He sent complete skeletons to Sir Arthur Keith at the Royal College of Surgeons in London, but he only found two or three of these. For the rest, Hawley did identifications himself. In the best of circumstances, diagnosis of cremated bone (age and sex) is a tricky business. We have to accept that Hawley's notes on the cremation burials are just as likely to be wrong as right.

As if that wasn't enough, there is a cruel indication of what we have lost regarding the unburnt human bone. In August 1936, Frank Stevens, Curator of the then South Wiltshire and Blackmore Museum (now Salisbury and South Wiltshire Museum), wrote to Dr A. J. E. Cave at the Royal College of Surgeons. The year before he had sent the College a collection of Hawley's Stonehenge bones ('from the bottom of the ditch'). He had thought them better stored in London, and had been keen to hear what the museum's conservator had to say about them. He had attached a note:

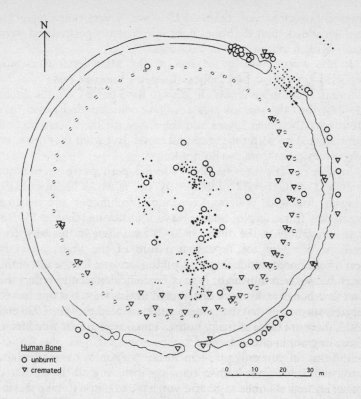

N

Figure 25. Stonehenge Phase 2: by around 4400 years ago, the ditch had partly refilled (natural silting and deliberate levelling of bank), and Aubrey posts were gone. The smaller post holes – across the main entrance, in rows aimed at the south entrance and in clusters in the centre – are undated. It is assumed they are mostly contemporary and belong to this phase. Also thought to predate the arrival of megaliths are human cremation burials (almost every excavated Aubrey Hole – now silted up – has at least one) and much of the unburnt human bone. Symbols outside the ditch indicate ditch finds that cannot be precisely located. The north-west side of the site has not been excavated. *After Cleal et al.*

The numbers on some of the pieces – 1922.112 etc – refer to the Diary pages kept by Mr R. S. Newall. 29 BGL means 29 ins [74cm] below ground level.

If Stevens had known where the bones came from, when they came back to Salisbury that information was lost. His letter elicited the desired report, but it is only a list of identifications ('19. An indeterminate piece of a thick cranial vault. 20. Ditto – a tiny fragment', etc). Stevens thanked Dr Cave. 'I very much regret to say', he added, 'that the bones were insufficiently packed and were badly broken in transit from you to us.'[234]

It gets worse. Wilfrid Jackson, at the Manchester Museum, reported on the animal bones. Like the human bone sent to London, Jackson's animals all seem to have come from the ditch. He described the various creatures he could see, and noted that from both the upper layers and the lower silt there were human bones mixed up with the sheep and cattle. But what they were, or where they came from, we do not know.[235]

So if we can't be sure *who* Hawley found, perhaps we can be more confident of numbers? Unfortunately, no. When he began in 1919, Hawley followed William Gowland's techniques precisely: a measuring frame to plot finds, and careful sieving (chapter 9). His first excavations in the ditch (1920–2) were done in this way. But perhaps tiring of the repetitive nature of the finds, certainly receiving a bored response at his London lectures, for the rest of the ditch he was less thorough. It may be coincidence, and reflect the fact that bones really were distributed in this way; but one has to say it is suspicious that in the segments excavated between 1920 and 1922, there are twice as many human remains as are recorded from those dug out in later seasons.[236]

But this isn't the only problem. Jackie McKinley has studied the surviving Stonehenge human remains, including all the cremated bone. She has also, she says, and you have to pause to take this in, examined 4000 cremation burials from archaeological digs of all dates (not least Saxon). About one in twenty of these contained bones from two people, and a very few from three.[237] In the only modern study of a complete cemetery of comparable date to that at Stonehenge, at Dorchester-on-Thames, Oxfordshire, nearly half the deposits of cremated bone contained more than one person; one even had five.[238]

In a funeral pyre a skeleton survives more or less intact: the bones may be broken and discoloured, but they're still there.[239] It's what happens next that can confuse. There will be nothing to dig up in the future, unless something is buried. What is done will depend entirely on custom. A large bagful of bones and charcoal can be collected; yet many of the particular bones that help the archaeologist determine the deceased's age and sex can remain in the pyre. If the pyre site was a permanent fixture, the odd identifiable bone from a completely different occasion could be innocently scraped up with the newly cremated.

So 4000–5000 years later, along comes William Hawley. In common with other archaeologists of the time (and, indeed, with many today), he believes that cremated remains have little to tell. After all, were the bones not all burnt? Weren't the objects with the corpse destroyed in the pyre? He gives cremated bone less attention than he would an unburnt skeleton laid out in the ground. Look at his excavation diary:

25 March 1920. 'We sieved the cremated bones [from Aubrey Hole 9]; keeping the larger ones and casting away the sifted remnant after thoroughly searching.'

7 November 1922. 'There were odd pieces of cremated bone met with occasionally and at one spot about a handful in a small mass.'

And so on. Such is the database for cremation burials at Stonehenge. Hawley stored the saved bones, but no one saw them again until they were taken from the shelves, packed in hessian bags and dumped in Aubrey Hole 7.

There is, however, an important exception to this rule. Atkinson's field records are deplorable, but this man knew how to dig.

In 1950 three friends, a youthful thirty, forty and fifty compared to Gowland and Hawley, who were both working at Stonehenge when more than twice the age of the youngest, convened for their first excavation. Richard Atkinson, Stuart Piggott and Marcus Stone were 'an informal committee' appointed by the Society of Antiquaries.[240] It was a quarter of a century since Hawley had stopped digging, and archaeologists were none the wiser. These three men brought great experience. They would consider all Hawley's finds, and, where necessary, conduct small new excavations. The science of modern archaeology would sort out Stonehenge.

They worked on and off through the 1950s, initially with Stuart Piggott as leader. Stone died suddenly in 1957, and Atkinson gradually took over as sole co-ordinator.[241] In 1954, a typical year, they excavated some bluestones, an arc of a missing stone circle and a small stretch of the encircling bank. They also dug four trenches close to the main ditch entrance, two in the ditch and one each on the inner and outer banks. When you start to think about what they found there, one's whole perception of Stonehenge begins to change. But you do have to think about it.[242]

On cue, they found a cremated bone deposit – the only one available from the whole of the ditch for Jackie McKinley to study.[243] One and a half kilos of bone had been collected and buried after the cremation of a woman aged twenty-five. From the same context, Jackie identified other human remains (all unsexed): 4.4gm from the cremation of a subadult or adult, and 0.8gm from the cremation of an adult; an unburnt ankle bone (adult) and a toe bone (young/mature adult).[244] This is the sort of collection, perhaps representing five people, that Hawley might have described as 'odd pieces of cremated bone'. In addition, Jackie identified from the two trenches a further twenty-five to twenty-seven small cremated fragments and one to three unburnt human bones. Many of these could be from the main burial. Or yet another, disturbed deposit.

Jackie noted that the woman's body had been well cremated, and that most of the bone remaining after the burn had been collected and buried, the commonest fragment size being about 1cm across. This degree of recovery would have taken some care. These features – high degree of cremation, and a lot of bone collected – are typical of burials found in the centre of round barrows. Burial mounds like those around Stonehenge, most if not all later in date than Phase 2, are complex monuments. The initial construction usually marked the burial of one or a few people, with considerable ceremony. Subsequently, cremated remains were often buried in the mound and surrounding ditch. These later burials appear to have been more modest events, the only evidence frequently consisting of a small pit containing the potted bones.

By analogy, Atkinson and Piggott's cremation burial, and perhaps the others in the ditch, represent the sort of people for whom, at a later date, a barrow would have been dug, not those folk whose remains accumulated around the founder monument. In other words, perhaps not everyone got the chance to be buried in the Stonehenge ditch.

A quarter of a century after the Atkinson–Piggott dig, when Margaret Ehrenburg was sorting their finds, she came across some human toe bones. John Evans had just found the man laid out in the upper ditch fill, his bones scarred with fatal arrow wounds. Although Atkinson had not spotted the burial pit, his trench had cut through one end. Evans recovered a complete skeleton – except the feet. They had been sitting in the basement at Cardiff University, unwashed and unrecognised, but perfectly recorded.[245]

So the 1954 excavation confirms our suspicion that Hawley's record almost certainly underestimates the number of people, however incomplete, found in the ditch. And he found them elsewhere, too.

Of the thirty-four excavated Aubrey Holes, twenty-four contained at least one cremation burial, amounting to thirty-two people in all.[246] Certainly most, possibly all of these burials occurred after the posts had gone. Hawley also found at least eleven cremation burials when he 'trenched' his way between the bank and the stones on the eastern side. We don't know exactly where these were.[247]

So to summarise, we know of seventeen finds of cremated bone in the ditch. The remains of thirty-two people were found in Aubrey Holes, and a further eleven close to Aubrey Holes. That makes up to sixty cremation burials in about half the monument. Hawley's record is undoubtedly incomplete, an intuitive judgement reinforced by Atkinson and Piggott's ditch section, and there is still some unexcavated ground in this half (virtually all the bank, for example). Let's double this figure: 120. Suppose burial occurred randomly around the entire circuit of the earth circle.[248] Double again: 240 (figure 25).

Two hundred and forty people, perhaps specially selected people, laid out on wooden pyres, burnt, their remains carefully collected and buried in holes in the ground on the edge of the circular Stonehenge enclosure. This figure is of course entirely hypothetical. But I believe it gives the right flavour. We are talking significant funerary rites: flame, fire, grief, ceremony, the effort of collecting wood and building pyres, wakes, perhaps paying off mourners, retainers or family, visits from afar, who knows. And we are not even guessing the number of people represented by bodies that were not burnt. We are talking big place, big events.

So when did this happen? We're largely guessing here, too. Associated artefacts are rare. There are no useful radiocarbon dates. We know the cremations were buried after the ditch had begun to fill and after the Aubrey posts had gone, but there are no relationships between burials and standing stones.

Objects first. There are a few bone pins and other simple trinkets, a beautiful stone 'macehead' (a perforated stone object of completely unknown function) and a funny little ceramic thing that looks like a touristic ashtray in Grooved Ware.[249] McKinley found some green staining on a bone from Atkinson's cremation burial, which may indicate that a copper or bronze object accompanied the body in the pyre (figure 26).[250]

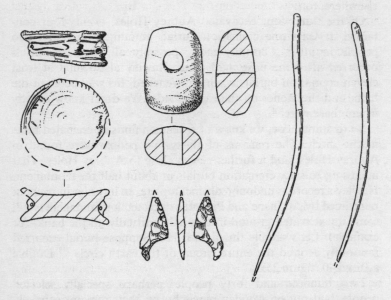

Figure 26. A selection of Stonehenge artefacts: a unique ceramic object with three small lugs from a cremation burial in Aubrey Hole 29; a beautifully finished 'macehead' in black and white folded gneiss found with a cremation near the South Barrow; two bone pins found with cremations; a flint arrowhead of the type commonly found with Grooved Ware, from the stone floor excavated in 1980. The macehead is 5.5cm long. *After Cleal et al. and Pitts.*

This isn't entirely useless for dating. We know the burials aren't Roman: in fact, all indications are they are contemporary with Stonehenge. The question is, which Stonehenge? There is another clue in the stone debris that Hawley called 'the Stonehenge Layer' (chapter 11). The stone chips found all over the site occur in the top of the ditch silts and the upper filling of the Aubrey Holes, but rarely actually with cremation burials.[251] If these chips do come from shaping megaliths, then by implication most of the cremations were buried before the stones arrived in Phase 3 (chapters coming up).

So after much thought, Ros Cleal decided that the burial of cremations began in Phase 2, but continued into Phase 3.[252] Phase 2 saw the slow filling of the ditch, between around 5000 and 4300 years ago, an era estimated by Bayesian statistics to be anything between 460 and 740 years long.[253] This makes Stonehenge not only one of the earliest cremation cemeteries in Britain, but easily the biggest in Hengeworld.

The largest group outside Stonehenge is at Dorchester-on-Thames, south of Oxford. Work started there in the late 1940s under the direction of Richard Atkinson, and included pioneering use of geophysical surveying equipment (chapter 2). With their ring ditches and refilled pits, these sites look individually like smaller versions of Stonehenge. Altogether, and all have been completely excavated, the burnt remains of about 170 people have been recovered.[254] So was Stonehenge just a focus for funeral rites, or was there more going on in this Phase 2?

As the ditch was filled with chalk and dirt, probably taken from the bank,[255] other debris – animal bones, charcoal, broken flint tools, antler picks, the occasional piece of roughly carved chalk and a few tiny sherds of Grooved Ware – got in there too. All this could derive from activity associated with the practice and ceremony of cremation, or it could mean more.

Phase 2 at Stonehenge is when the earthworks and timber rings of Hengeworld started to become common all over Britain. The radiocarbon evidence is nowhere as good as that at Stonehenge itself, but it looks as if the huge ditches at Avebury, Marden, Durrington Walls and Mount Pleasant, the ditch around the timber henge at Mount Pleasant, and perhaps Silbury Hill, as well as the modest henge at Coneybury,[256] a mere 1.5km to the south-east, were all dug at this time.[257]

Partly because of this synchronicity, some archaeologists came to believe in the existence of a huge circular timber structure in the centre of Stonehenge. We had known that there were many post holes scattered about the place. Fifty-odd pits, popular with researchers seeking sun and moon alignments,[258] but which probably are more to do with restricting and controlling human access than star-gazing, lie across the main north-eastern entrance through the ditch. Four large holes run across the Avenue in front of the Heelstone. Several holes occur amongst the stones in the middle, and a plethora fill the space between stones and outer ditch on the south side.

These last used to appear on the fold-out plan in the official guidebook, which was, believe it or not, until the recent English Heritage monograph the best accessible record. For the third edition of this guide, published in 1959 and in print into the 1970s, the plan was tidied up with the removal of post holes.[259] Nonetheless, the idea grew that there might have been a timber structure in the middle that preceded the stones, encouraged by the observation that Stonehenge has the architectural appearance of something more normally carved out of wood.

In 1951, Stuart Piggott said there was 'just possibly a central timber structure on the site of the present stone settings'.[260] Atkinson noted more specifically the 'possibility that some timber structure, in the form of a setting of posts, or even a small roofed building, may have existed ... in the centre of the monument'. Piggott and Atkinson knew more about Stonehenge than the rest of us, and this hesitant prediction grew by repetition (notwithstanding Atkinson's rider that 'Admittedly there is no evidence').[261]

Aubrey Burl described a 'Stonehenge hut', 'an enormous timber building ... just under 100 feet [31m] across, thatched, with an entrance at the north-east and a second, narrower, opening at the south where it was approached at an angle by a long, roofed passageway'.[262] Rodney Castleden drew a view of this 'roundhouse' ('25m [82 feet] in diameter'), and imagined decorated textiles hanging on its walls.[263] John North, on the other hand, envisaged a 'timber henge ... of the order of 30m across'. Scoffing at 'archaeologists with more fantasy than Hawley [who] have shown a predilection for imagining roofs completely spanning such rings of posts as these at Stonehenge', he went on to describe rings supporting timber lintels.[264]

Now the data have been studied and published, we can understand the disagreement about the size of this structure: it wasn't there (figure 25). There are indeed a lot of post holes, and some are very large, but there is no sign at all of a circular building.[265] The nearest we get to any coherent 'structures' are rectangular arrangements, one underneath sarsen stones 8 and 9 and another further south. There is a clear suggestion that the latter is some sort of passage aligned on the southern entrance. The problem is that we do not have, and sadly are unlikely ever to have, a sufficiently complete plan to help us make sense of the pits in the middle. Too much of the central area has been dug over without record, destroyed by the excavation of massive pits for megaliths, or remains unexcavated by archaeologists.

Individually, like the cremation burials, most of these post holes are undated. Some in the middle are plainly older than the megaliths, as stone pits were dug through them. Others were dug into stone pit ramps, and thus cannot predate the stones. Several of these were probably for scaffolding and supporting timbers when stones were being moved about.[266] Some were cut away when Y and Z Holes were dug, large pits we will come to later, dating from around 3700 years ago.

Few post holes have stone fragments in them, suggesting, like the cremation burials, that most were dug before stones were being dressed on site. Cleal proposed that, unless contrary evidence exists, post holes be put into Phase 2, that is, contemporary with the slow filling of the ditch and the placing of cremation burials.[267]

The fact that the Stonehenge posts can't be squeezed into a large timber henge is interesting. At other sites, we would expect the henge. There are occasional lines that look like fences or screens (most clearly at Durrington Walls), but the vast majority of posts fall into concentric rings.[268] It is tempting to link these two unusual features, the large cremation cemetery and the many scattered post holes.[269] It may be that there were some buildings, but also we can imagine memorial posts, posts hanging with bones or offerings, fences controlling what people or spirits could see or where they could go. At this stage in its long history, around 4900–4400 years ago, Stonehenge was dedicated to funeral ceremony, the earth replete with the dead, the space above alive with spirits.

We have spent much of this chapter bemoaning the loss of bones, and the information they might have given us. Hawley found only three complete human skeletons. One of these was in the ditch not far from the north-east entrance, close to the turf, suggesting it was no older than Roman.[270] Another lay in a grave south-east of the stones,[271] and a third, much disturbed, in a pit right in the centre.[272] Unusually, we cannot blame archaeologists for the loss of these three. Hawley sent at least two of them to Sir Arthur Keith in London, whose brief notes we are privileged to have, for Keith knew where he was with human bones.

No, it was not archaeologists who did for these skeletons. It was Adolf Hitler. Or at least that's what we'd all thought for the past sixty years.

16

Some Bits Have Gone Walkabout

It began near Salisbury, at the offices of Wessex Archaeology. I knew they had a copy of William Hawley's excavation diary, a key source about his work at Stonehenge. I suspected that while researching *Stonehenge in its Landscape* they had also collected other documents that would help me understand what it had been like for Hawley at the remote place that Stonehenge was in the 1920s. Karen Walker showed me a bulging file of recent correspondence. 'You might find something useful in here', she said, thumbing paper that represented months of work. I wouldn't have bothered, except my eye caught the letter heading of the Royal College of Surgeons.

Anyone who knows Avebury – not least every local child taken there on a school trip – knows the story of the barber-surgeon. A medieval itinerant man, so it is said, assisting in the burial of prehistoric megaliths early in the fourteenth century, was entombed with the stone that trapped and killed him as it fell. Archaeologist Alexander Keiller dug him up in 1938. The objects on his person – coins, a pair of scissors and an iron probe – are still in the museum that Keiller founded in Avebury. But he sent the bones to the Royal College of Surgeons for a report. Then, final ignominy, only three years after the barber-surgeon had been excavated from his impromptu grave, the College took direct hits in the London Blitz, the devastating wartime bombing, and he was finally and definitively destroyed.[273]

The barber-surgeon was not the only ancient body lost in that particular raid. The Royal College of Surgeons had amassed quite a collection of prehistoric, Roman and medieval skeletons, all donated by archaeologists. It was a small war tragedy that only archaeology could have created.

Having spent five years as curator of the Alexander Keiller

126

Museum in Avebury, I could hardly pass by this letter. It was from the College's Museum Secretary, Muriel Gibbs. She had written in January 1996. *Stonehenge in its Landscape* had been published the previous October.

'Dear Dr Allen', her letter began, 'I really must apologise for the overlong delay in replying . . .' Mike Allen had written to Gibbs in August 1995, asking if she knew of a skeleton found by Hawley at Stonehenge. 'It is possible', he had added gloomily, 'that this skeleton was destroyed in the war along with that of the barber-surgeon from Avebury.'

In his published description of the skeleton, Hawley quoted Sir Arthur Keith, Conservator at the College's Hunterian Museum. Keith was an eminent anatomist, famed for his newspaper columns and public lectures as much as for his research and teaching, with an interest in race and eugenics typical of the time.[274] He is one of many people accused of the Piltdown hoax (with little justification, but that is another story). Archaeologists gave Keith their skeletons. He reported back with sex, height and age at death, and an assessment of date and race based on detailed skull measurements. The bones were then returned or, 'particularly when the specimens submitted appear to be of real historical value',[275] were added to the museum's collections. If Hawley's skeleton had been kept in London, it was now presumably destroyed. But if he had taken it back, there was a chance it could still be found somewhere.

Well now it had been, by Muriel Gibbs: it was still in London, in the basement of the Natural History Museum in South Kensington.

The Stonehenge book was published, and the archaeologists were working on other projects. Wessex Archaeology had not pursued this new trail. I tried to remain sceptical: any researcher learns from experience that caution is a frustrating but well-advised tactic. I spent the day poring over notebooks and letters from Hawley's time, acquiring a strong impression of a conscientious, thinking excavation director, far from the mindless navvy so often portrayed.

A few days later, I phoned Robert Kruszynski at the Natural History Museum.

I had met Rob when I was researching the Boxgrove story in 1995.[276] He was proof-reading an academic paper. 'This is what matters to me', he had said. 'But I'm a curator. Cataloguing into the computer is what the people upstairs want.' I knew what he meant. I had been there myself.

They had a lot of fossils in the Human Origins section of the Palaeontology Department, but I had never thought of Stonehenge Man as the sort of thing they collected. I explained about the letter from the Royal College of Surgeons. It was a bit of a long shot, I felt, but did he know anything about this Stonehenge skeleton?

'You mean catalogue number 4.10.4?' he shot back. There was a pause. 'You might be wondering', he continued, 'how I can recall this skeleton so clearly from the twenty thousand in the collection.'

It had crossed my mind.

As Rob explained, my thoughts raced over how it was that such an important item (to prehistoric archaeologists) had been sitting quite happily all these years in one museum, while other museums – and every living archaeologist – were completely unaware of its existence; and the fact that the remains clearly did exist, thus almost doubling the quantity of unburnt human bone from Stonehenge available for study. That the only skeleton examined in modern times was full of arrows hardly tempered my excitement.

It was all because of a Mr Winston Peach, Rob was saying. About 1975, Peach had told the Natural History Museum (so how had he found this skeleton?) that the man from Stonehenge was King Arthur. He was so convinced that he had personally paid to have the bones radiocarbon-dated.

Rob laughed.

'He was proved quite wrong.'

The radiocarbon date came out at about AD 150. So it wasn't King Arthur, who, if he existed at all, was active around AD 500. But Keith, who had said the skull was probably Roman, was apparently right. I couldn't help but feel disappointed, having developed a sudden interest in this lost body from Stonehenge that I had always assumed to be prehistoric. No flint arrows in this one, then.

'Didn't make any difference. Still thought it was King Arthur. Yes, I would say he was a bit obsessed.'

Before long I was in London, looking at typed lists prepared for the Natural History Museum by Muriel Gibbs. My hunch was right: there was much more there than a Roman skeleton from Stonehenge. Some places had catalogue numbers, some didn't – perhaps reflecting the chance survival of skeletons in the Blitz.

There were many names familiar to me as the sites of digs between the wars. Amongst these – I could hardly believe my eyes – was Woodhenge. With catalogue numbers.

Stonehenge is a bigger site, and half of its ditch (the source of most of the human bone) has been excavated. Maud Cunnington only dug out five ditch sections at Woodhenge, the widest less than 10m across. Nonetheless, there is a familiar ring to what she found: the child in the centre (chapter 4), an adult in the ditch, a few other unburnt bones, and a single cremation burial in the top of a pit that had once held a post. Not a cemetery, but, as at Stonehenge, something had been going on there involving human corpses. The two skeletons had been sent to Keith for his report, so, of course, they must have been destroyed in the Blitz – or so we all thought. The catalogue had only one entry for Woodhenge. Was it the child, or the man in the ditch?

There was another line that caught my special interest: 'Overton Hill Long Barrow (M. E. Cunnington). 4.0372/PA SK 48.' What was this? I was not aware that Maud had excavated a long barrow on Overton Hill – or indeed that there was a long barrow there at all. There was a site on this hill she had dug, however: the Sanctuary. They found a single human burial, at the foot of one of the megaliths. Lost in the Blitz.

My eyes scanned many sites I knew would interest other archaeologists as much as Stonehenge and Woodhenge interested me. But the most extraordinary – shocking – entry was not for a prehistoric skeleton at all. The archive, read the entry, included four photos, a report by Dr Cave, and six letters. It read: '1938. Avebury. 14C skeleton. Sender Alexander Keiller.' Otherwise known as the barber-surgeon.

By now all thoughts of caution had gone. I had come to London hoping – but hardly believing it possible – to find confirmation that a Stonehenge skeleton was in the museum collection, although it held limited interest for me. Not only did that appear to be so, but there was also evidence that they had a skeleton from Woodhenge (which one?), the only skeleton from the Sanctuary (although that needed confirmation) and, astonishingly, the great folk-hero of Avebury, darling of tour guides and teachers, the barber-surgeon himself. Although I was not then able to look at anything in the store, I'd seen enough. As soon as I emerged back into daylight outside the grand front of the Natural History Museum, I phoned Jackie McKinley. Doing my best to sound coherent, if not calm, over a bad line, I asked Jackie if she'd be able to look at some more bones with me. In London.

'I've never tried sexing', said Louise.

'That is a pretty wide angle', said Jackie. She was holding up a pelvic bone. 'I mean the mandible is masculine', Jackie continued. 'But I'm not all that happy about the pelvis – it could be one or the other. It's a bit too wide to be positive.'

'I think', she said, looking round at me, 'we're going to have to leave the sex open.'

Not an auspicious start. Keith had examined the skeleton and reported it to be that 'of a lad of about fourteen years of age'.[277] Aubrey Burl disagreed: it was a girl, because the head was pointing south when the body was laid in the ground.[278] Jackie McKinley was not prepared to say. The jaw was masculine, but the 'sciatic notch', a sharp curve in the pelvic bone that in the female partly defines the birth canal, was wider than 90°. This would suggest a female hip. But the individual was still young, and things can change as both hip and jaw develop. All in all, Jackie felt, it was safer to leave the sex undecided.

Still, the good news was that this skeleton definitely was from the Sanctuary. This adolescent had been buried at the base of one of the megaliths; the bones had been excavated in 1930 (having somehow survived destruction by fire of the adjacent stone around 1720[279]) and sent up to London for examination; they had come through the Blitz in 1941; and finally they had ended up – first the skull in 1951, then the body in 1955 – at the Natural History Museum, in a subterranean bunker. It is an accidental irony that the ancient skeletons that endured the bombing of the Royal College of Surgeons should now be shelved in a cramped, dark store whose reinforced concrete walls were built as a secret communications centre, for use in the same war that destroyed more than half the College's collections.

Laid out for us with great care on sheets of rubber foam were the more or less complete skeletal remains of five people. Here was the adolescent from the Sanctuary. To the right the skull and a few other bones from some ring ditches near Woodhenge (the Cunningtons called the site Durrington Circle I). To the left, skeleton 4.10.4 from Stonehenge, and beyond this the barber-surgeon's bones from Avebury. Round the corner, hidden behind a stack of shelves, was – not the child from the grave pit, but the young man from the ditch at Woodhenge.

It was a strange gathering: me, Jackie, Louise Humphrey, who had popped in from her office upstairs to see how we were getting on, and these silent representatives from other ages. The bones had an antique air about them: not just because they were genuinely old and fragile, but, having all been dug up over sixty years ago, they had acquired a patina of dust and browning varnish. The Woodhenge man's ribs (the only prehistoric ribs to have survived the journey) were still carefully laid in cotton wool inside a colourful Rowntree's Pastilles box (blackcurrant ovals).

'The brow is quite thin and narrow, which looks female', said Jackie, gingerly holding the Sanctuary skull. 'But it's still young. It could become masculine as it grows.'

If, that is, this person cut down in adolescence had lived a little longer. Keith had suggested death at fourteen. Jackie felt a range was safer, about thirteen to fifteen – definitely under sixteen, as parts of the acetabulum (the leg socket in the hip bone) are not fused at all. The skull was squashed when they found it in 1930. Maud Cunnington had had a go at gluing it. It's not easy to tell now, said Jackie, whether the skull is warped from pressure underground, or just badly reconstructed.

She noted a black staining on the arm and leg bones. William Young described in his diary how 'slight traces of charring were noticed on the upper side of the large limb bones', although Maud made no mention of this in her published report.[280] I wondered if this could have been caused by the burning of the megalith in the eighteenth century. Jackie thought not. She favoured the presence of something organic, like leather, slowly decaying against the bones in the soil. And she spotted a slight periostial infection of a tibia (lower leg bone), which might have been caused by an infection elsewhere in the body, but not by anything dramatic.

Thus Jackie worked round the bench.

'4.0373. Incomplete skeleton from a Beaker burial, male, in the centre of Durrington Circle I.'

The Cunningtons dug two sets of ring ditches, probably once enclosing barrows, after they'd finished at Woodhenge. At the first they found some pits or post holes containing Grooved Ware, perhaps part of a squarish structure beneath the second mound, and Grooved Ware was also found in one of the ditches. In the centre was a grave containing a Beaker pot, an 'axe hammer' and this skeleton.[281] There's not much left of him now, but Jackie hazarded an age between twenty-five and thirty, and noticed calculus on his teeth. He had a healed fracture in his left radius (lower arm).

The bloke whose chest sat in the wooden pastilles box had a bit more to say for himself. Archaeologically, he is rather special: a rare example of a complete skeleton from a primary context in a henge ditch. The Cunningtons chanced upon him in their east Woodhenge section, lying crouched up with his head to the south, in a pit dug on the ditch bottom possibly within days of its excavation.[282] It was good to see how well his bones had survived.

Jackie started on the skull.

'Male.' She brandished a large leg bone. 'You're not going to get women with legs like that.'

She noticed that his upper teeth were worn to a rising curve.

'Now that is odd.'

Although he's a young adult, eighteen to twenty-five, perhaps no more than twenty-one (some of his epiphyses, the articular ends, are not quite fused to the long bones), he's still got deciduous molars, teeth he should have lost at around eight or ten years old. The teeth that would normally have grown up and pushed these temporary teeth out have not erupted. The milk teeth are a bit broader at the top than the missing pre-molars, so have cramped the other teeth, pushing his front teeth (incisors) up a little. The result is that the raised incisors in his lower jaw have worn a curve into his upper teeth.

There are some lines of hypoplasia on the teeth. Looking a bit like tree rings running parallel to the gum, these are caused by deficiencies when the teeth are growing during childhood. It might be that the child was ill, so that food absorption was affected, or that his diet was inadequate. He also has those little holes in his eye sockets that we saw in the Stonehenge skeleton excavated in 1978 (chapter 12) – cribra orbitalia; again, suggesting a poor diet.

Jackie was intrigued by the face.

'He's very long between the nose and the teeth. His mandible's very narrow, too. He's got a narrow face with a flat forehead. Quite distinctive. He looks a bit like my mate Dave.'

Working down the body, she found a small piece of pelvis and only five of the twelve thoracic vertebrae.

'Some bits have gone walkabout.'

There's slight strain damage visible in these vertebrae. He might have had a little lower back problem. His arms and legs are big (albeit his right arm is missing).

'Yep, big lad. These are strong bones, not just long.'

His feet and hands were jumbled together in a cardboard box. Working through these one bone at a time, Jackie continued to be impressed with his condition.

'I don't think he's going to have any arthritis. He had big hands. He could've been wiry muscly, rather than hefty muscly. My mate Dave is six foot seven, and lanky. Big feet as well. Very long . . .' She laughs. 'Toes.'

Jackie got out her callipers, and measured the skull. She calculated his height at 1.76m, and his cranial index at 67.3, a measure that underlines the long and narrow shape of the head. Keith came to similar conclusions.

Well, that was it for the Hengeworld skeletons. The Woodhenge remains were of the young man in the ditch, and not the supposedly sacrificed child in the central pit. So, unless something unexpected turns up (it's worth hoping), we won't know about the child's fate – the better assumption being that it died naturally.

Jackie and I had, of course, to have a look at the barber-surgeon. His bones were well preserved. As Dr Cave had noted in his report, they had been skilfully excavated by Keiller. It has always been assumed the man died when a megalith fell on him.[283] But looking at the bones neatly laid out in the Natural History Museum basement, this evidence for traumatic death was not immediately obvious. 'All we can see now is fresh breakage', said Jackie. The pelvis has been fixed with plaster of Paris. 'But it has to be said that the broken parts are those that so often are broken and damaged.' Just from lying in the ground.

I would need to go back to the detailed excavation archive to throw more light on this. But the seed was sown that we might be about to destroy a myth. Perhaps the barber-surgeon was not killed by the megalith.

There was something else. Cave had clearly written 'There are no signs present of ante mortem [i.e. before death] injury or disease.'[284] Yet here we were, with the same skull examined by Cave, staring at a huge, healed cut wound, clear as a pike staff. There could be no question it was the same skull. Keiller had seen this wound. Indeed, he'd seen all sorts of things, which his secretary typed out in standard triplicate.[285]

The man was a 'beetle-browed, low-forehead type I do not think that I have ever seen outside an asylum'. – 'Rubbish', Cave had written on his copy of the letter.

His nose had been broken 'from a short arm jab or a right hook'. – 'No', scribbled Cave.

'I note that at some time or another', opined Keiller, 'he has received a really fine crack on the right side of his head'. – 'Tripe'.[286]

Later in the year, when Keiller received Cave's considered report, he noticed the absence of any reference to the skull wound that the two men had only recently corresponded about. He wrote back the same day. Cave replied with an addendum to his original report. 'There is evidence', it began, 'of ante mortem injury, of the nature of two non-penetrating incised wounds . . .'[287]

It is a remarkable incident. With unguarded enthusiasm, the archaeologist saw all sorts of non-existent injuries, while the anatomist, more interested in racial characteristics, had completely forgotten about a dramatic scar. Looking at the skull, sitting there on its sheet of pale khaki foam, it was difficult to imagine how anyone could miss such an obvious wound. But then archaeology is full of surprises.

17

A Walk through the Stones

Stonehenge Phase 3 (earlier): Approximately 4550–4300 years ago

3	Stoneholes D and E
3a	Stone 97 and Heelstone
3b	Stone 97 removed, Heelstone ditch dug (bluestone near bottom)
	Station Stones and 'Barrows'
3i	Q and R Holes
3ii	Sarsen Circle and Trilithons (c. 4300 years ago)

It's not everyone, if I may be so immodest, who can claim to have discovered an unknown megalith at Stonehenge. We'll come to that soon, though I should say that I didn't find the stone itself, just the pit that held it up. There are several stones missing, but many are still there. For some years now, it's not been possible for the casual visitor to move amongst them. What would you see if you began at the Heelstone by the road, and walked into the middle?

The Heelstone is a rough thing, 4.5m high, leaning but never fallen, a pockmarked mass of naturally shaped steel-hard sandstone weighing 35 tons.

Sixty paces away is an apparent wall of carved megaliths. Although the uprights are now mostly set in concrete, the grassy scene is almost exactly as recorded over 400 years ago. About halfway there, as we cross the causeway through the circular ditch and banks, now slight but clearly visible, we pass a fallen slab, the Slaughter Stone. Twenty-eight tons.

At the great ring, towering above, are four of the seventeen stones that still stand. Eight more lie fallen, five missing. Twenty-six tons each, except one, which is both narrower than the others and under 3m tall. The rest stand 4m above the turf. The first four support three horizontal, touching lintels. There are five more lintels: three in the air, each on an isolated pair of uprights, and two

135

on the ground. Originally, like the uprights, there were thirty, all dressed to shape, sides curved to follow the ring. Seven tons each.

Through the doorway and across the others inside the circular arena, the largest megalith, smooth, straight, tall and alone, stands 7m high. On the ground beside, in two pieces, lies its twin. Forty-five tons each. Beside the broken stone is the fallen lintel that once completed the pi-shaped trilithon (trilithon: from the Greek, meaning 'three stones').[288] Nineteen tons.

There are four more trilithons, two on either hand, twelve stones in all. Seven of the eight uprights are standing; to the right, one lies in the grass, broken, in three pieces. The closer pairs are slightly shorter, at 5m, than the further, 5.2m. Forty tons each. Of the four lintels, the right-hand one is on the ground, broken, the others high above. Sixteen tons each.

There are two more stones, smaller, away from the others, each under 10 tons.

The once perfect circle of thirty standing and thirty horizontal stones, and the five trilithons in horseshoe plan: 1500 tons.

These are the local stones, from no more than 30km away. Sarsen, a hard, bitter stone that lies in swelling slabs on and just below the ground and interferes with shallow excavations – house foundations or cable trenches – is found scattered over parts of south and east England, but nowhere in such concentrations or sizes as are still found in north central Wiltshire, around the headwaters of the River Kennet. The very term 'sarsen' is a local dialect word. This is where the stone rings and rows of Avebury are found – all presumably local sarsens – and is probably where this 1500 tons of Stonehenge came from.

The other stones, the smaller 'bluestones', are not local. Collectively their mostly igneous nature contrasts with the sedimentary sarsens, but they do not share the uniformity of the local rock, consisting of dolerite (particularly the famous 'spotted dolerite', a blue-green stone with small, circular whitish blobs), rhyolite, altered volcanic ash, tuff, calcareous ash and micaceous sandstone.[289] They come from a small spot in south-west Wales, on or near the Preseli Hills, by a route at least 300km long, perhaps much longer.

Like a thin crowd, the bluestones stand, lean against each other, lie fallen or break the turf in buried stumps. In a circle echoing the surrounding sarsens are twenty more or less complete pillars of rock (a further nine stumps have been identified below ground).

Most, unlike the sarsens, appear to be shaped only by nature. Likewise inside the sarsen five-trilithon horseshoe, another horseshoe: fourteen small and lintel-less bluestones. These stones appear to be carved into rough rectangular posts. Thirty-four bluestones: 3 or 4 tons each. In the centre, in front of the tallest sarsen, is the largest bluestone, the Altar Stone. This is green micaceous sandstone, prone in two pieces under parts of the fallen great trilithon. Six tons.

Once there were perhaps sixty or seventy in the bluestone circle and nineteen in the horseshoe. Around 300 tons. In ton-kilometres that's only about half as many again as the enclosing sarsens.

These, then, are the stones of Stonehenge (figures 27 and 28, plate 19).[290]

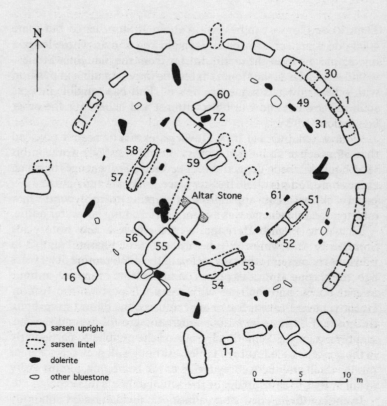

Figure 27. The present arrangement of stones in the centre of Stonehenge. *After Cleal et al.*

Figure 28. Average heights of stones standing at Stonehenge.

Sarsens	Feet/ins	Metres	Bluestones	Feet/ins	Metres
CIRCLE			CIRCLE		
16 stones	13' 1"	4.0	8 stones	4' 4"	1.3
HORSESHOE			HORSESHOE		
5 stones	16' 8"	5.1	6 stones	7' 4"	2.2
stone 56	22' 7"	6.9			
Heelstone	15'	4.6			

After Cleal et al. 1995, 547–8

There's not a lot we can be certain about at Stonehenge, but some 4000-odd years ago someone – it might be the man whose longest resting place was in the ditch, not far from the Slaughter Stone – would have seen all the stones that we now see, standing in position with others now missing, quite new.[291] This is a tangible fact, as solid as the stones now dribbled in mist and lichen. It's the other bits that are tricky.

We saw (chapter 11) how Hawley's excavations first revealed that Stonehenge had a rich history. Using Hawley's work, in his 1956 book Atkinson defined three successive Stonehenges in which every stone and post hole had its place.[292] By the time of the 1979 paperback, with two appendices attempting to incorporate new information, the scheme was as useful as a leaking hot water bottle.

Thanks to English Heritage, we now have a new history for Stonehenge that works. We have dealt with Phases 1 and 2 in previous chapters: (1) the excavation of the ditch around 5000 years ago, the placing at various points on the bottom of special, antique animal bones, and the ring of fifty-six tall posts in the Aubrey Holes; (2) over the next five or six centuries, the filling of the ditch, the erection of posts in various enigmatic groups around the site, and the placing of cremation burials on the periphery, particularly in the now backfilled Aubrey Holes. Although all previous schemes put the ditch and the Aubrey Holes at the beginning, almost every detail in this, to say nothing of the actual dates, is different.

In the continuing new story, Phase 3 is divided both temporally and spatially. This is because the inner and outer parts of the site are almost impossible to correlate with confidence.[293] We have 'sub-phases' 3i to vi for the inner stone arrangements and 3a to c for the periphery of the monument. These 'sub-phases' are not nine successive events, but three outer and six inner that run in parallel.[294] For example, we know (from my own excavation) that a megalith used to stand beside the Heelstone, and that after this was erected, and probably after it had been taken away, the Heelstone was surrounded by a small circular ditch. But we can do little more than guess whether these events occurred at the same time as, say, the construction of the sarsen circle or of an arrangement of megaliths that preceded it.

It must be said that even this cannot be the full story. Listen to William Hawley. Alone at Stonehenge, battered by weather, frustrated by slow arrival of equipment and all but ignored by archaeologists in London, even the determined Lieutenant Colonel must sometimes have wondered why he was there. Describing his work in 1924 amongst the stones, he found 'an extraordinary state of things':

> The ground was honeycombed with post-holes and craters of all sorts, sizes, and depths, many of them having been cut into another apparently in successive periods of digging and suggesting a series of changes. The long-continued burrowing of rabbits had increased the general confusion, making the difficulty of distinguishing the outlines of the holes far greater. I frankly confess that I have no explanation to offer in elucidation of this tangle, and I doubt if anybody will ever be able to explain it satisfactorily.[295]

Who can be dogmatic with evidence like that?[296] But we can try our best.

The first stone monument at the centre of Stonehenge was almost completely demolished by its builders or their immediate descendants or compatriots. So what this structure actually looked like is a mystery. Amongst the refilled pits in the central area are several packed with hard chalk and dug through by other pits, indicating an early place in the sequence. Nine or ten of these occur in distinctive dumbbell shapes. There are impressions of missing standing stones at the bulbous ends, and a narrower trough packed hard with clean chalk between. All but one of these pits lie on two imprecise arcs on the east side. Richard Atkinson, who first identified them, called them Q (outer end of the dumbbells, which have a radial alignment) and R holes (inner end). Atkinson noted that some of the stone impressions contained tiny chips of dolerite, suggesting that bluestones had once stood in them (figure 29).

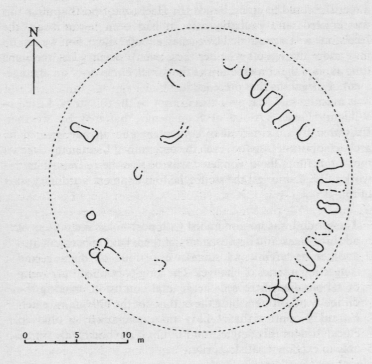

Figure 29. Stonehenge Phase 3i: Q and R holes. The dashed ring in this and subsequent plans is the inner edge of the sarsen stone circle (not yet built at this stage). *After Cleal et al.*

A handful of other pits may be contemporary, but even allowing for yet to be excavated features, it's not possible to extend the known plan to make bluestone circles. The most that can be justifiably imagined is a slightly rectangular arrangement open to the south-west.[297] At the open side was a large pit, astride the axis, which Ros Cleal suggests held the Altar Stone. If she is right, this now collapsed and broken stone may be the oldest megalith on the site still near its original position.

These Q and R holes, and what stood in them, constitute Phase 3i. There is no direct dating evidence, which is a bit of a problem because we cannot be certain that these stones were not standing in Phase 2 (chapter 15). The midsummer sun (the approximate site alignment was established right at the start with the excavation of the ditch) could have risen through the maze of posts standing in the pits across the ditch causeway, and shone on the flat face of the Altar Stone. It's more that, with all the post holes, there is a sense that there just wasn't room at that time physically and perhaps metaphorically for a load of stones as well.[298]

We do, however, have a much better idea of what came next, not least because half of it is still standing.

They might look timeless. Indeed the present arrangement is as shown in the oldest known realistic depiction of Stonehenge, drawn around 1570.[299] In fact, most of the sarsens were moved in the twentieth century. Of the nine high lintels apparently still as placed by the original builders, strictly only two got there by Neolithic technology. The three together on the north-east side were removed and stacked on the ground by the Office of Works in 1920, so that supporting megaliths could be straightened and set in cement. To the east, lintel 122 fell and broke in two in 1900, and was repaired and replaced in 1958. Lintel 107 was taken down in 1919, and put back after its megaliths were made safe. Lintel 158, on the ground since the trilithon of which it was part fell in 1797, was winched back into place in 1958. Lintel 154 was moved briefly in 1964 when trilithon 53/54 was concreted. Only 152, on the north-east trilithon 51/52, and 105 in the sarsen circle can claim to have remained in place for over 4000 years.

A disappointment for the romantic, perhaps, but a bonus for archaeology. For all this repairing has allowed archaeologists to delve into the foundations. As a result, we know quite a bit about how stones got into their pits, what holds them up, and, thanks to objects found with them, when Stonehenge was built. Let's deal with the last point first. This is one of the standard questions asked about Stonehenge, typically by someone on a quick visit: the one-date answer we seek is for the classic silhouetted ruin, the sarsens. By now, you might expect me to say there is no simple answer. This is of course the case. But it's fun to have a shot.

There are now ten radiocarbon dates for standing stones at the site. They are listed in Appendix 1, but it is convenient to bring them together here. Ten may sound a lot, but given the number of stone arrangements and uncertainty surrounding some of the samples, it's not enough. Below the dates, I have listed the Wessex Archaeology team's Bayesian estimates for events dated by more than one sample (figure 30).[300]

Atkinson quite reasonably argued that circle and trilithons were contemporary, although trilithons 'are far too big to have been manoeuvred once the outer circle was in place', so must have gone up first.[301] Radiocarbon dates, however, don't fit this, and

Figure 30. Radiocarbon dates for Stonehenge megaliths, arranged into structural groups.

Context	Material	Lab ref	BP (radio-carbon age before 1950)	cal BC range (95% confidence)	years ago (cal BC +2000)
SARSENS					
Stone hole E	antler	OxA-4837	3995±60	2832–2313	4575
Stone hole E	antler	OxA-4838	3885±40	2469–2204	4335
Sarsen circle hole 27	bone	OxA-4902	5350±80	4345–3979	6160
Sarsen circle hole 1	antler	UB-3821	4023±21	2618–2470	4545
Sarsen trilithon hole 53/54	antler	OxA-4840	3985±45	2618–2350	4485
Sarsen trilithon hole 56	antler	OxA-4839	3860±40	2465–2200	4335
Sarsen trilithon hole 56	antler	BM-46	3670±150	2469–1642	4055
BLUESTONES					
Bluestone hole 40c	antler	OxA-4900	3865±50	2469–2145	4305
Bluestone hole 40c	bone	OxA-4878	3740±40	2284–1983	4135
Bluestone hole 63a	antler	OxA-4877	3695±55	2275–1920	4100
PHASING (Allen, Bayliss and Bronk Ramsey)					
Stone hole E				*2480–2270*	*4375*
Sarsen trilithons				*2440–2100*	*4270*
Bluestone circle				*2280–2030*	*4155*

See Appendix 1 for details.

something has to give. You can say sarsens date from around 4500 years ago, relying on the dated antler from circle stone 1 (the other circle date can only be an old bone from unrelated activity, if not the remains of something curated from earlier generations). The antler from trilithon pits 53/54 fits. This is the line taken by English Heritage.[302] In this view, it is necessary to assume there is something 'wrong' with the other two trilithon dates. This is not impossible. All samples are from old excavations, and none really has the detailed provenance we would like.

The other way, proposed by archaeologist Humphrey Case, is to

Figure 31. Radiocarbon dates for Stonehenge megaliths, arranged into statistically similar groups.

Context	Material	Lab ref	BP (radio-carbon age before 1950)	cal BC range (95% confidence)	years ago (cal BC +2000)
RESIDUAL					
Sarsen circle hole 27	bone	OxA-4902	5350±80	4345–3979	6160
Stone hole E	antler	OxA-4837	3995±60	2832–2313	4575
Sarsen circle hole 1	antler	UB-3821	4023±21	2618–2470	4545
Sarsen trilithon hole 53/54	antler	OxA-4840	3985±45	2618–2350	4485
Bluestone hole 40c	antler	OxA-4900	3865±50	2469–2145	4305
SARSENS					
Stone hole E	antler	OxA-4838	3885±40	2469–2204	4335
Sarsen trilithon hole 56	antler	OxA-4839	3860±40	2465–2200	4335
Sarsen trilithon hole 56	antler	BM-46	3670±150	2469–1642	4055
	3 sample weighted mean		3865±27	2461–2205	4335
BLUESTONES					
Bluestone hole 40c	bone	OxA-4878	3740±40	2284–1983	4135
Bluestone hole 63a	antler	OxA-4877	3695±55	2275–1920	4100
	2 sample weighted mean		3724±32	2267–1983	4125

See Appendix 1 for details.

say that the youngest dates are the important ones, and assume that others are older objects accidentally incorporated in the fill of stone pits – the Aubrey Hole 7 principle (chapter 13).[303]

In the next figure, I have rearranged the dates, grouping the youngest, statistically indistinguishable results from each structure. Others are relegated to a residual bag (figure 31).

By including stone E (thought to be one of three stones that included the Slaughter Stone[304]), we have three dates for sarsens that combine to give an estimate for a sarsen 'event' of around 4300 years ago (4461–4205 at 95 per cent confidence). Likewise, we have a bluestone 'event' (not the first, which involved the Q and R holes) of up to two centuries later (4267–3983).

So where are we? Were the sarsen trilithons and circle – Stonehenge Phase 3ii – erected 4500 or 4300 years ago? The question's significance lies in what other events then become contemporary with the sarsens. If we accept the younger date, not only do the sarsens broadly share time with the earthwork Avenue and the much more precisely dated burial in the Stonehenge ditch, but also with the large timber henge at Durrington Walls, the ditch around Woodhenge, the timber enclosures at West Kennet, and perhaps Avebury stone circle. The earlier date puts the Stonehenge sarsens before all of this.[305]

The recent date seems more appropriate: Stonehenge as a culmination of tradition, not an initiation. Without more excavation and the retrieval of better dating samples, there's not much more we can say. So, when needing a quick answer to the question 'How old is Stonehenge?', go for 4300 years.

'But,' you might wish to continue, 'if you'd like to buy me a drink . . .'[306]

I have been quite informative about excavations: the archaeologists (not all with us to put their view) would not necessarily feel flattered by my versions of events. It's only fair, then, that I should say something about my own little dig (strictly, two little digs). They were both extremely productive, but I admit that had I been in total control, things would have happened differently.

It started when the Prince of Wales, once an archaeology student at Cambridge University, decided to see Stonehenge. Late on a Friday afternoon in 1979 some senior Department of the Environment officers, waiting for the delayed red helicopter, couldn't help noticing a small bright yellow excavator throwing clumps of earth and rock into the air, metres away from the famous Heelstone. A secretary in London passed the message to my office in Avebury, and I drove down to investigate.

The machine and its operators had left when I arrived, but the hole they had made was all too visible. I had no idea what was going on (custodians at the site later told me a telephone cable was being laid – for the new Stonehenge Exchange[307]). But it was obvious (to me, at any rate) that it had to stop. I was only a few weeks into my new job as Curator of the Alexander Keiller Museum. No one dug holes that close to Stonehenge without proper archaeological investigation – indeed the hole should not have been dug at all. It was simply a matter of stopping the contractors and mounting a dig.

Today there is a proper awareness of the sensitivity of the archaeological landscape at Stonehenge. There is no doubt, however, that this understanding was hard won from the experience of incidents such as this. It is absolutely vital that the lesson is not forgotten in the years ahead, when major works at and around Stonehenge are likely to take place. Any ground disturbance has to be thought about with very great care.

The reality in 1979 was anything but simple. The Post Office (who then ran UK telephones) were helpful. Once I had spoken to the manager in Salisbury, the men were moved to another part of the cable route to give me time to investigate the ground they had yet to dig up beside Stonehenge. This was Monday morning. As the workmen started before the Salisbury offices opened, they had been digging for an hour before they could agree to stop. By then they were 7m from the Heelstone, and no more than a pace from what turned out to be important prehistoric deposits.[308]

My problem was that while agreeing to give me a week or two to investigate, my superiors had no money to meet the costs of doing this. Salvation came from friends at the Department of Archaeology at Southampton University, in particular Arthur ApSimon. Arthur arranged for a number of students – and a few staff – to gain some rather special (not to say unusual) field experience, and helped me out with equipment. I picked up the bar bills.[309]

We set out a narrow trench where the Post Office had still to lay their cable. For them it must have seemed singularly unfortunate, for a day's further work would have seen them done and gone. My knowledge of Stonehenge led me to expect at least two features: the small ditch around the Heelstone, and the eastern of the two Avenue ditches. The chance to look at these structures was extremely welcome (not least because results of previous work on them were then inaccessible).[310]

I was nervous. It was a small project, but then it was also Stonehenge. I had years of experience working on excavations, but apart from the sort of grubbing about in my own back garden that every adolescent archaeologist goes in for, I had never before actually directed my own dig. And the word from above was that 'expert advice' said it would be a waste of time. Who, after all, would expect to find anything useful on the verge of a busy road?

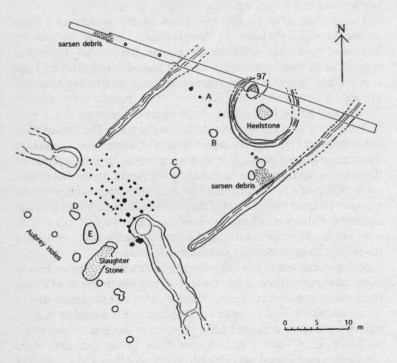

Figure 32. Hawley excavated most of the area outside the main entrance at Stonehenge in the 1920s, but his records are not detailed. The long thin trench passing the Heelstone was excavated by me in 1979–80. Pits D, E and 97 (with a megalith impression on the bottom) are stone pits, but it is unclear whether B and C are even artifical. The sarsen debris in my trench consisted of rock fragments broken up for a hearth footing; Hawley excavated something very similar closer to the Heelstone. *After Cleal et al.*

For that was where we were planning to dig: on that thin patch of grass between the Stonehenge perimeter fence and the busy tarmac of the A344.

We did get the sections through the ditches I had hoped for, and very useful they were. Sadly, there were no antler picks, so the chance to add to what was then a tiny collection of radiocarbon dates for Stonehenge came to naught. But we also found something we hadn't expected. It had been predicted by earlier archaeologists,[311] and it made sense that it should be there. But naive and impetuous as I was, it still hadn't occurred to me that we might actually find it.

The Heelstone is one of a handful of megaliths that, standing alone rather than as part of circles and horseshoes, are difficult to relate to the grander scheme of things. Being singular, they have each acquired completely arbitrary names. A large sarsen known as the Slaughter Stone lies in a shallow open pit at the north-east earthwork entrance. When Hawley excavated in that area in 1920 and 1922, he found two empty stone pits that he labelled D and E (figure 32).

His interpretation was that three stones had stood in a row across the causeway, of which only the Slaughter Stone survives, albeit flat on the ground. Hawley thought the stones contemporary with the causeway post holes; Ros Cleal suggests stones replaced posts.[312] Two antlers from pit E have been dated. As we saw above (figures 30 and 31), the results were separated from each other by around two centuries. Treating the older as residual leaves a single date compatible with Phase 3ii.

There are two low mounds (known as the North and South Barrows, although they did not contain burials) whose ring ditches squash up against the large circular bank of Phase 1, approximately north and south of the inner megaliths. Excavation has shown that both had standing stones in the centre. The Heelstone is surrounded by a similar small circular ditch. It is assumed that all three ditches were dug some time after the stones had been erected (figure 3).

The missing stones are numbered 92 and 94. Completing a rectangle that perfectly straddles the sarsen circle are the surviving two Station Stones, 91 and 93. These are apparently undressed sarsen of moderate size, fallen and sunk into the turf.

On old plans, two large pits appear between the Slaughter Stone and the Heelstone. Labelled Stone Holes B and C by Hawley, his descriptions of the pits are quite brief. After further consideration, he was 'inclined to think that [C] was a hole in which a thorn bush may once have grown'.[313]

These are not the only questionable pits that Hawley dug out. Some years ago, I pointed out that three of his 'bush holes', combined with the Station Stones, produce a plan of seven pits in a ring remarkably similar to the map of the 'cavities' sketched by John Aubrey. I suggested that, rather than representing a few of the Aubrey Holes, these cavities were indications of an all but lost ring of small stones around the edge of the earthwork.[314] This idea met with polite silence from my colleagues! The fact is, there are several features on the periphery of the monument, as well as in the interior, that remain unexplained.

About one pit, at least, there is no doubt. On 1 June 1979, I was about to start digging it out.

There at one end of our trench (less than 1m from the Post Office cable gouge) was an enormous hole in the ground. It was full of hard chalk rubble, but the conformation of this packing was subtly different to the undisturbed chalk around it. We first noticed it on the eighth day of the dig, when we thought it might have been a natural irregularity. The chalk under Stonehenge, at least that near the surface, is not the hard white rock you see in the cliffs of the English Channel. Rather, after centuries of freezing and thawing in the tundra conditions of the last ice age, it is a broken mix of off-colour chalk and silt. Picking out ancient excavations backfilled with chalk rubble can be a challenge, as much today as it was for William Hawley.

The next day, however, 2 June 1979, we found a sarsen flake in this packed chalk, and we knew the hole had to be artificial. 'Now beginning to look like a large pit', I wrote in the site notebook. '? stonehole.'

Over the following ten days we removed the chalk fill, finding nothing but a few tiny pieces of sarsen, an even smaller grain of pottery and a few flint flakes – and no antler pick for radiocarbon dating. But we were certain this was prehistoric. Not only were the flint flakes very fresh (two of them actually fitted back together, so they must have been struck by a prehistoric knapper in the close vicinity), but on the west side the compacted chalky rubble had been dug away by the excavation of the ditch around the Heelstone.

This meant the pit had been dug and refilled before the Heelstone ditch, something we already knew to be part of the ancient Stonehenge.

When we got to the bottom, about 1m from the ground surface, we saw the unmistakable signs that it had once held a large standing stone. This was the first large stone pit to have been excavated at Stonehenge for at least fifteen years, and the first substantial megalith site to have been discovered since Hawley found the smaller Pit D in 1922. Not a waste of time, then.

It was instructive to dig out the same things that Hawley described from his 1920s excavations. The pit was considerably wider than the stone it had held. Just as Hawley had done in pits of the sarsen circle, we found small post holes on the bottom, and parallel grooves pointing into a marked depression created by the weight of the stone in the soft rock. We even found, as Hawley had described in his Pit E (like our pit, a large excavation that no longer contained its stone), a long narrow hole that looked like a cast of a vanished wooden pole.[315]

Pressed for time as we were, we had dug out this wooden cast, if that's what it was, before we realised that it might have been something worth recording.[316] But the rest of what we found – two small post holes underneath where the stone would have stood, the grooves on the bottom that we interpreted as the sites of poles laid as a slide, the details of the stone impression and the strange deposit of what appeared to be once wet chalk thrown into the pit when the stone was taken out, and now hardened – was treated to a thorough record. This would be the best-described stone pit at Stonehenge.[317]

So, apart from a collection of stuff that will enhance a display if Stonehenge ever gets the full museum it deserves, what had we found?

The fill of Pit 97, as we called it, had been dug through by the Heelstone ditch. So the stone it was dug for had been removed before the digging of the ditch. We know from Atkinson's excavation nearby that the bank of the Avenue (this earthwork will be described soon) overlay the Heelstone ditch.[318] So we have a construction sequence, almost the only one on the monument periphery: first Pit 97, then Heelstone ditch (around the already present Heelstone), and finally Avenue. We don't know what intervals separated these three events, but the impression is the same as for the centre. It didn't all happen at once.

The Heelstone, then, may not always have been a lone megalith.

149

Indeed, it's possible it was one of three, like the Slaughter Stone. Pit 97 is massive, like Pit E. Pit D to the west of E is smaller, and a pit this size could lie outside the area of our dig, partly under the road (figure 32). As I said at the time, this discovery has obvious implications for the astronomical significance of the Heelstone, the monolith popularly imagined to have been erected to mark the rising midsummer sun.[319]

Meanwhile, the other side of the fence (by the time we had finished on 20 June, the day before midsummer's day, the tall mesh panels had been smothered in rolls of razor wire), another excavation had taken place. Finished the year before, its freshly backfilled shape was still enclosed with wooden split paling.

We knew John Evans had found the skeletal remains of a man. We didn't know, then, how he had died.

18

Patient Name: Stonehenge

On 6 March 1998, a woman confessed to having seen her husband beat to death her former live-in partner with a hockey stick. The assailant was convicted and sentenced to life imprisonment.[320] The trial was the conclusion of two years' work by the Hampshire Constabulary, who at first had nothing to go on but a body in a shallow grave at a farm near Southampton. As their plea to the public put it, the man later identified as Harjit Singh Luther, naked but for a T-shirt, had been 'beaten about the head with a blunt instrument'. His face was invisible.

The conviction was obtained after analysis of thousands of phone calls, extensive forensic evidence and interviews in India. But none of this would have happened had it not been for the work of Richard Neave, Artist in Medicine and Life Sciences in the Faculty of Medicine, Dentistry and Nursing at the University of Manchester. He was asked by the Hampshire police to reconstruct the face of the unidentified man.

Neave built up modelling clay, layer by layer, on a cast of the skull. To mimic the flesh and muscle on the victim's head, he used statistics acquired during a century of research by scientists around the world, combined with his own intuition and experience.[321] The resultant face, which regionally could only be described as probably Asian or east European, was photographed by the police, and broadcast on national television. Did anyone, asked BBC TV's *Crimewatch UK*, recognise this man?

Someone did. They phoned in with a name and address. It took little time for the police to ascertain that the identification was correct.

Sometimes Neave's work, as in this case, undergoes a degree of testing that no archaeologist can expect to confront. We can deploy the most sophisticated science and argument to reconstruct Stonehenge, or we can fantasise with gusto: there is no danger that anyone will stand up and say no, actually, it wasn't like that (or, even less likely, yes it was) because they were there to see it. But the test of Neave's work is also a test of the same idea applied to faces of which no one alive has any recollection. If facial reconstruction can create a likeness that someone can recognise – at once a rigorous and deeply personal test – then it can do the same for a lost prehistoric face. We can create something that a fellow being would have known. It won't be the actual face; it won't reveal the life story, the personality or the idiosyncrasies of culture, age, health, genes – the sound of the voice, the sense of humour. But it will be a recognisable likeness, a mute portrait of an individual from a world where there was no direct representation.

So it was, on a grey day shortly before Christmas 1998, that I found myself seated on a Salisbury train to London with a brown cardboard box. The box contained the best-preserved head I had seen from Hengeworld: the mandible in a polythene bag, the hyoid bone from the tongue in a Post Office envelope designed for coins, and the delicate cream-coloured skull nestling in clean white paper tissue like a large fossil egg. Folded up at the top of the box was a yellow Loans Out form, completed by Andrew Deathe, Assistant Curator at Salisbury Museum. Valuation: £3000 (well, the form had this space, so something had to go in). Object Description: Stonehenge Murder Victim. We had an appointment to meet at the Department of Medical Physics and Bioengineering at University College Hospital, London.

I met Robin Richards when writing a medical story for the *Guardian*. BBC television's archaeology series *Meet the Ancestors* was on its first run, and they were scouting for publicity. The theme of each programme is that archaeologist Julian Richards (no relation to the medical researcher, but the same Julian Richards who directed the ancient landscape project around Stonehenge) visits an excavation where a skeleton has been found. The world in which that person lived is told through their eyes, as a face is reconstructed on the skull. Armed with a press release about a Roman sarcophagus, I'd gone to Medical Physics and Bioengineering. I found the research team were developing some pretty exciting technology.

Gus Alousi, a surgeon also at University College, had walked into the lab once and announced: 'I have a problem.' Computer games could model moving faces in three dimensions, but he couldn't: if he could, and establish accurate internal anatomy, the dangerous and stressful ear and face operations he performed would be transformed. So Robin Richards, Alf Linney and colleagues have been working on this for a few years. The biggest hindrance is the cost of the software – what Robin described as 'fundamentally a souped-up graphics card'. When games need something that powerful, they'll be cheap. Remember that on your next liaison with Lara Croft: you're helping advance medical science.

The relatively simple tasks of representing the surface topography of a face in the round – a portrait bust – and of rebuilding a face from skeletal anatomy, are in the can. Faces have traditionally been modelled in clay on skull casts, as with the man from near Southampton. But scientists like Peter Vanezis, at the Human Identification Centre of the University of Glasgow, and Robin Richards in London believe that a greater future lies in digital imaging, which is cheaper, quicker and, ultimately, they say, will be more reliable.[322] For my purposes, armed with a unique and fragile skull from Stonehenge, not only was the process relatively cheap and fast, but there was no need to risk damaging the skull by having to make a cast.

I followed Robin into a small, dark room, painted black to minimise light reflections. As he fixed the mandible to the skull with blobs of Blu-Tack, he commented on the high quality of the teeth. Demonstration photos of an early surgery operation to adjust a protruding lower jaw (before and after) and laser scans of skin and skulls decorated the walls like trophies. He propped the head on a block of black-painted polystyrene, which sat on a metal support in a black swivel seat reminiscent of something between the chairs at the dentist and on the TV show *Who Wants to Be a Millionaire?* On a small desk stood a computer screen glowing in the shadow cast by a concealed anglepoise lamp. And then it got weird.

With all lights off, the skull (Patient Name: Stonehenge) rotated mechanically in the laser beam of an optical surface scanner. The computer stored the digital data for around 250 vertical profiles at up to 300 points per line. On the third scan, Robin was happy with the result. I then obliged by sitting in the chair for the same treatment, so Robin could add my face to his data base. Thanks to clever software, the four scans – my face and the three skull versions – all fitted onto a single floppy disk.

Back in the lab, Robin loaded the data onto his Dell.

19

Extending the Trench

Stonehenge Phase 3 (later): Approximately 4500–3600 years ago

3	Stoneholes D and E
3a	Stone 97 and Heelstone
3b	Stone 97 removed, Heelstone ditch dug (bluestone near bottom)
	Station Stones and 'Barrows'
3c	Avenue ditches and banks dug (*c*. 4500–4000 years ago)
3ii	Sarsen Circle and Trilithons (*c*. 4300 years ago)
3iii	Poorly understood features predating 3iv
3iv	Bluestone Oval and Circle (*c*. 4100 years ago)
3v	Stones removed from Oval to leave Bluestone Horseshoe
3vi	Y and Z Holes (*c*. 3600 years ago)

I was back beside the Stonehenge road in 1980, to conduct a dig this time planned in advance. The occasion was the laying of a new cattle-trough water pipe. I had already cleared out the most promising area, close to the Heelstone. The verge now had a telephone cable duct between older water and electricity trenches, so there really was very little left. But it seemed, given what we had already found, that we had to return before yet another service trench was dug, removing what little undisturbed ground still survived. Just in case.

The timing was, again, dictated by the contractor. This year it was March.

'17 March. Monday. Raining hard a.m. & most of afternoon', reads the first notebook entry.

'18 March. Snowing hard a.m., raining p.m.'

'19 March. Dry all day. Very cold strong wind.'

And so it went on.

We began with a long, thin trench that extended the area we had dug the year before. I was looking for the other side of the Avenue, which we duly found. Unfortunately this time, what with a tangle of pipes and a delightful old milestone, there was little of the prehistoric silts left. Outside the Avenue, however, we found several pieces of sarsen, and a test trench we dug some 17m from the end of the 1979 excavation produced some igneous rock fragments. That we should find these so far from any known features was curious. We extended the trench.

We found more stone, we extended again. In the wet conditions, we found it difficult to distinguish between rock fragments of interest and lumps of natural chalk, and our sieves clogged up with mud. The solution was effective, if messy. A hosepipe with a garden spray nozzle allowed us to clean everything in the sieves. I was determined that we would miss nothing.

An old Stonehenge controversy concerned the nature of a layer of debris, usually found quite close to the surface, that Hawley had named 'the Stonehenge Layer'. He believed, as we saw (chapter 11), that these fragments derived from ancient stone shaping, so any pits below it were older than the megaliths. Atkinson thought it was Roman or (in the revised edition of his book then just out) seventeenth century AD. Before English Heritage's recent study of Stonehenge, there was little hard evidence available to judge between these points of view. Now, it seemed, we had the chance to look at this 'Stonehenge Layer' by excavating some of it undisturbed since the time . . . whenever it had formed.

We extended the trench (figure 32).

More than half the large pits holding sarsens in the circle and horseshoe have been at least partially excavated. This allows us to see that while they do have features in common, in detail every pit is unique (figures 33 and 34). It is, for example, interesting to note that where evidence was visible, of twenty-two pits only thirteen had additional erection ramps, excavated down into the chalk at the edge of a pit. These ramps, featuring in attempts to imagine how stones were put up, would appear to have enabled a large stone to be levered into a deep pit with greater ease. Yet nearly half the pits didn't have one. By contrast, of the largest post holes at nearby Woodhenge and Durrington Walls almost all had substantial ramps.

In another respect, the stone holes differ from typical post holes. The latter are generally regular, circular holes that, at least when a post pipe is present to tell us, seem to reflect the size of the posts they held. Stone pits, on the other hand, can range from gaping

Figure 33. Sarsen pits in Stonehenge circle (1–30) and horseshoe (51–60).

Stones	Average depth of stone base below chalk (m)	Excavated	Ramp	Packing stones	Post holes in stone pit
1–30	0.9	Hawley 1919–24	7 present	0–58	0–7
		Atkinson 1954–64	7 absent		
51–60	1.4	Gowland 1901	4 present	present	present
		Atkinson 1954–64	2 absent		

Data from Cleal et al. 1995, 188–201.

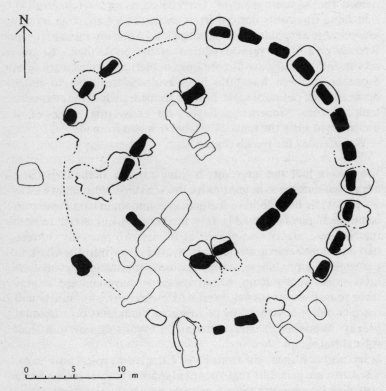

Figure 34. Stonehenge Phase 3ii. Sarsen circle and trilithons (stones still standing black, fallen stones white thinner line, stone pits thicker line). *After Cleal et al.*

amorphous holes to narrow, steep-sided trenches, yet hole width and depth are small guide to the shape of the contained megalith.

On the other hand, the occurrence of small post holes actually in the stone pits is common. These are sometimes beneath the stone (as we found in Pit 97), so whatever was in them must have been removed by the time the stone was in place. The most likely explanation is that the posts had something to do with stone erection. This being so, it suggests that stones were not so much thrown into their pits as manoeuvred under close control. It also reminds us of the plausible possibility that several of the post holes in the inner area, from which some archaeologists have contrived to create early circular timber structures, held megalith engineering poles.

It is quite common for the base of a megalith to sit, not on the pit bottom, but supported by chalk rubble and stones some way higher. The care devoted to straightening and smoothing the surfaces of the sarsens above ground did not extend to the invisible rock below the turf. Sometimes there is a substantial bulge just below ground, where stone removed higher up has been left in place. Stone 54, for example, has a 'foot' around twice the width of the rest of the stone. The fallen trilithon 55 also has a once underground swelling.

It was clearly important that the tops of the standing sarsens be level. With a relatively limited supply of stones (compared to the choice available to the lumberjack seeking large posts in the forest), it was sometimes necessary to achieve the desired height by propping up the megalith with care. On the other hand, if a stone stood just a little high, it was perhaps easier to extend the depth of the chalk pit than to remove a small amount of sarsen from the megalith.

The number of packing stones varies greatly from one pit to another. These stones often consisted of large hammers and mauls. It is probable that many were brought specially to the site. In pit 29, of the forty-seven stones listed by Hawley, one was flint, nineteen sarsen and the rest what he called Chilcot and Hurdcot ragstone.[323]

The megaliths themselves probably came from the Marlborough Downs. When considering the stone from my excavations, petrologist Hilary Howard wondered if analysis of grain size in sarsen (which is little more than well-cemented quartz grains) might help pinpoint potential sources. Not enough samples were analysed to come to any conclusions, but the results suggested a potentially fruitful approach to this problem, yet to be taken up.[324] A great deal of attention has been devoted to sourcing the bluestones, but curiously little to these stones whose mass is so much greater, and whose presence at Stonehenge is so much stronger. If petrology could identify possible sources, it may be that quarrying or preliminary dressing sites could be found. Perhaps different parts of the monument came from different quarries.

If precise quarries could be located, then the game of tracing a route for these sarsens could begin in earnest. As it is, the only part of the journey of which we can be reasonably sure is along the Avenue, the passage that runs from the River Avon up to the main entrance to Stonehenge. This remarkable earthwork,[325] a sort of cursus with a mission, consists of two parallel banks with flanking quarry ditches (figure 5). It begins (or ends) at the riverside by travelling north-west for 1km, then turns west in a 500m curve towards the ridge now occupied by the King Barrows, Bronze Age burial mounds that would not have been there when the Avenue was dug. Stonehenge comes into view at this point, where the distance between the ditches has dropped from around 34m to 25m. The Avenue descends the hill in a straight line, losing sight of the stones at the bottom of a small dry valley, and after 750m turns a relatively abrupt corner and climbs out to the south-west. The stones reappear on this last 530m straight, looming dramatically against the sky as they rise above you. At Stonehenge the ditches are 21.5m apart.

Discerning exactly what the purpose of this construction was would be greatly helped by precise dating. Is it actually the right age to be associated with the arrival of megaliths on site? Not for the first time, we are hindered by some confusing radiocarbon dates. There are four dates only for this long structure, and of these the youngest, around 4050 years ago, and the oldest, 4400 years ago, both derive from red deer antlers excavated by Hawley close to Stonehenge.[326] The older may be a residual antler pick, suggesting the ditch was originally dug here 4050 years ago (Hawley thought the ditch close to the sampling point had been dug through a post hole forming part of the group across the enclosure causeway);[327] or the younger may date a local re-excavation of the ditch four centuries after it was first dug 4400 years ago (in a section recorded in an electricity trench the other side of the road in 1968, the south-eastern ditch was thus recut, although the event is undated).[328] The two dates span Phases 2 and 3. In other words, the Avenue was probably there when at least most of the megaliths arrived. More than that we cannot say.

So, there are thirty sarsens in a circle supporting thirty lintels, and enclosing five massive sarsen trilithons. But what of the bluestones that stood before in the Q and R holes? They might well have been removed expressly to clear the ground for the huge engineering project of erecting the sarsens. Some of them, at least, are probably today standing amongst those same sarsens. But there is evidence that this was not their first new home. That lay in what is perhaps the murkiest area of the ancient Stonehenge.

As we saw in chapter 17, a postulated major sarsen event around 4300 years ago was followed two centuries later by a 'bluestone event' (figure 31). What was this?

There are two components, matching the circle and horseshoe in sarsen. The larger was a ring of bluestones 2.5m inside the inner face of the sarsens. About forty-seven stones or stone pits have been identified, of which the dated pit 40c is one.[329] The original total – Atkinson thought sixty,[330] though there could have been as many as seventy or even eighty – can only be a guess on available evidence.

The smaller, set within the sarsen horseshoe, consisted of twenty-three stones arranged in an oval, including pit 63a,[331] with a single additional stone standing just inside at the north-eastern apex (figure 35).

There are two things about these settings, designated Phase 3iv,[332] that suggest we are missing something. In the shadow of sarsen trilithon 57/58 is a handful of likely stone pits that immediately preceded the excavation of the bluestone oval, yet are not part of the older Q and R holes. And six or seven of the bluestones are dressed beyond the needs of their current position, suggesting they once stood in a different arrangement of finely shaped megaliths.

It's at this point that we stop looking for the right exit, and wonder which way the motorway is going. Ros Cleal's response was that of any good archaeologist. She designated a new phase, 3iii. But she admitted that this was not a 'real, coherent, and separate stage in the development of the monument':[333] more of a mystery ragbag.

The best of the finely dressed bluestones are both lintels, re-employed as free-standing megaliths in the circle of Phase 3iv.

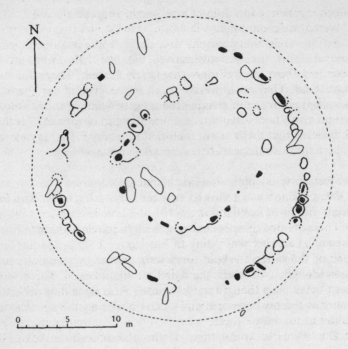

Figure 35. Stonehenge Phase 3iv. Bluestone circle enclosing bluestone oval inside standing sarsen circle (dashed ring) and trilithons (not marked) (stones still standing black, fallen stones white thinner line, stone pits thicker line). In Phase 3v, the bluestones at the north-eastern arc of the oval were removed, to create a horseshoe. *After Cleal et al.*

Stone 36, lying in the grass on the southern side of the circle, was excavated and lifted in 1954. It emerged as one of the finest carved stones from the whole monument – before being reburied, in a strict interpretation of the tradition of preserving the site without change (plate 10).

The other, stone 150, is also fallen and in the bluestone circle. Less regular than stone 36, this stone nonetheless has two clear mortise holes. The positioning of the holes suggests both stones stood as trilithons rather than in a continuously lintelled ring.[334] Two or three of the other carved stones (67, 70 and possibly 69) have indications of removed tenons. And two, 66 and 68, seem to have been carved to stand together in semblance of a larger, single stone: one has a protruding ridge the length of one side, the other (albeit in much reduced state) a groove of appropriate size.

We noted on our brief walk amongst the stones that most of the bluestone circle is undressed, while those in the inner setting are dressed. This itself is suggestive, but the half-dozen stones described above are yet more intensively carved. Where did they once stand? They could have been at Stonehenge in the Q and R holes, or part of an otherwise unrepresented arrangement inside the sarsen horseshoe. Alternatively, they might have come from a bluestone structure somewhere else on Salisbury Plain, leaving just sarsens at Stonehenge at this stage. One possible location is near the west end of the Stonehenge Cursus, where fragments of a number of types of bluestone rock have been found.[335]

Ros Cleal favours a missing structure at Stonehenge of lintelled bluestones (3iii), contemporary with the lintelled sarsens (3ii), so that sarsens and bluestones were always present together, once sarsen had first been introduced.

Some time later, the bluestones were rearranged, perhaps more were brought to the site, and the circle and oval of 3iv were constructed. But that was not the end. At a later date still, five stones at the north-eastern end of the oval, and the single stone standing just inside them, were removed. The remaining stones became what we know today as the bluestone horseshoe. This development constituted Phase 3v; bluestone circle, sarsen circle and sarsen horseshoe remained apparently unchanged.

With all that carving, you'd think there'd be a lot of stone litter about. That, at any rate, was what I was imagining as we carefully extracted one stone fragment after another from the mud in our narrow trench beside the road.

By 1980, following Atkinson, who made much of the difficulty Stone Age people would have had carving sarsen, the assumption was that most of the stone debris at Stonehenge was relatively recent.[336] So I knew, as I contemplated a heap of broken sarsen, that I would need good evidence if other archaeologists were to share my conviction that it was prehistoric. It did, after all, lie within a hand's breadth of the turf on the road verge, sandwiched between a water pipe, an electricity supply and a telephone cable.

About 25m from the 1979 stone pit, 12m outside the Avenue and 20m from the circular Stonehenge ditch, we had come across a dense concentration of rock debris spread over some 5m. There was no pit. These objects had just found their way to the bottom of the soil through worm action and had lain there undisturbed, if I was right, for thousands of years.

What made me so convinced? The first thing was that there was little indication of this debris in the soil higher up. So it couldn't have been that recent (for example, a dump from an earlier archaeological dig) or there would still be pieces slowly working their way down. The composition was also telling. Unlike published descriptions of the Stonehenge Layer, we had nothing that could not have been prehistoric: no Victorian rubbish, no Roman pottery. And when we began to wash the stuff, we found Neolithic artefacts.

We took the finds out of the cold and wet to my office in Avebury (or more correctly, it must be said, to the Head Custodian Peter Tate's office, where we could wash them in the sink at which he made his tea). At Stonehenge we had removed all soil from around the stones, leaving them in place on the chalk, before recording their positions and lifting them out. Now there were bucketfuls of rock in Peter's office. To avoid blocking his sink, I filled the first bucket with water, intending to swill it about and pour it on the ground outside. As I was about to go out, I noticed tiny black specks floating up to the surface. Charcoal. I was so confident that this deposit was prehistoric that it seemed only logical that the charcoal would be so too. I scooped it up, dried it and saved it. No one could argue with a radiocarbon date.

The stone fragments were not randomly mixed. The bulk of the sarsen was heaped over 4m of the trench. It looked burnt, cracked and reddened; the charcoal floating in the buckets came from the centre of this sarsen area; and the amount of burnt flint was ten times what it was elsewhere. There was also more dolerite there, the commonest of the bluestone types amongst the remaining megaliths. But tuffs, another type of bluestone, were more evenly scattered, and flint artefacts were mostly found 2m west of the sarsen and dolerite. When we looked at the fine sieving residue, we found tiny flint and sarsen spalls. These would not have been there if the debris was a dump from stone-working or wrecking from somewhere else.

The artefacts also confirmed that this stuff was not modern. There was a small sarsen pounder, fragments from ground objects of rhyolitic tuff, and a notched flint point. These looked Neolithic or Bronze Age. There was one flint arrowhead, the distinctive type seen at Durrington Walls. And there were a few tiny Beaker sherds.

We'd found a hearth, around which items of daily use had been dropped. Perhaps someone had collected some dolerite and a few large sarsen flakes, and used them like a fireplace, where they had broken up under the heat. In Britain, as much 4000 years ago as today, you don't build a hearth outdoors. The implication was that a roofed building had stood there. Perhaps it accommodated workers when part of Stonehenge was being built.[337]

As for the radiocarbon date, laboratory counting was not complete when my report went to press, but Bob Otlet at Harwell gave me what he described as a preliminary result, around 3700 years ago: prehistoric, if not quite as old as I had hoped (but the error term was large).[338] When the new English Heritage dating study was published, I discovered that my precious date had been dismissed! Alex Bayliss has a note from the Harwell lab saying the standard deviation I quoted in my report was a 'pure guess'.[339] Oh well, you can't win them all.

Still, I was pleased. We had shown that quantities of stone debris were around at the time Stonehenge was built. This didn't prove the Stonehenge Layer was ancient, but it did mean that some of it could be. Hawley had found something similar. South-east of the Heelstone, about the same distance from the Stonehenge ditch as our deposit, he excavated a 'large dump of sarsen chips' associated with burning. This was beneath the Avenue bank, indicating it was also contemporary with some part of the megalithic monument.[340] There has been no excavation anywhere else at Stonehenge this far outside the ditch.

'The BBC come along and expect you to give them the real face', complained Robin Richards, seated at his computer. 'But you can't do it. I wanted to blur the nose, but no one was interested.'

The television team wanted the complete person for their three million viewers, who were to witness the transformation from earth-covered bones to a clear-cut figure risen from the grave. But Robin Richards, in his lab at the Department of Medical Physics and Bioengineering in London, insisted this couldn't be done. Not even with an optical surface scanner and some highly sophisticated software.

The principle of facial reconstruction, whether practised in clay modelling or digital number-crunching, is the same. There are agreed 'landmarks' on the skull, points whose relative positions can vary significantly from person to person, which have a recognisable effect on a face. Richard Neave, the leading exponent of physical modelling, attaches small wooden pegs to a skull cast at these points. The length of each peg is determined by a century of measurements on cadavers. As the flesh is built up in clay, the peg tips come to sit on the face surface. Robin's computer does the same thing, using the same landmarks.

'With one or two others of my own', he explains. 'The computer needs every point, even if it's flat. Richard Neave can fill the gaps in his mind. The computer can't do that.'

Neither can the computer create a face like a sculptor. Robin has to give it faces. Lots of them. 'I would want a huge library of faces', he says, emphasising 'huge'. The little of his own face visible beneath his long hair lights up at the prospect. 'A huge database of thousands and thousands of normal subjects.'

Most of what he actually has are clinical data, face parts scanned in for specific medical reasons. With a vast number of whole faces and skulls, he enthuses, they could work out the means and variances, write the software, plug in the mystery skull and let the computer pick the near-perfect face so that fitting it would be just a matter of subtle digital tucking and pinching.

One day. Now he does it by eye and instinct – given the eye's ability to recognise the subtlest facial difference in a crowd of thousands, although Robin wouldn't admit it, perhaps nearly as effective as his digital dream. What he has to do is find a face – a human face scanned into his computer, just as he'd recently done mine – that in his judgement will fit the skull well. The computer can then stretch the face to fit. But only so far. 'Marilyn Monroe's face on my skull', he says, 'would look like Marilyn Monroe'. But then, he's not about to try to fit Marilyn Monroe to his skull. He's looking for a face that will match the beautifully preserved bones from the ditch at Stonehenge. A man killed violently 4300 years ago.

One of the oddest things at Stonehenge is also the last: a series of pits found by William Hawley in 1923. Like the Aubrey Holes, they were in rings surrounding the stones, and having (originally) called the former X Holes, Hawley named the new pits Y and Z Holes.

There were thirty pits in each circle, crowding so close to the stones that the presumed site of one in the inner ring, Z8, lies beneath a sarsen that has fallen outwards. We cannot be sure if this pit was dug, for the stone has not been lifted. Perhaps it fell early enough to prevent that.[341]

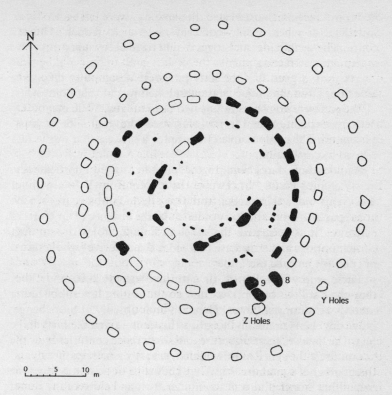

Figure 36. Stonehenge Phase 3vi. Y and Z holes dug around stones. Sarsens 8 and 9 are today flat on the ground. At this point there is no Z 8, and both 9 holes are further out than normal. I have reconstructed the sarsen monument on the assumption that 8 and 9 had fallen before the Y and Z holes were dug, but was then otherwise complete. *After Cleal et al.*

These squarish pits, shaped like old bath tubs about 1m deep and over 1m across, were laid out after the sarsens. They are roughly opposite the stones, not on a perfect circle marked out with rope from the centre (figure 36). Finds in the pits also point to a late date. There were pieces of bluestone on the bottom, and Iron Age and Roman pottery (and, indeed, medieval) higher up.

Y 30, the first to be excavated, could not possibly have had a post or stone standing in it, at least in the state that Hawley found it. 'Resting on the bottom were two stag-horn picks and three entire antlers. It was with difficulty they could be disentangled . . .' This and the other hole he excavated the same day were fresh and sharp, 'which leads me to think that they never held stones,' Hawley continued, 'as the sides and edges would have been ruined either by inserting or extracting them.'[342]

Atkinson argued that the sixty pits were designed to take sixty bluestones, but the project was abandoned just at that point when all the pits were dug but no stone had been moved. Well, maybe. Or perhaps excavation of the pits was itself the goal – or at least, excavation is the only visible evidence for a process that was in fact carried to completion.

Radiocarbon dates confirm the pits' age (they constitute the newly defined Phase 3vi). Two of the antlers from Y 30 are about 3600 years old; a third antler from this pit, and another from Z 29, are apparently over a century older.[343] In the absence of any further evidence, it is assumed that the Y and Z holes are in fact contemporary, and that these two older dates derive from residual or specially curated old antlers.

These empty pits, left to silt naturally so that 2000 years later they were still visible hollows that could accumulate rubbish, are among the strangest things. They are undoubtedly of Stonehenge. Nowhere else is there anything like this double ring of thirty large pits. The dates suggest they were dug some seven centuries after the sarsen circle they enclose was erected, yet they mirror its circuit and the number of its stones. Why were they dug, at this time when the megalithic Stonehenge was already ancient, and some of the round barrows, foci of funerary rituals in the generations after the last stone was put in place, were already grass-grown memorials? Are they something that happened long after Stonehenge, that really has little to do with it, or do they hold the key to the final role the stones played before they entered the world of myth and forgetfulness, symbols of a lost and timeless past?

'If the face fits perfectly,' says Robin Richards, 'nothing changes.'

The skull of the body pierced by arrows 4300 years ago, rummaged by badgers and retrieved accidentally by archaeologists, painted in gold, dances back and forth on the light green computer screen. As it rotates, you can see the prominent ridge above the eyes, the strong jaw and the missing tooth in the slightly rising bite.

'I look at the skull, I look at faces. The skin over the top half of the face is very thin, so it reflects the skull well. I have an immediate idea of what sort of forehead profile to look for. I look at facial proportions, the sort of nose, jaw shape. I look at them one by one, maybe ten to thirty faces. Normally I take two suitable faces and average them. If I'm really unhappy about it, I can change the face before I start. In this case, I did fiddle with the forehead a bit.'

Robin brings the initial face up on the screen. The changes wrought by the computer in fitting this to the skull are quite dramatic. In the Neolithic ghost, the mouth has turned down, the jaw is squarer, the midface has fallen in, bringing in the nose, while the forehead has pushed out.

'The ear is bigger', he explains, 'because the face there had to be bigger, so the ear went with it. Of course it could be right, but there's no reason for necessarily making the ear bigger.'

Since I last visited Robin, a new carpet has been fitted to the lab. They are still waiting for the ceiling to be painted. Most of their work is in plastic crates stacked on the floor. We don't recognise this face on the screen, because we've never seen it before. But there is something powerfully familiar, if forbidding, in those heavy cheeks and strong jaw. As fits the robust physique of the rest of his skeleton, the head has a large, muscular . . . this face is of a man.

No doubt about it. These eyes saw . . . If Stonehenge saw this face, it would recognise him. After all, he is one of us (plate 11).

PART III:

Avebury and How the Past Was Built

20

We Looked at Each Other and Said 'Why Not?'

We began by following the discovery of the timber henges and the 'superhenge' earthworks. We have now considered the monument of Stonehenge itself in some detail. Not least for a change of scene, for this next section we will move the 30km north to Avebury. Avebury has some of the biggest prehistoric earthworks, standing stones and timber structures found anywhere in Europe. This is a suitable place from which to ponder how these things were achieved, and to begin asking why.

Avebury today is a quite different place from Stonehenge. Stonehenge is a single, if complex, structure standing remote from the world – which is why we find the busy road and tatty facilities so offensive. Few people are aware of the rich ancient landscape around Stonehenge, of which it was once a part. In its isolation, it is easily appropriated. It is the symbol bar none for a primitive past; or, to the contrary, for a lost sophisticated civilisation; for alien visits to earth; for a dispute between establishment authority and people challenging convention; for the very appropriation of the past. Yet no such cause has any real interest in the people who built Stonehenge or the world they lived in. Stonehenge is an antenna for our own politics.

You can't do that to Avebury. It's too big, too rambling. The stone circle is so vast that its visitors could never be controlled (let's face it, farmers have trouble just keeping the sheep in). You can't even see all the stones of this circle at once: there are too many things like houses and trees and the very contours of the ground in the way. As you drive or cycle into Avebury, you cannot fail to be aware of other monuments in the landscape: the huge mound of Silbury Hill beside the A4, the more ancient West Kennet long barrow on the brow opposite, or the rows of standing stones of the West Kennet Avenue. Yet nothing quite connects. There are fragments of lost worlds muddled with the present, all asking the same question: What am I doing here, what do I mean?

Some writers tackle this with more confidence than others. Christopher Knight and Robert Lomas, presenting a model encompassing the whole of Late Neolithic Britain, are not among the modest. In *Uriel's Machine* they describe how Enoch, a mythical Old Testament character descended from Eve and Adam, foretold the arrival of a large comet that would cause a world flood. In Britain lived 'the Grooved Ware People' who possessed the astronomical skills to understand the future. So Enoch travelled north for help.[344]

Less encompassing but more specific is Michael Dames' notion that the Avebury landscape is a three-dimensional representation of a Neolithic 'fertility cycle'. The Sanctuary, for example, relates 'through symbolic architecture to the Great Goddess in her early spring state'.[345]

Paul Devereux, without strongly committing himself to much, runs through the gamut of female deity, strange 'earth lights', horizon alignments that become spirit flight lines, auras, sacred geography and shamans. Paul is a talented artist and photographer, and he illustrates his story with Avebury megaliths that appear to show human and animal faces – what he calls 'dreamstones'.[346]

This is a theme adopted with gusto by Terrence Meaden. I will not forget the day when Terry took me excitedly to see his vulva. There is a complex of quite natural grooves and wrinkles on the face of a stone in the southern inner circle, that with only a little imagination can seem quite gynaecological. Having spotted this, Terry had then noticed that the only tall thin stone in Avebury (described by Stukeley as 'the obelisk' in the eighteenth century, but since destroyed) once stood nearby, and, he imagined, cast a phallic shadow across the vulva on May Day. Thus was revealed 'the basic myth by which Sky God and Earth Goddess . . . mated at the beginning of time'.[347]

Devereux had already commented on these 'forms strikingly evocative of vulvic symbolism',[348] but Meaden's theory had a theatrical power that particularly appealed to me – not least because Michael Dames, whom Devereux not unfairly describes as 'besotted by the idea of the goddess',[349] had completely missed this piece of his great feminine landscape puzzle.

Emma Restall Orr is more subtle, if no less passionate. Regularly seen on television elaborating her vision of modern Druidism,[350]

Emma, like many of us, has a soft spot for Avebury. I once attended a party inside the stone circle at which she had been asked to bless a newly discovered monument (a cropmark, it may be a Neolithic burial, or it may be just about anything else.)[351] She talked about a skeleton found in the ditch around the stones, the founder dwarf priestess of Avebury.

Standing at the back of the marquee ready to take the microphone, I found myself in a tricky position. I didn't want to spoil the party, but I knew this deceased lady was neither dwarf nor founder. She was uncovered by Harold St George Gray in 1914 about 2m down in the ditch fill. Although the bones were poorly preserved, even before being kicked about by his men while Gray was away breakfasting, one tibia was measured to give a calculated height of 1.32m.[352] Even at a more recent estimate by Don Brothwell of 1.52m (5 feet),[353] she was not tall, but that is not the same thing as saying she was a dwarf, which is a skeletal condition. Furthermore, the fact that her grave was less than halfway down the ditch silts clearly indicates that the ditch was dug some considerable time before her death. This supposition is backed up by radiocarbon, which, in a small dating programme I initiated when curator of Avebury museum, suggested that the ditch was nine centuries old when she was buried.[354] I have to admit that I cannot remember what I said (it was a good party).

I could go on.[355] This is all very interesting, but also worrying. At least some of these writers believe in what they are saying, yet, like Emma Restall Orr's vision of the founder dwarf priestess, little derives from balanced study of archaeological evidence. At the extreme is *Uriel's Machine*, containing what we might politely call a radically alternative approach to Grooved Ware pottery ('there is evidence which suggests that the Grooved Ware People *did* produce giants who settled in China'), which includes in its bibliography such items as *Myths and Legends of Australia*, *Robert the Bruce* and *The Pleistocene Elephants of Siberia*, but not a single primary archaeological source for England (where, it has to be said, a great deal of Grooved Ware has been found).[356]

Are they right? Does the frustrating tendency of archaeologists to hold back on questions that ask 'why?' reveal a deep but depressing truth? Is archaeology actually incapable of tackling the really big questions? Is it necessary, indeed, to avoid contact with archaeology at all if we would get close to the real world of our ancestors?

Well, understanding something of the people who built these astonishing constructions is what we are about. It is easy to fantasise and to judge the past. We all do it, from Michael Dames ('Milk, bubbling and frothing as it rises from the underworld, makes Neolithic sense')[357] to Aubrey Burl ('Witch-doctors may appear somewhat ridiculous and ineffectual, rather disgusting and frightening, primitive, and yet the people of Avebury themselves were primitive . . .').[358] Academic writing is full of it – it's just better disguised by the language. It is altogether another thing to attempt justice to the reality of the past, to merge the evidence from the landscape with analogies from living people, and to know where to draw the line at ignorance.

Paradoxically, of course, we can only succeed in this venture in so far as we recognise that there can be no absolute reality. We can never recover the lost world; and anyway, there never was a single hard truth. Different people led different lives, understood different things. So today, if a writer claims to have found the answer to the mysteries of the past, we know we are confronting a charlatan: there can be no such truth, except in fiction.[359]

Two excavations took place in Avebury in 1999, as I was writing this book. It is fashionable in some archaeological circles to decry excavation, to see all such work as destructive and unnecessary unless the site is anyway going to be destroyed, for example by the construction of a new school. But the stuff we found in 1999 (the smaller dig was mine) would still be undisturbed and safely in the ground if we'd left it there. Clearly, we believed this work necessary and useful.

Over the next few chapters, I hope to show how the things that archaeologists find and interpret really are important in our quest to understand the past. As we consider the tale of ancient Avebury and beyond, we will also be thinking about what we are doing, about how it is we can claim to be revealing things about the lives of people long dead from apparently mute detritus. We will find that our attempt to understand the past is inextricably bound with our conceptions of who we are, what it is to be human. There are some good stories here: how an Avebury archaeologist nearly killed his workforce; how Stonehenge's most famous archaeologist was himself nearly killed by the object of his devotion; how, after centuries of cynicism, a brilliant antiquarian was dramatically proved right. But good as they are, the stories are not the end of it. To understand our ancestors, we need to look inside ourselves. This is no game. This is life.

It was in February 1999, after talking about the Sanctuary with Ros Cleal, the present Curator of Avebury's Alexander Keiller Museum,[360] that I had gone to Devizes Museum to look at William Young's diaries. They had originally been destined for Keiller's museum, but Young fell out with the Ministry of Works, who had employed him as the Avebury curator after the war, and left them to his friend Denis Grant King with instructions for their disposal.

I discovered that the first formal volume was written in the very year of the Sanctuary excavation. When he was on site, Young's diary took the form of an excavation notebook, such was the detail it contained. Apparently no one had noticed this remarkable record. But it wasn't just the Sanctuary entries that kept drawing me back to the dark loft in Devizes. There was something intriguing about this stilted scrapbook autobiography, whose eighty-eight volumes, so carefully filled in fountain pen at the end of the day's work, were packed onto the rickety shelves. If Young was emotional, he kept that side of himself out of his journal – this is a story of cups of tea and bus trips, not inner thoughts. Here was a man fascinated by archaeology, resentful of those spared his financial struggles by accident of birth, but brought up to be respectful, lonely but regularly making social calls on friends and family, pleased by simple incidents innocently described, and increasingly involved in the Catholic church as the years passed.

On 7 February 1940, Young went to London. This was the day Stuart Piggott gave his influential lecture about Woodhenge and the Sanctuary, the day from which timber henges became huge circular roofed buildings. And Mr Young had sat in the audience.[361]

He and Grant King (who had both worked with Piggott and Keiller on the Avebury excavations just before the war) took the 10.52 train from Swindon to Paddington. It had been a particularly cold spring, and somewhere near Reading, they saw army lorries massed in the snow. 'There must have been literally thousands of them,' wrote Young, 'parked together in long rows, close to the railway line.' When the archaeological meeting was over, they emerged from the Society of Antiquaries' rooms in Piccadilly into a blacked-out London – the Luftwaffe, Germany's air force, were spared illuminated advertisements.

'In his paper, which was illustrated by slides of his drawings, etc,' Young later wrote of the experience, 'Mr Piggott tried to show how timber circles could have grown from small beginnings, and how they could have been roofed over as well.'

When the talk was done, the Chair asked Young to open the discussion. He stood up, politely commended Piggott for his scholarship (making ineffectual excuses to himself for not speaking his mind), and sat down. Inside he was seething. Though the plans of the Sanctuary and Woodhenge were similar (as Young says, in each case the third of six post rings has the largest pits), Piggott's reconstructions were quite different. He turned the larger Woodhenge into a single building with an open centre, while the Sanctuary, he said, had been a succession of three small buildings, each different from the other.

'One point in particular', Young wrote back at home, 'I totally disagreed with. This was his maintaining that the double post holes at the Sanctuary [which occurred in two of the rings] were the result of re-placements carried out during the gradual growth of the hut, thus flatly contradicting the evidence which came to light when those post holes were excavated.' They had thought of this at the time, he said, and cut longitudinal sections. These 'proved that the two posts in each particular case had been erected at one and the same time'.[362]

This was completely new evidence, of key significance for the interpretation of the site. The Sanctuary has a number of post holes that are not circular, like all those at Woodhenge, but elongated, rectangular with circular ends. Some of them had a post pipe at each end. Piggott proposed that these holes were in fact two circular pits dug so close together that they had intersected: large posts had rotted and been replaced. This was the basis for the idea that the Sanctuary had evolved over a long time. But Young denied this.

A standard technique in archaeological excavation is to cut vertical sections through the fill of pits and ditches, so you can study the layers of earth and rubble. If the double post holes had been two successive circular pits, then you should have seen the vertical side of the second cutting through the layers filling the first. The Cunningtons rarely drew sections – there are none at all of any real use in Maud's Sanctuary report, and no indication that any were even dug. But here was Young writing that he had deliberately cut sections to examine the double post holes, and found the evidence argued convincingly for them being single pits.

And there was something else. To make sense of all the new data in Young's book, I had tabulated his pit descriptions against those of Maud Cunnington. The hardest part had been matching the two records, for they use different numbering systems. I was convinced I'd got it right (and Ros Cleal later came to the same conclusion), yet at times the discrepancies between the two were so strong as to suggest that Cunnington and Young were writing about different places.

Playing reinterpretation games with the Sanctuary was an old archaeological hobby, for amateurs, students and professionals alike. At least seven different versions had been published, and many more doubtless remained private.[363] There are enough post and stone holes to allow of almost endless varieties of structures, yet insufficient data to disprove almost anything.

My own view had been similar to that of Josh Pollard. In his doctoral thesis at Cardiff University, he had argued cogently that the Sanctuary was a single-phase structure of relatively brief duration, consisting of concentric rings of free-standing posts. The megaliths alone might have constituted a later addition to the site.[364] It was depressing, now, to come across new evidence that might be thought to help understand things, but in fact seemed to offer yet more confusion. There was only one way out. No one seemed to have thought of this before, but as I struggled to make sense of Young's diary, it became obvious what I had to do. It was time to go back to the Sanctuary and dig it up.

In March I filed my application for permission to dig. As you might imagine, this is now quite properly not simply a matter of asking the tenant farmer and getting out the spades. Avebury is a World Heritage Site (strictly, and rather bizarrely, part of the World Heritage Site that encompasses both Stonehenge and Avebury). The Sanctuary itself is a Guardianship Monument, the highest level of legal protection granted to ancient sites in England. In the guidance notes provided by English Heritage with the application forms is a telling sentence: 'Unless exceptional circumstances apply, permission to excavate is not normally given to directors with a significant backlog of unpublished excavations.' The lesson has been learnt.

With luck, I would hear from the Department of Culture, Media and Sport (advised in the matter by English Heritage) in July, in time to dig in August – if the permit came through. Meanwhile, another much grander Avebury field project was being planned for the summer. My colleagues Mark Gillings, Josh Pollard and Dave Wheatley, who had been quietly working in Avebury for a few years, were pulling the stops out. This time, they had decided, they were really going to find something different.

It began for them in Newcastle. Josh and Mark were doing post-doctoral research, and neither felt he was getting very far. They were chatting one afternoon, and found they had much in common. They were both interested in theories of landscape use and perception. Much had recently been written and spoken about landscape theory, by some prominent and highly regarded archaeologists. People were trying to get away from contemporary conceptions of landscape, and see if it was possible to look at the world through the eyes of past cultures. There was this idea that in the Neolithic people were consciously shaping the land around them, populating it with ancestors, values, meanings, and sculpting it with earthworks and timber monuments.

Writing specifically about Avebury, John Barrett had high-lighted a discrepancy between the way archaeologists usually described the ancient monuments – through plans, in views never known to people in the past – and the experience of modern visitors, who wandered about from stone to gate post, building up a personally idiosyncratic impression of a complex three-dimensional place rich with sounds, smells and movements. The latter, suggested Barrett, is much closer to the prehistoric viewpoint.[365]

Under the rubric of 'phenomenological analysis', archaeologists had attempted to show how this different way of looking at the landscape could be used to help understand the motivations of people in the past. Touring prehistoric tombs in Sweden, Chris Tilley had written that we experience both megaliths and landscape as sculpture. Distribution maps (much beloved of archaeologists) removed the tombs from this visual context. We needed a sense of place, given only by experience of the tombs in their landscape, if we were to understand what was going on.[366]

But it was mostly words (sometimes rather long ones), and like much academic writing was stimulating to read but left you wondering, what next?

Josh and Mark found they had a shared love of Avebury that went back to school days. 'We looked at each other,' Mark told me, 'and said Why not? Let's have a go.'[367] So in 1996, Gillings and Pollard hacked out a research proposal. Then Mark met Dave Wheatley at a conference. Dave had just finished his PhD on geographical information systems. He was impressed by Mark's ideas, and asked if he could come along. The next Easter they were all in Avebury, together with Glyn Goodrick. Glyn was the tiddlywink man.

While Dave did a digital topographic survey of the West Kennet Avenue, Mark and Glyn began recording the stones. Remarkably enough, just as at Stonehenge, archaeologists have rarely before looked in detail at the surviving megaliths – although for the average visitor these are undoubtedly the most important part of ancient Avebury. We can safely assume they also had some significance for the people who put them there.

Glyn Goodrick had figured how to capture 3D images of the Avebury megaliths using tiddlywinks. They stuck coloured counters on the stones at significant contouring points (we might call them 'landmarks'). They then digitally photographed the stones and recorded the counters three-dimensionally. Using methods developed by Goodrick, back at Newcastle University the computer merged the 'wire-frame' models with the photographs. The result is an eerily realistic Virtual Reality Modelling Language (VRML) model of the stones.

Meanwhile, Josh worked in the museum looking at Keiller's excavation records from the 1930s, and out in the circles created a full set of conventional drawn elevations of the stones – astonishingly, never done before.[368]

At the end of this spring excursion they were each about £100 out of pocket. The idea had been to get the project going – they called it 'Negotiating Avebury' – and get better funding for more work. And they sent a paper about it to a prominent British archaeological journal. But funding applications were all roundly rejected, as was the article. They did a further short trip the following Easter. Mark now had a post-doctoral Leverhulme fellowship at Leicester University, and money he received for a Distance Learning Module went towards the project. But talk had started to move to excavation.

Ros Cleal was interested in a recent air photo taken just to the west of Avebury that appeared to indicate an enclosure similar to those excavated at West Kennet a few years back by Alasdair Whittle. Whittle had shown that two massive timber palisaded enclosures had stood next to each other (or perhaps after each other) close to the Kennet stream south-east of Silbury Hill. The friends plotted a very small excavation. 'In wanting to create a 3D model,' said Mark, 'we had to know what the monument looked like.' And it was easier to get funds for digging.

This time they had a bit of cash, about four or five grand, principally from Southampton (where Dave worked) and Leicester, some of whose archaeology students attended the dig as a training project. By then Josh was working for an excavation unit in Cambridge; soon he was to be appointed to a lectureship at the University of Wales, Newport. It was a small dig, but the idea was not that it should be quite so small as it turned out. They couldn't afford to buy off the farmer's crop, still there at the time they had to work, so they laid out their trenches on the edge of the field where there was an old track. The air photo showing the enclosure had been plotted onto an Ordnance Survey map. But the field edge was where the photo was least clear. It was a bit of a gamble. And they lost.

'We dug more trenches than we made finds', said Mark. 'We missed it.'

Still, their article had at last been accepted for publication – by a Dutch journal.[369] They would have another go in 1999. Now they all had jobs, and were able to put together a full research proposal to the British Academy, as well as applications for smaller grants to private organisations. They got the lot. This time, they thought, we'll find the enclosure, we'll stir up the archaeology a bit: despite Alasdair Whittle's work at West Kennet, there was still a common feeling that Avebury's archaeology was complete, done and delivered. Well, Negotiating Avebury (at first a suitable name for a project without a grant) was about to gear up.

And all that was before the English Heritage geophysical team went out into the field in May, just to give the diggers a head start. Up in London keeping an eye on things, as he had been for the Stanton Drew survey, was Andrew David. Waiting for the phone to ring.

21

I Have Always Regretted Missing That Photograph

The archaeology of Hengeworld is about people and land: about earth, stones and timber. Only Brittany in France has megaliths on the same or a bigger scale, and there is no ring of stones as large as Avebury's. The palisaded enclosures at West Kennet consumed as much woodland as anything we have yet found in Hengeworld. Silbury Hill is the greatest mound in prehistoric Europe, and the ditch and bank around the stone circle may be the largest surviving earthwork of this age anywhere in the world.

Making these things, then as now, people would have been subject to basic principles of physics and organisation. By considering the mechanics of monument building, earth in this chapter, stone and timber later, we get a foothold in the precipitous cliff of the past. Twenty tons of rock is twenty tons of rock, and moving it then required the same energy as moving it now. And then, as now, twenty tons of rock can kill.

Young's description of his three weeks at the Sanctuary fills fifty pages in his case-bound diary. Hawley's journal of eight years at Stonehenge is a mountain of detailed notes. There are two little notebooks that I have not referred to, started in 1908 and finished in 1922. So small, yet their interest is as great as the others.

Harold St George Gray, curator of Somerset's Taunton Museum, was employed by the British Association as excavator in their project to date stone circles. The relationship between Gray and the British Association was much the same as that between William Hawley and the Society of Antiquaries. Committees ordered the research, oversaw the fieldwork and publication and channelled the funds. But in the stone circle project, excavator and committee came together in perfect partnership.[370]

Gray's route to Avebury in 1908 took him through the stone circle of Arbor Low, Derbyshire (1901), and rings on Bodmin Moor, Cornwall (1905). Negotiations to dig at Stenness in the Orkneys fell through. They rejected Stanton Drew because there was no ditch: like Geoff Wainwright, Gray hoped to find things in ditches. Only a century after the formation of the Age of Stone Circles committee in 1899 did English Heritage find a ditch at Stanton Drew.

Gray had a job (stone circles were holiday work). But like Young, he lacked the social confidence of the rich. His outdoor talks, name-dropping essays read from carefully typed sheets, must have been tedious in the extreme. His plodding style was opposed to Keiller's driven, obsessive enthusiasm, and it is no wonder the two men fell out when they came to work together. But Gray's work is distinguished: not only was it excellently published, but also he left an archive that is as good as that of any British excavator. It may be small, but the record of his Avebury work – the most precious group of photographs, notes, drawings and diaries – is one of the great treasures of Avebury's museum.[371]

Gray spent the 1912 season (with his wife and eleven-year-old son) surveying. The dykes[372] around the stones were known for their unique size. From crest to crest, they ascertained, the bank was 425m, and the distance along this crest 1.35km. It was inevitable the bank would have collapsed, but even in its weathered state the ditch was 5m below modern ground level, or well over 10m from the top of the bank.

No one, however, could have been ready for what Gray found when they dug down into this ditch. In a word, it was massive. If you visit Avebury today, and marvel at the turf-covered earthwork, you have to forcibly remind yourself of what Gray discovered. The silts in the ditch bottom, layers of chalk and earth collapsed and washed in from the sides, are typically 6m deep. That's just the silt, not the ditch: the Neolithic workers, equipped with antler picks and stone and wooden tools, dug 11m down through hard, rocky chalk, so that in excess of 20m separated ditch bottom from bank top – that's more than half the present height of Silbury Hill. And they did that for a circumference of more than three-quarters of a mile (figures 6 and 37, plate 12).

It began in 1911, when Gray planned to open a trench in the ditch east of the southern entrance causeway. Off the Taunton train on 22 April, he met Captain Leopold Jenner (then owner of the

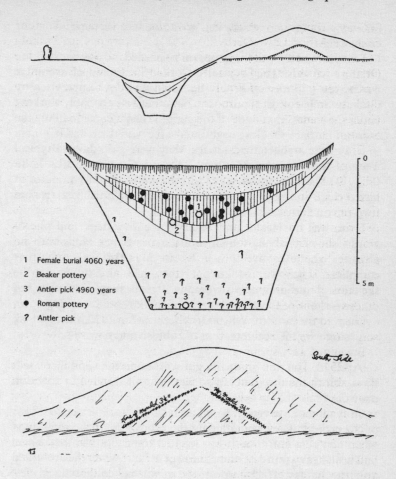

1 Female burial 4060 years
2 Beaker pottery
3 Antler pick 4960 years
● Roman pottery
? Antler pick

Figure 37. Avebury's superhenge earthwork is the best preserved anywhere, but there has been no modern excavation. Sketch at top is key to position of Gray's schematic ditch section (1908–22) and Leslie's bank section (1894, copied from an original drawing). Over half the ditch had silted up by 4000 years ago, when a woman was buried in the upper silts; Roman pottery close by indicates that silting was very slow thereafter. Leslie's drawing shows the buried turf he identified, suggesting that a smaller, older bank is hidden within the large bank we see today. *After Leslie, Gray, Pitts and Whittle.*

land he wished to excavate) at four o'clock in the afternoon. Jenner was helpful, granting permission to cut down bushes, and offering to lend wooden planks and a wheelbarrow. The tenant farmer was less enthusiastic. 'Interviewed Mr Parsons,' wrote Gray the following day, 'who would on no account give permission for excavating.'[373]

Two years later, with the approval he needed, he was back taking off the first sods. They typically worked in a team of around a dozen men ('13 men as usual', he noted one day), supervised by Gray for archaeological purposes, but otherwise probably working under the leadership of one of the gang. When it came to filling the excavations back in, Gray negotiated a fee with them and left them to it. For the archaeological work, they were paid daily: a typical week of thirteen men, Monday – Saturday, came to £12 3s 8d (£12.18). They started at seven am, broke for twenty minutes at nine o'clock and again for an hour at noon, and finished at five pm (two pm on Saturdays).

There was no Health and Safety Executive then, and photographs show terrifyingly high and narrow trench walls with no shoring. The excavation they began in 1914 was only part completed when war broke out (they had already found the skeleton of the diminutive woman). It was fenced around, but otherwise left open, with wide steps of chalk rubble reaching down over 8m to the bottom. When Gray returned in 1922, the first task was to remove the accumulation of rubbish and new silt.

It was a stormy spring.

'April 12. The rain gradually got worse and the wind increased. By 4 o'clock the men had got so wet, that we decided to abandon the work . . .'

Gray might have remembered an incident in 1908, the first year of the project. They were digging the other side of the road, west of the southern entrance. It was his first trench in the ditch. There had been heavy rain on the morning of 1 June, when they returned after the Sunday off. One side of the trench had collapsed. 'Several tons of material', he had noted, 'found to have "caved in" since the close of the work in Section I on Saturday.'[374] But they continued to dig – the trench side continued to fall in – and his photos show a teetering west face even when they reached the ditch bottom 5m down.

On 24 April 1922, they gathered for work at eight am. Three days before, Gray had taken one of the best-known of his carefully composed photographs on half plate glass negatives, and a second the following day (plate 12). Now he was preparing for a third shot, in which the ledges left in place for the gang to work from were removed to reveal a continuous straight section through the silts.

'It was', he later wrote for a lecture given to the British Association in 1931, a 'sloping face . . . in which the stratification was very finely represented.'

His camera was on its tripod on the causeway, its movements adjusted for convergence in a steeply angled view down into the depths of the ditch. The men were instructed to climb out for lunch. And then, just as the last of the gang hauled himself up from the two ladders (twenty-three and twenty-two rungs), it happened. It fell in. The face bulged out, split and sluiced down into the pit in an instantaneous rush, like water from a burst balloon. Then a second drop followed from the ragged loose edge, smashing one of the ladders to pulp: it was, he wrote in the diary, 'badly broken (in fact rendered useless)'.

No one was hurt. But Gray was not happy. 'I have always regretted', he read from his typescript to the British Association meeting, 'missing that photograph.'

The details of what happened at Gray's excavations would of course have been different from events there when the ditch was dug around 5000 years ago.[375] But comparisons can be made. All the organisation that Gray had to face – planning, agreements, a workforce, tools, compensations (at the least, food and drink), concern with weather and safety, clearing vegetation and so on – such things would have mattered as much to the Neolithic engineers as to the Edwardians. In particular, the actual manner of digging may have been quite similar.

As we have seen, Gray's men worked in a gang of twelve or thirteen. As they dug deeper into the chalk they cut ledges on the working face, providing a series of platforms. Two or three men worked on each ledge, picking and shovelling up onto the ledge above. In this way, the silt and rubble could be raised from the bottom of the ditch to the turf 8m above using only shovels, arms and backs. At the top, men barrowed the spoil out of the way.

It is often said that Neolithic people used cattle shoulder blades for shovelling chalk. This is an old idea that dies hard, despite experimental evidence from forty years ago that proved such a bone useless for the task,[376] and the absence of anything that actually looks like a prehistoric shoulder blade used as a shovel.[377] They might be OK for sandcastles on the beach, but huge engineering projects in hard rock are another matter. There is evidence for the manufacture of wooden shovels in Neolithic Europe, in those rare waterlogged contexts where wood survives.[378] There is no dispute, however, that red deer antlers were used on a truly grand scale. We have noted the 400-odd 'picks' from Durrington Walls, and hundreds more have been recovered in excavations at Grimes Graves flint mines in Norfolk – by extrapolation, there must be tens of thousands of antlers discarded and buried in the mines.[379] Some 130-odd antler implements survive from excavations at Stonehenge, and they were abundant in Gray's trenches at Avebury.[380] They obviously worked well. But how exactly was that?

We do not use deer antlers for tools today, any more than we use flint. This may seem an obvious point, but archaeologists are only just beginning to realise that antler technology may have been quite sophisticated, such that fully understanding it now may need more experimenting than has yet been done. For the people of Hengeworld, it was an old technology. The oldest antler tools in the world are flint-knapping hammers from Boxgrove in Sussex, where half a million years ago hominids who had not yet evolved into Neanderthals were using antlers from giant deer now long extinct.[381] More directly, the ancestors of the people who dug the Avebury ditch were using red deer antlers in the same way at least 2000 years before.[382] These were tools people understood.

Male deer grow a pair of antlers every year, and shed them in the early spring. As the stag matures, each year the antlers get bigger, until old age sets in and they grow back. There was a clear selection of antlers for tools from mature stags, and most were shed rather than cut from the skulls of killed animals. The typical proportion of unshed antlers (10–20 per cent) is considerably exceeded at Stonehenge, however (figure 38).

It is likely that collection of these antlers was a major operation. In theory shed antlers could be found at any time of year, but the quantities sometimes required may have meant that competition for them led people to go on expeditions in the spring when a 'crop' was newly available.[383] The antlers were trimmed down with flint tools, often with the assistance of a piece of burning wood to weaken the tough bone. Both ends were used, the crown as a 'rake' and the beam (more commonly) as a 'pick'. In the latter, one or more of the tines were frequently cut away, leaving one as a working point (typically the brow tine).

Most picks show battering on the back of the beam close to the burr. There are two possible explanations. The pick may also have been used as a hammer; or the pick may have been hammered into the chalk, before the beam was used as a lever to prise the rock

Figure 38. Red deer antlers in later Neolithic excavations.

Site	% shed	% unshed	Number
Grimes Graves (1971–2)	90	10	65
Durrington Walls	87	13	332
Avebury	85	15	34
Grimes Graves (1972–6)	82	18	282
Stonehenge	65	35	79

Data from Clutton-Brock, Gray, Legge, Serjeantson/Gardiner.

apart. At Avebury in particular, some of the antlers are very heavily worn, sometimes to the extent that half of the thickness of the beam has been bashed away. Used with strength and skill, these could undoubtedly have been formidably efficient tools.

Turf and topsoil would respond well to shovelling, but this is not the best way to move chalk rubble. It is likely that hands and rakes were used to pile chalk into containers, such as baskets, that could be handed up or carried out on the back. So armed with tools, protective clothing, supplies and shelter, how, 5000 years ago, would these people have gone about digging out the ditch at Avebury?

The Avebury earthwork was not created in one go. The evidence for this came when the then owner of much of Avebury, Sir Henry Meux, had a trench cut through the bank in 1894.[384] Some years ago in Devizes Museum I discovered a manuscript sketch of what they found, made in 1914 by the supervisor Thomas Leslie shortly before he died. About halfway down inside the chalk bank was a very clear line marking a former turf surface (figure 37). This means at this point there are actually two banks, one inside the other. That such a thick soil developed on top of the original bank suggests there was some time between its construction and its later burial when the bank was enlarged.

Clear support was found by Faith Vatcher in 1969 (though she didn't recognise it), when the new village school was built near the bank on the west side. Faith found a turf core about 2m wide at the base, suggesting that the first act was to deturf and expose the chalk, and set out the course of the earthwork with a small mound. Chalk and marl were then piled on until the bank reached 2.5m high – about half the height of the present bank. We can but assume that the quarry ditch for this chalk lay approximately where the present ditch is.

It's often said by tour guides that Avebury is older than Stonehenge. Maybe. But we'd need to know 'which Stonehenge', and now you can see we'd also need to know 'which Avebury'. When was this first bank constructed? There are three dates from the turf below the bank that should at least provide an age limit after which the bank has to have been built. The 95 per cent confidence range of these is 3633–2495 cal BC – anything from 4500 to 5600 years ago.[385] We might say this means the bank was built at the earliest not much before 5600 years ago, but unfortunately we can't be sure that any of these dated samples came from beneath the older bank, rather than all from under the later extension. So if we don't know, what would we guess?

There is a low hill to the north of Avebury, famous to archaeologists as Windmill Hill, crowned by three concentric ditch rings dug around 5500 years ago.[386] The ditches are full of rubbish (hence the fame), including pottery of a general type common in Britain, but long gone out of manufacture by the time of Hengeworld. Such earthworks as those on Windmill Hill are known in large numbers, and are typically found on hilltops. They are frequently referred to as 'causewayed enclosures', on account of characteristic interruptions in the ditch circuits. These people do not seem to have built large monuments in valleys, so a fair assumption is that the first Avebury bank and ditch dates from sometime between Windmill Hill and the second Avebury earthwork.

There is only one date for the latter event, from an antler pick in the bottom of the newly deepened ditch. This came out at around 5000 years ago (within a range of over seven centuries),[387] similar to, but much less precise than, the date of the construction of the ditch at Stonehenge. If future dating confirmed the second Avebury ditch to date from 5000 years ago, then we might imagine the first to have been dug two or three centuries before that. Which, for the benefit of tour guides, would indeed be older than Stonehenge (just remember there are no stones there yet).

The ditches at Windmill Hill and Stonehenge share a construction feature: they are irregular in shape, and in plan look like badly made strings of sausages. But, says archaeologist Bill Startin, these are informative sausages. They tell us how the ditches were dug. Starting from the premise that prehistoric engineers would have developed skills commensurate with the materials they used and the scale on which they worked (a supposition that only deep familiarity with both academic and popular literature exposes as highly radical), Startin argues that Victorian construction gangs – working on canals and railways before the advent of heavy machinery – provide a good model for their remote Neolithic predecessors. So while Richard Atkinson employed boys from private schools in an experiment floating a replica Stonehenge megalith,[388] Startin turns to dusty, ageing work manuals with titles like *How to Estimate* and *Useful Rules and Tables*.[389]

Startin's important ideas need to be developed, and tested with experiments that, for example, determine exactly how best to use antler picks. Nonetheless, they already bring some crucial insights. Not least on those sausages. There are, he says, two ways to dig a ditch: 'pit-digging' or 'trench-digging'. In the former, a large workforce is loosely organised into small teams who each dig separate pits. Joining the pits creates a more or less continuous ditch. In the latter, a single gang dig a pit and work from a moving face along the route of the ditch.

Although a circle can be drawn within the two edges of the Stonehenge ditch on a plan, from close to it is quite irregular. It staggers along in a series of round pits (which Hawley called craters) and connecting trenches. Cleal distinguished twenty-eight 'segments' in the ditch Hawley dug out, but these are only distinctions where changes in the sides or bottom are clear. There were probably over 100 small excavations in the chalk that were broken through into each other to form a more or less continuous ditch, from whose spoil perhaps a more finished bank was constructed.

There are two ways this could have been dug. A small team, perhaps five (one to dig, one to shovel or lift and three to carry), could have slowly worked their way round the circuit. Or several teams could have worked in parallel. At the extreme there might have been as many teams as there were pits, so the whole thing could have been dug in a few days by 600 people. At an informed guess, around 200 antler picks were abandoned in the excavation of the ditch, a figure compatible with a rapid attack by many workers.[390]

In his excavation into the great ditch at Durrington Walls, Geoff Wainwright found a group of fifty-seven deer antlers. 'It would have been a very human reaction', he commented, 'to throw one's implements into a heap in the relief of having completed such a major undertaking'.[391] Whatever the reason for disposing of antlers in this way, this implies at least fifty-seven workers on site together.

At Avebury, where there has been little excavation and where only a small part of what may be the original ditch has been found,[392] we can only guess its appearance. But coming between the excavation of the classically pit-dug ditches at Windmill Hill and Stonehenge, we can imagine that it too was dug as a series of interconnecting pits by a large number of small teams working together. It is possible to fit a circle of about 380m diameter into the ditch of the south-east sector of the earthwork, but this cannot be done with the adjacent sectors, which have straight segments. As with the rings on Windmill Hill (the outer of which is about the same diameter) perfect circularity on this scale was not apparently an issue.

The Avebury henge is anyway one of the biggest known, but when the first earthwork was dug there seems to have been nothing comparable anywhere in Britain. As we saw in chapter 13, there are only two other henge-like enclosures in Wessex dated to this time. Both are circular, and about a quarter the size of Avebury: Flagstones in Dorset, and Stonehenge itself. So we might imagine that, before any megaliths were brought to the site, before construction of the huge earthwork whose eroded remains we see today, already a workforce had gathered at Avebury of a size rarely encountered before.

When this earthwork was enlarged by deepening the ditch and raising the bank, it's possible that the by then overgrown ditch silts and undisturbed chalk below were removed by trench digging, much as Gray's men had worked. Gray was very struck by the wide, flat base of the ditch he emptied, and, at least as it was cleaned out by his men, the sides were steep and regular. Three or four gangs could have worked in each ditch sector, reinforcing the straight, segmented nature of the original ditch as they went. If we allow twelve people in each gang, we have a workforce of around 150–200.

But Gray was only heaping the spoil in the ditch beside his excavations, and he had the help of wheelbarrows. Five thousand years ago, the task was to lift the chalk to the top of the bank, a considerably more demanding task. We might, then, double the number of people required: 300–400. Gray's Cutting I was excavated over eighteen days.[393] Assuming the original ditch was similar in scale to the profile of the silted-in ditch we see today, then the Neolithic builders would have been faced with digging out the same amount of material as was Gray's team – over the entire ditch circuit. So we can extrapolate from Gray's schedule[394] to say that, other things being equal, one gang with basketers could have dug the entire circuit in around 400 weeks.[395] If there were three or four gangs working together in each sector (our 300–400 people), they would have taken around twenty-five or thirty-five weeks. This great henge, with sufficient labour and good organisation, could have been built in less than a year.[396] With a single gang working around each ditch sector at the same time (that is, four altogether), it would have taken two years.

Conventionally, archaeologists have supposed that such organisation would require a political hierarchy – somebody to take control, in an extreme form as seen in popular images of slaves piling up Egyptian pyramids. Writing of Stonehenge, Richard Atkinson imagined 'a single man, who alone could create and maintain the conditions necessary for this great undertaking'.[397] Colin Renfrew wrote of 'chiefdoms' in Neolithic Wessex, with powerful individuals coordinating work and accumulating and redistributing supplies.[398]

It didn't have to be like that, and these days archaeologists are less confident about saying exactly what sort of society was responsible for these great constructions. The tendency is to think more in terms of community endeavour than ranked control.[399] It is instructive to hear what a contemporary Egyptian archaeologist has to say about ancient pyramids:

> We often describe pyramid-building in terms of labour recruited in military fashion or the wage-labour of a large modern engineering project. Coupled with this is a popular notion of the pharaoh as totally autocratic. Both images obscure the way in which pharaoh's power was woven through the fabric of ancient Egyptian society, and the degree to which labour for large-scale, 'public' works was organised by towns, villages, estates and households . . . Pyramid building was perhaps regarded as a ritual act embedded in social custom and tradition.[400]

There is, of course, good independent evidence for a political hierarchy in ancient Egypt, but the implication is that such a hierarchy is not itself a necessary precondition for complex works. In Britain, there is no direct evidence from Hengeworld for the accumulation of wealth and power by a very few.

But there is a pyramid.

*

Just the other side of the small hill south of Avebury, not far from the spring that feeds the nascent River Kennet, rises Silbury Hill, another great chalkwork piled up from the excavation of a ditch. Most investigation at Silbury has been a forlorn search for rich burials in the centre (which nonetheless might still be there somewhere). Not every archaeologist would agree, but I believe that this site is ready for excavation on a large scale, not least in the ditch, which should prove a treasure house of historical and environmental information. For now, we must make do with what we have: a confusing set of radiocarbon dates, and Richard Atkinson's poorly recorded tunnel, incomplete ditch section, and unmapped trenches on the top. Other, older, excavations are next to useless.

There is a lovely story about Silbury. Atkinson's team, watched by viewers of BBC television, found plant and animal remains exceptionally well preserved in the peculiar airless conditions beneath the tons of chalk. Amongst the insects recovered were a particular ant species, *Myrmica rubra*, some of which had their mating wings of late summer. So we may not know precisely what year Silbury was built, but we know what time of year, or thought we knew. Sadly this has now been challenged. Mark Robinson, who re-examined the insects in the recent study of Atkinson's dig[401] (helped considerably when specimens were found in 1992 in sweet jars in the basement of the London Institute of Archaeology), confirmed the ant identifications. But, he said, the late summer story is a myth. Yes, some ants probably did have wings (although they are now lost), but there is no saying when they died: the corpses could have been at least several months old when they were buried by the mound.[402]

More positively, insects and plant remains confirm what John Evans proposed, from different evidence: that at the time the earthworks at Silbury and Avebury were built, the Winterbourne, the small stream that today runs from below Windmill Hill into the Kennet south of Silbury, was dry. At most, the valley was marshy at certain times of year.[403] Silbury was not surrounded by water, and neither was Avebury beside a stream (as yet there is no evidence for the status of the Swallowhead spring south of Silbury, but it cannot be assumed that that was there either).[404] This is a most unexpected conclusion, as it has been an axiom of archaeologists that all big henges are beside rivers.

Excavation at Silbury has mostly revealed what we might expect.

It is a mound of compact chalk rubble, with an inner core of turves, gravel and clay such as would have been removed from the vicinity at the start of construction. Try and imagine away the road (at the latest, a Roman intrusion: engineers probably sighted from the top of the hill). You can see that Silbury stands on the end of a small north-facing spur. It is on the eastern side of this spur tip, so that when builders cut away chalk rock, carving back the natural contours and piling the rubble onto the growing mound, they had more to remove on the west side. So the wide 'ditch' at the base of the hill extends further to the west than the east or north.

What looks like the base of the mound, then, especially on the south side, is actually undisturbed 'clay with flints' (a natural deposit on the chalk) and chalk rock. Atkinson's trench on top revealed rough concentric walls of small chalk boulders, creating a box structure into which smaller material was dumped. This would have given greater stability than random dumping, but we don't know how far down this construction device goes. A very similar wall was found by Keiller in a small excavation into the bank of the henge at Avebury.[405] This might have been a local technique, or perhaps one used throughout the chalk district of southern England.

The distinctive step just below the top of Silbury is well known. This, and a now largely filled-in step lower down, are probably constructional features that both strengthen the sides and provided working platforms for builders. There is clear evidence that these terraces were cut back and fenced round in relatively recent times (a coin of Aethelred the Unready was found on the second step, *c.* AD 1010), apparently when the mound was used as a fort. On current evidence, we cannot tell whether the top of Silbury had its present terraced appearance when it was completed in the Neolithic. The steps may all have been filled in, to give the mound a smooth profile.

When was Silbury built? There is a single date of material from turf beneath the mound of about 4600 years ago (within a range of over five centuries), and two dates from antlers near, but not at, the bottom of the ditch of about 4300 years ago.[406] On the face of it Silbury is a few centuries younger than the earthwork at Avebury, which we tentatively dated to around 5000 years ago. But the latter is dated by only one sample, and we have ignored seven other dates from Silbury, which for one reason or another are problematic.[407] There may be good cause for mistrusting these other dates, but the situation is not satisfactory. Both the absolute and the relative dating of Avebury and Silbury still contain a significant element of hypothesis.

What is not in doubt, however, is Silbury's size. Bill Startin's estimate is that its construction would have taken four million hours: that's eight times his calculation for the henge at Avebury.[408]

Although the construction of Silbury could have been protracted, there is no indication that it was completed as a smaller mound and then enlarged by later generations: there is no buried developed soil such as has been found within the bank at Avebury. This is a huge undertaking, whether it was done by, say, 1500–2000 people in a year, 300–400 over five years or even 60–80 over twenty-five years.[409] The much older long barrow on the hill above, West Kennet, with its impressive stone chambers, consumed 250 times less labour.[410] Indeed, it is a considerably larger task than, again by Startin's calculations, the erection of the great sarsen monument at Stonehenge. So whatever the relationship between Silbury and Avebury, it is perhaps unlikely that these two earthworks were under construction at the same time.

There has been no excavation into any of these chalkworks, which are unusually well preserved in the Avebury district, with a specific view to understanding how they were built. But we should have no illusions as to Neolithic earth-moving skills. The one place these have been well considered in recent times is at the flint mines at Grimes Graves in Norfolk, which were in use at about the same time Avebury henge and Silbury Hill were constructed, by people making the same type of Grooved Ware pottery.

Here the extreme conditions were matched by special skills: a great deal of labour was required to reach the deep, valuable flint, and the working environment would have been mortally dangerous for any but the experienced miner. It took modern professional miners, a Dutch team led by Joseph Felder, joined by British Museum archaeologists in the 1970s, to reveal just how skilled the ancient miners had been, extracting the maximum amount of flint commensurate with safety and effort.[411] Neolithic mines – and there are several in southern England[412] as well as others elsewhere in Europe – are amongst the most extraordinary industrial relics anywhere in the world.

Tiny little arrowheads might have been made with flint from these mines. Skilled engineering was applied to big stones, too, and it is to these we now turn. How were they moved? By proposing a possibly false journey of bluestones from Wales, have we exaggerated the achievements of the megalith-builders? Or have we, indeed, underestimated them?

22

Ye Same to Some of the Stones
in ye Inner Circle

Andrew David may have the ideal, reserved personality for the job of chief geophysicist at English Heritage. With all the new-fangled technology, making these extraordinary discoveries, it would be too easy to jump the gun, to be on the TV excitedly proclaiming the latest find, only to find a few days later that it was a figment of some computer's imagination. And figments abound in this business.

June 1998. It's nine months since the Stanton Drew survey. They're out at a stone circle again. It's a bit different now, thanks to the publicity Stanton Drew attracted. A television crew want to be in on this discovery, and Geoff Wainwright wants to see that if there is a grand discovery, then English Heritage get the credit. The TV people want an exclusive. So no one is quite sure what they are supposed to know or say. Makes for interesting evenings in the pub.

A few kilometres north of Avebury, just up the hill from the village of Winterbourne Bassett, is a stone circle. At least, William Stukeley said he'd found a circle in the early eighteenth century, about 70m across. Today it looks like a promising jumble of sarsens in an old meadow. There's been no excavation, no geophysics survey. Everyone's hoping for another revelation: another timber henge in a stone circle. Andy Payne, on the English Heritage team, is buzzing with excitement. 'I've been looking forward to this ever since I came up here with Rosamund Cleal when we were surveying the Avebury quadrant a couple of years ago. I knew we'd get here one day. I wouldn't have missed this survey for anything.'[413]

His boss is a little more circumspect. 'One of our objectives', says Andrew David, carefully unfolding a copy of a nineteenth-century survey, 'must be to establish if this is a real stone circle.'

The wind ripples the grass and pulls at the oak trees, the ropes are laid out, the gadgets carried and wheeled about, and the laptop plots pored over. A torrential storm holds up work. There's something wrong with the survey grid. Initial hopeful patterns on the computer screen disappear in later scans. They'll have to return. This Winterbourne Bassett circle, if that's what it is, turns out to be a bit of a tough nut.

No matter. May 1999 and Andy is back in Avebury, this time with a relatively new lab recruit, Louise Martin. Louise finished her archaeology degree the year before, and joined English Heritage in November. They're in a field to the west of Avebury, at a place they surveyed ten years before. Andy was on the team then, too.[414] They think they can improve on the old survey. Archaeologists are digging there in the summer, and one of them, Josh Pollard, has asked if they might have another look at the field for them.

There's a crop of young barley, like grass. Wrapped in layers of thick clothes, they soon steam up in the mild weather. They carefully measure out a 60m square grid, do the resistivity survey, and the batteries start to die. So they rush to the National Trust office in Avebury to recharge the computer. While they sit with cups of tea discussing the work with Ros Cleal and Chris Gingell, an archaeologist who also happens to be the Trust's Avebury property manager, the plot comes up on the reviving laptop. Andy Payne's got it this time. Bang in the middle of the grey screen are four dots, like the face of a die with four spots – one white and three black. 'This is why I got into archaeology', Andy tells me, remembering the moment, his eyes sparkling.[415]

You see, they hadn't just found four dots. They'd found four stones – well, that's what they looked like. And these four stones might be the harbinger of the greatest lost megalithic structure in all of Europe. Or, as Andrew David put it in the report he wrote a month later: 'The reversed anomalies do raise suspicions.'[416]

Megaliths embody in their substance and their mass some record of the physical effort required to get them into position. At Stanton Drew, which includes the largest circle after Avebury, there are a variety of different rocks which a nineteenth-century study suggested could all have come from within 10km.[417] North of Avebury in Oxfordshire, at the Rollright Stones, principally a stone circle some 31m in diameter, the megaliths are all oolitic limestone that could apparently have been taken as boulders from the surface of the ground from no more than 500m away.[418] There are some big stones at these circles, but not so big that it's difficult to imagine Neolithic people moving them those distances.

It's different at Stonehenge and Avebury. We saw (chapter 17) how these great communities of megaliths consist of two different groups of rock: Wiltshire sarsens and Welsh bluestones. Is it possible that Neolithic people could move these stones, some of those at Avebury weighing more than 60 tons, over considerable distances? Could they transport a total of 300 tons of bluestones to Stonehenge all the way from Pembrokeshire, a journey almost certainly involving a water passage as well as more than 200km overland?

Archaeologist Aubrey Burl thinks not. He dismisses the notion of 'a floating platform without sails' piloted by 'kamikaze crews', and makes the point that anyway 'prehistoric societies' did not go great distances to fetch megaliths. They used stone conveniently to hand.[419] Burl has some geologists on his side. Geoffrey Kellaway disputed Herbert Thomas's pioneering claim, made in 1923, that all the bluestones had been carried from or from near the Preseli hills by people. Writing thirty years ago, Kellaway found it 'incomprehensible' that the builders of Stonehenge would have gone all the way to Wales for stone when they had suitable material close by.[420]

More recently, and with more authority, having completed the most intensive geological study ever conducted of the Stonehenge megaliths, a team from the Open University at Milton Keynes concluded that the bluestones had been brought to the Stonehenge district by glaciers hundreds of thousands of years ago.[421] William Judd, the geologist who examined rock fragments from Gowland's excavation in 1901, would have agreed.[422] And in case any archaeologists had missed the point, two of the team, Richard Thorpe and Olwen Williams-Thorpe, wrote a separate paper titled 'The myth of long-distance megalith transport'.[423]

This is an old controversy. It is a fascinating story involving detailed geological argument, notions of people who died thousands of years ago, and a garden ornament at a country house. At stake is the engineering skill of our ancestors – and on trial are our preconceptions.

Let us begin in the garden. We met William Cunnington, wool merchant of Heytesbury[424] near Salisbury and archaeological companion of Sir Richard Colt Hoare, in chapter 9. In 1801 Cunnington dug a mound on Salisbury Plain known as Boles Barrow, a few kilometres north of his house. Inside he found a heap of rocks covering a mass of human skeletons. He took ten of the stones to his garden, and later realised that one of them was a 'Blue hard Stone . . . ye same to some of the upright Stones in ye inner Circle at Stonehenge'.

The significance of this is that Boles Barrow is a long barrow, of a type common a thousand years or more before the stones were put up at Stonehenge, but no longer being built when bluestones were erected as megaliths. Either some, perhaps all, of the bluestones had been portaged to Salisbury Plain long before Stonehenge was thought of, or, on the face of it more likely, the stones were already on the plain when the old barrow itself was built – that is, they'd been dropped by glaciers. That this single bluestone was jumbled up with more local sarsens, without any apparent significance being accorded to what one might have thought to have been a special stone, supports the geological thesis. Aubrey Burl picks on this as 'the most compelling evidence for glacial transport of the bluestones'.[425] As well he might: we will see later that it is the only evidence.

We have four elements in this deed.[426] There is the barrow where William Cunnington found some stones. There is his garden in Heytesbury, where some stones were arranged in an ornamental ring. There is a second garden at Heytesbury House, in which a stone was discovered in 1923. And there is a stone in Salisbury Museum, said to be the one from the garden that was originally in the other garden that had been found in the barrow. If that sounds complicated, it gets worse. Geologist Christopher Green recently argued with some persuasion that the stone in Salisbury did not come from Boles Barrow at all, but from Stonehenge.[427] With a little elaboration from me, this is his case.

We can hardly dispute the stone. It sits on the floor of the museum, too heavy to be lifted into a display cabinet. It was donated by the writer Siegfried Sassoon in 1934 when he moved into the village, and, in a blind analysis of a fragment off the block, none other than Herbert Thomas proclaimed 'there is no doubt that the specimen . . . [is] identical with the spotted Blue stones of Stonehenge'.[428] The stone was found in the garden at Heytesbury House by Ben Cunnington, Maud's husband, who ascertained that it had been there since before 1860, and that it had been known to the occupants as the 'Stonehenge Stone'.

Meanwhile, up the road at William Cunnington's residence, there was once a ring of stones at the bottom of the lawn around a weeping ash. One of his many granddaughters, Eliza, remembering this in 1864, noted that the stones had come from Boles Barrow. She does not say what type of rock they were. She does, however, refer to another, larger block of stone, a piece of granite from Dartmoor. This was not, she says, 'as has been supposed, a stone brought from Stonehenge, but was presented to Mr Cunnington by Sir Richard Colt Hoare'.

Finally, the evidence from the barrow is in a letter William sent to one H. P. Wyndham, MP for Wiltshire with an enthusiasm for antiquities, who encouraged Cunnington to dig on his land. Wyndham's sister lived at Heytesbury House.[429] 'The Stones that composed so large a part of this ridge over the Bodies', Cunnington wrote in July 1801, describing the excavation of Boles Barrow, 'are of the same species of Stone as the very large Stones at Stonehenge.' That is, they were sarsens. He continues by offering a few comments on sarsens in general. 'I have brought away Ten', he says, leaving us to guess whether he means from the barrow or from 'the vallies in our Downs', 'to my house'.

Then, at some later date, he added the already-mentioned footnote to his copy of the letter: 'Since writing the above I discover amongst them the Blue hard Stone also, ye same to some of the upright Stones in ye inner Circle at Stonehenge.' He stuck in another footnote, this time to say 'the stones were from about 28 lbs to 200 lbs weight' (13–90kg).

The pedigree of the museum stone is far from clear. If we accept that the stones Cunnington says he took to his garden did indeed come from Boles Barrow, we have to deal with the issue of size. Even his largest is a long way from the 611kg of the stone in Salisbury.[430] That's a significant difference. At the barrow, they had to leave hastily when the rocks tumbled down into the trench. Would not Cunnington have remembered if one had been that big? And as his comments on both the 'Blue hard Stone' and the weights were written some time after the dig (we have no idea how much time), is it not likely that his impression of size would have been influenced by what he could still see in his garden? And even if we override these objections, we have to imagine that at some time this particular bluestone made its way from Cunnington's garden to the other garden, while sarsens still remained *chez* the Cunningtons to be seen in the 1920s.

An alternative hypothesis is that what the owners of Heytesbury House knew as the Stonehenge Stone was just that: a piece of a bluestone taken from Stonehenge (and the story of the granite block suggests there was some confusion, at least amongst later generations, exactly where the stones did come from). With Cunnington in the village, and the antiquarian interests of Wyndham, it is easy to imagine how his sister's garden could have become the beneficiary of one of those incidents of Stonehenge vandalism of which writers complained throughout the nineteenth century. Burl's argument that no stones have been removed since 1740 (comparing Petrie's nineteenth-century survey with John Wood's earlier one) may or may not be correct, but it does not deny the possibility of part of a stone having been removed.[431] It could also be a stone taken before even John Wood's plan.

I noted (chapter 17) that the five hollows described by John Aubrey in 1666, supposed to represent the sunken fill of fifty-six 4000-year-old pits found in 1920, had gone only a century or so after Aubrey's visit. It still seems to me that a likely explanation is that standing stones had been recently removed. Perhaps the Boles stone was one of them. Alternatively, Hawley believed at least one stone had been removed from the bluestone circle in the seventeenth century, evidenced by part of a glass flagon in the trench dug 'for the robbery'.[432]

As for Cunnington's footnote about the discovery of a piece of bluestone in the barrow, this need refer to nothing more than a fragment of stone axe. Throughout the Neolithic people had a good knowledge of Britain's rich surface geology.[433] After all, they were dependent on this knowledge for their stone tools and their pottery (which required not just clay but also filler, material to add to the clay to give it resistance to sudden changes in temperature). Potting and stoneworking are both sophisticated technologies that demand very particular raw materials (see also chapter 25).

Types of stone known to have been quarried for axeheads could have been confused with the materials of Stonehenge bluestones. Richard Atkinson did this at Silbury Hill. At the time of the dig, he announced the discovery of a piece of stone 'apparently identical with one of the varieties of Stonehenge bluestone'. This identification was quietly dropped and the piece is now lost.[434] Cunnington says he found something 'ye same to *some* of the upright Stones': there are several types of bluestone, of which spotted dolerite is only one. Even were his identification correct, it still need not have been spotted dolerite.

So all in all, Aubrey Burl's case comes off pretty shaky. But, looking again, perhaps not. Christopher Green has his own agenda. Just as Burl cannot believe that primitive people went all the way to Wales to get megaliths, so Green is convinced, not least from years of his own geological research in the field, that Salisbury Plain was never glaciated. He needs to argue that the Boles blue-stone was not on the plain centuries before Stonehenge was built.

The evidence that the museum stone did come from Boles barrow is not all bad. Going backwards again, we know the stone came from the garden at Heytesbury House. There is an account passed on to Ben Cunnington in 1923 by Lord Heytesbury, that it reached there from No. 108 Heytesbury, almost opposite the front gates of Heytesbury House, where William Cunnington lived. Heytesbury's aunt, the Honourable Mrs Hamersley, told him that the stone had been taken from the late Mr Cunnington's garden, that it was known as the 'Stonehenge Stone', and that it was placed under the beech tree where Ben found it.

We have already accepted that to suggest the ring of stones in William Cunnington's garden (where he also had a model of Avebury made with pebbles) did not come from Boles Barrow requires special pleading. So what about the great weight of the stone? It turns out that when William dug Boles Barrow, he had a larger than usual gang to help him. The dig took place at the invitation of the farmer, who offered him two or three men as assistants. So when they excavated through the mound Cunnington had four men under him. Perhaps they could have lifted out such a large stone. Perhaps Farmer Fricker provided yet more labour. Perhaps, then, although you have to admit it can hardly be called proven, Aubrey could be right.[435]

Boles Barrow today, in the midst of the army's Salisbury Plain training area, is remote as it was when William Cunnington rode out in 1801. It's a large, high mound, rising like an elongated wart from the rolling chalk grassland. I went there in the summer of 2000 with Dave Field, an English Heritage archaeologist who had been surveying the Plain's ancient riches, and who knew how to steer his landrover around unexploded shells. I had been contemplating a new dig. Perhaps a modern examination of the barrow would throw light on the bluestone controversy.

The remoteness, the logistical challenge of mounting a large dig so far from the modern world, negotiating with soldiers and conservationists, such things appealed immensely. But, at least for now, I had to abandon the idea. The archaeology of Boles is a mess.

Three large, but unmapped, digs took place in the nineteenth century. Early in the next century the army built a water tank on top and a pond to one side. Trees sunk roots deep into the ancient tomb. Rabbits and badgers took extensive advantage of the convenient bank. The badger sett, still active, would have to be moved, at huge cost, before any dig could take place. And such has been the damage, there could be no guarantee of finding undisturbed deposits.

The old digs threw up many questions. The archaeologists saw evidence for a forgotten massacre: the human skeletons were all male, and cut-wounds, perhaps from swords, were abundant. But they found nothing to indicate when the mound was built, not a single distinctive artefact except for a bronze buckle in a grave on the top, clearly dug when the barrow was already old.[436]

The human remains were saved, however, and recently I went to museums in Cambridge and Devizes, shortly followed by Mick Wysocki and Rick Schulting from Cardiff University, to examine them. The bones make an odd collection. There is extensive evidence for heavy weathering, perhaps caused by percolating rainwater after the bones were buried, and some nice ancient chewing by animals like dogs or foxes. But, said the Cardiff archaeologists, the supposed sword wounds are imaginary, no more than mis-identified natural erosion scars. And there are women there as well as men.

This new study did not help us with the question of when these people died. We don't know exactly how the mound was built – was there an early structure of stone rubble, later covered in chalk, perhaps itself preceded by a timber burial chamber? – and we don't know how extensive was the much later use of the mound as a cemetery, perhaps in Saxon times. In sum, even were we to believe the Boles stone did come from the Boles barrow, we could not answer the more precise, but highly significant question: which Boles barrow?

The Boles stone is the only piece of Welsh stone yet found in Wiltshire, not at Stonehenge, bigger than a tea cup – and all others have been in an archaeological context of some kind or another. Further evidence for a glaciation of Salisbury Plain is so convoluted as to be not worth repeating.(To give you a flavour: geologists Richard Thorpe and colleagues quote from an unpublished letter from Kellaway, in which he reports a meeting with Robert Newall – deceased – at which Newall told him he had found rocks that looked like glacial erratics, but Hawley would have none of it; Newall kept the rocks, and gave one to Kellaway; 'we are attempting to trace this piece', say Thorpe and his colleagues, '. . . for further examination'.)[437]

Suffice to refer briefly to a study that should have settled the argument for good twenty years ago. Christopher Green analysed river gravels in Wiltshire and Hampshire and found a 'complete lack of glacially derived material'. The gravels were all of rocks in the local areas from which the rivers still draw their water. If there aren't even gravel-sized 'erratics', what chance of there being erratic megaliths? As Green said, his data 'show conclusively that the "Anglian" ice never invaded the basins of these rivers . . . ice cannot therefore be invoked to explain the presence of large and medium sized Welsh rocks . . . on the Wiltshire Chalk'.[438]

So you see, it's only prejudice that can be invoked to say that people didn't bring them. In one sense, Burl, Williams-Thorpe and the others may be right. The journeys that took eighty stones to Stonehenge from Wales, and seventy-five massive sarsens from somewhere in Wiltshire, may be unique in the annals of primitive peoples. Which just shows how primitive, illogical and uninformed these Hengeworld folk were.[439]

23

Fantasies and Maggots

The visitor's Avebury was created by Alexander Keiller in the 1930s. He removed buildings, trees and fences, re-erected megaliths and set concrete markers over sites of missing stones. From a relatively little-known archaeological site dominated by local, rural lives, Avebury became a public park.

Yet it is not Keiller who did the most important fieldwork in Avebury, but an eccentric doctor and country parson, the 'simple, droll, absurd, ingenious, superstitious' antiquarian, archdruid Chyndonax, alias William Stukeley.[440] Keiller's work in Avebury – on the West Kennet Avenue, the west side of the stone circle and near the United Reformed chapel in the south-east sector of the henge – took place over five years, in 1934–5 and 1937–9.[441] Stukeley was in Avebury for a similar period, staying in the area (sometimes at the Catherine Wheel Inn which used to stand near the Cove inside the stone circle) for a number of weeks between 1719 and 1724 (figure 39). The excitement his manuscripts betray, and the deep distress at the destruction taking place before his eyes, suggest that for Stukeley, as for Harold St George Gray, Avebury was a very special experience.

And for us, his records are very special indeed. We have seen (chapter 5) how he recorded the Sanctuary just before its demolition. Many often superbly drawn sketches of Avebury and the West Kennet Avenue provide us with invaluable information about the megalithic remains there. But most intriguing are his notes on a huge component of the Avebury monuments, of which little if anything still survives, and which has been much discussed – and frequently dismissed – over the centuries.

He believed that the West Kennet Avenue was not alone, but that a second avenue extended from the stone circles for a similar distance to the west, skirting the hamlet of Beckhampton and ending somewhere on the downs in what are today horse gallops. He imagined the two avenues to be part of a whole, a processional route and symbolic serpent that arched from its tail beyond Beckhampton via the henge to its head at the Sanctuary on Overton Hill (figure 7).

Of the West Kennet Avenue there were numerous stones still standing, and its course had already been sketched by John Aubrey in the mid 1660s.[442] But no one had recognised the other avenue. Stukeley recorded two stones where it joined Avebury, but after that it was mostly boulders or depressions in the ground marking fallen or missing megaliths, beginning with the sites of two removed stones opposite the churchyard. From there, he said, the avenue continued across the Winterbourne stream (where stones had been used in the bridge), through the row of houses on the south side of Bray Street and out into 'open plow'd fields' where it joined the only two megaliths still standing west of Avebury, known, then as now, as the Longstones.[443]

Stukeley thought the western Longstone was originally part of a cove, like that in the centre of Avebury, at which three stones stood on the sides of an open square, in this case facing south. In a little sketch he showed the existing stone, a second fallen on the ground (since gone) and the third standing on the west side, already 'deftroyd by Richd. Fowler'. Opposite these three stood a fourth, on the south side of the avenue, also taken by Fowler. The eastern Longstone he noted as the only stone in the entire avenue still standing, and a scatter of further fallen stones marked the passing route of the two parallel rows (figure 7).[444]

A few collapsed stones indicated its continuing path just south of the large barrow now north of Beckhampton roundabout,[445] from where its final conclusion was impossible to ascertain. First Stukeley imagined a temple like the Sanctuary (standing at this end, as Maud Cunnington put to advantage two centuries later, he could see the stone rings on Overton Hill), but after an exhaustive search failed to deliver, he decided it merely fizzled out into nothing.[446]

Of this huge alignment of megaliths, perhaps 100 each side, only one stone was in place. Stukeley's head was famously riddled with fantasies and maggots. Is it any wonder that later antiquaries dismissed this snake's tale as the figment of a piebald imagination? That in 1999, if asked to put money on it, few archaeologists would have said that Mark Gillings, Josh Pollard and Dave Wheatley would prove Stukeley right?

Avebury's best observers – from the vicar Bryan King in 1879,

Figure 39. William Stukeley in Avebury. He was aged 32 in 1719.

Year	Date	Events
1719	19 May	First visit to Avebury and first sketch plan of circles
	(18–19 May	First visit to Stonehenge)
1720		Sees stones recently removed from West Kennet Avenue
1721	August	Draws plan of Avebury
	16 August	Measures circumference of henge ditch, draws Cove and other views
1722		Recognises Beckhampton Avenue
		Writes first draft of 'a fine tour' of Avebury
	26 July	Draws views of Avebury and sketch of Tom Robinson
	August	Draws several views of Avebury
1723	8 July	Draws the Sanctuary
	10 July	More views of Avebury
	11 July	Draws Silbury Hill
	12 July	Draws stone circle
	14 July	Draws Beckhampton Avenue
	15 July	Draws views of Avebury
	17 July	Draws West Kennet long barrow
	19 July	Draws Silbury Hill and views of Avebury
1724	12 May	Draws distant view of Avebury
	13 May	Draws Silbury Hill and sees stones carted away from the Sanctuary
	14 May	Draws view of West Kennet Avenue
	15 May	Draws views of West Kennet Avenue, Beckhampton Cove and Sanctuary
	16 May	Draws West Kennet long barrow
1743		Publication of *Abury: A Temple of the British Druids*

Simplified from Piggott 1985.

through Isobel Smith in 1965 to Aubrey Burl twenty years ago – had in print come down strongly on Stukeley's side.[447] Yet talk was different. No archaeologist had actually incorporated this second avenue into any interpretation of ancient Avebury.[448] Nobody had before tried excavation to test the idea. When Chris Gingell, cup of tea in hand, looked at Louise's and Andy's laptop with the four spots in the centre of its screen, he was expressing wide opinion when he mused: 'Didn't the first geophysics survey show it's not there?'

You might think erecting megaliths a lost art practised by primitive and superstitious peoples, but you'd be wrong. Many stones have been put up this century in Wiltshire alone. The events mostly have been quite public affairs. With reason, at the erection of every megalith, the media have been there as witnesses. The most recent exercise was televised around the globe.

The first to be moved, in September 1901, was the only complete stone in the great trilithon at Stonehenge. It was propped up at an angle of 60° by a bluestone, so this was only half, and the easier half, of the job required in the Neolithic. It was still a major operation, devised by a Mr Carruthers and supervised by a Mr Blow, that took eight days.[449] Carpenters constructed a special timber frame that was fitted around the smooth-faced stone, and cables connected this cradle to two powerful winches. They raised the stone a few inches at a time, after which heavy larch struts were wedged against the frame. By this means it was uprighted from the south-west, and a hydraulic jack was used to get the megalith vertical from the south-east as well.

Ten years later, an Avebury stone fell flat onto the ground. Adam, the western and larger of the two Longstones (no prizes for the name of the other), crashed into the chalky earth, throwing out small boulders used to pack its base.[450] Re-erecting this would be a bigger challenge.

Ben and Maud Cunnington did their first excavation at Avebury, the pit which had held the fallen stone. It was a big hole, 4m by 2m in plan, and 1m deep, but the megalith had only penetrated the chalk by 75cm. They removed around 150 packing stones, some weighing over 50kg. Close by they found a human skeleton accompanied by a decorated Beaker. It was so close that it would have been damaged if it had been there before Adam, but could have been buried at any time after, even immediately. This was the first useful evidence as to the date of the stones at Avebury.

Chivers of Devizes were contracted to move the stone, with the additional aid of three jacks (two of 40 tons and one of 50 tons strength) loaned from the Great Western Railway works at Swindon. A fund was promoted through *The Times* and local papers, raising £95 – enough to pay to re-erect another stone as well, on the West Kennet Avenue.

The idea was to jack the stone up part way, then use two steam-powered traction engines to haul it upright with wire cables. Though tested to a strain of 50 tons, the ropes snapped without moving the stone at all. So the job was continued with the jacks (designed and built to manoeuvre components of iron steam engines in the Swindon workshops), timber beams being wedged into place as the stone slowly lifted. It cost more this way (even then it was cheaper to do a job quickly with machines than slowly with men), but it worked. If the Cunningtons' estimate of 62 tons for this stone is correct, then not only would it have been harder to manoeuvre than the great trilithon at Stonehenge, being rough and irregular in shape, but it is also significantly heavier. It is one of the largest surviving megaliths in Avebury.

The Kennet Avenue stone was a more modest 17 tons, and was soon standing in its new concrete foundation. Twenty-three years later, Alexander Keiller decided the stone had been erected upside-down, moved it and, as he saw it, redid the job properly (complaining profusely as he did so). But this was only one stone. In 1934 and 1935, his team erected twenty-seven stones in the West Kennet Avenue. Later, at least twenty-six were stood up inside the henge. For most of these megaliths, hired machinery similar to that used by the Cunningtons was employed. But at one, a small 8 ton stone on the West Kennet Avenue, timber, ropes (albeit steel) and men alone were applied in a re-enactment of prehistoric engineering.

Keiller was waiting for the delivery of modern equipment loaned by the Office of Works, but as the foreman ('old Griffiths, who had so much to do with the Stonehenge Stones') was already there, they put the first stone up using what Keiller 'could purchase or raise by loan on the spot'. Apart from steel ropes and iron staples (whose job Keiller said could just as well have been done by hides), they 'employed no equipment which would not have been at the disposal of the original builders of the Avenue'.

It was a spectacular success. Under the experienced foreman and sub-foreman, twelve untrained men raised a stone in four days (plate 16).[451]

What do we learn from this? First, even with wheels, cast iron and diesel, erecting stones is a difficult and dangerous task. Richard Atkinson was nearly killed at the centre of Stonehenge, in an incident no writer could have invented. During one of the Ministry of Works consolidation projects, a huge crane was brought in from

Bristol, where it had been specially constructed for moving the enormous, pioneering but ultimately doomed Brabazon airplane. Atkinson took the opportunity for a leisured examination of the underside of a newly exposed stone hanging from the crane. But something went wrong, and the stone suddenly began to plummet towards the recumbent archaeologist. The operator, unfamiliar with the machinery, grabbed a bar and plunged it into the works. It held.[452]

Second, although you might think this self-evident, apparently not everyone does: it is possible for a gang of ordinary people with rope and timbers to erect a rough stone without resorting to mysterious lost powers or the help of aliens. There's no mystery, but there is magic. Erecting even the smallest stone is an event. It requires planning and organisation, people and equipment. It attracts attention and bequeaths stories – it generates a buzz. It gives an anonymous rock a unique identity. In a word, it creates a megalith.

These stones were ready to re-erect because, thousands of years ago, people had brought them to where they were. How did they do that? Let's start with the hardest to imagine. How did Aubrey Burl's 'kamikaze crews' transport 4 ton rocks on sail-less platforms without going to the bottom of the Bristol Channel?

Atkinson argued convincingly that water transport would have been easier than overland.[453] Whether or not wheeled vehicles were available when Stonehenge was built – it is a possibility, albeit unproven – they could not have been strong enough, nor the ground surfaces firm enough, to carry the weights of heavy stones. Thus whether power was human or oxen – again, an untested possibility – on land, stones would have had to be dragged: bound to sledges and pulled over the ground, along fixed wooden rails, or across movable timber rollers. Friction would have made this a more labour-intensive task than floating stones on some suitable raft or hollow craft. As to what these were, we do not know. But there can be no question that the people of Hengeworld were capable of making good, seaworthy vehicles. After all, we've found them.

Well, not the precise boats that carried stones, nor indeed boats of precisely the right date. But in the world of ancient materials, where timber survives only through some fluke of preserving conditions, the identification of six sophisticated craft around the shores of Britain dating from up to 3700 years ago should be enough to silence the doubters.

Remarkably, three of these were found in the Humber estuary near Ferriby, Yorkshire, the first in 1937 and the most recent in 1963. These are among the oldest and most important maritime finds made in north-west Europe.[454] A few boat planks have been found at Caldicot and at Goldcliff in the Severn estuary (as it happens, close to any likely sea route connecting Preseli and Stonehenge),[455] and an astonishingly well preserved boat was uncovered in Dover in 1992.[456] These are all similar structures: large oak planks (at Dover, the planks are as long as the craft, all of 15m) bound with yew withies and wooden joints, and caulked with moss.[457]

These are far from specimens of spontaneous amateur carpentry. Roy Switsur thought them the 'culmination of perhaps centuries of development'.[458] They are complex pieces of engineering, embodying skills that could only have been learnt in apprenticeship, that were directed at producing tough, working craft that could plough the open sea. If there were any doubt about this (naturally, archaeologists and maritime historians do not all agree), the discovery by Keith Muckleroy of a large spread of scrap metal of approximately the same date as the boats, out to sea off the coast of Dover, should settle it. If you belong to the primitive and ignorant school of thought, you could, I suppose, argue that these went down with a canoe that strayed dangerously far from shore and got its come-uppance. But then you'd have to explain the presence in the boat of bronze objects made not in Britain, but on the other side of the Channel.[459]

These boats were made with metal tools. We can imagine, although research is badly needed on this, that things can be done to wood with metal tools (not least with joints) that could not be done with stone tools. We will be looking at this issue again, but for now we can ask, would the people who took stones from Wales to Stonehenge have had access to metal tools and the marine carpentry these would have facilitated?

Let's look at radiocarbon dates. In chapter 17 we described a bluestone circle and oval erected inside the existing sarsens around 4000 years ago (Stonehenge Phase 3iv). This is not thought to be the first time bluestones were on site. That earlier event (involving the Q and R holes in Phase 3i) remains undated. It predated the sarsen event, which we put at around 4300 years ago, and was not significantly before the main ditch filling, complete a century or so before that. Perhaps, then, somewhere between 4400 and 4300 years ago, give or take a century.

211

The best dates we have for early metalwork in Britain come from graves where people were buried with Beaker pots and little pieces of precious metal: gold and copper ornaments and copper daggers and knives.[460] Where the very skeletons have been dated, we can be confident that the metal objects were in use at the time suggested by radiocarbon (unless they were already antiques). The three oldest dates we have (they are still quite rare) fall into this period of 4400–4300 years ago.[461]

They are not normally found in graves, but simple copper axe blades were also being made at this early date. There is a timber structure in Ireland bearing the marks of metal blades, dated by dendrochronology to within a decade either side of 4259 years ago.[462] It looks likely, then, that our Stonehenge navigators could well have benefited from the earliest metal carpentry kit to have reached Britain. Indeed, you might argue that the imperative to get those stones from Wales could have boosted boat technology and seamanship.

On the other hand, as Sean McGrail has said, the journey could as well have been done with logboats. To be in Britain in the first place, these people had to be descendants of settlers from mainland Europe who had survived 'some of the most difficult seas in the world'. His preferred choice is three logboats joined in parallel, a stone on the central boat and paddlers either side.[463] A Cornish fishmonger, Mr R. Wallington, discussed the issue of Neolithic seamanship with local fishermen who had spent all their lives working a notoriously difficult coastline. They were agreed that Neolithic people would have had no problem with such seas.[464]

As for the routes taken and the precise mechanisms, we can only guess. No one has yet replicated the journeys.[465] Atkinson proposed a route that hugged the coast of south Wales, crossed the Bristol Channel and reached Stonehenge via three rivers, the Bristol Avon, the Wylye and the Hampshire Avon ('avon' is simply a pre-English word meaning 'river'), leaving relatively little overland portage (figure 40).[466]

The home straight is marked by the Stonehenge Avenue. There is no reason to think that the entire land route was not prepared in some way. These stones could not have been dragged through gardens and villages, across unexplored marsh and into strange woodland. The Somerset levels are crossed by substantial pedestrian wooden trackways preserved in the peats, some older than Hengeworld, that run for several kilometres.[467] None could

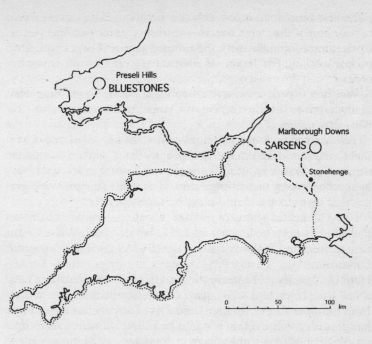

Figure 40. Hypothetical stone routes to Stonehenge. Bluestones: overland from Preseli to the Bristol Channel, along the Somerset Avon, the River Wylye and the Wiltshire Avon, with a small portage between the Avon and the Wylye; or a longer sea route around the Cornish peninsula and up the Avon from the Dorset coast. Sarsens: overland from the stone fields of the Marlborough Downs. *After Atkinson.*

take a megalith, but clearly there was a tradition of investing effort in permanent constructed paths. A passage for the stones must have been surveyed in advance, involving negotiation with a variety of peoples, and quite probably numerous political and religious ceremonies. Perhaps local people in some way assisted as the stones passed through their territories.

Some interesting maths has been proposed for assessing the number of people required to erect megaliths. I am not a mathematician, so I will just quote an example. A. R. Whiteman, writing about the destroyed stone circle at the Devil's Quoits in Oxfordshire, calculated figures for a stone weighing 17 tons. He needed at least thirty-six people to move it over turf on a sledge.

Forty-five people, equipped with five wooden poles as levers, could lift one end of the stone. Erecting it from a leaning position on an earth ramp continuous with the ramped side of the pit required 55 people working five levers, or alternatively 261 people using five ropes.[468]

Working experience is also essential if we are to get near what really happened at the erection of a stone. In this respect, the 1994 BBC experiment is almost in a class of its own. A replica of the largest surviving Stonehenge megalith, stone 56 of the Great Trilithon, was dragged by 130 people for 150m on a wooden slipway. It was then stood upright with some clever but very Neolithic-looking technology, and a concrete 10 ton lintel was dragged up a ramp and into place by ninety people.[469]

I said almost in a class of its own, because a similar experiment had already been conducted in 1991, beside – where else? – the Otava river, on land provided by the town council of Strakonice, Czechoslovakia. Pavel Pavel, with drawings from English Heritage, 'money and construction materials from local firms', and a few friends, erected a full-scale concrete replica of two sarsens from the outer ring (3.9m high) and a five-ton concrete lintel. Pavel had this idea that the lintels could be raised by sliding them up a couple of poles (oak trunks 40cm in diameter), rather than going to the trouble of building a solid ramp. It looked easy on a clay model, so he tried the real thing. That worked, too. Just ten labourers were able to drag the lintel up the poles, using ropes and levers, although it was easier with two teams of ten each ('The lintel fell down during one of our tests'). It was up in three days.[470]

In the case of both sarsen and bluestone, the rock naturally breaks into slabs and boulders that can be lifted and taken away for megaliths. Most sarsens, and apparently several bluestones, at Stonehenge and Avebury are just that: natural, uncarved boulders. Despite a continuing faith in some quarters that the Avebury stones are dressed,[471] there is absolutely no evidence for this. There are occasional patches where the stone has been pecked or rubbed, and these need studying properly. But that is a completely different thing from carving.

At Stonehenge, though, almost all the sarsens are artificially shaped. Atkinson stressed what a time-consuming job this must have been. Just the finer dressing, he said, would have occupied fifty masons working without break ten hours a day for two and three-quarter years. Then they'd have to polish the surfaces and shape the joints – and they'd already completed rough dressing, removing several tons of stone.[472]

I am hesitant here. When Stonehenge was built, Europe had had a technology of working stone to produce tools for at least half a million years. It had arguably reached its apogee. Drawing on a sophisticated practical understanding of fracture mechanics and raw materials, stone workers used a variety of ways of hitting, applying pressure, drilling, grinding and polishing (and quite probably careful heating). Sometimes these skills were directed at producing highly functional tools, sometimes at beautiful objects so fragile that they cannot possibly have been made for anything other than their value, however that might have been perceived.[473]

Almost all we now know about this technology comes from attempts by archaeologists and others – sometimes pretty successful – to replicate the extinct tradition.[474] Some 4300 years ago a bunch of people sit down and decide to build Stonehenge. They've done similar stuff before with timber, but never in stone. Among the many things they need to consider is this question of how the stones are to be shaped. Nothing like it has been attempted in Europe before, and Stonehenge cannot be done without lengthy discussion and experiments. It is inevitable that among those consulted are the most experienced and skilled flint-knappers and stone-workers. The latter include people well versed in shaping sarsen. This stone has been used for generations for grain-milling querns, not least on the Marlborough Downs, where so many huge sarsen slabs lie on the surface of the ground.

We owe an insight to Herbert Stone, writing eighty years ago. He had detailed knowledge of Stonehenge and experience of gneiss quarries in Hyderabad ('many years ago, when in the service of the Government of India'), and conducted experiments with a funeral mason in Devizes, Mr W. L. Morgan.[475] Many of the bluestones, he wrote, have a conchoidal fracture similar to flint. This was exploited by the Neolithic masons, who treated 'the blue stone as if it were to form an enormous flint implement'.[476]

Strong conchoidal fracturing, literally breaking like a shell when struck, is one of the things that makes flint such a good material for tool manufacture. In skilled hands, it can be used to great advantage, giving the knapper close control of otherwise extremely tough material. Stone was proposing that the small bluestones could be thought of as giant flaked tools. The same approach can be taken to the much larger sarsens. Sarsen, too, has a conchoidal fracture (as we discovered excavating the stone floor in 1980: chapter 19). Technologically and conceptually, Stonehenge is an arrangement of absurdly massive stone tools. And if the people of Hengeworld knew how to breathe, they knew how to make stone tools (figure 41).

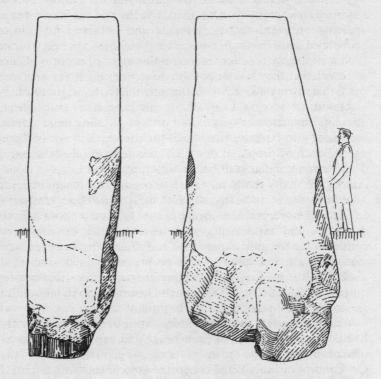

Figure 41. Stonehenge sarsen stone 30 drawn after adjustment in 1920, showing massive flaking below ground (east side, outer face). *After J. A. Wright/Office of Works.*

That is the architectural genius of Stonehenge. Taking a small everyday object, using everyday technology, but in ways previously unimagined, people created something on an unprecedented scale. As the designers of the new London Eye, the Statue of Liberty or indeed the ancient pyramids of Egypt understood, expanding scale does more than just make something bigger. Handled with skill it can transform the banal into the awesome.

It is also a play on materials. Timber turned to stone, and a well-known local rock joined by alien geology. Stone and timber are the steel and plastic of Hengeworld, the stuff of housing, religious structures, tools for eating and tools for killing. People knew the language of stone and wood in ways we do not.

If you look closely at the megaliths, you see that not only are sarsens and bluestones kept apart, but the various bluestones are also set up with apparently deliberate pattern. All fourteen identified stones of the horseshoe are dolerite (all spotted, bar one), while of the thirty known stones in the wider circle, only eighteen are dolerite: the others are volcanic ash or tuff (five), sandstone (two) or rhyolite (five). We can note that dolerite, on the one hand, and tuffs and rhyolites, on the other, both materials much used for tool manufacture in highland parts of Britain, have different working properties and are suited to the manufacture of different types of implement.[477] It is a practical distinction that the average contemporary observer is likely to have known.

Stonehenge is a play on space. Unlike any other stone circle, gaps between sarsens are similar in size to the stones themselves. So if we look at the sarsen circle through the eyes of contemporary British artist Rachel Whiteread, who makes casts of spaces between objects, and turn space into mass and stone to light, we see a ring of thirty squared uprights, without lintels, in direct echo of the sarsen circle yet also speaking for otherwise universal free-standing stone circles. People would have known how much labour, how much time – how many deaths, how many careers – had been spent on placing those massive stones. In teasing opposition, columns of weightless nothing rise between, as real as the stone that in turn becomes unreal.

For us Stonehenge is mysterious and unexplained. For the people in whose imaginations Stonehenge arose and lived, it was a stunning play on the familiar. For us its crude grandeur evokes a primitive ancestry glimpsed in the simplifying mists of time. For its creators Stonehenge was pushing at the limits of technology and organisation.

In all these things, architecturally Stonehenge is quite unlike Avebury. People who have lived inside that great stone circle (of whom I am one) often say that the artificial horizon created by the earthwork gives the space a comforting domesticity within the expanse of the open downs. The natural, irregular shapes of the stones deny human involvement, encourage one to see each megalith as an independent entity rather than part of a grander scheme. The whole is less forbidding, less didactic.

Yet its sheer scale still has the power to impress. And never more so than on one damp morning in 1999.

The permit for my Sanctuary excavation came through in July. Early Monday 23 August 1999, I sat in my car in the lay-by, waiting for delivery of security fencing. I watched the wind blow loose straw across the tarmac and a flight of rooks rise over the circles of concrete markers all but hidden in the grass.

Meanwhile another, much larger excavation was starting 3km to the north-west, on lower (and less exposed) ground between the hamlets of Avebury Trusloe and Beckhampton. It was going to be big (we all knew it was going to be big), but at the moment the small size of the archaeological trenches set a weird tone beside the two enormous standing megaliths and the field of giant round straw bales. Later that day, when the low sun came out from under the cloud, bright and yellow on the baled straw, I thought of the artist Paul Nash, who had visited Avebury in 1933 and again, after Keiller's restorations, ten years later. In 1934 he created a stylised landscape with two standing stones, his first painting of Avebury, and by the following year in another oil megaliths had become giant wooden drums against a square gridded panel out on the Wiltshire downs. In this field with the stones, the bales and the small holes in the ground, Nash would have known where he was.[478]

The little square holes were just testing the earth, checking up on the geophysics plots, ascertaining the depth of ploughsoil and the nature of the chalk beneath. In two days the machine would come in. They had enough money for one excavator and its operator, which was all they needed to take off the soil at a leisurely pace, so they could watch what was happening, be in control. Thanks to the new geophysics survey done by Andy Payne and Louise Martin, they had a good idea of exactly where to look.

The new magnetometer survey showed the enclosure ditch, first revealed in the 1997 air photo, particularly clearly. In fact, when English Heritage reprocessed their 1989 survey data – new software, higher-resolution printers – they could see it there, too. It had been in the numbers, but invisible in the plots. However, when Louise looked at these old illustrations, unhindered by experienced caution, she thought she could see a whole avenue of stone pits.

Three of the four that had come out so clearly in May were there, but, Louise suggested to Andrew David, there were several more. Andrew agreed to add two question marks to the plan, and the archaeologists were able to flag six possible stone sites with surveying poles.

So on Wednesday, when the machine took away the earth and revealed the top of a filled-in ditch, there was anticipation, but no surprise. They knew it was there. The next day, they would look for stone pits. Mark Gillings, ever confident, was convinced they would find the avenue, but the others were less sanguine. Dave Wheatley reckoned their chances at 50 or 60 per cent – before the spring's geophysics survey, he'd put them at only 10 per cent. Josh Pollard was the same. Until the new survey, he'd been thinking of the Longstones as part of an independent structure, nothing to do with an avenue. This was an old idea of the doubters: perhaps there'd been a stone circle there? Now he was just waiting, and hoping.

The machine started to peel back the field on Thursday. The chalk under the soil was not white, but dirty and fissured, and shallow ditches and ploughmarks from a medieval system of ridge and furrow cultivation – or rig – sprawled across the area, smudging older features. But the spots in the geophysics survey started to appear.

'We had these two anomalies partly obscured by the rig', said Mark, downing champagne with the team at the end of the dig. 'Then further up, the machine's bucket was slowly dragging over, and it made a different kind of noise.'

'But it could've been a natural sarsen', said Josh.

That was the third day of machining. It had been all right for Mark, who came rushing over screaming 'Yippee!' On the fifth day, there was no doubt. There they were: six diffuse brown splodges in the surface of the chalk, each about 5m across, precisely matching the geophysics predictions. In one of them, where the bucket had scraped something hard, you could see patches of a large sarsen. And the distances between them, 17m from side to side and 25–30m between the pairs, were the same as between stones on the West Kennet Avenue.

The machine done, they scraped away at the chalk with pointing trowels to make any features stand out. Apart from medieval fields and the six large pits, however, there seemed to be little there. Some of these were big holes, big enough to bury stones weighing perhaps up to 6 tons, in one case so that the highest part of the stone was still 60cm below the depth of the plough. 'We're the first people to see this', said Dave Wheatley as he and I stood on the edge of a pit looking at the top of a megalith rising out of the earth like an iceberg, 'since William Stukeley' (plate 18).[479]

Over sixty years ago, as we saw in chapter 16, Alexander Keiller had discovered that several complete megaliths had been felled and buried. Beneath one were the bones of the barber-surgeon. The three early fourteenth-century coins on his person are the best evidence we have for when this unexplained stone burial took place. Keiller also found copious evidence for the destruction that so appalled Stukeley. The sites of several once proud megaliths were marked by pits full of burnt straw and stone fragments.[480] And so at Beckhampton in 1999, laid out for a new generation of archaeologists and public, there were three megaliths in their medieval pits, and two shallower hollows (the original stone pits, as Keiller had found in Avebury, were not deep) packed with charcoal and burnt stone debris. The sixth pit was empty, the stone removed whole. Only the buried megaliths had survived the need to build.

It's impossible to exaggerate the impact these discoveries had on those of us who had spent much of our working lives thinking about the archaeology of Avebury. Few of us wanted to doubt Stukeley, but the fact was there hadn't been any proof for this avenue, and there was plenty of contrary gossip. Isobel Smith was sent running to her book to see if she'd got it right thirty-five years ago: naturally, she had.[481]

The work has only just begun. The stones were reburied in the ground, and soil samples and small finds await analysis. There will be more excavation. But the impact is greater than the parts of the discovery. For decades archaeologists have been arguing about old excavations and even older manuscripts, sitting at desks while cow parsley brushed against the megaliths outside. Suddenly the landscape had come to life. As Mark Gillings said: 'We've put a couple of thousand volts through the World Heritage Site.'[482]

The university-based team are a contemporary manifestation of Alexander Keiller and his private wealth. While Keiller assembled his staff ('The Morven Archaeological Institute') at home at Avebury Manor and employed men to do the heavy work, Negotiating Avebury housed student volunteers in tents at a barn hidden away on the downs, courtesy of local farmers Gill and Robin Swanton.

Keiller was fascinated by new technology: he was that creature that only archaeology could generate, a Spenglerian mechanaut obsessed with reviving the past. His wealth allowed him to have the best cinematic camera, Kodachrome colour film in the year it first appeared (Avebury Museum has a fat file of correspondence with Mr Wallace Heaton in London, whose business is still a major photographic retailer), and to exploit the latest scientific techniques for the study of his finds. So Dave Wheatley had a digital camera at Beckhampton, putting video clips of the dig onto the world wide web even as they worked.[483] They held guided tours for locals, just as Keiller had done. And as happened in Avebury in the 1930s, so today there was a strong sense of intellectual companionship, of an exciting quest into unexplored territory. The greatest difference, I believe, is that ultimately Negotiating Avebury promises to tell us more about the story of ancient Avebury than Keiller was able to achieve – even as it marshals increasingly clever science, it knows the futility of conviction.

And it's not afraid to ask Why? In the next chapter we will consider what is undoubtedly the most popular answer to this question in respect of ancient megaliths: astronomy. But there is a contradiction, for people also like to think of these prehistoric scientists as more in touch with nature than us, more intuitive and less calculating. Some argue they were also hallucinating on mushrooms. In other words, they were less scientific. How do we square this?

24

Seeing Stars

Many think the people who erected megaliths in ancient Britain were accomplished astronomers and mathematicians. Yet it is also commonly believed (not infrequently by the same people) that our Neolithic forebears were seriously into mind-altering substances. How can you be rigorously technical about space when you are spaced out? Let us first consider the presence of astronomy in Hengeworld.

While I was researching this book, Europe experienced some relatively unusual celestial phenomena: a comet that hung clearly in the sky for a week or so, and a total eclipse. The opportunity was there for a bit of author-promotion. On the world wide web, one writer explained how Stonehenge was used to predict eclipses ('The idea that Stonehenge may have been a centre for some kind of worship', he confided, 'has occurred to many').[484] Another launched a book in which, proclaimed the *Sunday Telegraph*, 'The mystery of Stonehenge may finally have been solved.' It was an early warning system for meteor storms. 'Something must have really worried the early Stonehenge people for them to have invested so much in its construction', mused the writer, 'an authority on comets'.[485]

Meanwhile, while we were staring at the sky, a Canadian astronomer told us the world's oldest map of the moon had been carved on a megalith inside the great Neolithic tomb at Knowth, Ireland. 'The people who carved this . . . knew a great deal about the motion of the moon', said the map maker. 'They were not primitive at all.'[486] I looked up the carved stone in my library, and found the astronomer had arbitrarily selected a few markings from a rich complex, even then producing a most unconvincing moon (figure 42). 'It took the eye of an expert to see it for what it was', said the BBC Online Science Editor. Indeed.

Astronomy and Stonehenge have an odd relationship. On the one hand, so much nonsense has been communicated on the topic

1. Avebury. © Mike Pitts.

2. Stonehenge. © Mike Pitts.

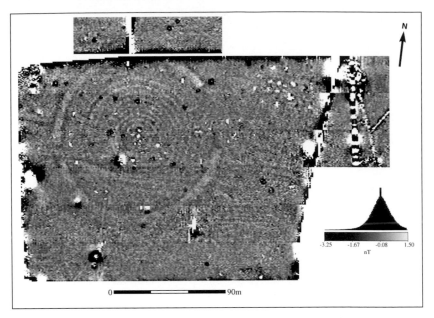

3. Stanton Drew: magnetometer survey (Sept 1997).
© Ancient Monuments Laboratory.

4. Stanton Drew: caesium gradiometer survey (Oct 1997).
© Ancient Monuments Laboratory.

5. Hawley (with moustache, seated right), Stonehenge 1920.
© Stonehenge Archive Wessex Archaeology.

6. Straightening stones 6-7, 1919-20.
© Stonehenge Archive Wessex Archaeology.

7. Straightening trilithon 53-54, 1964.
© Stonehenge Archive Wessex Archaeology.

8. *(left)* One of the four Station Stones at Stonehenge. © Mike Pitts.

9. *(right)* Sarsen 16, Stonehenge. © Mike Pitts.

10. Bluestone 36. © Stonehenge Archive Wessex Archaeology.

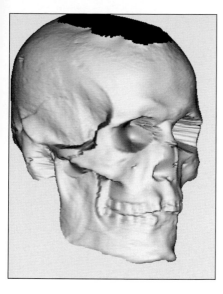

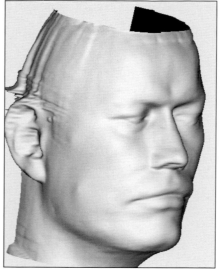

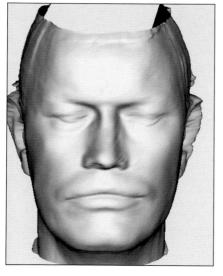

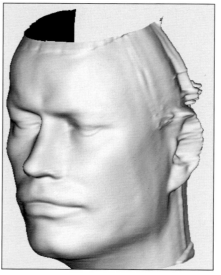

11. Digital reconstruction of
the face of the neolithic man
from Stonehenge.
© Mike Pitts.

12. Gray's excavations at Avebury stone circle. © Alexander Keiller Museum.

13. The Sanctuary in 1723 as drawn by Stukeley.

14. The Cunningtons' excavation at the Sanctuary, 1930. © Alexander Keiller Museum.

15. The author's Sanctuary excavation, 1999. © Mike Pitts.

16. *(above)* Re-erecting a stone on the West Kennet Avenue. © Alexander Keiller Museum.

17. *(above)* Excavating Seahenge, 1999. © Mike Pitts.

18. Beckhampton Avenue excavation, 1999. © Mike Pitts.

that the cynical, not least the weary academic, is wont to dismiss the issue. Personally I am moved to anger at some of the ignorant, racist, patronising claims made about our ancestors – without science like mine, runs the clear subtext, these guys were savages. On the other hand ('no smoke without fire') it is now widely taken for granted that Stonehenge did, in some vague way, have celestial connections. This is an important issue. Maybe Stonehenge *was* an observatory. We'd have to fit that into any explanation of what it meant to the people who built it.

So was it?

We are fortunate that a mathematician and astrophysicist turned archaeologist has spent the past twenty-five years researching 'archaeoastronomy' in Britain, and has collected his thoughts into a large and recently published study. My assessment relies heavily on the fruits of Clive Ruggles' work, which displays unparalleled attention to detail in both its archaeology and its astronomy.[487] To pre-empt the review, Ruggles' answer to our question is clear: no . . . but.

Most claimed evidence for deliberate orientation or alignments of monuments on bodies in the sky comes in the form of often complex statistical argument. But occasionally the archaeology and the astronomy combine so clearly that intuition alone is enough to convince. Sometimes you just step in it. That happened in 1998 when an archaeologist excavating a Neolithic tomb at Crantit in the Orkneys fell into the previously unexplored burial chamber. In the dark a small shaft of light came from the direction of the blocked entrance. Looking close, he could see the horizon on the hill across the valley.

A rough arrangement of stones over the small entrance passage had created a little window. Colin Richards was convinced this was a deliberately constructed 'light-box', through which, at mid-February, the rising sun shone into the recesses of the tomb. Beverley Ballin-Smith, Richards' co-director at the dig, disagreed. The key slab, she said, was too rough. 'I would have expected, given their skill with stonework, that they'd have removed a few bumps and made it squarer.'[488]

But as to the inspiration for Richards' light-box there is little doubt. At the huge Neolithic tomb of Newgrange in Ireland, built perhaps 5100 years ago,[489] there is also a window above the entrance through which the rising sun shines on a particular day. From above, the mound looks like an apple cut in half, 85m across.

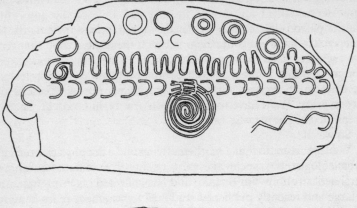

Figure 42. Moon maps. The large stone from Knowth, Ireland, has twenty-two crescents ('new moons') and seven discs ('full moon'); Brennan also points out that the snake across the middle has fifteen loops, all of which suggest to him mapping of a lunar cycle, which, given ethnographic study suggesting that most people are aware of lunar phases, is not unlikely. The smaller Knowth stone bottom left (obscured by another stone or the ground where dashed) was read to be a map of the moon's surface as drawn by Stooke (right). While Stooke's interpretation stretches credulity, Brennan's reading also needs to be considered alongside the many other Knowth stones that have similar carvings that do not represent the same pattern. *After Brennan, Eogan and Stooke.*

From the dimple where the stalk would be, a passage lined with standing stones that support a slabbed roof runs inside for 25m, ending in a cruciform chamber with an impressive corbelled dome. A large rock, covered in swirling spirals, blocked the passage entrance, but higher up there is a narrow window topped by a slab decorated with dots and circles. On midwinter day, the just risen sun shines through this opening, down the passage and onto a large, decorated stone basin on the floor at the back of the chamber.[490] Outside at the back of the mound is another heavily decorated stone. A broad vertical line cuts through the abstract swirls at the point where the continuation of the sun's rays would split the stone.

If somebody 5000 years ago had wanted to leave a message to say, look, we knew about the shortest day and the sun on that day was important to us, they could not have put it more clearly.[491] Maes Howe is a large stone chambered tomb within a round mound (built around 4700–4500 years ago, during Phase 2 at Stonehenge[492]) on the same island as Crantit in Orkney. On the shortest day, the sun shines down the tomb passage, this time when it sets.

Less well known is a group of stone circles clustered in Aberdeenshire in north-east Scotland. They were singled out for study by Aubrey Burl, and Clive Ruggles followed up with a detailed field survey. Although undated, they are thought probably to be broadly contemporary with Stonehenge (that is, sometime between 5000 and 4000 years ago), which would make them not quite as old as Newgrange. But like Newgrange, they combine a clear orientation with a distinctive construction. And there were over 100 of them; Ruggles examined sixty-four.[493]

These rings are known as 'recumbent stone circles': each has one of its stones not standing, but propped up on a long side to present a table effect. Sometimes, while other stones in the ring are local, this recumbent megalith has been brought from further afield, and scatters of white quartz fragments are common on the ground in the vicinity. Prominent stones stand at either end. In every case, this triad (a sort of upside-down Stonehenge trilithon) is on the south-west side of the circle. 'There is absolutely no doubt', comments Ruggles, 'that the orientation of [a recumbent stone circle] was of the utmost importance to its builders.'

Ruggles' fieldwork revealed that the lines of sight from inside the circles over the recumbent stones towards the horizon were unusually clear. The locations had been chosen so that this horizon was never as close as 1km. The wide foresights presented by the recumbent stones and their flanking uprights meant that it was not possible to pinpoint a precise astronomical event, but there is, says Ruggles, 'good reason . . . to suspect that observations of the moon were of particular importance'. The idea was to have the full moon pass low over the flat stone around midsummer.

So we have two striking but very different examples of astronomic orientation that it would be churlish to dismiss, one concerned with the midwinter sunrise, the other with the full moon around midsummer. These are not just events picked out by a computer. They are, first, alignments that would be easy for anyone to have made (midwinter/midsummer, compared, for example, to the equinoxes, which are less apparent to the observer than to the academic with astronomic tables). Second, archaeology offers corroborative support: the light-box construction and the decorated slabs, in addition to the general orientation of the chamber passage at Newgrange; and quartz fragments and clear horizons at the Aberdeen stone circles, as well as the highly prominent arrangements of three stones.

Is this 'science'? Consider Maes Howe, aligned, as we saw, on midwinter sunset. Victor Reijs has calculated on the basis of his own observations that when the tomb was built, the midwinter sun would have flashed inside repeatedly over a period of forty-four days.[494] So no, the precision in the alignments is too low to be called scientific.[495] There can be no doubt, though, that some people, at some time in this little corner of prehistoric Europe, were aware of systematic patterns in the movement of the sun and the moon. It is good to have this demonstrated by archaeological evidence, but it should occasion no surprise. In a review of the literature, archaeologist Nick Thorpe found that around the world it is extremely unusual for people, regardless of their technology or type of society, not to take some interest in the heavens.[496]

Thorpe made several interesting findings. Many of the claims for ancient astronomy in Britain posit sophisticated scientists concerned with detailed, technical observations of the type made famous by, for example, the ancient Maya.[497] Such science did exist, wrote Thorpe, but it was not the norm (and when it did, it was still but part of a wider system of belief, philosophy and politics). More typical was relatively simple time-keeping by movements of sun and moon ('there are very few peoples that have no knowledge of a regular lunar month'), and observation of star constellations. People used basic equipment that would often leave little for future archaeologists (sticks and shallow markings in the ground, nondescript portable artefacts and so on). He could find no documented use of anything resembling a stone circle.

The conclusion, then, is that it is more than likely that the people of Hengeworld observed the heavens, used simple astronomy to build a calendar, and did some things for purposes that we can never discover. Our task is, first, to see if they did anything more than that, and second, to establish as best we can just what they did do and how that fitted into other practices of the time. So was Stonehenge really a computer?

'Despite persistent popular belief,' says Ruggles, 'detailed reassessments of the ideas of C. A. Newham,[498] Gerald Hawkins,[499] Fred Hoyle[500] and others have shown that there is no convincing evidence that, at any stage, constructions at Stonehenge deliberately incorporated a great many precise astronomical alignments, or that they served as any sort of computing device to predict eclipses . . . there is no reason whatsoever to suppose that at any stage the site functioned as an astronomical observatory.'[501]

That sounds like 'No' to me. But I will repeat the point. No studies that have taken a proper note of archaeology, statistics and astronomy have found any evidence whatsoever that at any time any celestial observations that might have been made at Stonehenge were other than symbolic.

Douglas Heggie, in a thoughtful review twenty years ago, came to the same conclusion. He found it 'very hard to square this bleak record [which he had determined for astronomical observation] with the enthusiasm and confidence with which most accounts . . . are usually coloured'.[502] It doesn't matter how many times the claims are made, how superficially persuasive they look or how apparently convinced their promoters are of their veracity, they are all complete fantasy. When we read these accounts, we have to ask ourselves, what do we really want to do? Learn about the people who built Stonehenge? Or play games?

This should not be a surprising conclusion. Stonehenge is an old structure, ruinous, with many components missing or not fully understood. We are unsure about which posts or stones or holes in the ground were precisely present at the same time (a prerequisite for inclusion in alignments). The gaps between stones and posts, and the stones themselves, are large and irregular, and potential markers are close together. These things militate not only against our chances of establishing that there were precise alignments, but also strongly against their existence in the first place.

Most archaeologists have been unhappy with attempts to find complex scientific thinking among the motivations of the people who built Stonehenge. This is not because we are blind to their abilities (ironically, Richard Atkinson, who originally believed Stonehenge could not have been conceived by 'howling barbarians',[503] came round to some of the more extreme hypotheses). The reticence stems more from respect. The committed astronomer or mathematician reasons as if only the possession of a post-industrial-style scientific logic would redeem the primitiveness of our ancestors. It would not occur to a modern archaeologist to dismiss other people as 'primitive' just because they were different to us. We know that scientific logic is special to certain parts of our own culture (the very literature claiming complex Neolithic astronomy in itself often illustrates the point that few of us today really understand celestial observation). Science does not make us better than anyone else, any more than its absence demeans others. The people of Hengeworld had their own world-view, and it's our job to establish what that was, not to patronise them by demanding that they wear our clothes.

The same argument can be mustered against notions of a precise unit of measurement with which stone and timber circles were supposedly laid out. It is manifest in the very existence of structures like Woodhenge or the Sanctuary, let alone Stonehenge, that people were able to survey and count, and probably employed a measuring system, if only – and possibly not even consciously – by pacing. These were after all humans, and people do things like that. But in the 1960s and 1970s, Alexander Thom and his family made claims that went much further.

The Thoms divined a 'megalithic yard' of 82.9cm (precise to within less than 1mm from Orkney to Brittany) from study of hundreds of their own surveys of stone circles. All attempts by others to prove the Thoms right by informed statistical analysis have failed.[504] A stone can only be reduced to a point on a plan to a precision of its width, perhaps 1m, not 1mm. Yet the case for the 'megalithic yard' is entirely dependent on mathematical patterns fitted to such stones (or in the case of Woodhenge, of huge concrete markers placed after the site had been backfilled), in which the 'proof' is dependent on matching the abstract geometry to imaginary points much smaller than the megaliths. The megalithic yard is a figment.[505] This does not mean, in Thom's words, 'Megalithic man was our inferior in ability to think.'[506] It just means they were not us (and as I would say to my school maths teacher, his superior ability to grasp trigonometry did not make him better than me).

So if we dismiss notions of a precise unit of measurement, and of Stonehenge as a scientific observatory, does that leave anything?

The original earthwork, dug around 5000 years ago, had two smaller entrances to the south and its most prominent to the northeast. This north-easterly orientation is also seen at the approximately contemporary henge of Coneybury. The alignment of the two sites is far from identical, however. Long ancestral burial mounds are common on the chalk of southern England.[507] The best-known in Wessex is the West Kennet long barrow at Avebury, but there are several others, not least around Avebury and Stonehenge. Built between 6000 and 5000 years ago, these were mostly closed up and, if not abandoned, no longer maintained by the time of Hengeworld. The larger, access ends of the mounds show a strong tendency to face in an easterly direction throughout Britain.[508] The north-eastern orientation of Coneybury and the major gap through the Stonehenge earthwork may have been an echo of this ancient pattern. There is no unequivocal indication of an astronomical event.

Following suggestions from several writers, Ruggles considers the possibility that this earlier Stonehenge embodied lunar alignments. He dismisses many of these on astronomical grounds, but finds some 'can not be entirely discounted'; he allows a 'tentative working hypothesis' that there was 'lunar symbolism in Stonehenge 1 and 2'.[509] Archaeology, however, offers little support. There are a number of interesting features on the eastern side of Stonehenge. Cherry-picking from these (this group of cremations marks moonrise at the southern limit, so is significant; these cremations mark nothing, so we will ignore them) does not convince. A number of Wessex henges are characterised by this apparent emphasis of ritual activity on their eastern sides. Like the north-easterly orientation of the earthwork, explanations couched in tradition and ritual seem more relevant than astronomy.[510]

Set against this background, the reorientation of the site onto a precise alignment on the rising midsummer sun looks significant. It appears at the start of Phase 3, with the erection of the Altar Stone on an axis of declination +24° to the NE and −24° to the SW (which is midwinter sunset). Other features, not all necessarily added at the same time, emphasise this alignment. Sarsen circle pairs 15/16 and 30/1 and the trilithon 55/56, as well as the horseshoe as a whole, sit astride the axis. It continues between stone pit E and the Slaughter Stone at the earthwork entrance and stone 97 and the Heelstone a little further out. It also cuts through pits B and C, possible stone pits between these two pairs, and bisects the earthwork avenue, whose passage at Stonehenge is partially over the older enclosure ditch, largely refilled by this stage. Ruggles calls this the 'solar corridor' (figure 43).[511] The orientation of the timber rings at Woodhenge is similar.[512]

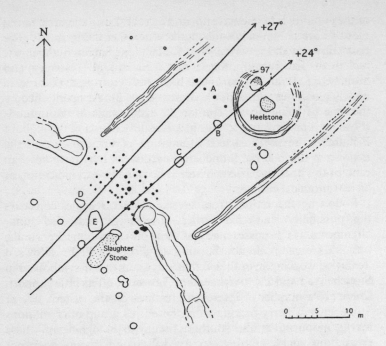

Figure 43. Stonehenge is famous for the alignment of the Heelstone on the rising midsummer sun. This is not precise, however: it is better to think of a 'solar corridor', in Ruggles' phrase, than a line. Computer-aided design established slightly different axes for the Phase 1 earthwork (declination 27°) and the stones of Phase 3 (24°). *After Cleal et al. and Ruggles.*

Maud Cunnington was the first to point out similarities in the plans of Woodhenge and Stonehenge, and she proposed a 'foot' of 11.5 inches (29cm) used to lay out the Woodhenge posts in ovals of long diameters of 40, 60, 80, 100, 130 and 150 'feet'.[513] Curiously, Alexander Thom discerned almost the same pattern in the *circumferences* of the rings, measured in his quite different 'megalithic yards' (40, 60, 80, 100, 140 and 160 'yards'). The dimensions are not in fact so regular (for example, ring D is not 80 Cunnington 'feet', but 77.2) and the measurements selected are arbitrary, as the posts are not arranged on perfect ovals but appear, rather, to be grouped in segments. Nonetheless, the numbers of posts and stones that occur in some of these sites do suggest deliberate counting and the repetition of particular quantities.

To return to the Scottish recumbent stone circles, Aubrey Burl noted that 70 per cent have 11 or 12 stones, including the prone megalith itself.[514] At Woodhenge the posts in the rings progress from 12, through 18 (two rings), 16, 32 and 60. Similar numbers are seen at the Sanctuary: 6, 8 (twice), 12, 32, 34 and 42 (the last two each have pairs at the 'entrance' that stand out from the others, so may be represented as 32 + 2 and 40 + 2). Again, at Mount Pleasant: 16, 24, 36, 48 and 52.[515] Here there are four clear segments, each consisting of 4, 6, 9, 12 and 13 posts.

Different numbers occur at Stonehenge. There are 30 sarsens in the ring (with 30 lintels), and 15 stones in the five trilithons. The only other structure whose numbers we can be sure about is the bluestone oval: the 18 stones that will remain as the horseshoe, and the wider spaced arc of five across the north-east end that is later removed. The Y and Z holes, which give the strong appearance of having been dug opposite sarsens, naturally consist of 30 in each ring (allowing for Z8 missing or hidden by a fallen sarsen). At Avebury, it looks as if the two inner stone rings each have around 29 or 30 stones, while the large outer has around 100. More work is needed before we can be precise about these figures.

Jeremy Dronfield published his first study, a pilot, in an academic book about rock art (that's art carved and painted onto big rocks). The next year, 1994, he finished the PhD and over the following two published further papers, extending the analysis to take in more art, in more detail. Cynics whined, the converted applauded, but mostly, it seemed, nothing changed. He wanted to continue the research, to look at different types of evidence, to ferret out seeds or spores, perhaps identify skeletal clues, but he couldn't get a job or a fellowship, and writing began to dominate his work. Before going to Cambridge he'd bummed around the music scene – writing and arranging in another Welsh band you never knew about – and now, after a publisher took his latest novel, he's moving into commercial literature.[516] Was no one interested in his archaeology?

I met Dronfield at a pub in the centre of Cambridge, laid back in collarless black shirt with his coke and lemon, Gitanes and silver lighter, grey-blue eyes peering through boyish fringe. The fingers on his left hand are nicotine-stained.

What happened? There were no breaks, he says. He'd been passionate about archaeology, yet three years on the dole after finishing the PhD ground him down. Oh yes, he believed quite strongly in his work (well, I had to ask). The tunnels and near-death visions, he believed in that too, though maybe not quite as firmly. When he started, no one thought he would produce a result. And when he was done, few were convinced. It was entertaining, but, well, not proper archaeology.

Perhaps it was just so obvious that people weren't ready to have it dissected and proved. A bit like the astronomy. While most of the mathematical stuff was incomprehensible, and was anyway intuitively unlikely – and so it proved, most of it – there was a kernel that wouldn't go away. Yet it remains mostly on the edge, not part of archaeologists' world-view of the past. So, as I write, rests Jeremy Dronfield's work on altered states and subjective visions: on the edge. Ready to be picked up, perhaps, by a writer with poor understanding of archaeology and used to their own ends so that no archaeologist would consider it again. Which would be a shame. Because it is an important body of research, and it adds a layer to our understanding of Hengeworld without which we'd be that little bit further out from the centre of the party. It's not a joke: some of them, it seems, really were stoned.

An early idea in recent discussions of altered states by archaeologists concerned Beaker pots. You will remember that these pots were once equated with invading peoples, but that this interpretation gave way to less sweeping links with peculiar social sects or fashions (chapter 10), or, perhaps, beer-drinking cults. The evidence for brewing consists only of an apparent increase in the cultivation of barley at the time Beakers were being made. Maybe there was a cult, involving not beer, but plant hallucinogens? Possible contenders include ergot, deadly nightshade, henbane and the mushroom, fly agaric, all native to Neolithic Britain. Marijuana and opium poppy, though not indigenous, could already have been introduced at that date. Some writers promoted fly agaric, *Amanita muscaria*, as a drug of choice associated with early historic shamans across vast areas of Asia and Europe. There were reports that urine from suitably grazed reindeer was prized as a naturally concentrated form of the chemical. Perhaps the Beaker pots were containers of hallucinogenic liquids?[517]

Archaeologists had been looking at the rock art of certain hunter-gatherers in southern Africa, where there was historical evidence for the types of ceremonies and the roles of trance and hallucinogens. Perhaps decorated caves in Palaeolithic Europe, at the end of the last ice age, might also reflect shamanic practices and trance ceremonies. The search was on for abstract 'entoptic' design elements, geometric symbols perceived by subjects whose minds are affected by certain trance-inducing substances. It was noticed that much of the 'art' in Neolithic tombs in north-west Europe fell into this category. Institutionalised altered states of consciousness, the uses of hallucinogenic substances as part of formal ritual and ceremony, were, it was said, extremely common around the world. Why should Neolithic Europe be any different?[518]

This argument has begun to spiral out of control. Claims are being made that *all* peoples (except us, out of touch here as in so many things) used psychedelics for ritual and spiritual purposes. On the more eccentric fringes, 'out-of-body experiences', powerful visions of flying, are treated as genuine physical phenomena, and Neolithic peoples seen as more 'in tune' than us with natural 'energies'.[519] Mircea Eliade's 1951 book on shamanism has become a key text in this arena. It is instructive to see how he worked.

While placing much emphasis on his study as history, in fact Eliade is completely ahistorical – in the sense that an archaeologist would use the word 'history'. His argument is that shamanism, associated with 'archaic techniques of ecstasy' (as the subtitle of the English edition puts it), was such a widespread practice across Eurasia, with occurrences elsewhere around the world, that it can be seen as the survival of a once universal primitive religion. The argument is false. If he finds a particular mythic practice, rather than attempt to relate it to similar practices amongst neighbouring peoples or at earlier or later times, charting the changes that characterise historical process, Eliade sets it up as proof of something that occurred thousands of years before. The story of why one of Thor's goats limped illustrates this well.

Out travelling, Thor stayed at a peasant's house overnight. So they might dine, Thor slaughtered his two billy-goats. As Thor and the peasant's family sat down to eat, Thor laid out the two hides and asked his hosts to save the bones on them. Too late: Thjalfi, the peasant's son, had already cracked a thigh bone for the marrow. Still, he cast the split bone onto the hides. The next morning, Thor swung his hammer, and the two goats sprang to life, good as new – except one was lame in a hind leg.

'This episode', claims Eliade, 'bears witness to the survival, among the ancient Germans, of the archaic conception held by the hunting and nomadic peoples' thousands of years before. Of course it does nothing of the sort. It is an early example of an idea that is, indeed, quite common, that the life of a creature resides in its bones, not its flesh. But to say that such an early occurrence is itself a survival of something much more ancient is utter whimsy. Eliade musters no evidence at all.[520]

It is in the context of such literature that Dronfield's research is so important. First he devised a technique for analysing abstract 'art'. He divided shapes into two classes: one where the patterns were diagnostic of 'subjective' visual experience (images produced spontaneously in the brain, by a variety of processes including trance, hallucinogenic intoxication, flickering lights, migraine or epilepsy) and the other where the images were not so created. In general he found that 'subjective' images were irregular or chaotic, while non-subjective designs were simple and geometric.[521]

He then used these design elements to analyse cases where the inspiration for the art was known: four in which subjective stimulus was known or suspected (of which one was a large sample of clinical studies); and five in which consciousness-altering was not present. The relationship between the two classes of designs and the different inspirations for specific examples of art was striking. This gave Dronfield the confidence to apply the analysis to art where the impetus was not known, specifically abstract designs pecked into large stone slabs at Neolithic tombs in Ireland, constructed some-time between 5300 and 5000 years ago.[522]

We have already been to two of these tombs, at Knowth and Newgrange, where at the latter we saw reason to believe that some elements in the designs were related to the rising midwinter sun. Dronfield's analysis makes no claims for the meaning of the designs, merely the mental conditions under which at least some of them were developed. At the eleven tombs whose designs he analysed in detail, there is convincing indication that the art was inspired by altered states of mind.

Two questions follow: what was the cause of the altered states, and how far beyond Ireland can the results of the analysis be extended? By further reference to clinical trials, Dronfield determined that three factors were likely to have been present behind the Irish tomb designs: migraine, flickering lights (such as could have been created simply by waving the hand in front of the eyes while looking at a bright source of light), and hallucinogenic substances of the lysergide group, probably derived from *Psilocybe* mushrooms.[523]

Dronfield found similar patterns, though less strongly, in some Neolithic tombs in Brittany, but the problem in trying to extend the

Figure 44. Later Neolithic decoration throughout Britain has a family feel, in which abstract geometric patterns prevail over rare facial representations. Clockwise from top left (not to scale): pecked designs on stone slab at Knowth; polished flint 'macehead' from Knowth (length 8cm); engraved chalk plaque from Amesbury, near Stonehenge (height 7.5cm); Grooved Ware pots from East Anglia (shown in section on left sides); two of three carved chalk drums from Folkton, Yorkshire; another plaque from Amesbury; carved antler 'macehead' from Garboldisham, Norfolk. *After Eogan, Harding, Piggott and Simpson.*

geographical scope of the study is that the richness of the designs on the Irish tombs is rarely repeated. There is a range of simple abstract designs – spirals, diamonds, parallel lines and so on – that occurs throughout Hengeworld in a wide variety of media, including stone slabs at tombs (in Ireland and Scotland), objects of bone, stone and antler, and pottery – and probably, one imagines, materials that do not survive, such as fabrics and carved timber, body paint and tattoos (figure 44). There was clearly a community of design concepts which, in parts of Ireland at least, was partially inspired by altered states of mind, but elsewhere the relative simplicity of the surviving 'art' does not allow Dronfield's complex analysis. For example, Carrowkeel Ware, decorated pottery found around the Irish tombs, and the Grooved Ware that succeeds it, convey no evidence for altered states. Thus the absence for this inspiration in the 'art' (such as we also see in Grooved Ware in Britain) does not prove that altered states of mind were not present in certain ritual contexts.

There is no direct evidence for altered states of mind in Wessex at the time of Hengeworld. However, we do have two relevant observations. The great majority of human societies practise some form of consciousness-altering (rarely if ever in the purely secular and hedonistic fashion that characterises our own world).[524] Second, there is convincing evidence that this was occurring in nearby communities of similar age to Hengeworld (the Irish tombs are roughly contemporary with the first phase at Stonehenge),[525] using similar technologies and constructing houses and religious monuments of analogous forms. Thus it seems we are justified in hypothesising that altered states were indeed a component of some ceremonies of Hengeworld. This may sound circumspect, but it is a great deal further than previous studies have been able to take us. It remains for archaeology to provide the evidence for the actual use of hallucinogenic plants, which has as yet only tentatively been suggested for henbane, found with a Grooved Ware sherd in Scotland in a context difficult to interpret.[526]

What is the answer to the contradiction posed at the start? As drugs for us are a plaything, an expensive commodity of style, status and escape from reality, so most writers on astronomical observations in Hengeworld imagine a context removed from social meaning, games for boys in a clinical world. It would never have been thus. If some form of celestial observation was present, which it clearly was, and if mind-altering practices were a component of some ceremonies, which they seem to have been, then all this would have been part of a rich mix of ritual, tradition and occasion that had meanings far beyond the rarefied, nerdy discussions that characterise so much of the literature.

So yes, they knew something about 'astronomy'. Yes, they probably sometimes deliberately induced altered states of mind, perhaps helped by drugs. But they were not scientists. They were people, members of that particular society at that particular time that I have chosen to call 'Hengeworld'. Understanding what the astronomy meant, what they hoped to gain from experiencing altered states, are not technical questions, but part of our grand project to enter their world. It is time to move on to the last component of our material triad: earth, stone, and now timber.

25

The Lintels Are All Wonky

Jennifer Garofalini, a Canadian research student in Wheatley's department at Southampton University, was creating a virtual reality model of the Sanctuary. I saw the site as free-standing posts rather than roofed buildings, and using the new information in Young's diaries I had supplied Jen with ideas about how it might have been.

Among the distinctive features of the Sanctuary are two rings of 'double post holes'. Maud Cunnington described a post pipe at each end of most pits in the Bank Holiday ring. But the oval pits in the smaller Ten-Foot ring had a pipe only in the outer end. Young disagreed. He was confident that the Ten-Foot ring also consisted of pits with a post at each end. If posts were all standing together, these inner post pipes in the Ten-Foot ring would be a timber circle not described before.

But the diaries were getting confusing. I had realised there were two sets, the shorter derived from the longer, yet this revised edition seemed to contain the odd new snippet. Only a few days before we stripped the turf, I found scraps of a third set in Avebury Museum – the original draft that had to have once existed. Written in pencil on a variety of pieces of loose paper were a few days' notes that, by apparent good luck, included the single post hole section drawing that appeared in the longer fair copy.[527] Yet this draft too had something that the other versions did not: a plan of the sectioned post hole. Did it hold the key to the contradictions between Young's record and Cunnington's? Only excavation was going to sort this out.

When I went to see Jen at her computer, it was clear she was unhappy about the model. 'It just doesn't work', she said. Rising from a virtual turf was a mass of virtual wood-effect posts and genuine Avebury megaliths. It was impressive. By pressing the buttons you could move among the posts and stones. I had never seen anything like it. After years puzzling at two-dimensional plans, here was the real thing. My imagination took me away: images of intricately carved poles I had seen in north-west Canada, of dried cattle skulls hanging from posts in Madagascar, of rain lashing freshly barked wood . . .

'It just doesn't work. There's no space to walk around. The double posts obstruct everything.'

I could see what she meant. There were so many posts, so close together, that you could make no sense of anything. Even with the help of the lintels I had suggested – some connecting the double posts, others in rings – it was impossible to disentangle one ring from another. And we had the advantage that we could fly over it. Which was just as well, because on the ground we had difficulty getting in through the ring of stones and posts that presented an almost solid wall.

'And the D ring', she continued. 'The lintels are all wonky. It's sort of like somebody put it in the wrong place.'

No, there was something here that didn't add up.[528]

Although very few people actually visit the Sanctuary (you can see concrete bollards in your supermarket car park) it's almost as well known as Silbury Hill or the stone circles in Avebury. Since Stukeley saw it as the head of his serpent, it's had a role. One I particularly like was described to me by a visitor to the dig (well, we *had* just been on breakfast TV). The Sanctuary, he said, was a charnel house where the bones of the dead were stored. When a birth took place, the ancestral remains were carried ceremonially down the West Kennet Avenue into Avebury, so they could greet the newborn. Has to be.

Down in the valley between the Sanctuary and Silbury there used to stand, around the same time as these two contrasting essays in circularity, timber structures that vastly outscaled the Sanctuary. They were spotted in 1950, only twenty years after the original Sanctuary excavation, in an air photo. In 1973 the then Avebury Museum curator, Faith Vatcher, confirmed that at least one of the ditches was approximately contemporary with the stone circles, and that it had held large posts (a pipe trench had been dug through it). Alasdair Whittle dug the first of several trenches there in 1987 which eventually revealed the site to be spectacularly large.[529] Yet it is still little-known (figure 45).

If an earthwork is big enough, it gets noticed today. You can't

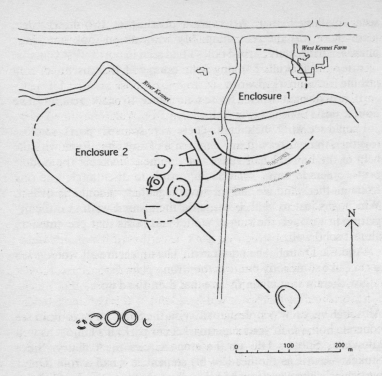

Figure 45. The two timber palisaded enclosures at West Kennet, Avebury, and associated timber structures. *After Whittle*.

miss the megaliths in Avebury. But you need to be reminded that there were some very large timber structures in Hengeworld, too. It wasn't just large stones – megalithic – but large trees too: megadendric. We saw (chapter 4) that Cunnington had estimated some of the Woodhenge posts were 9m long and weighed over 5 tons. An actual Neolithic oak was pulled from the peat of the Cambridgeshire fens in 1961, in which the trunk had risen for over 20m before branching.[530] Like megaliths, these could be heavy, impressive things.

The two West Kennet enclosures, rising as much as, or even more than, 8m above the ground, were set out in irregular ovals, the eastern having two circuits. As well as three smaller rings inside the western enclosure, there were various straight lengths of palisade, including one that ran over 200m towards yet another ring palisade. That's a lot of timber.

At Mount Pleasant, Wainwright estimated that to build the palisade enclosure, similar in size to one of those at West Kennet, people would have needed to search 360ha of oak forest.[531] Just Phase 2 of the Southern Circle at Durrington Walls consumed over 250 tons of oak.[532] All these places are dwarfed by Hindwell, however. Recent excavations by Alex Gibson at this cropmark site in Powys have identified this as another Neolithic palisade, enclosing an enormous 34ha.[533]

Mount Pleasant and Durrington Walls are beside the River Avon, so timber could have been floated at least part of the way to the construction sites. But at West Kennet, even if the present stream was there, of which we can't be certain (if it was, it would have flowed through the middle of the eastern enclosure), there was no navigable water. All timber would have been dragged overland. Indications are that when the Kennet enclosures were built, much of the surrounding landscape was grassland.[534] It is not improbable that acquiring so much timber meant spreading out over quite a wide area of the local landscape, or even further afield.

Because they leave no trace above the surface of the ground, timber structures are found only by chance. It is more than likely that others lie undiscovered in the Avebury district. Geophysics inside the north-east sector of Avebury henge have identified some marks that are strongly suggestive of a timber henge there, but excavation is needed to prove it.[535]

How was all this timber cut and shaped? There was a tradition extending back through the Neolithic of making heavy-duty axeheads with a variety of stone types. Some of these axes, probably through a combination of exchange and the movement of owners, travelled the length of the British Isles. But generally, the best local materials were used, for example flint in south-east England, or metamorphosed sediments (such as porcellanite in Antrim) in northern Ireland and Scotland.

The axes were made by flaking and pecking, and finished by grinding, which, particularly with the more brittle rocks like flint, greatly increased their working strength.[536] Many people have cut down trees with replica or original stone axes, but new experiments are needed. Most of the work has been done by men unskilled in the peculiar use of a stone axe, and almost all has been with small trees.

Nonetheless, it is clear that these tools were effective at tree felling, and a pine tree of, say, 25cm girth could be felled in a matter of minutes.[537]

Using an axe he made with flint, and another with fine green rock from the Lake District, Phil Harding has cut down a few dozen trees, the largest being a 45cm silver birch.[538] Some Neolithic bone tools have been found in Denmark which, in replica, were effective at carving out a mortise in a small softwood pole;[539] it's possible that bone chisels found in Britain, including one from Stonehenge, were used for carving fresh wood.[540] Limited experiments have suggested that hardwoods blunt stone much faster than softwoods.[541] The large oaks used in Hengeworld – 50cm across (at West Kennet) or even 1m (Arminghall, Norfolk: chapter 5) – would have commanded considerable time from skilled lumberjacks with a range of tools.

It is often noted that post pipes are lined with oak charcoal. One idea is that posts were charred in a belief that this would extend their life in the ground. Another possibility is that fire was used to tidy up tree boles, removing small branches and bark.[542] Again, there is scope for large-scale experiments.

For the time being, however, building timber henges was something we were doing in hyperspace. But we *were* getting dirt up our fingernails.

Excavating at the Sanctuary completely changed my ideas about the place, and has made me wonder about other timber henges. There were several surprises (plate 15).

We sieved all the soil we removed, so we could see what the Cunningtons had left, however small. Until quite recently, archaeologists tended to discard all flintwork unless they could see it was an implement, like an arrowhead. In this way a great deal of information was lost, and it is likely that quite a few tools were missed – at the best of times, identifying flint artefacts is not easy. Nonetheless, it was a surprise to find so much stuff: quantities of knapping debris, suggesting stone-working on the spot, and a remarkable collection of arrowheads. The Cunningtons found four or five on the whole site in 1930 – we found nine in their backfill of this tiny part of the site. Even for the most hardened field archaeologist, the discovery of a beautifully made 4000-year-old flint arrowhead is an exciting moment.

But all this sieving slowed us down. At first it was difficult to know exactly what we were doing. The concrete posts told us where the Neolithic pits were supposed to be, but we found that that was not necessarily where they actually were. In one case, a post had been broken and replaced twice, ending up nearly 1m from its original location. It was as if the site were still alive, far from the fossil it appeared.

Offerings had been buried near some of these posts, including polished stones bought from the souvenir shop in Avebury, crystals, beads and coins whose dates suggest this is a recent phenomenon: ten were less than five years old, and all but one of the other eight were no older than 1986. The number of foreign coins suggests either an international following, or parsimony on the part of British worshippers offloading holiday change! There was one other coin, away from the others, a 1930 US cent. It may be that the Cunningtons themselves left this as a calling card. Their ancestor William Cunnington used to put little metal plaques with his initials (WC) and the date of the dig at the bottom of his trenches. Perhaps Maud did the same with ready-minted coins?

Not only did these finds slow us down, but when we got to the bottom of the topsoil it was clear that identifying the top edges of the post pits was going to be difficult. None of the records told us what to expect: the impression is of nice discrete pits. The chalk, it turned out, is not clean and hard, but crumbly and fissured with dirt. We had to take it slowly, because this would be the last chance anyone had to examine these post holes. We halved the area of our trench, leaving two large pits for future investigators.

Eventually we found the tops of the eight post holes we were to excavate. It was difficult to believe that each had held a post simultaneously, they were so close together. Some undoubtedly had been dug across others. If the Cunningtons had not excavated before us, we would have put strings out all over the ground, and cut sections down that would have told us which pit had been cut through which. Now we couldn't tell. I thought of Jennifer Garofalini's VR model, and the impenetrable maze of posts. She was right: they *weren't* all standing at once.

I had been hoping that there might still be some Neolithic fill in the pits, mistaken for solid chalk in 1930. Young's diaries showed they did sometimes have difficulty distinguishing rock from hard backfill. We were in luck. One of the double post holes had a step at one end, 50cm high.[543] Like our predecessors, we thought it was rock. It was only after the hole had been open to the weather for a week, and I had plucked up the courage to start hacking out what still seemed like solid chalk, that we were all proved wrong. It was Neolithic pit fill, almost pure, hard-packed chalk. When I dug it out, there was still a step, half the height of the original. The next day I found that this too was in fact Neolithic packing.

Josh Pollard and I thought hard about this. What did it mean? It seems to me the best way of explaining everything we found is to imagine that what appeared to all of us as a large, oval-shaped pit was actually the combined effect of at least five circular post holes dug very close together.

In his diaries, Young had described the adjacent pit in detail, the only one for which we have a section drawing. Comparing our records of the two pits, you could be forgiven for thinking that we were in fact talking about two completely different places. But eventually it all came to make sense. Young had described 'recesses' at the end of these big double pits, and it was in these that the inner post pipes were found. We could now see that these 'recesses' were in fact what Cunnington described as a separate ring of pits, her Seven-Foot ring. You don't get this from the published record, but in fact the pits of this ring cut into (or were cut away by, we can't now tell which) the oval pits. Young described the whole lot as if it were one big pit. So in fact the double pit only had one post pipe, 25cm across, at the outer end, as described by Maud Cunnington; the other one in his diary was inside the Seven-Foot post hole.

Were all these five big pits dug to hold posts, despite the fact that there was only one pipe? And how do we reconcile Young's fervent conviction that the entire fill of this hole was in fact simultaneous? The answer, I suggest, is that many circular pits were dug and refilled in rapid succession. There was no time for timber to rot, for soil to fall into the pit and contaminate the chalk, for packed chalk rubble to become cemented by percolating rainwater. The purity of the fill might even suggest that the site had been completely stripped down to a chalk surface. If each pit held a post, an idea I favour, these were removed. Only the last was left to decay in place.

This could hardly have occurred beneath a heavy thatched roof, confirming the idea that these sites were displays of free-standing posts (figure 46). It is time to recognise the force of the new evidence. At Stanton Drew, the rings are so vast they cannot possibly have been roofed. At Durrington Walls, where the old ground surface around the post holes was better than normally preserved, the archaeologists looked for but did not find evidence for water running off a roof, implying that the rain fell uninterrupted between open poles. Here at one of the smallest timber henges, the posts at the Sanctuary were also standing free. We are looking at a tradition of timber henges, as Maud Cunnington originally envisaged at Woodhenge itself – could we but see them complete, structures comparable to Stonehenge, in wood.

Figure 46. In 1940, Piggott published a photograph of John White's 1585 watercolour of people in Virginia, USA, 'wth. strange iesturs and songs dansing about posts carued on the topps lyke mens faces' (looking remarkably like Elizabethan court dancing through White's eyes). However, Piggott preferred the image of 'great dim raftered halls of magic and ritual' as interpretation of sites like Woodhenge and the Sanctuary, to 'the forests of naked posts in which we have all so long and so dismally wandered'. *After White.*

But more than that, this extraordinary process of pit regeneration encourages us to look at the Sanctuary in a new light. It suggests that the old way of identifying discrete 'phases' misses the point. There were many phases, there was one phase. This was not a building like a cathedral, architectural styles succeeding one another over centuries. It was not a monument at all: it was a process.

The day I turned up to backfill, there were two women seated in the grass outside our little security fence. They had thrown some fresh herbs over the top, and one bunch had fallen into an excavated pit. We talked, and I brought them inside to show them what we had found. I offered to split the herbs, and put a piece at the bottom of each pit before I backfilled. So my final poking about was done with a strong smell of lavender filling the Neolithic post holes.

That's what the Sanctuary is about: ceremony, not concrete. So in the Neolithic, the important thing was the observance, the activity. Going out into the wildwood to find the tree, felling it, dragging it to site, carving it, digging the pit, hauling the thing into place (the absolute minimum required). And this process was so important that to allow it to continue, the post had to be removed and the pit filled. Then the cycle could begin again. A continuously repeating megadendric ritual.

At the end of a huge processional way – the West Kennet Avenue – what could be more appropriate than a place of ceremony, movement and effort? Perhaps the present state of the Sanctuary, an airy waste populated by eccentrics, visionaries, past spirits and the occasional excavator, is nearer an ancient truth than any of us imagined.[544]

We have been blinded by monumentality. In Europe medieval churches and cathedrals impress us with their mass, their architectural power and their permanence. Yet we forget that when they were built, they were not treasured antiques, but centres of vision and activity: of music, singing, chanting, speech; of ceremonies, from inductions of bishops to the burial of kings; of the largest gatherings of people ever seen in their districts. And the buildings themselves were constantly changing, as successive priests set their architectural mark and minor monuments and memorials came and went. Like a modern town centre, a typical Gothic cathedral must almost have had the appearance of a permanent construction site, where unparalleled engineering feats, sky-reaching scaffolding with a high death record, and huge stocks of timber, stone and sand pulsated under swarms of people and clouds of dust.

So, even more so, it must have been in Hengeworld. The timber and stone rings were not just silent ruins before the decay. They were parts of places where people focused their thoughts and efforts, accumulating traditions and memories and inspiring imaginations. As we begin to draw everything together, we need not only to think of all the new ideas, finds and dates – the timber henges and the superhenge earthworks, the integral position of Stonehenge, the certain knowledge that people brought stones to Wiltshire from Wales, and that Stonehenge is engineered like wood not because its architects knew no other way but because that's how they chose to do it, the possibility that some ceremonies demanded altered states of mind, a symbolic but definitely not scientific interest in the sun and moon, and the recurrent presence of human remains – we need to think not only of such things, but also of the living people themselves, their thoughts and their actions.

And the best way to do that is to embrace the stones and get out there with them.

PART IV:

Stonehenge of the Ancestors

26

All for the Ancestors

I want to tell you two stories about stones. The first was researched by anthropologist Miriam Kahn, working in Papua New Guinea twenty or so years ago. It is a moving tale set in a coastal village named Wamira.[545]

Once, long ago, when people first came to this stony shore, two lineages settled close to each other. From the start there was a little controversy over which lineage was the senior, but it was established – the Aurana people say through trickery – that the Maibouni people with their leader Tauribariba were the 'elder brothers'.

Some time later both groups moved a few kilometres down the shore. On arrival, they looked around and noticed that their leader Tauribariba was not to be seen. Someone realised he was still back at the old village, so a canoe was sent to fetch him and his sister, Tauanana. On their return, some large waves caught the canoe and Tauanana fell into the sea. A crowd of people managed to save Tauribariba, and carry him to the safety of the village centre, where, all these years later, he still stands, one of several stones in a circle about 5m across. He watches over the taro gardens, and walks about at night. Wherever you see a column of smoke rising into the air, there goes Tauribariba, for he can make fire from nothing.

'But look,' Kahn was told by a Maibouni man by the name of Osborne Kaimou, 'today he is not there!'

Although Kaimou described Tauribariba as if he were still in the village, in fact about forty years before, Mr Bodger, a priest from the Anglican Mission a couple of kilometres inland, had demanded the stone, so that he could cement it into the wall of his new cathedral. Tauribariba, wrote the triumphant Anglican cleric at the time of the deed, 'is safely embedded in concrete and its wandering days are over. Even so have the children of darkness and superstition become living stones in the House of God's building – His Church.'

'When Father Bodger took Tauribariba,' Osborne Kaimou said to Miriam Kahn, 'he did not just take a stone. He took the entire identity and spirit of the Wamiran people.'

On the western edge of the Indian Ocean, high in the mountains of Madagascar, are megaliths that would not be out of place in Avebury. One day in 1989 Arsène Randrianasolonjanahary took me to see the largest standing pair of stones in his village of Andina. As he talked, the tune to 'Abide With Me' drifted across from a Victorian pedal organ in a modest iron and timber Adventist church, the first Christian building to appear in Andina. Chapel and megaliths rose in isolation, away from houses.

Stones are normally erected in pairs, said Arsène, one taller and squarer (male), the other squatter and rounder (female). These two had been brought from the quarry – he gestured vaguely to the west – to the accompaniment of ox sacrifices every 20 to 100m. The larger stone had proved particularly difficult to erect, so the priest determined that a human sacrifice was required. Accordingly a slave was killed, and buried in the stone pit. His name was Lavavelo, and the place is known as Lavaville. Three hundred bulls were sacrificed, Arsène told me, when these two stones were put up.

Tauribariba, once in a circle but now walled up (Tauribariba, it must be said, is only 15cm high), and the 4m high megalith on Madagascar have a message for us before we embark on a final tour of our own stones. Archaeologists, astronomers, guidebook writers, anyone looking at the stones today, see grand sweeps: circles, avenues, rows, patterns in the landscape. The stones get lost in the crowd. Yet each megalith, a major investment in organisation and time, and with who knows what narrative associations, would once have had its own identity.

We can create a personality for a stone, by looking at its peculiar history (much of it often the recent story of its archaeology), its unique physical characteristics, its location and so on.[546] But that has little to do with its original persona, just as, only a few generations after the stones in Papua New Guinea and Madagascar were erected, already their stories are being reworked (and just as medieval folk tales about British stone circles have absolutely nothing to do with the original monuments). We can never know those lost prehistoric sagas, but we must remember that once they were an important part of the world we would understand. And not just the stones: every post, every tree, every bend in the river, every pot and bone had its meaning, and every person brought their own experiences and personality into an ever-changing world whose richness we can imagine but never know.

To make sense of the past, we need to know which events occurred at the same time. To this end, I have compiled tables of radio-carbon dates. Dates need to be assessed critically, as has occurred at Stonehenge, a process that would reject many and in some cases improve on the precision of the bare dates.[547] This is a huge task, beyond a book like this. I have selected dates relevant to the story of Hengeworld, particularly in Wessex, and listed them without judgement. This glosses over potential problems, but it's enough for now. It is, I believe, the largest such general listing of calibrated dates yet assembled. The detailed information appears in Appendix 2, where sites are listed alphabetically, and the dates are combined with those from Stonehenge in Appendix 3, where they are listed in chronological order.

So, let us begin with dates for what most interests us, the area around Stonehenge when the megalithic monuments were being built (figure 47).

After all that fieldwork and excavation, it comes as a shock to find how much in the dark we are: for the Stonehenge area at this period of around five centuries, we have fewer than twenty dated events! Most of these are at Durrington Walls and Stonehenge itself – only three of the hundreds of round barrows are even approximately dated. The complex South Circles at Durrington Walls are 'dated' by only two 'contexts': the single post hole 92, and a bulked sample from five different holes. The 95 per cent confidence range for the mean of these samples spans 270 years, but common sense suggests we should allow a yet higher guesstimate range for activity at the site. That is not to say it was busy for centuries, just that centuries blanket the precise time of that activity. The conventional interpretation of the South Circles is as a two-phase structure. Things may have been much more complex.[548] We still have a great deal of work to do on dating the Stonehenge environment.

Bearing in mind that the earliest stone structures at Stonehenge (the bluestone-holding Q and R holes) are amongst the *undated* features, it is clear that, over a number of generations, large stones and posts were being moved about at Woodhenge, Durrington Walls and Stonehenge. It is possible to pick a date, say 4200 years

Figure 47. Radiocarbon dates for Stonehenge area at time of stone monuments.

Site	cal BC: calibrated date range (95% confidence)	years ago (cal BC mean +2000)	Stonehenge phase
Durrington Walls ditch, primary	2617–2304	4460	
Durrington Walls North Circle	2836–2038	4435	
Stonehenge, Avenue at Stonehenge	2571–2239	4405	3
Stonehenge, end of ditch filling	2460–2210	4335	End 2
Stonehenge, Avenue 900m from Avon	2466–2201	4335	3
Durrington Walls South Circle	2471–2201	4335	
Stonehenge, large sarsen structures	2461–2205	4335	3ii
Stonehenge, human skeleton in ditch	2398–2144	4270	3
Woodhenge ditch, primary	2394–2039	4215	
Amesbury 51, burial + Beaker, bronze awl	2294–1978	4135	
Stonehenge, bluestone circle and oval	2267–1983	4125	3iv
Stonehenge, Avenue 42m from Stonehenge	2326–1919	4125	3
Durrington 7, 2 juveniles, 1 cremated	2456–1777	4115	
Stonehenge, Avenue at Stonehenge	2281–1832	4055	3
Amesbury 39, cremation with amber and jet	2272–1741	4005	
Durrington Walls ditch, secondary	2196–1697	3945	

Amesbury 51, Durrington 7, Amesbury 39 are round barrows. See Appendices 1–3 for details.

ago (2200 years before the Christian era), when the sarsens and bluestones at Stonehenge, the Avenue earthwork, Woodhenge and the superhenge at Durrington Walls as well as posts at the South Circles might all have been standing together. At this time also the earlier round barrows may have been appearing. One's view on this depends on how much one sees the relationship between Grooved Ware and Beaker pottery as exclusively chronological (Beakers succeeding Grooved Ware: see figure 12). If this is the case, then most round barrow burials, perhaps all, would be slightly more recent. If early Beakers are seen as wholly funerary vessels, however, they may have been buried at the same time as Grooved Ware was in use at Durrington Walls. The details can be confusing, but generally we are in the land of simultaneous megalithic and megadendric ceremony.

If we look at individual sites, we find that posts and stones are often together in one place. The conventional spin is that stones were erected a few generations after posts, by people wishing to perpetuate the sanctity of a place with their own, more permanent mark.[549] This idea was inspired by Stonehenge, where Aubrey Hole posts predated the megaliths, and where nearby Woodhenge was seen as a Neolithic precursor to the Bronze Age megaliths. Radiocarbon dates for posts and stones at Mount Pleasant in Dorset seemed to confirm the sequence: first posts, then stones.

Things look different now. We know Stonehenge was not an anachronistic Bronze Age flowering of a Neolithic idea, but an integral part of Hengeworld, contemporary with many large timber henges. With this different perspective, if we look again at timber henges with megaliths we see it is realistic to think of posts and stones as contemporary.

In southern England it is only at Mount Pleasant that we have radiocarbon dates seeming to indicate a timber to stone sequence. The picture is not as clear as we would like. Not one of the 166 excavated post holes nor the fifteen pits that may have held stones is dated. We know that the ditch surrounding them was dug around 4400 years ago,[550] and we assume that the posts were erected at the same time. When the posts were showing signs of significant decay, if they hadn't completely disappeared, quantities of sarsen flakes were thrown into the ditch. The excavator, Geoff Wainwright, interpreted this as evidence for stone-shaping, and thus erection. Grooved Ware pottery (common in the centuries around 4500 years ago: see figure 12) is found at the bottom of the ditch, but Beaker pottery (4000 years ago) higher up, at the level of the stone debris. In 1970 Stonehenge was still thought of as Bronze Age, so the sequence of Stone Age wood, Bronze Age stone seemed to have been confirmed.

However, it is equally possible to read the evidence as indicating that stones had been erected at the same time as posts, but were smashed up – hence the debris – around four centuries later.[551] The only clear case we have in the whole of the British Isles for extensive stone-dressing is at Stonehenge. The debris at Mount Pleasant lies in the ditch with heaps of charcoal: burning is more likely to accompany destruction than carving. Even the stone pits have bits of broken megalith in them. If we look at the plan we see that the megaliths were carefully arranged within the four sectors of the posts, never once going so close to a post that it would have been difficult for them to have stood together (figure 20).[552]

We see the same subtleties of plan at other sites. At the Sanctuary there is a megalith, like the two at Woodhenge, standing between posts, aligned parallel with the post rings. One ring consists of alternating posts and stones; never do stone pits get so close to post pits as to interfere. The whole arrangement is enclosed by a ring of stones, just as at Stanton Drew – where we await excavation with bated breath – and the stone circle neatly fills a space between the hundreds of wooden posts and the ditch.

The sequence at Stonehenge may not be so relevant. The single ring of posts in the Aubrey Holes is unlike the multi-ring henges, and may be significantly older. As for the stones, carved into shape with tongue and groove and ball and socket joints, they embody wood technology in stone: they are timber made stone.

If posts and stones were standing together, this begs the question, why? What was it that required both materials, so different in sourcing, handling, appearance and subsequent weathering? And not just stones, but sarsen and bluestone from so far away. What did they mean?

One answer to the use of both stone and timber, the answer we will run with, was given by Madagascan archaeologist Ramilisonina. Brought to England by Mike Parker Pearson and the BBC,[553] shivering in his thick black coat and woolly hat, he walked into the centre of Stonehenge and exclaimed:

'This is all for the ancestors!'

Ramilisonina and Parker Pearson developed their ideas in a controversial paper that emphasised the role of ancestors at Stonehenge and proposed that stone was associated with the dead, while wood was used in ceremonial sites for the living.[554] The theory was not just plucked from the air – and as we shall see, it can help us make sense of these enigmatic monuments. So why stone for the ancestors?

In some respects the people of Hengeworld were much like us. They needed to eat, sleep, keep warm, have sex. We can make more probabilistic statements derived from consideration of different human societies. Perhaps, for example, most people, regardless of historical context, believe in a continuation of existence after death, and revere their ancestors (there are cross-cultural studies claiming just that).[555] This being so, then funerary rituals in Hengeworld may in part tell us about how people related to their ancestors and perceived the afterlife. On the other hand, every group of people has its special history, its own blend of technology, natural resources and so on. Archaeology can illuminate this, and effect a blend of the particular and the general to tell the unique story of a specific time and place. Along the way, anthropology can again be useful in helping us to understand various details, such as the movement of megaliths, that we do not encounter in our normal lives.

Archaeology, then, depends on analogies between different societies.[556] Parker Pearson and Ramilisonina made such an analogy between Neolithic Wessex and recent Madagascar. But why accept this one, and not another? With good reason, they say. Standing stones are common and important in many parts of Madagascar, and are intimately associated with rites involving the ancestors. Ancestral rites do seem to be a very common concern in kinship-based societies, so to make the leap from stone/ancestors in Madagascar to a parallel connection in Britain may not be as dramatic as it at first seems. Centuries before Stonehenge was built, sarsens in the Avebury district had been used for chambers in burial mounds, and in areas of Britain where hard stone is common, earlier Neolithic tombs are often stone-built. On this evidence, archaeologists had already suggested that stone might have stood as a metaphor for ancestors.[557]

The way in which stone is seen as a material that brings people together in Madagascar may also apply to Neolithic Britain. Using large stones requires organised, team effort, in Britain just as in Madagascar. And stone, by definition, is hard, dry, durable and solid, a material analogy for the timelessness and permanence of the ancestors that contrasts with the soft, perishable wood of houses for the living and memorials for the recent dead.

We can draw on a completely different analogy, with the recent peoples of the north-west coast of America and Canada. Documented particularly well in the nineteenth century are the huge carved cedar poles that were erected for various reasons, often memorial and sometimes for the physical containment of human remains. Despite the effort that went into producing and shaping these 'totem' poles, and in many cases the supreme quality of the craft and art, they were not maintained but left to decay, physical reminders of the passage of the dead from the world of the living to that of the ancestors. However we interpret it, this physical distinction was a given in Hengeworld. Timber perishes, stone lasts. Posts at the Sanctuary were removed and replaced and, within a few years, were gone; if they hadn't been broken up for housing three centuries ago, stones would still be standing.

Official 'Christian' funerary ritual in our world does not dwell on it, but in reality death is rarely encountered as an event. For those still living, someone is not 'alive' one minute and 'dead' the next, but enters a liminal world where objective knowledge of a person's physical demise conflicts with a lingering sense that they are still present. This experience can be the more powerful depending on how close the deceased was to the individual, and how strong was their position in the community at large. Many societies clothe the occasion in intense ritual, helping, as they see it, the newly dead to escape this liminal tie to the living, and people to make the psychological and social adjustments.

In Madagascar structures of wood, which include posts beside tombs and megaliths, are associated with the recent dead, and stones with the ancestors who have made that ultimate transition. Carved wooden poles erected in the south commemorated individuals (in some cases with sculpture of astonishing virtuosity, left outside, like memorial poles on the Pacific coast of Canada, to fade gently with the memories). Conceptually, the bones in stone tombs are not so much groups of people as collective ancestry.[558] Ramilisonina and Parker Pearson's proposal is that the same material connections can be made in Late Neolithic Wessex.

Back on Salisbury Plain, most of the stones are at Stonehenge, while most of the posts are 3km to the north-east at Durrington Walls and Woodhenge. The model suggests that on one hand we have a place for the dead, on the other for the quick: what Parker Pearson and Ramilisonina termed the 'domain of the ancestors' and the 'domain of the living'. Without any reference to stones, but instead to finds made in excavations, Josh Pollard had already labelled Woodhenge and Durrington Walls as places for celebrations of everyday existence, and Stonehenge for ancestors.[559]

Looking at these relatively well-excavated sites – Stonehenge, Durrington Walls and Woodhenge – we notice several things that need explaining:

There are large quantities of pottery and flint arrowheads at Durrington Walls and Woodhenge, but very little of either at Stonehenge.

At Durrington Walls and Woodhenge animal remains are predominantly pig, at Stonehenge cattle. There are more bones from wild animals at Stonehenge and Woodhenge.

At Stonehenge, Woodhenge and probably the South Circles at Durrington Walls, most signs of activity are on the east sides.

Stonehenge and Woodhenge are orientated on midsummer sunrise, Durrington Walls is not.

Approximately opposite the earthwork entrance at Woodhenge are two megaliths surrounded by posts; opposite the main entrance to Stonehenge is a stone carved to look like wood.

Human remains are common at Stonehenge, less so at Woodhenge and almost absent at Durrington Walls.

Consider the evidence. Despite the large area excavated at Stonehenge, pottery was scarce – why radiocarbon alone was able to cause such a dramatic change to our perception of its age. By contrast, at the Walls South Circles, there was so much of it, often in the form of large, fresh sherds (Grooved Ware is typically soft and friable), that archaeologists have imagined pots were deliberately smashed and buried. There was also a unique feature immediately beside the South Circles known as the Midden (figure 17). This was a flat 12m-long hollow terraced into the chalk rising to the north, filled with black, ashy soil containing masses of artefacts and bones. Nearly 1000 sherds, mostly Grooved Ware, included twenty-five pieces of Beaker, otherwise rare at the Walls (suggesting the radiocarbon date of around 4900 years ago may be misleading, as this would be much too old for Beakers).[560]

Downslope from the Midden, opposite two unusually large posts in the outer ring, was a platform of chalk rubble and flint gravel. Fires had apparently been lit here, and archaeologists recovered further quantities of rubbish – including no fewer than twenty-six flint arrowheads, two of them broken barbed and tanged types and the others the sharp cutting ones typically found with Grooved Ware. This is far more than have been found anywhere at Stonehenge. The only Stonehenge specimen of a distinctive type with a long barb down one side was found *outside* the earthwork, in the stone floor I excavated in 1980 (figure 26): there were eight of these in the Walls platform, and a further four of very fine quality were found in a single post hole.[561] No features like the Midden or platform were identified at Woodhenge, but nonetheless finds of pottery and flintwork were numerous. It also should be said that the way Woodhenge was dug, it's possible that if there were such heaps they may not have been noticed.

Animal bones present a similar picture. At the South Circles at the Walls, the quantities of animal bones are so great as to suggest pork feasting on a grand scale. 'Feasting' is a contentious word: perhaps there were just a lot of people living inside this superhenge, and over time their rubbish accumulated to give a false impression of large-scale butchery. But it is not just the numbers of meat bones that are striking.

Julian Thomas had a detailed look at the remains, and confirmed the original analysis.[562] Many unfused epiphyses (the articulating ends of bones in young animals) were still in place, meaning these bones had to have been buried with tissue still attached (or the epiphyses would have come adrift). The absence of dog gnawing indicated this was done pretty quickly. Yet there was little evidence for butchery in the form of flint scrape marks, and many bones had not been split for their marrow.

The suggestion was that there was so much meat about that a lot remained unconsumed, and flesh still adhered to bones when they were carefully and immediately buried. Further study has revealed the curious fact that some of these pigs (over 95 per cent, incidentally, domestic and not wild)[563] were apparently killed by archery. The tips of some of those arrowheads are embedded in pig bones.[564] Pigs do not like to die, and make this fact pretty obvious. There must have been some spectacularly noisy and messy occasions in the vicinity of these large timber rings.

In the wild, pigs are a woodland animal (remember those medieval illustrations of peasants knocking down acorns for their swine?). Four thousand two hundred years ago at Durrington Walls, however, there was not a lot of forest left: the immediate landscape was dominated by grassland. So why pigs? The answer is probably partly in their fecundity, making them an ideal creature for repeated mass slaughter. Compared to cattle and sheep, pigs have larger and more frequent litters. A herd can be killed down and bred up again with little threat to its continued existence.[565] So pigs were the chosen animal for celebrating the living. But the ancestors had their chosen flesh, too: cattle.

At Durrington Walls, nearly two-thirds of the animals were pig, and less than a third cattle. Of the bones saved from the ditch around Stonehenge, the figures are reversed: two-thirds were cattle, and less than a fifth pig.[566] But there's more than that. We saw how radiocarbon dating at Stonehenge revealed the remarkable fact that a collection of bones from the ditch was already some two centuries old when buried. There were two jaws, a tibia and a skull. The tibia (leg bone) was from a red deer. The other were cattle. Even older was a bone found in the pit holding one of the sarsens in the circle – some six millennia.[567] It's difficult to imagine people looking after ancestral bones for several thousand years, then burying them, but it's possible; perhaps this old bone had been found in the ground, an ancestral animal from the world of the ancestors. This bone was probably also cattle.

There is another difference between the two collections. At Stonehenge there were an unusual number of wild animals. Out of nearly ninety cattle from Durrington Walls, there were only three aurochs, the huge wild cattle still present out there in the Neolithic forest. From the far smaller collection of bones at Stonehenge there were four or five from aurochs. The size of the bones from Stonehenge also suggested that larger animals, probably bulls, were chosen in preference from the domestic herd. Again, there were more wild boar at Stonehenge, animals notorious for their strength and ferocity.

There was also an unusual collection of wild cattle bones from Woodhenge. The Cunningtons planned to dig out the whole ditch, but realised this was impossible when they found out how big it was. In only five trenches, they found four aurochs bones on the ditch bottom, three of them just east of the entrance causeway. There was a fifth bone in the bank.[568]

It's not only around Stonehenge that we see a peculiar relationship with cattle. One of the most extraordinary barrows to have been excavated in recent years was at Irthlingborough in Northamptonshire.[569] An adult man had been buried in a pit with a bunch of precious things: a wrist guard, as was found with the man in the Stonehenge ditch (but no arrows in this one), flint tools including a dagger, five jet buttons and an amber ring, a boar's tusk, other bone and stone tools and a Beaker pot. He had been covered by a round mound, but immediately above him were the decayed remains of cattle. Lots of cattle: the heap originally contained at least the skulls, jaws, shoulder blades and hip bones of forty animals, with further skulls from around 145 more. It is preposterous to imagine that amount of meat being consumed at one go, so what was going on?

We see the familiar signs that these cattle bones were already old when the man died. The number of incisors, front teeth, was far fewer than would be expected from all those jaws. These are teeth that fall out relatively easily, and are likely to have got lost if the skulls and mandibles had been preserved, for example hanging on wooden poles. And as at Stonehenge, radiocarbon dates confirm this. Although the man died around 4000 years ago, the cattle appear to have predeceased him by up to six centuries, that is some time before Phase 3 at Stonehenge.[570]

The boar tusk is interesting. We don't find them in Wessex, but in parts of the Midlands and northern England are graves from a time before the appearance of Beaker pottery containing several bodies and rich collections of artefacts – exceptionally fine flintwork, pots, jewellery – and often boar tusks. The best-known is Duggleby Howe in Yorkshire, where a huge round mound (nearer in scale to Silbury Hill than the typical round barrows of the Early Bronze Age) covered numerous burials. One of these was an adult accompanied by six flint arrowheads (interestingly, of the type found at the Sanctuary), a bone pin, two beaver incisors and twelve boar tusks.[570] These are personal belongings, symbols of feasting and danger in life, perhaps of hunting prowess. The contrast between this and the mound of ancient cattle bone at Irthlingborough is striking.

Two smaller henge-like sites suggest that deer antlers were caught up in this web of meanings. At Radley, Oxfordshire, and East Lavant, West Sussex, antlers seem to have been carefully placed along the bottom of ring ditches. At Radley there were also two cattle limbs in the ditch, diametrically opposite each other, and nearby some pits containing Grooved Ware pottery and large amounts of pig bones; radiocarbon dates these to around the time of early Stonehenge Phase 3.[572]

In view of the proposed connection between cattle and ancestors, and pigs and the living, the occurrence of immature pig skeletons at Stonehenge is interesting. Parts of four young piglets were found in the ditch, two near the southern entrances with the ancestral cattle bones, and two to the right of the north-east entrance (near where the human body was later buried). Only one of these was found in the lowest silts, the others appearing to date from Phase 2.

Nonetheless, the pattern is striking: the animal of life represented by newborns, the ancestors by large, and often wild, mature creatures.

If we include all the identified cattle bone from the bottom of the ditch – a row of teeth suggesting a decayed jaw, and a further nine bones – we find that these, like the dated bones, are at or near the south entrance. Without radiocarbon, we cannot tell if these other bones are also older than the ditch or contemporary with its excavation – the state of some of them suggests they may not be so old[573] – but either way, the association of the south entrance with cattle is reinforced.

Reference to entrances brings us to the observation that most evidence for activity at Woodhenge, the South Circles at the Walls and Stonehenge occurs on the east – at Stonehenge, that's between these two entrances. At Woodhenge, almost all the antler picks come from the east, as do the rough carved chalk objects and most of the animal bones, whether cattle, pig or other rarer creatures such as deer or wild cat (figure 48). At the South Circles there is a similar concentration of debris, not least at the Midden and platform.[574] Because that part of Stonehenge excavated is more or less the eastern half, we are prevented from assessing finds in this way. Perhaps there are more antler picks there? More small objects made from bluestone? Without further excavation, we cannot know, although cremation burials do seem to thin out as we begin to progress round to the west.[575] But there are some things we can see. There are a number of odd features about the stone circles on the south-east side.[576]

First, where the pits of the Q/R holes of Phase 3i are normally dumbbell-shaped, with a bluestone at each end, at positions 10 and 11 it looks as if the paired stones each stood in isolated pits. Just outside the ring is a large pit thought to be contemporary that is unmatched elsewhere. This is suggestive of something strange at this south-east point, but perhaps not too much should be placed on it. The whole Q/R structure is poorly understood, and in fact on the opposite side, to the north-west, there is also an anomalous pit – a crescent-shaped feature inside the Q/R ring that may have held two stones (figure 29).

But perhaps it is significant. It is here that the later stone 33e of the bluestone circle (Phase 3iv) was erected at right angles to the ring, unlike every other stone on the site which stands on the circumference. It was here that sarsen stones 8 and 9 (Phase 3ii) fell

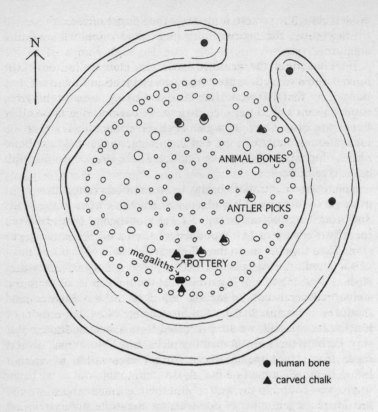

Figure 48. Excavation of the whole of Woodhenge by the Cunningtons revealed that ancient activity focused on the east side of the site. *After Cunnington and Pollard.*

outwards and broke (or were they pushed?). The later still Y and Z Holes (Phase 3vi) seem to respect the fallen sarsens: there is a kink in the two rings at this point, and Z8 (which should be near fallen sarsen 8) may never have been dug. The collapse may have occurred in the time of Hengeworld.

It is also near here that the only really substantial post pit was recorded at Stonehenge, complete with ramp and pipe where timber had rotted in situ. At over 1m deep, this is a respectable pit, and one of few that approach the scale of post pits at Woodhenge or Durrington Walls, or even, indeed, the Sanctuary. Like most of the posts at Stonehenge, we can do little more than guess its age, but it is possible it stood at the same time as the sarsens.[577]

If we move a little around the sarsen ring to stone 11, we find a diminished, stumpy thing, less than 3m high compared to the normal 4m (figure 27, plate 10). Was this always thus, or was it broken down some time after erection? Excavation should tell, but we can note that destruction in place, yet leaving a respectable erect stump, seems beyond any realistic stoneworking operation. If it *was* put in place like that, which does seem more likely, there are some serious implications. It could not have held a lintel connecting to the two adjacent full-size stones, despite the fact that both have ball joints ready for a lintel's sockets. Were the joints routinely carved onto all sarsens, to be adjusted at final fitting – in these two cases something that never happened? Were these two designed to connect with an outsize timber lintel that bridged the space above stone 11? Or was there perhaps a timber extension to stone 11 to support two timber lintels?

Whatever the case, there would have been a significant visual block to the otherwise apparently continuous ring of standing stones and lintels (which I guess means all those reconstructions should be redrawn). Richard Atkinson wrote of an 'entrance' into the circle between stones 30 and 1, the solar passage, indicated by a gap wider than normal by a few centimetres. What is that compared to this huge interruption in the normal flow of sarsens? Here, surely, is a major symbolic entrance or exit.

And this symbolic gateway is opposite the south entrance to the earthwork, where the ancestral cattle bones had been buried around seven centuries before.

Furthermore – and can this too be coincidence? – it is between these two areas, the odd stones in the circles and the southern earthwork entrance, that the rows of post holes seemingly marking out a passage are found. As we saw, these are thought to be from Phase 2, but it has to be said that we don't really know when posts stood in most of these holes. It could have been in Phase 3.

Several of the sarsens have carvings on them. Apart from the single dagger that we have already come across (chapter 3), there are engravings of numerous copper or bronze axeheads with their blades facing skywards. By far the most highly decorated stone is number 4, due east of centre.[578] Adjacent stones 3 and 5 also have a few axes.

The carvings are crude and weathered, and have yet to be properly surveyed. This makes dating even harder than it might be,

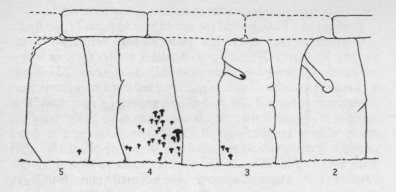

Figure 49. Axe carvings at Stonehenge are most common on the outer face of sarsen stone 4; the position of the single carving on stone 5 is hypothetical. The 'female' and 'male' grooves on stones 3 and 2 seem to be completely natural. *Carvings after Newall.*

as the only chance of that is by reference to subtleties of metalwork design. I consulted leading Early Bronze Age specialist Stuart Needham, who told me the splayed blades and in some cases what look like protuberances on the sides of the shafts suggest parallels with objects not found before around 3900 years ago. This could make them contemporary with the Y and Z holes.[579] So if they are later than the era we are considering (a hypothetical moment 4200 years ago), perhaps their positioning on the east side perpetuated the memory of an earlier significance (figure 49).

Terry Meaden found sexual symbolism at Stonehenge as well as Avebury (chapter 20). Here, he says, the shadow of the Heelstone phallus penetrated the inner femininity of the sarsen ring at midsummer dawn.[580] In my experience, the shadow is far too limp to pull that one off. But he missed a trick. If we regard Flinders Petrie's description of the paired sarsen tenons as 'worked to an irregular mammiform shape' as mere turn of phrase,[581] we may be less keen to dismiss the significance of a huge phallus-shaped natural hollow that droops across the outer face of sarsen 2, especially when we notice that the adjacent face of stone 3 has a comparable hollow ending in a female pudendum (figure 49).[582] You can of course see what you like in these irregular stone surfaces. But who knows? Carved portable chalk phalluses are a regular feature of henges in Wessex. There is a possible piece from

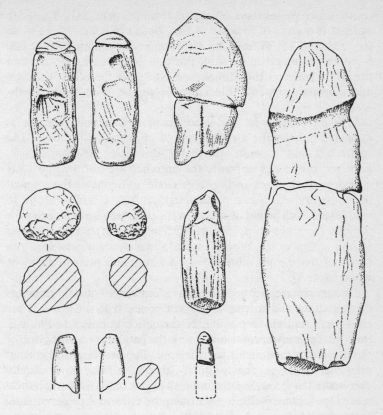

Figure 50. Not quite the indigenous answer to the Elgin marbles, but the common occurrence of carved chalk balls and willy-like objects ('phalluses'), often found in ceremonial contexts, has led some archaeologists to believe them to be representations of male sex organs. Clockwise from top left (drawn to scale): two pieces from Windmill Hill, Avebury (the chalk 'figurine' is a rare item), Maumbury Rings, Dorset (length 22cm), The Trundle, W. Sussex (bone), a Stonehenge phallus, two balls from Stonehenge and a phallus from Windmill Hill. *After Smith, Bradley, Piggott and Cleal et al.*

Stonehenge itself, although it's less convincing than some, for example that from the henge ditch at Mount Pleasant (figure 50).[583] Like the artificial carvings, these two natural hollows are on the outer faces of stones on the east side.

We cannot know what the two absent megaliths at Woodhenge looked like, but their location is interesting. They are both on the south, which places them off-centre from the main axis. There are at least two ways of looking at this, both symbolic – there is no suggestion of any meaningful astronomic orientation. On the one hand, the stones are in the same position as the south entrance and the cattle bones in the Stonehenge ditch. On the other, they are approximately opposite the entrance to the Woodhenge earthwork.

Unlike Stonehenge, at Woodhenge midsummer sunrise is indicated only by the arrangement of uprights into an oval. The earthwork has a more northerly direction. At Stonehenge, however, the stones opposite the entrance are also on the solar corridor. At the back of the large circle, only one of the original pair has survived. It is a particularly distinctive sarsen. Stone 16 stands to the full height of others in the ring, but tapers to a narrow top. Its faces are conspicuously faceted in a style that suggests adzing of timber. At Woodhenge are two stones almost lost in a forest of timbers. At Stonehenge is a megalith pretending to be wood (plate 9).

Human remains are prominent at Stonehenge – untold numbers of cremations and scattered unburnt bones. If Ros Cleal and her colleagues are right in placing the cremation burials into Phase 2, then this funerary episode may mark the path of transformation of the site into a monument to ancestors. The people in the ground may be close to the original ancestors later symbolically represented in stone. Significantly, there are only two human finds from Durrington Walls, a tibia from the ditch and pieces of skull from a post hole.

At Woodhenge there is the fully articulated human skeleton we saw in the Natural History Museum, laid on the ditch bottom. Although the quantities are not as high as at Stonehenge, there are quite a few other human remains, including a cremation in a post hole. It looks as if at Woodhenge the boundaries between the living and the dead were less clearly drawn. And once again, the location of finds seems significant. Human remains among the posts are restricted to a corridor along the axis that links the two stones with the entrance that divides east from west. The biggest concentration of Grooved Ware is also on this axis, around the two stones.

An idea is emerging. Suppose the living and the recently deceased, fresh from large celebrations inside the Walls, enter Woodhenge to the north-east. They move to the left (east) and participate in a variety of activities that leave intriguing but indecipherable traces in the ground as they progress. They pass that fit young man buried on the bottom of the ditch. They reach the two stones at the south, and enter a liminal world between the living and the ancestors. Whatever they do after that leaves little for us to dig up (figure 48). But a journey has begun.

Let us suppose that 4200 years ago, an old woman – perhaps in her late fifties – dies, in her sleep, at home in bed. There will be some shock, some emotional distress, drawn from the pit of instinct that all people contain within them. But most of what happens, most of what is felt and said, is determined not by gut responses but by culture and tradition, what everyone, individually and together, has learnt to do, learnt to express.[584]

So what happened next?

27

The Mountain Comes to the Monument

What did they do with her body?

Curiously, given the great scale of engineering devoted to Hengeworld ancestors in general, we have little idea what happened at this time to most individuals. Two millennia before, as at the West Kennet Long Barrow at Avebury, bodies were collected in long mounded tombs and selected bones were removed for ceremonies and reburial elsewhere.[585] In later generations, people were given more personal attention, first at the centre of relatively small round mounds, where their undamaged corpses were laid after a variety of domestic-scale ceremonies, and subsequently in graves in and around these founder barrows.[586] But in Hengeworld we have evidence that confuses. They are not prolific, but there are odd human bones all over the place: we would be surprised to find no human remains, if only just a few disarticulated bones, at any large excavation of a Late Neolithic site, whatever its functions. And we might find almost anything in the way of apparently more deliberate burials.

We have already been to Duggleby Howe, where a dramatic mixture of inhumations and cremations hints (from a poorly documented nineteenth-century dig) that some of the people may even have been intentionally killed in funerary rites. Nothing like this has yet been found in Wessex, but there are complete skeletons, sometimes, as at the henge of Gorsey Bigbury in Somerset, in peculiar situations. Here it is thought that an adult male and female were buried together in a stone cist in the ditch just to the west of the single entrance, and later the cist was dug out and some of the remains reburied in the ditch the other side.[587] At Flagstones in Dorset, at the centre of the older ditch ring that itself contained a variety of human remains, a young man was buried beneath a small sarsen megalith.[588] At Wyke Down in Dorset, pits in small rings contained a variety of disarticulated and cremated bone.[589]

But none of this adds up to a pattern, a common ritual process fossilised in the ground. What happened between the moment of death and the process of joining the ancestors is, for the most part, still a mystery. However, it does seem that these two transformations – from living to dead, from dead to ancestor – were different in time, scale and place. The complex of monuments around Stonehenge is large, and its construction would have involved very large numbers of people – far more than would have lived in the immediate vicinity. There is a contrasting scarcity of evidence for substantial settlement in Hengeworld, and some archaeologists believe that people were living a partly mobile existence, following herds (both wild and domestic), cultivating temporary fields and gardens and harvesting wild foods at places that changed with the seasons.[590] So not only to create the infrastructure, as it were, but also to conduct the ceremonies, to perpetuate the traditions, now and again people would have gathered in unusual numbers from a wide area. Unlike the living, and, apparently, the physical remains of the dead, the ancestors assembled in one place, and stayed there.

So people gather inside Durrington Walls for grand celebrations and feasting. Perhaps the woman's corpse was earlier ceremonially exposed near where she died, to rot and fall prey to scavenging animals, so now she is represented only by dry bones. Perhaps her body has been brought entire, or perhaps her presence is immaterial, a mixture of memories, spirit and mementoes such as clothing. The strong identification of both Woodhenge and Stonehenge with the longest day suggests the time is midsummer.

To enter the Walls people have to approach from the north-west or the south-east. There is significance in this orientation, for on the one hand it contradicts the north-east–south-west axis of Woodhenge and Stonehenge, and on the other it links with the focus of activity we have noted at these two sites on the south and east sides (figure 51).

It is then surely not coincidence that the timber rings just inside the southern entrance at Durrington Walls are facing the same way. This forest of huge oak posts, carved and painted and festooned with objects in ways we can only guess, has a clear focus on the south-east (figure 17). Here there are areas of rammed chalk and gravel inside and outside the rings; in the outer ring two exceptionally large posts rise above an area where animal parts,

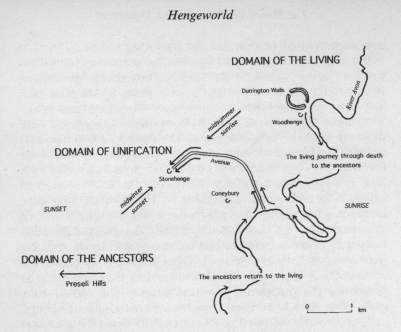

Figure 51. Stonehenge 4200 years ago, as a place where the living met the ancestors. After ceremonies at Woodhenge, the newly dead travelled down the river and up the Avenue to Stonehenge, coming from the east/sunrise direction. Bluestones, ancestors embodied in the world of the living, travelled overland or up the river from the south, coming from the west/sunset. *Adapted after Parker Pearson and Ramilisonina.*

pots and arrows are smashed and buried. In the rubble that packs posts into their pits, and on the ground around the standing timbers, in this area unusual quantities of pottery, antler picks and flint tools have been deposited.[591]

Given that we are making a specific identification of this axis with the movement of the living, it is interesting that Roy Loveday recently suggested that henges with two entrances, and Durrington Walls in particular, are linked to long-distance land routes. In many cases, he found the axis of these henges paralleled that of adjacent Roman roads which, it seems fair to imagine, would often have followed already used routes. Durrington Walls lies close to a series of medieval tracks that cross Salisbury Plain from the north-west and continue to the east the other side of the River Avon.[592] The river itself, of course, was probably a thoroughfare, linking different territories to north and south.

The dead are there to make that all-important journey from the world of the living to that of the ancestors. But the route, the dangerous passage from which the dead must not be allowed to deviate, is tightly controlled. Once inside the Walls, a huge ditch and surrounding bank, gleaming white when new, keeps them in the arena of noisy, sweaty ceremony. The slaughter and feasting is a reflection of the wider process, death and regeneration. Throughout the world, symbols of fertility and rebirth are common at funerary rituals.[593] The death of the woman is also the birth of an ancestor. To the screams of dying pigs we can almost certainly add chanting and drumming, if not other forms of music as well: some years ago, anthropologist Rodney Needham noted a common association between rites of transition (birth, weddings, initiations, funerals) and percussive music. Good funerals are noisy affairs.[594]

Then, at the right time, inside Woodhenge the woman is led around the rings of posts and past the standing stones, past the ancestors in this outpost of the living. They are her guide on her passage into their world. The woman comes from the east, the direction of life and the rising sun and moon. She moves to the west, where sun and moon set, the direction of the ancestors.[595]

West is also the direction of the mountain in Wales whence came the ancestral bluestones. Surely everyone knows this. Those extraordinary alien megaliths assembled at Stonehenge have been brought from beyond the setting horizon, from the place where ancestors live and the dead travel, to meet the new dead in the land of the living. The stones *are* ancestors, ready to receive the woman into their circle, and their world. Woodhenge *is* Preseli.

It hardly rises into the mist, but locally Woodhenge is a high point in the gently rolling landscape. From inside the chalk bank, seeming taller than it really is because of the deep intervening ditch, 4200 years ago the view out is nothing but sky. From the South Circles below, even the tall Woodhenge poles rising above the bank are invisible, hidden by the steeply climbing ground and the truly massive superhenge bank. This chalkwork hides also the river to the east, only a quick walk away, swirling muddily further down-slope and at the bottom of a steep bank.

The stones, the ancestors, journeyed from the toothy peak of the Preselis down to the sea. So the new dead make the same journey from the memorial poles, the oak-planted summit, to the river. The river is the sea. Woodhenge is Preseli, the river the sea, the Avenue, the last leg of the journey, the great portage from the Bristol Channel to Salisbury Plain. At Stonehenge east meets west, stone wood, ancestor the new dead.

Water is also a metaphor for change and transition, the river that is always present but never the same, the purifying, dissolving liquid without which we all die but which in excess will kill us.[596] The would-be ancestors travel down this meandering, flowing symbol in a muddle of orientations, a practice often seen at funerals, where the unsettled spirits of the dead are deliberately confused so they cannot find their way back to the world of the living. The final loop of the river takes the woman due south-east, and then back north-west, paralleling the axis of Durrington Walls. This direction is continued overland, as she climbs the hill along the wide white-banked Avenue. The route gently curves around and down into the valley, where quite suddenly it turns towards Stonehenge, and onto the ancestral north-east–south-west axis. The 'ancestral initiate' is about to go home.[597]

At Stonehenge she enters through the main gap in the earthwork, passing the piglets in the ditch to the right and perhaps already the murdered man. Now the resonance of the arrow-studded corpse with Christian saints, Sebastian whom Roman emperor Diocletian ordered shot by archers yet who recovered to confront his murderer, or Edmund who died in a hail of arrows proclaiming his love of Christ and whose beheaded body miraculously repaired itself and defied decay, seems perhaps meaningful. Perhaps similar stories embraced this man who saw the stones rise, an emblem of death and regeneration.

As at Woodhenge she progresses around the circles to the left. Here there are not just a couple of megaliths almost lost in the trees. Here there are sentinels, guardian stones on the edge, and in the centre, the grandest construction of them all, wood made stone, soft hardened, the living become ancestors. It is an extraordinary climax, most of whose ceremony and symbolism is lost, but a flicker of which we see in the tallest stones of all, the sarsen trilithons.

As we move round these stones in the same direction, from left to right, we pass five pairs. One of these (59/60, the last in the circuit) is broken and fallen, and difficult now to assess. The stones of the tall central trilithon are both exceptionally well shaped. But the others reveal a consistent pattern: in each pair, the first we come to is more heavily dressed than the second.[598] We might say that the first is better finished. But we could say, metaphorically, the opposite: that the first is more timber-like, carved and smoothed as yielding flesh, while the second in its heavy cross-sections, its roughness of surface and its angular shadows that move over the course of the day, is revealing its true and ultimate nature as stone. Stonehenge is timber turned to stone, people to ancestors (figure 10).

We can see this same pattern in the whole structure of Stonehenge. The only completely undressed sarsens are those on the edge: the Heelstone and the two surviving Station Stones. As we move towards the centre, stones become more shaped, the sarsens in the ring patently carved yet less well finished than the trilithons, among which the tallest at the focus of the horseshoes, on the solar corridor, are the smoothest. The outer bluestone circle is undressed, contrasting with the carved stones of the bluestone horseshoe.[599] Similarly the older cremation burials, the remains of people seeking ancestral permanence, are all on the edge of the site.

And in the trilithons, do we not see the newly dead joined, by the lintels, with the ancestors?

Which takes us to the final act in this eternal drama.

As we enter the henge and go round the ring, we begin an endless circuit, emphasised particularly by the bluestones and sarsen circles, and the ring of sarsen lintels – with its symbolic break at the ancestral southern gate, and the timber become stone at sarsen 16, a great chrysalis awaiting the midwinter sun. Life and death are a continuous process, an unending dance from one state to the next. In this place of death and ancestors, symbols of procreation shaped naturally by the earth mark the first stones in the cycle. There are thirty sarsens. Could this be a month? A moon cycle, from black to full to black again. A repeating rhythm that is broken only twice a year, at midwinter when the sun sets in the shadow of the axis, and at midsummer.

On the longest brightest day the sun both rises and sets the furthest north it ever reaches. Not until the shortest darkest day does it rise so close to where it sets. At midsummer and midwinter east and west, rise and set, living and ancestor almost touch. Weather permitting, on midsummer dawn the sun rises bright, high-climbing and white along the white Avenue earthwork, over the Heelstone, through the stones standing across the ditch causeway, into the sarsen ring, through the bluestone ring and into the open arms of the bluestone and sarsen horseshoes. The first, indeed perhaps the only thing it strikes is the Altar Stone.[600]

This Welsh stone is different from the others. It is the largest bluestone, its 4.9m total length contrasting with average height above ground of little more than 2m for other bluestone horseshoe stones (which are themselves larger than those in the circle).[601] And, almost uniquely for these stones, it is not igneous or metamorphic, it is not 'blue', but a pale green sandstone, flecked with glistening mica. From our modern geological perspective, it could be said to be a metaphorical 'sarsen bluestone', a sedimentary rock from Wales. They may not have seen it in these terms, but is it not possible that 4200 years ago, people were conscious of that symbolism, a stone that brought together the two ancestral rock grounds? And towering above it, framing the continuing passage of the midsummer sun, is the central trilithon, the smoothest and tallest sarsens of the lot, the dead and the ancestor rising above all, now joined in perfect harmony by a huge lintel in that explosion of white light.

Something familiar? On the shortest day, when west comes round to meet east, we are seeing an echo of the older alignment at Newgrange, where the rising midwinter sun seeks out the window and bursts down the passage to shine on carvings in the burial chamber, an act repeated at Maes Howe on the same day by the setting sun. Indeed, archaeologists have suggested the alignment of the Maes Howe tomb on the setting sun, and nearby houses at Barnhouse on the rising midwinter sun, might indicate an association in the Orkneys that anticipates what I am here suggesting for Stonehenge around five centuries later: sunrise with houses of the living, sunset with houses of the dead.[602]

At Newgrange Jeremy Dronfield found evidence in the carvings for altered states of mind, 'subjective visions' possibly brought on by hallucinogenic mushrooms. People see all sorts of things when their minds are hallucinating, but something that frequently recurs is the tunnel, the sensation of moving down a dark passage, attracted to a distant and bright light. In certain circumstances, such visions are associated with dying: the life-changing 'near-death experience'. Perhaps, thought Dronfield, the concentric spirals carved onto the stones and the tomb passage itself were metaphors for these visions, physical expressions of the possibility of moving between the world of the living and the world of the ancestors.[603] Assisted by mind-altering drugs, light effects, music or who knows what, and the symbolic carvings that acted as doors between the two worlds, like wardrobes or looking-glasses, people could make that journey out and back, people who in other contexts we might call shamans.

The tunnel of stones and the receptive horseshoes and rings, the gleaming chalk-lined Avenue and the bright of the rising sun: at Stonehenge we have the final denouement, where the sun breaks the endless cycle on earth and the near-death vision is written on the landscape for the newly dead and the living to walk into, join hands and transcend materiality to rise with the sun into the timeless sphere of the ancestors (figure 51).

28

Avebury Reciprocates

Stonehenge, you might say, with its megaliths carved out of stone like timbers, is always going to look good in a story that plays the contrast between wood and stone. What of other places, where this doesn't happen? Surely the real test is to see how well this all works elsewhere?

Several times we have commented on the variety of practices in different parts of Hengeworld. While there is an astonishing community of pottery style that extends from the Orkneys to Wessex (Grooved Ware, which looks increasingly to have originated in the far north), we do not see precise replicas of spiritual sites, of ceremonial landscapes. Nonetheless, with something as powerful as the vision we have painted for Stonehenge – a vision that entailed bringing stone from west Wales as well as Avebury, and timber and whatever else from who knows where – we should expect some sign of the same concerns at other places.

Of the other great ritual territories that have been well investigated, Avebury is the nearest. If we are to explain the presence of sarsens at Stonehenge, we need to understand Avebury, whence they came. What happened there? Let us begin as we did before, by considering timelines, now with a few key events from Stonehenge (figure 52).

The sobering conclusion is that we have even less of an idea what happened, and when, at Avebury than we do at Stonehenge, a point reflected in the diagram at the front of the book (figure 8). We should soon have some new dates for the ditched enclosure excavated at Beckhampton in 1999, and possibly even a date or two from the Sanctuary. But we still have a big problem. Almost nothing is securely dated. The series from the West Kennet timber enclosures is confusing. Silbury Hill has but one date (and we have ignored several contradictory 'experimental dates'), Avebury and the stone avenues are dated by a ridiculously small collection of

Figure 52. Radiocarbon dates for Avebury area.

Site	cal BC: calibrated date range (95% confidence)	years ago (cal BC mean +2000)	Stonehenge phase
West Kennet long barrow, NW chamber	3783–3373	5580	
West Kennet long barrow, SW chamber	3709–3363	5535	
West Kennet long barrow, NW chamber	3709–3363	5535	
West Kennet long barrow, NE chamber	3646–3345	5495	
Avebury old land surface under henge bank	3633–3104	5370	
Avebury old land surface under henge bank	3345 – 2879	5110	
Stonehenge, excavation of ditch	*3015–2935*	*4975*	*1*
Avebury, henge ditch primary	3304–2625	4965	
West Kennet Avenue, Pit 1	3304–2582	4940	
Avebury old land surface under henge bank	3007–2495	4750	
Avebury stone circle	2906–2466	4685	
West Kennet Enclosure 2, ditch	2874–2407	4640	
Silbury Hill, turf under mound	2896–2354	4625	
West Kennet Enclosure 1, outer ditch	2827–2208	4520	
West Kennet Enclosure 1, outer ditch	2573–2144	4360	
West Kennet Enclosure 1, inner ditch	2569–2142	4355	
West Kennet Enclosure 2, outer radial ditch 1	2470–2200	4335	
Stonehenge, end of ditch filling	*2460–2210*	*4335*	*End 2*
Stonehenge, large sarsen structures	*2461–2205*	*4335*	*3ii*
West Kennet Enclosure 1, outer ditch	2552–2069	4310	
Avebury stone circle	2575–2039	4305	
Silbury Hill, S ditch secondary	2398–2141	4270	
West Kennet Enclosure 1, outer ditch	2459–2046	4255	
Hemp Knoll round barrow, aurochs scapula	2399–1980	4190	
Stonehenge, bluestone circle and oval	*2267–1983*	*4125*	*3iv*
Avebury, secondary burial in ditch	2295–1830	4065	
West Kennet Enclosure 2, ditch	2196–1771	3985	
West Kennet Enclosure 1, outer ditch	2137–1783	3960	
Hemp Knoll round barrow, coffin in pit	2134–1744	3940	
West Kennet Enclosure 1, bone deposit	2032–1747	3890	
Stonehenge, Z Hole 29	*2013–1742*	*3880*	*3vi*

See Appendices 2–3 for details.

samples from old excavations, and from one of the largest groups of round barrows in Britain we have two dates from one mound!

Does that one antler pick from the Avebury ditch really date the excavation of what we believe to be the second of two ditches, separated by a considerable space of time, to the same era as the excavation of the Stonehenge ditch?[604] Which date do we believe for the stone circle, 4700 years ago or 4300 – if either?[605] If we are to proceed, we have no choice but to assume that most of the monuments were conceived together, at the same time as events were proceeding at Stonehenge. This is hardly satisfactory, for if it cannot relate the details, archaeology does suggest a process of historical development that is at least as complex as that in the Stonehenge district.

Silbury is one of the most interesting parts of Avebury, for there is nothing like it at Stonehenge. It used to be thought unique, but though exceptional in its size, we now see large round mounds as part of the Neolithic landscape. We might begin to wonder why there is not one at Stonehenge.

Down the River Kennet at Marlborough a 20m-high stepped chalk mound lurking in the grounds of Marlborough College is unexcavated and undated, and may yet (although I would be surprised) turn out to be medieval.[606] Inside the henge earthwork between Avebury and Stonehenge at Marden (chapter 7) was the Hatfield Mound, once at least 150m diameter and 7m high, also undated. But at Mount Pleasant is a mound radiocarbon-dated to the same era as Silbury.

The Conquer Barrow (that many of these mounds have names is testament to their unusual size) at first sight appears to stand on the henge bank, just north of the west entrance. When excavating the henge in 1971, Geoff Wainwright dug a few small trenches to locate the surrounding ditch, about 50m in diameter, and found an antler pick dated to around 4600–4700 years ago.[607] The mound, reaching some 7–8m from the ground, was apparently constructed about the same time as the henge earthwork. It was partially buried in the newly extended bank 500 years later when the entrance was narrowed (figure 19).[608]

Between Stonehenge and Mount Pleasant is another complex of henges, which we have not referred to before because there has been no substantial excavation or revealing geophysics. This is to say the least unfortunate, as a large part of this important group of monuments is under plough. At Knowlton in Dorset there are three or four earthwork enclosures, ring banks with internal ditches, one of which is still a substantial standing monument, hiding the ruins of a medieval church. As at other henge sites, there is a concentration of what are assumed to be Early Bronze Age round barrows in the area. But one of the mounds, close to the church henge, is atypical: indeed, it is, with the Conquer Barrow, the largest round mound in Dorset, 6m high and with a henge-like surrounding ditch about 100m in diameter, earning it the name the Great Barrow.[609]

So at three of the four great Wessex henge complexes there are round mounds of exceptional local size. Further afield, aerial photography revealed that the great mound at Duggleby Howe is sited at the centre of a large henge earthwork. Maes Howe in Orkney is surrounded by a ring ditch with outer bank about 150m across at its widest point. Geophysics has just revealed a henge-like ditch and double palisade 175m by 210m across, inside which stands the Mound of the Hostages at Tara in Ireland, a large stone-chambered round tomb.[610]

Archaeology tells us little about these mounds in Wessex, but Silbury has a tantalising suggestion. As well as the mound there may have been rings, of small sarsen stones, and of wooden stakes. Eight sarsens were found by Dean Merewether in 1849, spaced out at intervals ranging from 2.5m to 100m, around the edge where they would have been visible against the white chalk. Atkinson's team found another sarsen inside the mound, about 45cm across, lying on the buried ground surface. 'This looks like a kerb-stone,' says the site diary, 'and recalls similar sarsens described ... by Merewether ...'[611]

Near this sarsen they also found a stakehole, one of four that may be part of a ring around an early stage of the mound. Merewether found this inner mound covered in a layer of small sarsen stones. These may have been slight constructional devices in what remains a poorly understood monument. But they may have been more than that, the first manifestation of stone and timber in a circle in Wessex, whose presence beneath that enormous mound may have given them greater significance than their apparent flimsiness suggests. Could we be seeing the origins of the stone and timber symbolism?[612]

Silbury stands in the valley immediately below one of Britain's largest Earlier Neolithic long barrows. The contrast between the two is striking. The West Kennet long barrow, although on a hilltop, is inconspicuous in the landscape, quite unlike Silbury's strong presence. The barrow has a visible burial function, built into it with what at the time of construction would have been amongst the largest megaliths in Britain. The mound, the flanking quarry ditches and the chamber entrance are strongly orientated to the east. Silbury, on the other hand, is visually no more than a mound of chalk, with no obvious front or back.

The largest megalith of all at West Kennet blocks what had been an opening into the tomb used by both dead and living. Silbury's blind circularity might be a deliberate front to the eastward thrust of West Kennet, a monumental contradiction to a long architectural tradition, symbolising change in the organisation of beliefs. Apparently bereft of actual bodies, could Silbury represent the creation of an artificial lineage, a claim to a new mythology as old families were laid to terminal rest, new ancestors and new lives in circular embrace within the engineering project that brought together more people than ever before assembled in the district?

This is pure guesswork, and does nothing to help us understand other mounds or the absence – although one might yet be discovered – of one near Stonehenge. But we are on more familiar ground with the huge stones and timbers. We've been there before.

In earlier centuries, long mounds were foci of activities involving the human body, places where the transitions from living to corpse to ancestor were eased and celebrated.[613] At the West Kennet long barrow, the best-understood of several of these mounds (two-thirds of which, as at Stonehenge, point between north and east), skeletons were disarticulated, and some parts removed. Across the valley to the north on Windmill Hill, the ditches of the three concentric enclosures contained large quantities of bone, much of it human. Deposits continued to be made at West Kennet when people were using Grooved Ware and subsequently Beaker pottery, but by then the chambers were nearly full, and there is little evidence that complete bodies were still brought there. As at Stonehenge, when we get into the time of Hengeworld we lose these distinctive houses for the dead; instead, we find odd human bones scattered about in a variety of places.

Enough has been excavated to indicate a pattern remarkably like Stonehenge. Where there are stones there are human bones; where there is only timber there are none, but here, at the sprawling complex of rings, passages and enclosures at West Kennet, there is feasting on young pigs.

There also appears to be a tradition associating the burial of cattle parts with people, even at two long barrows *instead* of people, going back to at least 5500 years ago. In one telling instance on Windmill Hill, a child's skull was buried with an ox skull and two horns, and deer bones. At the South Street and Beckhampton long barrows, in the field where today the two megaliths of the Beckhampton Avenue still stand, there are no human remains, only cattle: four shoulder blades in the former, three skulls in the latter. Much later, around 3900 years ago, the round barrow at Hemp Knoll was thrown up over the grave of a man with a Beaker pot. In the pit, but outside the coffin, were the head and four feet of a domestic cow, thought to be the remains of a complete hide. These bones were not radiocarbon-dated, but in chalk from the mound was a wild cattle shoulder blade dated three centuries older than the burial.[614]

There is a suggestion of the special nature of red deer antlers, too, in a find made in 1894 in the bank around the stone circles. We have seen how antlers were used to dig ditches, but occasionally circumstances imply there was more behind their deposition than the simple discarding of worn tools.[615] Tools are typically from shed antlers, yet at Stonehenge many had been taken from the skulls of slain deer.[616] The Avebury find combines these characteristics: several antlers were found together in the bank (not the usual position at the bottom of a ditch), apparently protected by large blocks of chalk; and they were not shed but taken from dead animals.[617] A shed roe deer antler had been placed into the grave pit at Hemp Knoll.

Yet in the details there is much difference. Gray found a variety of scattered human bones in the ditch surrounding the Avebury stone circle (chapter 16), at first sight comparable to the bone in the Stonehenge ditch. The odd thing is that here the earthwork itself is more like Durrington Walls, which encloses not stones, but timbers. The post holes and ditch at the Walls were full of pottery, bones, flintwork and so on, yet at Avebury excavations have revealed few finds. By contrast, at the West Kennet enclosures is the largest group of Grooved Ware pottery from the district, as well as examples of the distinctive flint arrowheads that we saw were so common at Durrington Walls, and, in a few cases at least, had been the cause of death of pigs.

Can we make sense of this, using the Stonehenge model? Perhaps. The original Avebury earthwork may have been the equivalent of those at Stonehenge and Coneybury. The newly discovered ditch enclosure at Beckhampton has much in common with the Stonehenge ditch, not least its single entrance opening to the north-east. While all stone at Stonehenge had to be imported, at Avebury there were vast fields of natural sarsens, probably mostly in old woodland – again, that juxtaposition of stone and timber. Perhaps the presence of these stones, both physically and metaphorically, encouraged profligate use. So at Avebury we have not one stone circle, but at least three. And we have at least two avenues made not of chalk, but of standing stones, as well as other smaller and little-understood stone circles outside the Avebury henge. What happened at the end of the Beckhampton Avenue is a mystery, but the West Kennet Avenue turned into two stone circles: where Woodhenge has its enclosing ditch and back, at Avebury, again, they used megaliths. Yet there are some remarkable similarities between Woodhenge and the Sanctuary.

Both sites have six concentric rings of posts, and several rings have the same number of posts. At Woodhenge, ring B has thirty-two, C has sixteen and F twelve. At the Sanctuary, the Fence ring has thirty-two (excluding the two much larger posts at the entrance), the Stone-and-post ring has sixteen and the Bank Holiday ring twelve; the other three rings have half these numbers (Ten-foot and Seven-foot have eight each, Six-foot has six). Of course there are also sixteen stones in the Stone-and-post ring.

Most notable, however, is something about the Sanctuary apparently not noticed before that links directly to Woodhenge. Woodhenge's oval shape points at the midsummer sunrise, but the circularity of the Sanctuary, like that of Silbury, defies direction. It is there, however, and, like Woodhenge and Stonehenge, that direction, perpendicular to the axis of the avenue entrance, is towards the rising sun at summer solstice.

The posts of the outer Fence ring are unevenly spaced, but typically are about 2m apart. There are three places where this pattern is broken, and the location of each one is significant. Apart from the two stone circles, there was a single megalith just east of south, comparable to the two stones at Woodhenge. Unlike the Woodhenge stones, which were placed inside timber rings, this stone stood between two rings, but had a pair of posts either side. Two of the anomalous post spacings in the Fence ring are by this stone. Posts 23 and 22, and 25 and 26 are only 1m apart, suggesting entrances or passages into the ring at this point (analogous to the southern entrance at Stonehenge).

The other small gaps are either side of post 8, where again the distance between it and its neighbours is only 1m. In other words, post 8 is superfluous to the normal pattern. Why is it there? One answer is that, seen from the centre of the site, it appears to be indicating the point of midsummer sunrise (figure 53).

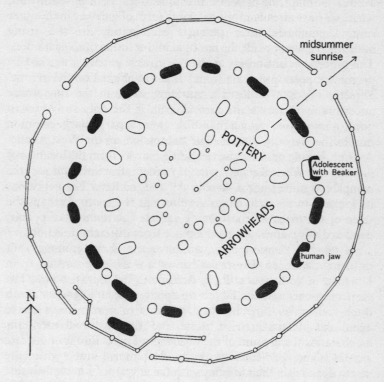

Figure 53. In this plan of the inner area of the Sanctuary at Avebury, I have drawn ring B as a fence (as originally envisaged by the excavator), including a screen around the lone megalith on the south-west side. There is a 'surplus' post on the north-east, which is approximately on the midsummer sunrise line from the centre. Artefacts concentrate on the east side. *After Cunnington and Pollard.*

As at Woodhenge, the focus of artefact deposition at the Sanctuary was on the east side.[618] The Sanctuary lies south of Avebury, connected by an avenue. The stone rows twist and turn, particularly close to Avebury, repeating the meanderings of the

River Avon and the chalk avenue that connect Woodhenge with Stonehenge to the south. But direct comparisons end there.

To gain access through the Sanctuary's inner stone circle, which presents an almost solid wall of posts and stones, requires some tricky manoeuvring between the post and stone just right of the avenue entrance, or opposite the lone stone on the south-west, where we have already proposed some form of gateway in the outer ring. Ceremonies here, perhaps culminating in the rising midsummer sun, include the removal and erection of large timbers. The procession out begins at the north-west gateway, marked by prominent posts and circle stones that are aligned on the avenue. Directly opposite, beneath a standing stone in the ring where ancestors and living stand arm in arm, is the only stray human bone, a lower jaw; human mandibles were a particularly common find in the Avebury ditches. The procession up the West Kennet Avenue, having passed close to and then away from the location of feasting at West Kennet, where timber structures mirror the complex of stone rings at Avebury[619] and the River Kennet begins its journey to the east, enters Avebury at the south. Perhaps the scale of the megalithic structures reflects the number of people, dead and alive, approaching the place from different directions.

At Mount Pleasant also, we have the same grammar but different dialogues. The collection is not as large as that from Durrington Walls, but still pig dominates the animal bones. The earthwork-enclosed Site IV has no apparent solar alignment, both ditch and timber rings pointing just east of north. But we have again the juxtaposition of stone and timber, small megaliths emphasising the division of the five rings of posts into four discrete sectors (figure 20). Here this carefully planned arena where the recent dead begin their journey with the ancestors is actually inside the large henge ditch. Elsewhere along the east–west ridge are other monuments whose roles in the process remain unclear.

On the immediate west is the Conquer Barrow. The henge at Maumbury Rings, orientated to the north-east, is 2km away. Halfway between Maumbury and Mount Pleasant are the flattened remains of a round mound enclosed by a 45m diameter ditch that had once covered three Neolithic-looking grave pits dated to around 4300–4100 years ago.[620] In one, a barbed and tanged arrowhead lay on the body's hip, and cattle bones surrounded it: a shoulder blade under the head, a neck bone under the feet and two further scapulae in the grave fill. Close to Maumbury is the massive timber ring at Greyhound Yard. Nearer Mount Pleasant is the circular Stonehenge-like earthwork at Flagstones (chapter 7).

What we find, then, is that elsewhere the data are not up to the level of detail we have read into the Stonehenge landscape. This is partly because of inadequate fieldwork, but it is also because, ironically, Mount Pleasant and Avebury, the only other Wessex henges where the archaeology can stand any interpretation, are more elaborate than Stonehenge. Gaps in our knowledge are compounded by the sheer complexity of the texts.

So let us rest content for now with the little progress we have been able to make in bridging that chasm of millennia and culture that separates us from these particular ancestors of ours, and ask: what happened next?

29

A Relic Ripe for Manipulation

One of the saddest things I witnessed while writing this book was archaeologist Mark Brennand, sunk to his calves in marine sludge, frantically trying to save his excavation as the light faded, the temperature dropped and the tide rushed in. Not that there was a problem with the tide, for they knew about it, and you can't argue with the sea. Nor the mud, for it had preserved this unique archaeological find. It was one of the most extraordinary things to have turned up in British archaeology in the twentieth century, and Mark Brennand, proud and excited, had the job of retrieving it for posterity.

His problem was that what should have been the highlight of his still young career had become a nightmare. It was a well-organised Norfolk Archaeological Trust project, but Brennand was in danger of losing it completely. Some well-meaning eccentrics, utterly unaware of what was going on, had tried to stop the dig. Two local men, a journalist and an earth-moving contractor, saw a cause to support, the national media arrived and the archaeologists had to work their brief shifts under the glare of police, women chanting unrepeatable doggerel, Druids looking like escapees from a nativity play, and assorted protesters for whom the plot was never really an issue. At one point, tired of screaming 'Leave it, leave it!', a woman rushed at the site and had to be tackled into the mud and handcuffed. I didn't even have that at my Stonehenge dig (plate 17).[621]

But it was saved, and it was worth every drop of sweat. When first exposed, 'Seahenge', the ring of timbers scoured out by the tides at Holme next the Sea, Norfolk, was one of the eeriest, most compelling sights that any archaeologist might face. Now it is gone, conserved in water tanks at Flag Fen Museum, it is a relic dating from a key moment in our history, whose importance cannot be exaggerated.

A ring of fifty-five split posts surrounding the upturned root stump of an oak tree 150 years old when it was felled, Seahenge preserves in its timbers the oldest-known use of metal tools in Britain, signalling the start of a new tradition in carpentry that culminated in the spire of Salisbury cathedral, Elizabethan framed buildings and the fighting ship the *Mary Rose*. Drawing on old customs, yet reworking these into a new form, and now surviving as silent focus for our imagination, Seahenge also presents the perfect symbol for the passage of Hengeworld. If it hadn't been excavated and retrieved for conservation, it would soon have gone, victim of tides, moving sands and tunnelling molluscs. You did all right, Brennand.

The great thing about real wood is that, with skill, you can get real dates. Dendrochronology and radiocarbon, juggled with Bayesian statistics, tell us that the tree was felled (perhaps by windblow) in the early summer 4050 years ago (i.e. 2050 years before the Christian era). The posts in the outer ring were cut down the following year, 4049, between April and June.[622] That means that Seahenge was probably built immediately after the last stones were put in place at Stonehenge, and a few centuries before the Y and Z holes were dug to enclose those stones (figure 54). We will consider two things about these posts: the use of metal axes to cut them, and their place in the Hengeworld tradition of timber circles.

The very marks left by the axes in the wood connect straight to Stonehenge. We would expect to find evidence for the use of early copper axes in the shape of the blade scars, and that is indeed the case. What is a surprise is to find that those scars indicate an axe with a wide, splayed blade edge, exactly as we see in the blades pecked into the sarsens at Stonehenge. This emphasises the difficulty we noted earlier (chapter 26) of dating these carvings. Perhaps they are contemporary with Seahenge, which would make them not that much older than the stones. They may have been part of the symbolism that turned timbers into megaliths. If the stones had to be worked with stone, like giant stone axes, then metal axe blades could be carved into their surfaces to represent the metaphorical dressing of timber. The carvings are hieroglyphs.

Metal is around throughout Phase 3 of Stonehenge (although we should be cautious of the few radiocarbon dates and their wide ranges) – not, at least among actual dated finds, as working tools, but as precious ornaments and display items such as knives and daggers. The 'Iceman' who died in the far north of Italy over 5000 years ago possessed an axe cast from native copper, but at the moment there is no reason to think that metallurgy reached Britain that early. The flint mines at Grimes Graves, Norfolk, amongst the largest in Europe, were being actively worked in this same period (figure 54).

Even the soft-bladed pure copper axe has an advantage over flint. When Channel 4's *Time Team* built a replica Seahenge, Phil Harding and Damian Goodburn found a copper axe could work twice as fast as a stone axe.[623] In a large timber construction project, copper could substantially reduce the labour requirement, and the sharpness of the blade might also encourage more sophisticated carpentry. This presents two possibilities for the impact of copper axes in Hengeworld.

If axes were available early enough, they might have been instrumental in encouraging the whole tradition of large-scale timber carving (as was once, erroneously, thought the case for the impact of imported European iron axes on wood-carving on the north-west coast of Canada and the United States). However, as seems more likely on present evidence, if the axes arrived at the tail-end of the tradition, their effect might have been more to diminish its power. Less labour means less 'cost', making the possibility of constructing a timber henge available to smaller groups of people. The archaeology suggests that this is indeed what happened, and Seahenge is the perfect example of this development.

At a maximum diameter of 6.7m, Seahenge is on a different scale from the large henges. This is not a grand project where large sectors of the living population connect with the community of ancestors. This is a personal memorial, perhaps a family statement where individuals sought to join local ancestors.[624] Yet there is an intriguing survival from Hengeworld cosmology. The oval of the oak ring is orientated north-west–south-east. Opposed to this, on the south-west, is a single 'gate', formed by a post that branches into two as it rises from the ground, creating a sort of knot-hole in the metaphorical trunk of serried split posts with their outwards-facing bark (the posts opposite this hole are the largest in the ring). The people of Holme had made a single, large oak as their link to eternity. And the entrance, on midwinter day, would be penetrated by the rays of the setting sun.

It is interesting to note that had this site been a conventional excavation, with nothing but filled pits, this gate would have been missed, for it exists only in the branching wood above ground. But many small timber post rings have been found, commonly buried

Figure 54: The end of Hengeworld.

Site	cal BC: calibrated date range (95% confidence)	years ago (cal BC mean +2000)	Stonehenge phase
Ötztal, Italy: the 'Iceman'	3358–3122	5240	
Amesbury 71, barrow with stake rings	2865–2141	4505	
Grimes Graves, Greenwell C Gallery 105–106	2548–2345	4445	
Radley 919, burial + Beaker and copper rings	2620–2147	4385	
Grimes Graves, Greenwell Gallery 108–109	2468–2294	4380	
Shrewton 5k, burial + Beaker and copper knife	2471–2208	4340	
Grimes Graves, Greenwell Gallery 104–107	2470–2202	4335	
Stonehenge, large sarsen structures	2461–2205	4335	3ii
Radley 4A, burial + Beaker/gold ornaments	2616–2042	4330	
Grimes Graves, Greenwell A Gallery 200–201	2460–2153	4305	
Corlea, Co Longford, metal-cut timbers	2259±9BC	4260	
Grimes Graves, Greenwell C Gallery	2459–2039	4250	
Grimes Graves, Greenwell Gallery 101–102	2462–2001	4230	
Grimes Graves, 1971 shaft	2462–1981	4220	
Chilbolton, burial with copper knife and gold	2456–1919	4190	
Barnack, burial with copper dagger and gold	2291–2041	4165	
Stonehenge, Bluestone circle and oval	2267–1983	4125	3iv
Mount Pleasant, palisade event	2139–1979	4060	
Holme next the Sea ('Seahenge')	2050–2049 BC	4050	
Radley 4460, burial + Beaker and copper knife	2194–1834	4015	
West Heath III, round barrow with stake ring	2287–1695	3990	
Buckskin II, barrow with stake rings	2201–1687	3945	
Gallilbury, round barrow with stake ring	2271–1605	3940	
Stonehenge, Z Hole 29	2013–1742	3880	3vi
Amesbury 61, round barrow with stake ring	2137–1605	3870	
Edmondsham, 'Wessex' barrow	1934–1642	3790	
Stonehenge, Y Hole 30	1876–1687	3780	3vi
Norton Bavant, burial with 2 bronze daggers	1862–1621	3740	
Llandysilio, round barrow with 6 stake rings	1883–1525	3705	
Hungerford, pit circle with Aldbourne cups	1741–1523	3630	
Stonehenge, Y Hole 30	1687–1525	3605	3vi
Hove, 'Wessex' barrow	1594–1322	3460	
Earl's Barton, 'Wessex' barrow	1521–1324	3420	
Edmondsham, 'Wessex' barrow	1430–1133	3280	

Amesbury 71, Radley 919 etc. are round barrows. See Appendices 2–3 for details.

under or within round barrows, and a few of these have been dated (figure 54). Amesbury barrow 71, at around 4500 years ago, seems early, but the 95 per cent confidence range reaches to 4140. The other five are all contemporary with or more recent than Seahenge, and it may be that Amesbury 71 lies at the young end of its radiocarbon range. It seems the large timber henge tradition turned into a more repetitive (there are many undated examples), more personal concept associated with round burial mounds that served smaller communities.

What happened to the monumental customs, and the ceremonies and rituals? Did they slowly fizzle out, imperceptibly transform into something else? Or was the change more dramatic, violent even? Archaeology raises the possibility of the latter.

You'll remember how we argued that the stones and timbers at Mount Pleasant, conventionally interpreted as dating from different eras, were in fact contemporary. The case rested on saying that sarsen flakes and charcoal in the ditch at Site IV were not construction debris, but came rather from the destruction of the stones (chapter 26). Who did this, and why?

It's early days, but if archaeologists try to disprove this idea, we'll get closer to understanding what was happening. There are three events at Mount Pleasant that radiocarbon dating suggests occurred at the same time. These are the destruction of the stones at Site IV, the extension of the henge bank and ditch to reduce the large west entrance to a small gap, and the construction of the huge timber palisade, which was shortly substantially slighted by a combination of severe burning and uprooting. The five radiocarbon dates are statistically indistinguishable, and combine to give a date of around 4100–4000 years ago for what I have called the 'palisade event'.[625]

Other monuments along this Dorset ridge were destroyed in prehistory. A strange linear earthwork at Fordington, in which an aurochs skull had been buried and at a later date human cremations, was ploughed flat. The huge timber ring at Greyhound Yard was under fields in the Bronze Age.[626] This process whereby unenclosed open landscape was divided up by fences and ditches into systems of fields and settlements that could not easily be moved seems to have occurred throughout southern Britain at this time, not least around Stonehenge.[627] If Mount Pleasant was defended and attacked, it is difficult to think what other forms of evidence we might now have: perhaps the one thing we miss are quantities of flint arrowheads. This may not be particularly significant, however, as the types of deposits that produced most of the arrow points at Durrington Walls – well-preserved, deep Neolithic strata – are less common at Mount Pleasant. On the other hand, if it was the monument that was being slighted and not the people around it, perhaps arrows would not have been loosed. Perhaps, as a place for ancestors, there were no living people there anyway.

Once we imagine such a dramatic event, other things we might not have noticed seem to gain significance. If you walked around Durrington Walls or Mount Pleasant today, you would need someone in the know to point out the courses of what were once enormous earthworks. They are all but gone, which is why it was only modern archaeology that rediscovered them. Yet at Avebury, an earthwork of similar size is still a substantial presence. A few weeks before I write this, after a snowfall, the dykes at Avebury were alive to the sound of villagers tobogganing. You couldn't trip over the other banks if you tried.

Could it be that they were deliberately pushed into their ditches, something that did not happen at Avebury where the ditch had actually been deepened? At Woodhenge, the two stone pits contain fragments of burnt sarsen. Could these stones have been destroyed at the same time as those at Mount Pleasant?

And there is something else. At Avebury, where megaliths stood in their hundreds into the Middle Ages and the earthworks still impress, we have a clear phenomenon of individual human burials, complete bodies, at the base of standing stones, typically accompanied by a Beaker pot, that ceramic that comes into wide circulation at the end of Hengeworld. There is the adolescent we saw in the Natural History Museum from the Sanctuary. There are bodies along the West Kennet Avenue, inside the stone circles and on the Beckhampton Avenue. Somehow Avebury survives, because its expansive wide-reaching cosmos is subverted for personal, family needs.

The association of these occurrences at both Mount Pleasant and Avebury with Beaker pottery is a big tease for archaeologists, who have been arguing for over a century about precisely what the appearance of this ceramic, and other things like the barbed and tanged arrowhead, signal (chapter 10). A recent study attempted to reassess the evidence of both archaeology and cranial anatomy (often in the past claimed to indicate an immigration of people), but was unable to find a solution to the issue.[628] Dramatic change does not need invasion, but it has to be said that the immigration hypothesis was rejected in the 1970s as much as any reason because of academic fashion. The possibility that at this time in Europe certain people were on the move, in search of land and other resources, needs to be revisited.

Stonehenge, naturally, was caught up in this change. Once a gathering of the ancestral community from distant worlds, it becomes, I suggest, a huge symbolic burial mound, the final resting place for a single entity, a man elevated from leader to god.

The strange, empty Y and Z holes were dug outside the stones some time after these were erected, in imperfect rings that follow the sarsens (chapter 19). A slight deviation in the circuits suggests that sarsen stones 8 and 9 were flat on the ground before the Y and Z pits were dug (chapter 26). The converse implication is that all the other sarsens were still standing around 3600 years ago, seven centuries after they were put up.

People commonly speak of these pits as if they were meant to take megaliths in a plan that was abandoned, but as we saw (chapter 26) it seems more reasonable to assume they were actually meant to be what they are: rounded, rectangular holes in the chalk 1.7m by 1m at the top (Y holes) and 1.75m by 1.5m (Z holes), and 0.9m and 1m deep respectively. They taper significantly as they go down, in what I referred to as a bath-tub effect.

There aren't any other *rings* of pits like this, but there are many individual comparable pits. They are found all over Britain, not least in a zone between about 1 and 2km from Stonehenge, beneath circular mounds. Normally they contain, amongst other things, human skeletons. Which is why we call them graves.

The people who excavated the Y and Z holes must have been aware of the similarity between these pits and barrow graves – the only other comparable pits they would ever have dug – just as their ancestors before them had to have known the bluestones came from the west. So, taking our cue from these symbolic graves, let's consider the implication that Stonehenge itself has now, around 3600 years ago, transformed into a piece of funerary architecture.

As so often happens, we would like to have many more dated sites than we do. Such as they are, however, radiocarbon dates suggest that the Y and Z holes are broadly contemporary with what Stuart Piggott long ago called 'Wessex' burials (figure 54).[629] These are bodies, often cremated, buried in pits under large round mounds and accompanied by a selection of precious craft goods that might include copper and bronze daggers, jewellery of gold, jet, amber and faience (blue glass), strange little pots (known as 'Aldbourne cups', 'incense cups' and other fanciful names) and other distinctive things. They are found all over Britain – and elsewhere in Europe, not least in Brittany – but are particularly common around Avebury and Stonehenge.

As many as half the surviving barrows at Stonehenge may cover burials of this type. The best-known, named the Bush Barrow by William Stukeley, was dug into both by Stukeley and later, in 1808, rightly suspecting his predecessor had not gone down deep enough, by William Cunnington. With the unburnt remains of a single man laid on his back the diggers found an extraordinary haul: two finely decorated gold sheets in the shape of lozenges, a gold belt hook, two or three daggers and an axe of copper or bronze, a polished stone 'macehead', thousands of tiny gold pins that had once covered the dagger handle, and several other small items. Fragments of wood and cloth preserved in metal corrosion products hinted at what else might have been placed in the grave pit (figure 55).

This is by any standard an exceptional grave, and for this reason it is sometimes suggested that the occupant directed the construction of Stonehenge. Not many years ago, while this was always a whimsical idea, it was at least in theory possible for part of the monument. Radiocarbon dating, however, now makes that more than unlikely. The Bush Barrow itself is not dated, but the types of objects in the grave were being made centuries after the stones were put in place – Stuart Needham suggests some time between 3900 and 3700 years ago.[630] If he did not see the stones being erected, however, the tomb's occupant might just have witnessed the excavation of the Y and Z holes.

Following the English Heritage study, I have said these pits are around 3600 years old. However, the four radiocarbon determinations range between 4000 and 3500 years ago.[631] We accommodate this range by assuming two of the antlers dated were already two centuries old when buried, an unsatisfactory position encountered previously with Stonehenge radiocarbon dates. So both Bush Barrow and Y and Z holes are floating in time in the centuries after the last megalith was erected.

Among all the objects in this grave, we have noticed there were perhaps three large metal daggers (one was destroyed on

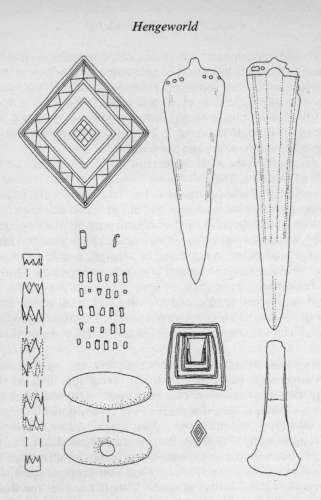

Figure 55. Some of the finds from the primary inhumation beneath the Bush Barrow, south of Stonehenge. They include (clockwise from top left): an intricately incised gold plaque, daggers of copper (left) and bronze, an axehead (copper or bronze), a heavy gold belt buckle and a small incised gold lozenge, a limestone 'macehead', bone mounts suggesting the former presence of a wooden baton, and bronze rivets. Also found were thousands of 1mm-long gold pins, which had decorated the handle of the smaller dagger. The burial is undated, but the style of the daggers suggests around 3900–3700 years ago. *After Annable and Simpson.*

excavation) and one axehead. While daggers are not uncommon in these graves, axes are rare. But it is a combination we see in the centre of Stonehenge: a single dagger carved on the face of stone 53, surrounded by a group of 'at least 14 axes', and further axes on the outer faces of sarsens 3, 4 and 5.[632] It is as if the stones have become a symbolic grave, the mythical corpse represented by carvings of precious and distinctive objects normally buried with people granted elaborate and expensive funerary rituals. If we follow Needham's suggested date for these carvings (not before 3900 years ago: chapter 26), rather than put them nearer the date of megalith erection (as above), their creation too might have been seen by the Bush Barrow man.

Let's look at them a little closer (figures 10 and 49). Just as the dagger is amongst a group of smaller axes, so the axes in the outer sarsen circle surround one outsize axe. In a variety of contexts across Europe, including rock carvings and burials, there is a reasonably confident association of daggers with men.[633] Axes have no such identified connections. It is tempting, however, to suggest that in this Stonehenge context, the large rounded axe is the counterpart of the carved dagger: it is, perhaps, a woman. It is a curious coincidence (only proper survey will establish whether it is more than temporary coincidence) that the number of axes presently identified in this group is the same as megaliths in the ring – thirty. There are three on stone 3, twenty-five with the large one on stone 4 and one on stone 5. Stone 3, you may remember, is the one with the natural feminine groove (figure 49).

Ros Cleal has suggested that an unusually fine Beaker, represented by six sherds from secondary contexts inside the bluestone circle, accompanied the skeleton excavated by Hawley in 1926 in the centre of Stonehenge.[634] Only radiocarbon could date this: prehistoric, Roman and later objects were found in the pit, which had been disturbed in recent centuries. The bones were at the Royal College of Surgeons before the war, and they have not been found (see chapter 30). But whether or not anyone was actually buried in the centre of Stonehenge is not the issue. As with the relics of a medieval saint, it is the symbolism that is important. Stonehenge has been usurped by a man and his retinue, accompanied by objects of mortal existence. The stones are no longer ancestors, but merely an extraordinary version of something everyday, the burial mound. The man is an extraordinary transformation of humanity, something alien to earlier cosmologies: a god.[635]

His symbolic tomb is enclosed by two rings of thirty graves, matching the numbers of stones and axe carvings, just as barrows for the living are surrounded by a ditch – or often two. Beyond Stonehenge, the hundreds of round barrows are also arranged in

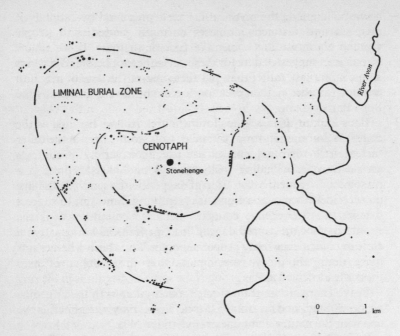

Figure 56. Stonehenge 3600 years ago, as focus of a funerary landscape. At Stonehenge the dagger is carved on the trilithon, and empty grave pits are dug around the stone circles. On the plain around, hundreds of burial mounds are arranged in a zone distant from the stones, focusing on two rings. *Based on Woodward and Woodward.*

two broad bands, as if in echo of the central 'barrow' so that the entire cemetery landscape becomes a symbol of this divine focus (figure 56).[636] Once a place where individuals came together at death to join the community of ancestors, Stonehenge is now a personal memorial, perhaps a political pawn, around which society expresses its aspirations for life and its achievements at death. Already, 3600 years ago, Stonehenge is a relic ripe for manipulation.

The new contexts for Stonehenge I have presented in this book envisage metaphor and symbol, not over-literal science; process and action, not rigid monumentalisation. This does not add up to 'the solution'. As I have said repeatedly, there are few solid answers to the many questions that strike us when we look at Stonehenge and similar places from the past. Faced with this uncertainty you can, as some archaeologists two or three generations ago did, pretend not to want to know. You can, on the other hand, plough ahead in complete defiance of what evidence there is and imagine whatever takes your fancy. Many non-archaeologists are now doing this, partly, I suspect, in frustration at the professionals' apparent lack of concern. What I have tried to do in this chapter, and throughout the book, is show how archaeology has created too much data to be ignored. Any satisfying story of the past has to recognise this. There is no excuse for ignorance now. With the publication of English Heritage's Stonehenge report, the information from the last century is publicly available. But the picture continues to change. That huge book, and this one, are a beginning, not an end.

Perhaps now, having read this far, you feel like having a go at working it out yourself. I recommend you do. There is something quite special about deep contemplation of our remote ancestors. I think they knew that, too.

But the story is not quite over. Another man was buried near the centre of Stonehenge, and his bones *have* survived. They are now, as Jackie McKinley and I discovered, in the basement of a London museum.

30

Loss of Innocence

Jackie McKinley picks up a long brown cardboard box full of bones. The base is covered in crumbs.

'A few more years', she says, 'and there'll be nothing left of the poor thing.'

In the concrete-walled basement of the Natural History Museum we've looked at the bones of people from the Sanctuary and Woodhenge and a medieval man from Avebury. Of least interest, it seems, is the one who started this particular quest, 4.10.4, the skeleton from Stonehenge that turned out to be Roman – if the date obtained by Arthurian fan Winston Peach is to be believed.

The head has been the victim of a creative act of restoration. There is plaster and glue everywhere. The once separated pieces of skull have been fitted back together in more or less, but significantly not quite, the right positions. A tooth has been jammed with a dollop of glue into the wrong socket. But the rest of the skeleton is well preserved. Thirty to forty years old, he has a distinctly masculine, square jaw – 'like the men in the razor adverts', says Jackie. 'Gillette jaw', she writes in her notes.

Jackie is going through the Stonehenge man's vertebrae – threaded onto a wooden stick like a large kebab – when she pauses and holds one out to me. 'Look at that', she says. I take it.

The bone is flattened on one side, as if it's been planed away. The penny doesn't drop. So, a bone is damaged? I'm really not that interested in this skeleton, it's Roman. But Jackie is talking to the bone. She's trying to prove, by argument, that the damage to the vertebra is modern. She's losing her case. OK, this neat truncation of the bone was not caused by the digger's spade. But I still don't get it. Jackie is examining the other vertebrae, turning them over one by one. She finds the bone that would have articulated with the one I hold in my hand. It's undamaged.

'So if the neck was bent forward', she says . . . Neck? For some reason I've assumed it was from the lower back. '. . . the sword

300

could've completely missed the third cervical.'

Beheaded.

It's obvious. In fact I'm wondering why no one has seen it before – not least the person who has, since the arrival of the skeleton in the Natural History Museum, written out pages of bone measurements.

As Jackie and I talk, my mind begins to race. Execution in the centre of Stonehenge. What – sacrifice? Murder? Punishment? Romans against natives? Modern against ancient in the centre of the ancient aliterate world's icon. For a century archaeologists have fought to dissociate Stonehenge and Druids (with about as much success as a pub landlord calling 'Time' at 11.30 pm on New Year's Eve). What will people make of this?

Images crowd my mind. Of the late Stuart Piggott, who had both excavated at Stonehenge and written what remains the best English-language book on Druids, who never knew. Of those archaeologists in the 1920s who thought Stonehenge itself was Iron Age. Of the old guidebook sacrifice clichés (well at least it was male, so we'd be spared speculations over virginity and bust size). Of modern judicial executions: by the end of 1999 more people would have been legally murdered in the United States than in any year for half the century; Saudi Arabia would have beheaded – a sharp, curved sword is efficient – nearly 100 people, over half of whom would not be Saudi citizens. Of the silvery grey megaliths rising from the innocent grass into the mist. None of us knew . . .

When Jackie and I looked at the barber-surgeon, we had wondered if the old story about him being killed by a falling megalith was really true.

'We're destroying one myth', I say, 'and creating another.'

'That's what archaeologists do', she replies.

Perhaps there'd been a mix-up. Suddenly it became important to know – to *really* know – if skeleton 4.10.4 was found by Colonel Hawley at Stonehenge. With all the to-ing and fro-ing, it was easy to see how things might have got muddled – labels lost, records confused. I had to trace this skeleton's pedigree through the years since its discovery. I had to confirm that what Jackie and I saw in the Natural History Museum matched descriptions of the bones written near the time of the excavation. I needed to know.

If it did come from Stonehenge, which of the three skeletons could it be?[637] The one in the ditch, excavated by Hawley in 1922?

From the grave outside the sarsen circle (1923)? Or from the pit close to the bluestone circle (1926)?

The 1922 find was clearly not in the running, as it was too incomplete to be 4.10.4. When Mike Allen wrote to the College of Surgeons he had asked about the skeleton found in 1923; Hawley refers to a report about this one by Arthur Keith. But with her reply, Muriel Gibbs had enclosed a copy of a letter from Keith to Robert Newall (the only original osteological documentation for all three bodies) that almost certainly refers to the 1926 skeleton. These two burials are superficially quite different, but looking closely at the records, I could see similarities. If one did prove to be 4.10.4, then perhaps the other might have been a contemporary and related death.

1926 was Hawley's last, abbreviated season at Stonehenge, and the documents are proportionately brief. The excavators were alerted to something interesting when they found 'a quantity of human bones . . . in a disordered mass, evidently thrown there carelessly'. They proceeded with caution, and recovered a wonderful assortment of rubbish typical of the centre of Stonehenge: medieval and prehistoric pottery, Roman coins and a horseshoe nail, Georgian tobacco pipes, bottle glass and a Victorian pin. Hawley thought an earlier explorer had disturbed the grave and thrown the contents back, leaving just enough to tell that the original pit had been 2.4m long (8 feet), 75cm deep (2½ feet) and lying between north-west and south-east. Judging by an arm bone still in place, the head had been at the northern end. This would mean the body had been astride the midsummer axis, close to the centre of the monument, an apparently significant location.

He was, wrote Keith to Newall, 'a stout-limbed fellow about 5 ft 6 in high [1.7m]'. The skull was damaged, but from other bones Keith suspected a 'lateish' Roman date. There is a nice Stonehenge touch to this: he also identified ox and sheep bones, and a piece of jaw from, he says, a prehistoric woman.[638]

We have more information about the 1923 burial. Hawley's diary records the discovery:

Friday 2nd November

Today I examined a spot where it sounded hollow yesterday. Player had taken off the turf and a dark patch of humus suggested another post hole in line with those found yesterday at Y [Hole] 9 and Y 10 . . .

After descending a little farther I came upon a large bone and almost immediately after a human patella [knee-cap] came out. I now saw that there must be an interment here.

I returned loose soil over the spot and directed Player to lay the top open for special investigation tomorrow and wired Newall to come.

Newall duly motored over the next day, and the two men excavated the grave. It was a shallow thing, only 65cm deep, 60cm wide at the shoulder end and 45cm at the feet. Hawley doesn't say it in so many words, but it sounds as if the body had been laid out straight, on its back. At 1.6m long (5 ft 4 ins) the pit was too small:

It was very roughly cut and only [sufficient] . . . to contain the trunk of the body . . . the neck and shoulders had to be forced into a curve and pressure seems to have been exerted upon the pectoral portion as all the ribs were contracted and forced together and all were in a broken state with the exception of two.

If this was 4.10.4 (whose ribs do not seem to have survived), the pit deficiency might be explained by its excavators wanting to dig no more than was necessary to take the headless corpse, squashing the skull in on top. The records do little more than hint at this. There are no photographs. Newall drew a section of the pit (figure 57), which shows the skull higher than other (unidentifiable) bones. Measured on the drawing, the top of the head is 40cm from ground level, similar to the 41cm (16 inches) Hawley wrote in the diary. The fact that Hawley commented (twice) on how close to the surface the skull was suggests it might well have been separated. Newall's drawing shows a similar pit depth to the diary, which is really too shallow for there to be much distance between head and body. This is an important point, as we shall see later.

After this, the story comes mainly from the Royal College of Surgeons, where Sir Arthur Keith, confident of his personal worth as much as of the value of his work, kept particularly detailed archives (bless him).[639] Seven months after it was dug up (during which time it was probably stored in one of Hawley's huts at Stonehenge), the skeleton was delivered to Keith by none other than Alexander Keiller. Keith wrote his study within less than a

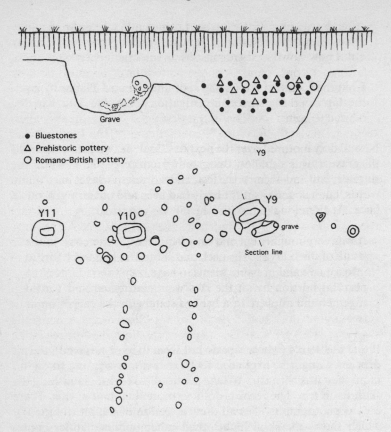

Figure 57. This section by Robert Newall and the Office of Works plan constitute the only visual record we have of the grave excavated in 1923. *After Newall and Cleal et al.*

fortnight, and a few days later, on 24 June 1924, Hawley addressed a London audience at the Society of Antiquaries. He described the burial. It was, Keith had told him (I have not found a copy of the original report):

> . . . the skeleton of a man and of a type he has become familiar with, occurring in the period about the time of the Roman occupation, or more probably in the centuries immediately preceding it.

Although only months before he'd confidently written in the diary that the burial was Neolithic (he'd also thought it was female), Hawley was now happy to go along with the expert anatomist, referring to Roman and Iron Age pottery he'd found in the area. 'Perhaps', he said, 'a Roman-British squatter and his family made their abode in that quarter.'

This change of opinion is interesting. For an archaeologist reading Hawley's diary, the Neolithic date of the burial comes across as more of a fact than a whim. First, Hawley described the grave and post hole fills as being contemporary, while Y 9 'cut' one of these post holes: in modern archaeological parlance this would mean the post hole, and hence the grave, were older than the Y hole. He also says that despite sieving the grave fill they found only the skeleton and a thin 'Stonehenge Layer' above it. As we have seen, in common with Hawley, modern archaeologists take the absence of stone debris in pit fills as a suggestion that such pits were dug before megaliths were dressed on site.

Yet Hawley overturned his own records in deference to Keith (in favour of what admittedly only now would we call a highly dubious racial argument). The implications for Stonehenge are a little worrying. After all, at the moment our case that the Aubrey Holes are older than the stones rests largely on the same logic used by Hawley to say his grave was Neolithic. Fortunately, pursuing this is not our present task. We move on to 1938, and an astonishing piece of luck.

Keith retired as Conservator of the museum in 1933. In 1935, Dr A.J.E. Cave was appointed as Assistant Conservator. It became his duty to see the collection, of enormous medical interest, through the war. As well as equipment and records of famous early surgeons, the Hunterian Museum (as it was known) had amassed an extraordinary assortment of specimens from around the world. Even for the 1920s the accessions register is something to behold. Gorilla skulls, human cysts, tumours, hands, hearts and bladders, penis sheaths from New Guinea and antique stomach pumps, all pale beside the cyclopic double-headed duckling ('3 of clutch so: hen sat irregularly').[640] Beside such wonders, what were dirty, broken old bones dug up by archaeologists?

But to its eternal credit the college did not shirk its responsibilities. Prime Minister Chamberlain may not have expected war, but in September 1938, a year before it started, Cave began his preparations. Miss M. G. Collett was appointed

Temporary Anthropological Assistant to clean up the basement. Her duties included the 'general overhaul, repair and card-indexing of specimens' and the 'sorting and boxing of much archaeological material of uncertain value, deposited in past years by various field workers, and by them neither re-claimed nor presented to the Series [of Human Osteology]'.

In Miss Collett's lists is the following entry:

4.10.4 Skeleton, adult male, Roman-British, Amesbury, Stonehenge. Donor: Col. Hawley (Stores).

This is the first indication I have found that a Stonehenge skeleton (we are not told which one) had been accessioned by the museum. If this had not been done, it and the other skeletons later moved to the Natural History Museum are most unlikely to have survived what was to come.[641]

When war broke out the museum was closed down, most of the staff moving to Bristol to work at the Army Blood Transfusion Service. The college itself became a sub-station of the London County Council Fire Service. Bombing started in September 1940. The most precious specimens were stored in the basement, reinforced with gas- and splinter-proof shelters. Much of the library was moved to the country. In November heavy bombardment inflicted no more than door and window damage. Over at Bloomsbury, a few blocks north of the college, which is in Lincoln's Inn Fields, the British Museum had made its own preparations. Quantities of objects were removed at the outbreak of war, many of the heavier items making the short journey to the underground train tunnel at Aldwych.

On the night of 10 May 1941, incendiaries fell on the British Museum. The security effort was justified. But nothing could have prepared the ancient college buildings for what hit them. They got the incendiaries (a roster of roof-watchers had been assembled in readiness). They also got three high-explosive bombs. The rooms holding most of the comparative osteology collection were annihilated. The lecture theatre, the council room, the President's room, the room for this and the room for that were transformed into ragged boxes open to the sky, containing mounds of rubble under which there was no point in searching. A reinforced tunnel, used to store some of the specimens, collapsed under white-hot brickwork.

But, miraculously, not everything was lost. As people slowly sifted the chaos, helped by the American Ambulance Corps, some 40 per cent of the Hunterian medical collection was salvaged. Within five weeks of the raid seventy ambulance loads had been taken to seventeen different locations 'in the country'. In one of those vans, bumping out to one of those secret places, we can imagine were the boxed remains of skeleton 4.10.4.

What happened next is, for the moment, a mystery. There is no doubt that at the time archaeologists all believed their own stuff was completely destroyed. The link had been severed.

Rebuilding and expansion began soon after the war. In its redefined role, the college had little use for much of its older collections (not every organisation gets the chance to create space by donating a whale to the Natural History Museum, as they did in 1953). The archaeological skull collection was in a shed. It was accepted by the Natural History Museum in 1948, and seven years later the rest of the bones followed. If the head was still on the shoulders when the body was buried at Stonehenge, Arthur Keith definitively separated them. In 1999, following my request to view skeleton 4.10.4, Rob Kruszynski located both skull and long bone boxes, and after a varied and not uninteresting career, the man regained a sort of completeness.

I am now persuaded that this skeleton was dug up at Stonehenge. Close study revealed the numbers '4.10.4' on several of the bones; the ink is worn, indicating a certain age for this labelling. Even fainter is the word 'Stonehenge', written in pencil. Science would prove it, but I suspect the pencil on the skull is underneath varnish.

But none of this tells us which skeleton we have. This is where the bones come in. Anatomical features of 4.10.4, particularly the state of the teeth in the upper jaw and the way the skull is repaired, match descriptions in Hawley's 1923 diary. By itself, this would not be enough to identify the skeleton as Hawley's, but with the historical record it does make it as certain as we could hope that the bones are from the burial found at Stonehenge in 1923.

Case proven. A triumph, if I may say so, of archaeological and museum record-keeping, if abetted by outrageous luck.

So we can add an executed man to the lists of things found at Stonehenge. Who was he, and why did he die? Critical to answering this question is another: *when* did he die? Call Mr Winston Peach, King Arthur advocate of unknown origin and address.

*

Once I was satisfied skeleton 4.10.4 really was from Stonehenge, I approached English Heritage who agreed to fund a new radio-carbon date. Queuing for the laboratory takes several months. In the meantime, I would have to make do with what I had. The first edition of this book would go to press before I got the new date. I was going to have to stick my neck out.

In 1975, two large bones were almost totally destroyed for a single date (the same would be obtained today from a tiny scrape). The 'Mould Book' in the Natural History Museum confirmed the circumstances, with an entry describing the casting of a femur and tibia from 4.10.4 before radiocarbon dating.

About AD 150, said Kruszynski. Was this the raw date or a calibration? In 1975 calibration was still seen by archaeologists as an option, so it was probably uncalibrated. How 'about', and what was the standard deviation? I calibrated two dates, AD 100 and AD 200 with a deviation of 100 years. The result, with 95 per cent confidence, indicated that 'Arthur' died somewhere between about 50 BC and AD 550.

This was scary. The 'evidence' of the date obtained for Peach, as remembered by Rob Kruszynski, was enough to say the bones were not Neolithic or Medieval, but the range covered the whole of the Roman era in Britain, and even took in the mythic battle of Badon at which King Arthur is supposed to have won a historically significant victory against invading Saxons. This would perhaps have pleased Winston Peach, but it made life difficult for me. All I could do was explore the more likely contexts for a skilful decapitation at Stonehenge within these six centuries

I began at the stones. Apart from the burial, was anything else happening there at that time?

Most of the excavated coins were Roman: the oldest was struck around the time of Claudius's invasion and the rest covered the following centuries until the end of the fourth. Then there was a gap until a penny of Aethelred II (997–1003). Remarkably, more Roman pottery had been found at Stonehenge than prehistoric. Well over 6kg of small, weathered Roman sherds paralleled the coins with a story of people coming to the monument but leaving no other evidence for their presence: there were no known Roman holes in the ground.[642]

What did this mean? There was little evidence for any substantial Roman or Iron Age activity near Stonehenge. The river Avon to the east seemed to have been the local focus of settlement.[643] Some archaeologists had suggested that the dilapidation of Stonehenge – it remained unexplained why nearly half the monument was missing – might have occurred in the Roman era, perhaps as a deliberate slight to an indigenous pagan monument.[644] Archaeology threw no light on this. It was notable that many of the missing stones were the smaller, more portable sarsen lintels. Routine building with stone had been introduced by Romans, and future excavation might yet reveal a structure made with some of these missing lintels, perhaps at the small town on the outskirts of Amesbury east of the river.[645] It had to be said, however, that any substantial use of stones in this way would likely have been reflected in their later re-use in Medieval buildings, for which there was no evidence at all.

So with no more than a scatter of coins and small sherds, I could talk only in terms of casual visits or nearby farming that might have seen rubbish thrown onto fields with manure. An Anglo-Saxon or Medieval presence was even slighter, consisting of less than 0.5kg of pottery. To put this another way, there was nothing in the general archaeology of Stonehenge to give the slightest hint that there might have been an execution there in the first few centuries after the birth of Christ.

Medieval legends did not help. Queen Aelfthryth founded an abbey in Amesbury in 979 which later became the proud owner of what were said to be relics of Saint Melor.[646] I mention this because Melor was decapitated, after which a miracle occurred when his head rejoined his body by its own accord! Any parallel between this and 4.10.4, however, had to be coincidental. Melor was supposed to have lived and died in early sixth century Brittany, and the claim of Amesbury to have parts of his body was entirely unsubstantiated (as were most claims of this type).

I guessed Winston Peach thought 4.10.4 was King Arthur on the evidence of a tale written by Geoffrey of Monmouth around 1136. It begins with Hengist, the evil Saxon invader, and ends with Merlin building Stonehenge (with stones magically transported from an Irish mountain) to commemorate the slaughter of British men at the hands of Hengist's treacherous warriors. At his death the British hero king Aurelius Ambrosius is buried at Stonehenge, as later is his brother king, Utherpendragon. Uther is succeeded by his son, Arthur.[647]

It was all there for an imaginative mind: a famous king (in fact, two) buried at Stonehenge and a beheading (Hengist – was there once a Stone-Hengist? – was executed). But Arthur was not buried there, and as far as I knew (I couldn't help but think fortunately!) no Arthurian story related his decapitation. More importantly, this was legend and politically motivated creation of history, not fact. Arthur and Hengist might have been real characters alive in late fifth- or early sixth-century Britain, but Geoffrey's Stonehenge tale had been written for a twelfth-century audience. The association with Stonehenge was almost certainly a clever appropriation of a mysterious monument known only as something old and native.[648]

To proceed further, I needed to seek a wider context. Archaeology and history suggested three very different but equally intriguing possible connections. We'll start with the most recent, that closest to Arthur: this is a world of dragons, ancient burial mounds and the brutal murder of social outcasts.

That the decapitated man might not have come from Stonehenge at all was no idle fantasy. Shortly after the skeleton was acquired by Arthur Keith, his museum received a further sixteen, all of which had been beheaded, from two excavations not that far to the east of Stonehenge. It seemed to me there was a real possibility that one of these might have become muddled with the Stonehenge records. The College published detailed descriptions of them all, however, and not one fitted the Stonehenge skeleton.[649]

But what were these peculiar cemeteries of decapitated people? The two sites, Roche Court Down in Wiltshire and Meon Hill in Hampshire, had much in common. The bodies were all lying in shallow graves near the turf, in the top of silted up prehistoric ditches, on their backs, feet to the north. Some were decapitated but with the head still in place, some had the head down by the legs; others showed no signs of beheading. On several, blows had been delivered to the head, jaw and shoulder as well as neck. Hands were sometimes together, as if tied.

The locations were telling: Roche Court Down and Meon Hill had good views, were on parish boundaries and crossed by long-distance tracks. These were almost certainly the sites of judicial killings, where convicts had been hanged, beheaded and buried. The ages ranged only between twenty and fifty, and there was but one woman at each place.

On purely anatomical grounds, the College's Miss Tildesley thought these people were Romans or Saxons; there was little other indication of date. However, there is now wide archaeological support for Anglo-Saxon execution and burial in just that sort of place – at ancient burial mounds on hill-top boundaries. In a recent Oxford University thesis, Sarah Semple had shown that in Anglo-Saxon times, the eighth century and later world of Beowulf, there was a fear of remote barrows as places of evil, death and dragons. By committing certain offences, or at least by being believed to have done so, people put themselves outside society, and were fit only to end their days beyond the realms of normal life and death.[650]

My time frame did not extend into the eighth century AD, but Semple found something apparently yet more significant when it came to wondering if 4.10.4 might have been this sort of judicial murder. 'An analysis of the sources of the period', she had written, 'revealed a profound silence concerning stone circles'. Megaliths were not part of an Anglo-Saxon's cosmography. This conformed with Geoffrey of Monmouth's story: he would hardly have placed a stone circle centre-stage with his heroes if it had evil associations.

A few centuries before this, however, and well within the range of my radiocarbon 'date', decapitated bodies were being buried with the rest of the population. Perhaps here, in Roman Britain, I had a better context for the anonymous Stonehenge man.

Consider an older teenager, probably a girl, who had been laid to rest in a Roman cemetery in what is now Baldock, Hertfordshire. If her beads, bone hair pins and bronze finger rings were anything to go by, she had been, despite her unhealthy gums, one of the wealthier people in the community. Something else distinguished her. Although she was lying out straight, her head and her top two neck bones lay between her legs.

Examining her, Jackie McKinley had found the second neck bone, the axis vertebra, had six cuts; she had also found a cut mark on the jaw. The blows had all been delivered from the front, perhaps with a short sword like a machete, so the girl must have been lying on her back. There were probably hacks to the soft neck tissues before the bone was struck, and the final separation was achieved with a quick thrust back of the head, cracking the last of the bone.[651]

Why had this been done? The mode of burial did not seem to suggest she was an outcast. It hardly sounded like a murder: in fact, the young lady was probably already dead when her head was removed. The scene I imagined was less of a formal execution than of a butcher working casually in the morgue.

This type of thing was by no means uncommon in southern Britain.[652] There was generally little else to distinguish the people so treated from their fellow citizens. They might have been rich or poor, fit or healthy, male or female and, apart from the scarcity of children, of an age typical of the population. Almost without exception they dated from late in the Roman era, that is mostly fourth or even early fifth century.

In the absence of any historical record of what was going on, interpretation was a guessing game, and guesses had covered the lot, from sacrifice, murder and judicial execution to a variety of religious options, including the offering of another's soul to the gods as a substitute for that of a soldier killed in battle, and the ritual cleansing of an individual who had died from disease.

It was notable that the majority of bodies, like the girl at Baldock, had been decapitated from the front, and thus probably after death. None of this really sounded like the Stonehenge man. It could not be proved, but it seemed likely that decapitation was the cause of his death. His bent neck had been struck hard and with great efficiency from behind. His rapidly dug grave had only been long enough to take his headless corpse, yet the head had been unceremoniously buried above his shoulders. If, as seemed to have been the case in the majority of cemetery beheadings, the goal had been to achieve something after death, it made sense that the head should have been buried away from the neck, visibly signalling the act of removal. And finally he was, of course, alone at a remote and extraordinary location, not in the midst of the community that knew and reared him.

That left the final option: Druids. The third potential context for a decapitation at Stonehenge I had to consider was the meeting of two worlds, when parochial met empire.

It may be imagined that local feuds and alliances, between different communities and different strata in northern Europe, could have been redirected towards a wider common goal, to escape the Roman invader. For some people, this might have been better achieved through treaty. For others it was war. And as Tacitus vividly described at a confrontation on Anglesey in AD 67 (machine-tuned Roman soldiers were apparently so awe-struck by chanting Druids and black-robed torch-wielding women that they momentarily froze), for the north European, battle itself could be a religious event. Here was an opportunity not just for the petty empire builder, but also for the priest, the shaman, or the Druid.

Archaeology had long made it clear that Wessex was an area where indigenous and invader came to blows. A number of earthwork hill forts seemed to have suffered military assault in the first century AD. So it was in this atmosphere of rapid and unpredictable change, in which Druids might have led a sort of millenarian protest revolt,[653] that I could see a third setting for a beheading at Stonehenge.

There were two very different possibilities. The man could have been killed in a ceremony led by native officiants, a sacrifice dedicated to defeating the colonist, to appease gods and please onlookers. In such a case he need not have been an insignificant person. There are suggestions that some of the famous bog bodies dating from early Roman empire times, sacrifices thrown into bogs and lakes in which the means of death often focussed on head and neck, were relatively wealthy people.[654]

Or he could have been an important individual seized by Roman soldiers and taken to Stonehenge to make a political point. One possible explanation for the contempt with which Roman writers held Druids was that they provided a focus for religious and ethnic opposition to empire. Take the story, recorded by the soldier-historian Tacitus, of Mariccus, a member of the Boii people in what is now France. He had declared himself a god sent to restore Gallic liberty, assembled 8000 men to his cause and in AD 69 confronted an alliance of neighbouring Gauls and Roman soldiers. Captured in battle, Mariccus was thrown to the beasts. The animals in the arena had ignored him, but his triumph was brief: a soldier had stepped out and cut off his head.[655]

For either of these possibilities, Stonehenge did not have to function as a centre of religious activity. There was copious evidence from throughout northern Europe for a wide range of ceremonies that had left some fascinating and sometimes bizarre traces in the ground. But there was nothing to suggest either that people were building stone circles, or systematically revisiting them. Thus there was a scatter of Iron Age pottery at Stonehenge (people had passed by before Romans arrived), but there was no known nearby temple site. If we took Stonehenge away, we would be left with nothing to make us think the place had special religious significance a few centuries either side of the birth of Christ.

So whether 4.10.4 was a man sacrificed in a Druidic protest ceremony, or a politically prominent individual murdered by Roman soldiers, the roles of both the victim and the monument would have been similar. Both would have represented indigenous, timeless tradition, a claim to land and ancestry. If sacrifice, the purpose was to uphold and emphasise that stake. If murder at the hands of an alien power, it was the opposite: to demonstrate that native authority was dead, that the new world was Roman.

In February 2000, Channel 4 commissioned a film, to be broadcast in less than six months, that would tell 4.10.4's story.[656] What should we do, knowing we would not get the new radiocarbon date until, at best, the film was well into production?

I decided this was a chance to present science in the raw. We would give viewers the three possible contexts that archaeology and history suggested and conclude with the new date. Perhaps good archaeology would anyway point to the right era: but if not, the viewer could share in the fallibility of research. I don't remember that we ever discussed what we would do if a fortnight before transmission we were handed a Bronze Age date – or we were left still waiting for any result at all.

I felt the Roman funeral to be the least likely. The date obtained by Peach hinted at Druids rather than Saxons, and this was what, in his own way, Richard Atkinson himself had suggested forty five years before (the burial, he thought, dated from the Roman era). 'It is conceivable that Stonehenge was regarded by the occupying power as a dangerous focus for resurgent nationalism', he had written, 'particularly perhaps during the early years of the occupation, when the flourishing cult of Druidism was stamped out with unusual ferocity'. He was at pains, of course, to emphasise the absence of actual Druids, who were 'almost unmentionable in polite [archaeological] society'.[657]

In the meantime, perhaps we could learn more about Peach's old date? Indeed, I now had a new quest: who was this mysterious sleuth from Wales?

One evening, Mark McMullen (the film's producer), Jeremy Freeston (director) and I were reviewing progress in a London pub. Jeremy's most acclaimed project to date had been a film of *Macbeth*, so from the beginning I imagined 4.10.4 would be treated to more drama than academic discussion: I was not going to be disappointed. Then we got a call from Chris Stringer. He'd found a record of the original date.

That morning we'd been to the Natural History Museum to look at the skeleton. It was the first time that Chris, who is head of the Human Origins Group there, had seen the wounded neck bone. He was clearly impressed, and keen to help both with research and filming. Working late, he'd opened a box file marked 'Old Correspondence'. It contained two letters from a Mr Peach.

On 7 January 1976, Wystan Peach (as we discovered his real name to be) had written to Dr Stringer requesting more bone. Mr Otlet at the Harwell dating laboratory (Kruszynski's memory had been right on that) had told Peach that he needed a larger sample for a conclusive result. Chris had obliged, for four months later, he received another letter from Peach. 'Dear Dr Stringer', it read. 'Mr Otlet of Harwell gave me the provisional news of the investigation . . . of the skeleton as 760 AD'.

I stared into my beer. 760 was not 150: Saxon, not Roman. But yet more significant might be that word 'provisional' (and the absence of any further data, such as a laboratory number). It was a word with which the same Bob Otlet had described my Stonehenge date in 1980, the date that Alex Bayliss had thrown out in the English Heritage study on grounds that a final result had never been achieved. On the face of it, this date might be of no use at all.

We took an instant decision. The dramatic reconstruction of an early Roman beheading at Stonehenge we were planning would go ahead (with the help of English Heritage, still blissfully unaware of what we were about). But we'd also film a later Roman drama (the funeral rite). And a Saxon.

The next day I phoned Andy Reynolds, a colleague I knew would be excited by news of a possible Anglo-Saxon beheading at Stonehenge. He was even then publishing his work on early Medieval law and punishment, and he was married to Sarah Semple, whose work on Anglo-Saxon attitudes to ancient places had already attracted my attention. Then I went to the Natural History Museum to look at the letters Chris had found. Here was a further mystery.

Peach had written from a dental practice in Cardiff. He was delighted the radiocarbon date had proved experts wrong ('the anatomist of Cardiff' Dr Irvine – who he? – had inexplicably suggested dates of 1725 or 1890, although it's not clear in the letter if that should be AD or BC). The error range associated with a date obtained in the 1970s of AD 760 (albeit the letter held no news on exactly what it was) should have been enough to accommodate King Arthur. Yet Peach was unhappy. He argued, on no evidence, that the analysed leg must have come from a different skeleton, mixed up with the real Arthur's head. So what date *had* he wanted? I had to go to Wales.

From my experience as museum curator at Avebury, I knew

people with an archaeological obsession sometimes wrote long and often to professional archaeologists. I began my tour of Cardiff with a visit to my friends at the National Museum of Wales. There was indeed some correspondence. In 1961 the museum had returned to Peach a booklet he had written about Stonehenge (clearly more than a passing interest: this was fifteen years before he paid to date 4.10.4, closing a letter expressing his disappointment at the result with the memorable sentence 'I cannot give up the search yet'). The letters contained tantalising references to bluestones and folklore, and Peach had been admonished for incorrectly speaking of 'Celts or Iberians in the Britain of 1500 BC'. I felt none the wiser.

My next stop was the dentistry, now a Dental Surgery Implant Clinic. As I stood at reception, a frameful of grinning dentists with perfect white teeth eyed me suspiciously, but I was warmly received. Peach had been a lovely, popular man, with a little dog that attacked patients' ankles. He had given the new owners of the practice a copy of his Stonehenge pamphlet. Perhaps the boss would be able to find it, once he was back from spreading the smile at a conference in Cuba. Yes, Peach did have children.

In the public library I found what I needed: a death notice in the *South Wales Echo*, 24 March 1980. He had been 71 when he died, the 'loving father of Penrhyn, Gisela and Ceri'. I phoned Mark McMullen in Leeds, who began the search for living relatives. At last, it seemed, we were getting somewhere. And then in the university library (the fourth I'd visited) I found confirmation of his booklet, which was called, to the point if not very helpfully, *Stonehenge: a New Theory*. But still no copy.

I was writing up my notes that evening in a Cardiff pub when Mark phoned. He had found a website for Ceri Peach, an Oxford professor of geography. The next day he phoned again to confirm that Ceri was Wystan's son. The two of them had worked together on Stonehenge, not least diving off the Welsh coast looking for lost bluestones. Peach senior's interests had included left-wing politics, opera singing, hill-farming and dental training, but an enduring passion had been possible links between Stonehenge and the Mabinogion, a collection of Medieval Welsh tales. When Ceri's mother died, they had thrown out most of his father's stuff. But he thought his brother, Penrhyn, still had a few papers in a cupboard.

Meanwhile, English Heritage were proving unfailingly helpful, and on 11 April we shot our first film sequence: at Stonehenge in pouring rain (conditions we were to become very familiar with).[658] I had to collect a small soil sample for Paul Budd and Janet Montgomery, who had just set up in business as Archaeotrace. The sample was needed as a control in analysis of a tooth from 4.10.4. Was our victim a local man, or had he grown up some way from Stonehenge, perhaps, if he really was Saxon, even on mainland Europe? We would soon find out.

The soil sample delivered to Paul and Janet, our next stop, thankfully, was indoors: at English Heritage's offices in London. The news was that the first, provisional date had been released by the Oxford lab.

If you saw the film, you will know this result was handed to me on a piece of paper as I stood nervously in front of the camera. The scene was not faked! We had Peach's date of AD 760, but with little to encourage us to treat it too seriously, historical and archaeological argument for an early Roman context weighed heavily. But no more. The date was AD 591 ± 38. This, I later established, showed on the calibration graph with a strong peak around 650-700 (the second date came through in January 2001: the two averaged together give a calibrated range of about AD 600-680).[659] 4.10.4, we could now be in no doubt, was alive in Anglo-Saxon times (but too late to be Arthur). At that moment in front of the camera, quite suddenly, the man and his manner of death became very real for me.

A few days later Wystan Peach also rose from the texts and ephemera when a television crew invaded Penrhyn Peach's home in Rutland. Penrhyn was a charming retired Vulcan pilot. Not only did he have a cupboard-full of papers for us, but there was also a cine film of his father, happily walking outside his Welsh farm. Finally I was beginning to approach the man. If only, I felt, he could see us.

Lecture notes, press cuttings, letters and photos said almost all I needed to know. There was more on the radiocarbon date. Although still without a lab number, the detail of AD 760 ± 80 seemed to imply that this might have been a definitive result, although the lack of further information means that its value is limited.[660] 'I am positive my theory is right', he had told the *Western Daily Mail* in 1975. 'Mr Peach is not deterred', added the journalist, 'by the fact that most experts think his theory is wrong'. Indeed not. But such was the scorn of the 'cognoscenti', Peach had felt the only option was to 'plunge into print' with his booklet, illustrated with some striking contemporary-style graphics.[661]

The gist of his theory was that the Stonehenge circle represented the female sun, while the Heelstone and the stone horseshoes were the male earth. The purpose of Stonehenge was to marry Earth and Sun at winter solstice (and remember this was published in 1961, before Stonehenge astronomy became hot gossip – to say nothing of a similar idea trumpeted in 1992 as an original 'solution'). The first bluestone structure (known today as Phase 3i) was open to the solstice sunrise, with dawn ceremonies; at other times, the monument was directed at sunset.

This and more is described, thought Peach, or at least remains hidden for the perceptive reader, in oral stories handed down through the centuries to be recorded in the Mabinogion. So that was why Peach had dismissed the radiocarbon date: Arthur was a Bronze Age king, the architect of Stonehenge (another idea subjected to a modern book).

Frankly, I found all this quite fanciful, and could understand why archaeologists approached by Peach had been sceptical. But I liked the way he had constructed an imaginary Stonehenge world of ceremony and power struggles – such a contrast to professional ideas of the time conjuring a bare and silent fossil – and his consideration of the rafting of bluestones from the Preseli hills has yet to be matched in a modern study.

But most intriguing was a comment in one of his lectures (Welsh dentists, I felt, must have been well educated in the ways of Stonehenge) about a paper he had sent to the journal *Antiquity* in 1977 – that is, the year after he had dated 4.10.4. Did his text (I couldn't find a copy) refer to the skeleton and the date? It seems likely, not least because of how much the date had cost him. If so, in returning the submission which the editor considered not 'of sufficient national interest to be published', Glyn Daniel had missed an extraordinary scoop – news of 4.10.4 would soon have led to the realisation that all those other skeletons, including Avebury's barber-surgeon, were also still in London. I like to imagine that this was so. That, on behalf of all new antiquarians, ley-liners and mystic historical revisionists, Peach had scored against the Cambridge academic who railed bitterly against what he called 'the lunatic fringe'.

Towards the end of May, Paul and Janet had completed the tooth analysis and we went to Nottingham to film them at work. It was pioneering stuff. Teeth grow in early childhood, and become a sort of black box of a person's early life, containing all sorts of clues to health and diet. Our interest was in three trace elements: oxygen, strontium and lead. The oxygen in the water 4.10.4 had drunk as his teeth grew, and the strontium in his food (reflecting the soils on which plants and animals had lived) could both tell us something about where he had grown up. In Roman or Saxon times, lead crockery or pipes would have left their own fingerprint. The lead in his tooth also had a story for us.

It turned out, Saxon Brit though he was, he had not spent his childhood in Saxony. The ratio of two strontium isotopes in the tooth enamel matched the geology of central southern England, including the coast along to Kent, and a second area on the east coast of Lincolnshire and Yorkshire. The oxygen isotopes mapped an almost completely different zone, from west Scotland and central England down to the midlands, including East Anglia. There was but a small overlap, approximating to the Chilterns and north Wessex, 4.10.4's apparent home territory. He could even have grown up within sight of Stonehenge, a suggestion consistent with the carbon stable isotope values (obtained during the radiocarbon dating) which indicated he ate very little seafood.[662]

His tooth had a relatively high lead content, which suggested to Paul and Janet that he was ingesting lead with his food, perhaps from cups and plates. This might imply that he had been reared in a wealthy household.

It was all beginning to come together. It remained only to consider the wounds. Five of us, and a teaching skeleton wired so we could make it kneel on the carpet, assembled in a cleared room at York University archaeology department. Props man Ivan Williams had brought a coolbag full of sheep's necks from his local butcher, and the film crew circled like vultures. How much could we say about exactly how 4.10.4 had died?

David Sim is an experimental archaeologist from Reading. He has a variety of swords, made in his garage according to strict historical information, augmented by axes and other knives from historical re-enactment groups. Ivan sharpens the blades with an electric grinder, and David butchers the necks, one blade after another sweeping across a Health and Safety poster on the wall behind. After a time, we are picking little red flecks off everything. A bagged heap of severed joints grows on the floor. 'Can I have a cloth or something?' asks David.

Two months before, Malin Holst and Sarah King (who had studied late Medieval battlefield murders from Towton, Yorkshire) had examined 4.10.4 in London and found a small nick on the left side of the lower jaw. Their immediate thoughts were that this was not an execution, but a battle fatality. I had asked them if there was anything about the bones to suggest the skull and the rest of the skeleton came from different bodies. Quite the reverse: they showed me a rare feature of the first neck bone (technically, double condyles on the atlas vertebra), which fitted the skull perfectly. If they were from different bodies, aside from the size match, there was only a five per cent chance of getting this fit.

I hadn't bought the war wound: where were all the other men, and where the arm damage that typically occurs from failed attempts to protect the head? Now we have the chance to argue it out, Malin, Sarah, David and I and Chris Knüsel from the University of Bradford. Eventually we agree that the most likely story is a single blow delivered from behind by a right handed person, to a victim with a straight back, standing or, more probably, kneeling. The wounds were made with the very tip of the sword, suggesting to Malin and Sarah that the victim may have been moving away from the killer, perhaps running. But they accept that the Stonehenge location might imply a more formal execution. After a long stretch of filming, we break for coffee. The room empties, except for a clean white kneeling skeleton, in the centre of the carpet.

There was no carpet and no TV crew, then. Witnesses, tears, family? Rain or dust? Sheep or shrubs? Most of the details will forever remain unknown. But now we have a historical context, what of the generalities? Andy Reynolds, with a special interest in early Anglo-Saxon law and punishment in Wessex, sees the dismissal of a thief. With Stonehenge at the front of my mind I see more.

There are things that might make 4.10.4's death seem a result of some transgression.[663] In later Anglo-Saxon England grievances were aired at public courts (Aethelred published a code in AD 997 that refers to twelve men who for all practical purposes were jurors). The commonest punishment was a fine, but you could have a foot or hand removed for theft and be executed for a variety of offences, including travelling unannounced, minting false coins, plotting against the king or sorcery. But the laws of several kings prescribe capital punishment for theft too, especially if you were caught in the act.

As we saw earlier, execution sites were commonly in exposed, boundary locations, and gibbets could be erected on ancient burial mounds. Stonehenge, named for its resemblance to a ring of early wooden gallows, is not far from (if not precisely at) the meeting of three hundreds, local government units with their own courts. It's certainly remote and ancient. But I hesitate to say that is all there is to 4.10.4.

These laws, and the dated archaeological evidence for judicial execution sites, are mostly eighth century or later, not quite as old as our burial. And there remain the distinctive facts that the burial and the beheading are unique, and that these occurred at the unparalleled and dramatic monument of Stonehenge. I'm prompted to imagine a more political killing.

Seventh century Anglo-Saxon kings were no strangers to murder. In AD 626, King Cwichelm of Wessex sent an assassin with poisoned sword to see off Edwin of Northumbria. The plot failed, and the recovered Edwin marched against the West Saxons and killed five of their kings, with other supposed schemers. In 686 Caedwalla left Wessex to invade the Isle of Wight, and put to death the king and his two brothers.[664] We're not yet in full historical times, and it may be that we will never be able to say with confidence which kings held power at the time of 4.10.4's execution. But we might imagine that a death of this kind, the statement reinforced by the liminal location, is as possible as a more prosaic retribution for a criminal act.

This was a local man wealthy enough to feed from metal vessels. He would have had to have been walked from at least Amesbury, 3km to the east, implying the Stonehenge location was deliberate. A grave was dug for his body, and post holes at each end (figure 57) suggest a marker was erected. Is it not possible that Geoffrey of Monmouth's tale of warring Saxon and British kings, recorded around 500 years later, contains a garbled memory of real events (events perhaps, even, echoed also in Amesbury's story of the beheaded St Melor, despite what I said above)? That 4.10.4 is not Arthur, but, in some mythic fashion, Aurelius Ambrosius?

Like the time of the very creation of Stonehenge, this is a key era in our island history. Fundamental matters like an official religion (Christianity), language (English), kingship and the foundations of our modern judicial system were being settled. Whatever the original persona of 4.10.4 and the reasons for his death, for us today he is a nameless symbol of a transition from a prehistoric to a historic arena.

Stonehenge for me will never be the same. For half my life (in common with many archaeologists) I have imagined a place of Neolithic drama, that became a quiet ruin thousands of years ago. But when people killed a man there two or three centuries after the departure of Romans, Stonehenge could not have been an antiquarian curiosity. This was a real death at a place that gave the event certain meaning. The thoughts in the minds of people at Stonehenge in AD 650 were as real and as 'true' as those of their ancestors over two thousand years before, if quite different.

Why should it ever have been otherwise? I have proposed that Stonehenge was re-imagined in the early Bronze Age. Must not every generation have seen Stonehenge through different eyes? And are not those Stonehenges all 'equal', the real perceptions of real people? The extraordinary stones are a solid manifestation of Neolithic fancy, the crust around an abandoned bath-tub. But they do not speak to anyone: they mark the landscape, a focus for the new creativity of the living inspired by an invented past. And every summer, in the middle of the year, the same sun rises on the same axis, without censure or sanction, on the stones that defy time by never standing still.

When we go to Stonehenge today, whether to gaze in puzzled awe, to dream, to fight, to make money or even to cut the grass, we imagine we are at an ancient place. English Heritage want to remove the roads and car park – and may they succeed – to 'restore' some of the sanctity and peace of former times. In reality it's all now. The grass of Stonehenge is no more ancient than the concrete of a runway at Heathrow airport (under one of which, incidentally, lie the remains of an Iron Age temple). The stories we weave of our ancestors are testament to our detective skills and imagination: they are not stories told before.

But our 'now', and not just at Stonehenge, is quite profoundly infused by what came before. Over four thousand years ago, when people created that extraordinary sculpture in materials that would outlast unimagined generations, they reached out to a vision that added meaning to their lives. If, between that space and the megaliths, we can connect – in whatever way we choose – we show them, and ourselves, a respect that honours our shared humanity. And, from a bunch of old rocks, that's some inspiration.

Appendix 1: Radiocarbon dates for Stonehenge

Adapted from Allen and Bayliss in Cleal et al 1995, Table 64 and Bronk Ramsey and Bayliss 2000. Dates calibrated by OxCal 2.18 and Calib 4. They differ slightly from previous publications because the 1993 revision to the 1986 calibration data, used by Calib 4, was not officially accepted until after Allen and Bayliss's study. The 'years ago' figures are used in the text. The varied confidence ranges expressed in the cal BC column must be taken into account.

Context	Material	Lab ref	BP: radio-carbon age before 1950	cal BC: calibrated date range (95% confidence)	years ago (cal BC mean +2000)
Pre-Stonehenge					
Car park post pit A	charcoal	HAR-455	9130±180	8788–7806	10295
Car park pit 9580, secondary	charcoal	GU-5109	8880±120	8289–7602	9945
Car park pit 9580, secondary	charcoal	OxA-4919	8520±80	7706–7380	9545
Car park pit 9580, tertiary	charcoal	OxA-4920	8400±100	7597–7144	9370
Car park post pit B	charcoal	HAR-456	8090±140	7516–6643	9080
Sarsen hole 27	bone	OxA-4902	5350±80	4345–3979	6160
Ditch S entrance, curated bone	red deer bone	OxA-4833	4550±60		
Ditch S entrance, curated bone	ox jaw	OxA-4835	4455±40		
Ditch S entrance, curated bone	ox jaw	OxA-4834	4460±45		
Ditch S entrance, curated bone	ox skull	OxA-4842	4520±100		
Ditch S entrance, curated bone	*4 sample weighted mean*		*4478±25*	*3340–3030*	*5185*
Phase 1 (c.4950–4900 years ago)					
Ditch primary	antler	BM-1583	4410±60	3340–2897	5120
Ditch primary	antler	UB-3794	4432±22	3304–2926	5115
Ditch primary	antler	BM-1617	4390±60	3322–2886	5105
Ditch primary	antler	UB-3789	4430±18	3258–2927	5095
Ditch primary	antler	UB-3793	4393±18	3090–2920	5005
Ditch primary	antler	UB-3788	4381±18	3083–2918	5000
Ditch primary	antler	UB-3787	4375±19	3081–2916	5000
Ditch primary	antler	UB-3790	4367±18	3078–2915	4995
Ditch primary	antler	UB-3792	4365±18	3078–2914	4995
Excavation of ditch				*3015–2935*	*4975*

Phase 2 (*c*.4900–4400 years ago)

Ditch secondary, phase 2	antler	UB-3791	4397±18	3092–2920	5005
Ditch secondary, phase 2a	bone	OxA-5982	4405±30	3258–2918	5090
Ditch secondary, phase 2a	antler	OxA-4904	4365±55	3261–2883	5070
Ditch secondary, phase 2a	bone	OxA-4843	4315±60	3089–2787	4940
Ditch secondary, phase 2a	bone	OxA-4881	4300±60	3082–2708	4895
Ditch secondary, phase 2a	bone	OxA-4841	4295±60	3080–2706	4895
Ditch secondary, phase 2a	bone	OxA-4882	4270±65	3076–2677	4875
Ditch secondary, phase 2a	bone	OxA-5981	4220±35	2899–2698	4800
Ditch secondary, phase 2a	bone	OxA-4880	3875±55	2486–2145	4320
Ditch secondary, phase 2b	bone	OxA-4883	4300±70	3092–2702	4895
Start of ditch filling				*3110–2950 (86%)*	*5030*
End of ditch filling				*2460–2210*	*4335*
Aubrey Hole 32 cremation	charcoal	C-602	3798±275	2919–1519	(4220)

Phase 3 (*c*.4550–3600 years ago)

Sarsen hole 1	antler	UB-3821	4023±21	2618–2470	4545
Sarsen trilithon hole 53/54	antler	OxA-4840	3985±45	2618–2350	4485
Sarsen trilithon hole 56	antler	OxA-4839	3860±40	2465–2200	4335
Sarsen trilithon hole 56	antler	BM-46	3670±150	2469–1642	4055
Stone hole E	antler	OxA-4837	3995±60	2832–2313	4575
Stone hole E	antler	OxA-4838	3885±40	2469–2204	4335
Large sarsen structures (OxA–4838, OxA–4839, BM–46)				*2461–2205*	*4335*
Bluestone hole 40c	antler	OxA-4900	3865±50	2469–2145	4305
Bluestone hole 40c	bone	OxA-4878	3740±40	2284–1983	4135
Bluestone horseshoe hole 63a	antler	OxA-4877	3695±55	2275–1920	4100
Bluestone circle and oval (OxA-4877, OxA-4878)				*2267–1983*	*4125*
Human skeleton in ditch	bone	BM-1582	3715±70		
Human skeleton in ditch	bone	OxA-4886	3960±60		
Human skeleton in ditch	bone	OxA-5044	3785±70		
Human skeleton in ditch	bone	OxA-5045	3825±60		
Human skeleton in ditch	bone	OxA-5046	3775±55		
Human skeleton in ditch	*5 sample weighted mean*		*3817±27*	*2398–2144*	*4270*
Avenue ditch at Stonehenge	antler	OxA-4884	3935±50	2571–2239	4405
Avenue ditch 0.9km from Avon	bone	OxA-4905	3865±40	2466–2201	4335
Avenue ditch 42m from Stoneh.	antler	HAR-2013	3720±70	2326–1919	4125
Avenue ditch at Stonehenge	antler	BM-1164	3678±68	2281–1832	4055
Z Hole 29	antler	OxA-4836	3540±45	2013–1742	3880
Y Hole 30	antler	UB-3824	3449±24	1876–1687	3780
Y Hole 30	antler	UB-3822	3341±22	1687–1525	3605
Y Hole 30	antler	UB-3823	3300±19	1680–1520	3600
Last Y Hole				*1640–1520*	*3580*

Post-Stonehenge

Sarsen hole 8, upper fill	bone point	OxA-4885	2840±60	1210–834	3020
Palisade, human burial	bone	UB-3820	2468±27	774–409	2590

Appendix 2: Radiocarbon dates for selected henges and other sites

Calibrations as Appendix 1. Where dates for a single event are statistically indistinguishable they have been combined for calibration. 'Amesbury 39', 'Shrewton 5k' etc. are round barrows.

Site	Context	Material	Lab ref	BP: radio-carbon age before 1950	cal BC: calibrated date range (95% confidence)	Years ago (cal BC mean +2000)
Amesbury	chalk plaque pit	bone	OxA-3316	4250±80		
Amesbury	chalk plaque pit	antler	OxA-3317	4130±80		
		2 sample weighted mean		4190±56	2903–2581	4740
Amesbury 39	cremation with amber and jet beads	charcoal	HAR-1237	3620±90	2272–1741	4005
Amesbury 51	burial with Beaker, bronze awl etc.	charcoal	BM-287	3738±55	2294–1978	4135
Amesbury 61	round barrow with stake ring		HAR-6227	3520±100	2137–1605	3870
Amesbury 71	grave pit in barrow with stake rings	bone	NPL-77	3960±110	2865–2141	4505
Arminghall	post pit	charcoal	BM-129	4440±150	3622–2679	5150
Ashcott Heath	bow	yew wood	Q-598	4615±120	3645–2924	5285
Avebury	old land surface under henge bank	bone	HAR-10325	4640±70	3633–3104	5370
Avebury	old land surface under henge bank	charcoal	HAR-10063	4380±80	3345–2879	5110
Avebury	old land surface under henge bank	charcoal	HAR-10500	4190±90	3007–2495	4750
Avebury	henge ditch S entrance, primary	antler	HAR-10502	4300±90	3304–2625	4965
Avebury	henge bank, NW side	antler	HAR-10326	4160±90	2917–2471	4695
Avebury	great stone circle, 41	charcoal	HAR-10062	4130±90	2906–2466	4685

Site	Context	Material	Lab ref	BP: radio-carbon age before 1950	cal BC: calibrated date range (95% confidence)	Years ago (cal BC mean +2000)
Avebury	great stone circle, 44	animal bone	HAR-10327	3870±90	2575–2039	4305
Avebury	henge ditch, SE side, secondary burial	charcoal	HAR-10064	3690±80	2295–1830	4065
Barford	henge		Birm-7	4366±64	3326–2881	5105
Barnack	burial + Beaker, copper dagger and gold	human bone	BM-2596	3770±35	2291–2041	4165
Barnack	coffin round burial with Beaker	charcoal	BM-1412	3660±60		
Barnack	coffin round burial with Beaker	charcoal	HAR-1645	3570±80		
	2 sample weighted mean			3627±48	2138–1830	3985
Buckskin II	barrow with stake rings, central post	charcoal	HAR-8370	3590±100	2201–1687	3945
Caldicot Castle	plank sewn boat	wood	UB-3427	3430±19	1859–1664	3760
Cambridge Fens	bow	yew wood	Q-684	3680±110	2456–1744	4100
Chilbolton	burial + copper knife and gold ornaments	human bone	OxA-1072	3740±80	2456–1919	4190
Chilbolton	round barrow, secondary burial	human bone	OxA-1073	3780±80	2464–1959	4210
Chilbolton	outer ditch	hazel nut	OxA-2315	3740±80	2456–1919	4190
Condicote henge	inner ditch, lower secondary silts	charcoal	HAR-3064	3720±80	2399–1885	4140
Condicote henge	inner ditch, lower secondary silts	charcoal	HAR-3067	3670±100	2396–1747	4070
Coneybury	pit 1601	bone	OxA-1409	4370±90	3349–2764	5055
Coneybury	ditch primary	bone	OxA-1408	4200±110	3081–2471	4775
Corlea, Co Longford	timbers cut with metal blades		(O'Sullivan 1996)		2259±BC	4259
Lesser Cursus	Phase 1 ditch	antler	OxA-1405	4550±120	3635–2906	5270
Lesser Cursus	Phase 2 ditch	antler	OxA-1404	4640±100	3642–3039	5340

Site	Description	Material	Lab code	Date BP	cal range	
Dagenham	carved pine figure	wood	OxA-1721	3800±70	2464–1983	4225
Denny, Falkirk	bow	oak wood	Q-1196	3250±85	1737–1320	3530
Devil's Quoits	henge ditch, primary		HAR-1887	4010±120	2882–2147	4515
Devil's Quoits	henge ditch, top of primary		HAR-1888	3590±70	2139–1742	3940
Dorchester, Dorset	Church St, post pit	charcoal	HAR-5508	4060±90	2881–2346	4615
Dorchester, Dorset	Greyhound Yard, post pit 1631	charcoal	HAR-6688	4080±70		
Dorchester, Dorset	Greyhound Yard, post pit 1631	charcoal	HAR-6689	4140±90		
			2 sample weighted mean	4102±55	2878–2473	4675
Dorchester, Dorset	Greyhound Yard, post pit 4163	antler	HAR-6664	4070±70	2877–2462	4670
Dorchester, Dorset	Greyhound Yard, post pit 1635	charcoal	HAR-6686	4020±80		
Dorchester, Dorset	Greyhound Yard, post pit 1635	charcoal	HAR-6687	4090±70		
			2 sample weighted mean	4059±52	2861–2467	4665
Dorchester, Dorset	Greyhound Yard, post pit 4885	antler	HAR-6663	4020±80	2865–2303	4585
Dorchester, Oxon	Site XI: multiple ring ditch and pit circle	antler	BM-2440	4320±90		
Dorchester, Oxon	Site XI: multiple ring ditch and pit circle	antler	BM-2442	4320±50		
			2 sample weighted mean	4320±43	3078–2881	4980
Dorchester, Oxon	Site 2: penannular ditch, primary	antler	BM-4225N	4230±50	2916–2639	4780
Dorchester, Oxon	Site 3: post circle, outer wood of post	charcoal	BM-2162R	4100±120		
Dorchester, Oxon	Site 3: post circle, outer wood of post	charcoal	BM-2161R	4060±110		
Dorchester, Oxon	Site 3: post circle, outer wood of post	charcoal	BM-2164R	4120±120		
			3 sample weighted mean	4091±67	2879–2467	4675
Dorchester, Oxon	Site 3: post circle, pipe fill	charcoal	BM-2166R	4030±130	2898–2147	4525
Dorchester, Oxon	Site 3: post circle, cremation	charcoal	BM-2163R	4070±130	2915–2206	4560
Dorchester, Oxon	Site 3: post circle, cremation	charcoal	BM-2165R	3550±130	2277–1525	3900
Dorchester, Oxon	Site 4: paired ring ditches, grave pit	charcoal	BM-2167R	3690±130	2466–1695	4080
Durrington 7	grave pit with 2 juveniles, 1 cremated	bone	OxA-1398	3700±100	2456–1777	4115

Site	Context	Material	Lab ref	BP: radiocarbon age before 1950	cal BC: calibrated date range (95% confidence)	Years ago (cal BC mean +2000)
Durrington Walls	old land surface under henge bank	charcoal	Gro 901	4584±80		
Durrington Walls	old land surface under henge bank	charcoal	Gro 901a	4574±50		
Durrington Walls	old land surface under henge bank	charcoal	NPL-191	4400±125		
		3 sample weighted mean		4559±40	3491–3100	5295
Durrington Walls	Midden	charcoal	NPL-192	4270±95	3254–2582	4920
Durrington Walls	henge ditch, S entrance, primary	antler	BM-400	4000±90		
Durrington Walls	henge ditch, S entrance, primary	bone	BM-399	3965±90		
Durrington Walls	henge ditch, S entrance, primary	charcoal	BM-398	3927±90		
		3 sample weighted mean		3964±51	2617–2304	4460
Durrington Walls	henge ditch, N side, secondary	charcoal	BM-286	3630±110		
Durrington Walls	henge ditch, N side, secondary	charcoal	BM-285	3560±120		
		2 sample weighted mean		3598±81	2196–1697	3945
Durrington Walls	N Circle post hole 42	antler	NPL-240	3905±110	2836–2038	4435
Durrington Walls	S Circle base post hole 92	charcoal	BM-396	3950±90		
Durrington Walls	S Circle packing post hole 92	antler	BM-395	3900±90		
Durrington Walls	S Circle packing post hole 92	animal bone	BM-397	3850±90		
Durrington Walls	S Circle holes 133, 134, 141, 193, 194	antler	NPL-239	3760±148		
		4 sample weighted mean		3884±49	2471–2201	4335
Earl's Barton	'Wessex' barrow with bronze dagger		BM-680	3169±51		
Earl's Barton	'Wessex' barrow with bronze dagger		BM-681	3214±64		
		2 sample weighted mean		3186±39	1521–1324	3420
Edington Burtle	bow	yew wood	Q-669	3270±110	1872–1316	3595

Site	Description	Material	Lab code	Date	Calibrated	
Edmondsham	'Wessex' barrow		BM-708	3069±45	1430–1133	3280
Edmondsham	'Wessex' barrow		BM-709	4377±52	1934–1642	3790
Ferriby	Boat 1	wood	Q-3124	3020±40	1394–1129	3260
Ferriby	Boat 1	wood	Q-3043	2980±55	1389–1010	3200
Ferriby	Boat 2	wood	Q-3123	3120±45	1496–1263	3380
Ferriby	Boat 2	wood	Q-3044	3095±40	1434–1224	3330
Ferriby	Boat 3	wood	Q-3045	2975±45	1373–1023	3200
Ferriby	Boat 3	wood	Q-3047	2945±40	1293–1006	3150
Fir Tree Field Shaft	L6b hearth (Early Neolithic)	charcoal	OxA-8010	5150±45		
Fir Tree Field Shaft	L6b near hearth (Early Neolithic)	charcoal	OxA-8009	5045±45		
			2 sample weighted mean	5097±31	3967–3798	5885
Fir Tree Field Shaft	L5 turf (Peterborough)	animal bone	OxA-7986	4490±45		
Fir Tree Field Shaft	L5 turf (Peterborough)	animal bone	OxA-8007	4405±45		
			2 sample weighted mean	4447±31	3332–2925	5130
Fir Tree Field Shaft	L2a chalk dump (Beaker)	animal bone	OxA-7985	3775±45	2395–2037	4215
Fir Tree Field	Pit 11a (Grooved Ware)	antler	BM-2406	4140±60	2884–2497	4690
Fir Tree Field	Pit 32 (Grooved Ware)	antler	BM-2407	4080±50	2866–2471	4670
Flagstones	burial on ditch bottom, segment 19	human bone	HAR-9158	4490±70	3486–2919	5205
Flagstones	ditch primary, segment 27	antler	OxA-2322	4450±90	3486–2886	5185
Flagstones	burial cut into primary fill, segment 14	human bone	OxA-2321	4210±110	3084–2473	4780
Flagstones	ditch primary, segment 13	antler	HAR-8578	4030±100	2880–2236	4560
Flagstones	central burial	human bone	HAR-9159	3560±70	2132–1692	3910
Fordington Farm	Grave 61	human bone	UB-3306	3844±30	2458–2200	4330
Fordington Farm	Grave 59	human bone	UB-3305	3767±47	2330–2034	4180
Fordington Farm	Grave 70	human bone	UB-3304	3715±54	2285–1945	4120
Gallibury	round barrow with stake ring	human bone	BM-2232R	3560±120	2271–1605	3940

Site	Context	Material	Lab ref	BP: radiocarbon age before 1950	cal BC: calibrated date range (95% confidence)	Years ago (cal BC mean +2000)
Goldcliff	timber structure including boat planks	wood	CAR-1434	2720±70	1005–794	2900
Gorsey Bigbury	lower ditch fill	charcoal	BM-1088	3800±74	2466–1982	4225
Gorsey Bigbury	lower ditch fill	charcoal	BM-1089	3782±62	2458–1983	4220
Gorsey Bigbury	lower ditch fill	bone	BM-1090	3666±117	2456–1696	4075
Gorsey Bigbury	lower ditch fill	charcoal	BM-1086	3663±61	2201–1832	4015
Gorsey Bigbury	lower ditch fill	bone	BM-1091	3606±67	2140–1748	3945
Gorsey Bigbury	lower ditch fill	charcoal	BM-1087	3602±71	2191–1744	3970
Grimes Graves	Greenwell Gallery 101–102	antler	BM-1027	3855±40		
Grimes Graves	Greenwell Gallery 101–102	antler	BM-1261	3855±75		
		2 sample weighted mean		3854±35	2462–2001	4230
Grimes Graves	Greenwell Gallery 104–107	antler	BM-1049	3885±45	2470–2202	4335
Grimes Graves	Greenwell Gallery 108–109	antler	BM-1028	3925±40		
Grimes Graves	Greenwell Gallery 108–109	antler	BM-1044	3925±90		
Grimes Graves	Greenwell Gallery 108–109	antler	BM-1048	3880±40		
		3 sample weighted mean		3904±26	2468–2294	4380
Grimes Graves	Greenwell A Gallery 200–201	antler	BM-1050	3895±45		
Grimes Graves	Greenwell A Gallery 200–201	antler	BM-1068	3785±50		
		2 sample weighted mean		3845±33	2460–2153	4305
Grimes Graves	Greenwell C Gallery 105–106	antler	BM-1029	3860±55		
Grimes Graves	Greenwell C Gallery 105–106	antler	BM-1045	3950±45		
Grimes Graves	Greenwell C Gallery 105–106	antler	BM-1047	3975±45		
		3 sample weighted mean		3936±27	2548–2345	4445

Site	Description	Material	Lab code	Date	Range BC	
Grimes Graves	Greenwell C Gallery	antler	BM-1046	3800±55	2459–2039	4250
Grimes Graves	1971 shaft	charcoal	BM-778	3785±70	2462–1981	4220
Hemp Knoll	aurochs scapula in chalk from mound	bone	BM-1585	3760±60	2399–1980	4190
Hemp Knoll	round barrow, coffin in pit	charcoal	HAR-2998	3540±70		
Hemp Knoll	round barrow, coffin in pit	charcoal	NPL 139	3745±135		
		2 sample weighted mean		3583±62	2134–1744	3940
Holme	timber post ring	wood	(Bayliss et al1999)		2050–2049 BC	4050
Hove	'Wessex' barrow with bronze dagger		BM-682	3189±46	1594–1322	3460
Hungerford	pit circle with Aldbourne cups	charcoal	BM-2737	3360±40	1741–1523	3630
Irthlingborough 1	aurochs tooth above human burial	bone	OxA-2085	4040±80	2876–2346	4610
Irthlingborough 1	aurochs tooth above human burial	bone	OxA-2086	3810±80		
Irthlingborough 1	cattle tooth above human burial	bone	OxA-2087	3810±80		
Irthlingborough 1	cattle tooth above human burial	bone	OxA-2084	3610±110		
Irthlingborough 1		*3 sample weighted mean*		3768±50	2396–1986	4190
Knowth 1	burial	human bone	UB-3148	3681±47	2199–1921	4060
Knowth 1	mound	charcoal	GrN-12357	4405±35		
Knowth 1	soil contemporary with mound	charcoal	GrN-12358	4490±60		
Knowth 1	mound behind stone in E passage	wood	GrN-12827	4465±40		
		3 sample weighted mean		4440±24	3325–2927	5125
Llandegai A	cremation circle outside henge entrance		NPL-224	4480±145	3630–2766	5200
Llandegai B	cremations outside henge entrance		NPL-222	3740±145	2569–1742	4155
Llandysilio	round barrow with 6 stake rings, pit		CAR-666	3420±65	1883–1525	3705
Llandysilio	round barrow with 6 stake rings, OLS	charcoal	CAR-667	3310±70	1743–1431	3585
Loftus	palisade	charcoal	BM-2566	3740±60		
Loftus	palisade	charcoal	BM-2567	3700±50		
		2 sample weighted mean		3716±38	2269–1980	4125

Site	Context	Material	Lab ref	BP: radio-carbon age before 1950	cal BC: calibrated date range (95% confidence)	Years ago (cal BC mean +2000)
Maes Howe	ditch, N side	peat	Q-1482	3970±70	2831–2236	4535
Maes Howe	ditch, N side	peat	SRR-505	4135±65	2885–2493	4590
Marden	henge ditch, N entrance, primary	charcoal	BM-557	3938±48	2571–2291	4430
Maumbury Rings	top of Shaft 3	antler	BM-2281	3650±70	2265–1780	4020
Maumbury Rings	bottom of Shaft 1	antler	BM-2282	3460±70	2200–1777	3990
Meare Heath	bow	yew wood	Q-646	4640±120	3653–3021	5335
Meldon Bridge	palisade	burnt wood	HAR-796	4280±80	3092–2625	4860
Meldon Bridge	palisade	charcoal	HAR-797	4100±130	2921–2291	4605
Mount Pleasant	old land surface under henge bank	charcoal	BM-644	4072±73	2878–2462	4670
Mount Pleasant	Conquer Barrow ditch	antler	BM-795	4077±52	2867–2470	4670
Mount Pleasant	henge ditch, N entrance, primary	charcoal	BM-792	4058±71		
Mount Pleasant	henge ditch, N entrance, primary	charcoal	BM-793	4048±54		
		2 sample weighted mean		4051±42	2855–2469	4660
Mount Pleasant	henge ditch, N entrance, top primary	charcoal	BM-791	3891±66	2566–2144	4355
Mount Pleasant	Site IV ditch, primary	antler	BM-667	3988±84		
Mount Pleasant	Site IV ditch, primary	antler	BM-666	3941±72		
Mount Pleasant	Site IV ditch, primary	charcoal	BM-663	3911±89		
		3 sample weighted mean		3947±46	2573–2296	4435
Mount Pleasant	palisade trench (residual)	animal bone	BM-794	3956±45	2575–2307	4440
Mount Pleasant	henge ditch, W entrance, primary	antler	BM-645	3734±41		
Mount Pleasant	henge ditch, W entrance, primary	antler	BM-646	3728±59		
		2 sample weighted mean		3732±33	2273–1984	4130

Site	Context	Material	Lab code	Date BP	Calibrated range	
Mount Pleasant	palisade trench, construction	charcoal	BM-665	3645±43		
Mount Pleasant	palisade trench, construction	antler	BM-662	3637±63		
Mount Pleasant	Site IV ditch, secondary (sarsen flakes)	*2 sample weighted mean*		3642±35	2136–1888	4010
Mount Pleasant	henge ditch, N entrance, secondary	charcoal	BM-668	3630±60	2194–1780	3985
Mount Pleasant	henge ditch, N entrance, secondary	charcoal	BM-790	3619±55		
Mount Pleasant	henge ditch, N entrance, secondary	charcoal	BM-788	3506±55		
Mount Pleasant	henge ditch, N entrance, secondary	charcoal	BM-789	3459±53		
Mount Pleasant		*3 sample weighted mean*		3526±31	1939–1744	3840
Mount Pleasant	henge ditch, W entrance, secondary	charcoal	BM-664	3410±131	2108–1413	3760
Mount Pleasant	Site IV ditch, tertiary	charcoal	BM-669	3274±51	1685–1432	3560
Mount Pleasant	*Palisade event (BM-645, BM-646, BM-662, BM-665, BM-668)*					
Netheravon Bake	long barrow ditch	antler	OxA-1407	3681±22	2139–1979	4060
Newgrange	earth between passage roof slabs	charcoal	GrN-5462C	4760±90	3706–3358	5530
Newgrange	earth between passage roof slabs	charcoal	GrN-5463	4425±45		
Newgrange		*2 sample weighted mean*		4415±40	3262–2921	5090
Newgrange	turves in cairn	humic acid	UB-361	4535±105		
Newgrange	turves in cairn	vegetation	GrN-9057	4480±60		
Newgrange		*2 sample weighted mean*		4493±52	3363–2928	5145
Normanton Down	long mortuary enclosure	antler	BM-505	4510±103	3518–2903	5210
North Mains	Ring A post hole primary	charcoal	GU-1353	4105±60	2879–2472	4675
North Mains	Ring A post hole primary	charcoal	GU-1354	4040±70	2866–2352	4610
Norton Bavant	barrow burial with 2 bronze daggers	bone	BM-2909	3410±35	1862–1621	3740
Ötztal, Italy	objects found with the 'Iceman'	*8 sample weighted mean*		4546±14	3358–3122	5240
Radley 611	Ring ditch L14 (Grooved Ware)	antler	BM-2713	3950±80	2830–2202	4515
Radley 611	Ring ditch L13(Grooved Ware)	antler	BM-2712	3860±80	2564–2042	4305
Radley	Pit 917 (Grooved Ware)	bone	BM-2715	3940±60	2616–2208	4410

Site	Context	Material	Lab ref	BP: radio-carbon age before 1950	cal BC: calibrated date range (95% confidence)	Years ago (cal BC mean +2000)
Radley	Pit 3196 (Grooved Ware)	bone	BM-2706	3830±90	2558–1982	4270
Radley	burial with Beaker	human bone	OxA-1875	3990±80	2858–2236	4545
Radley 919	burial with Beaker and copper rings	human bone	OxA-1874	3930±80	2620–2147	4385
Radley 4A	burial with Beaker and 2 gold ornaments	human bone	OxA-4356	3880±90	2616–2042	4330
Radley 4460	burial + beaker and tanged copper knife	human bone	BM-2704	3650±50	2194–1834	4015
Fatfyn	Grooved Ware pit	bone	OxA-3318	3650±90	2287–1747	4015
Sarn-y-bryn-caled	outer ring, post pit 12	charcoal	BM-2807	3660±60		
Sarn-y-bryn-caled	outer ring, post pit 11	charcoal	BM-2808	3720±40		
	2 sample weighted mean			3701±33	2198–1979	4090
Sarn-y-bryn-caled	inner ring, post pit F	charcoal	BM-2805	3730±40		
Sarn-y-bryn-caled	inner ring, post pit E	charcoal	BM-2806	3670±40		
	2 sample weighted mean			3700±28	2196–1980	4090
Sarn-y-bryn-caled	primary cremation	charcoal	BM-2809	3900±40	2471–2208	4340
Sarn-y-bryn-caled	secondary cremation	charcoal	BM-2810	3660±40	2140–1917	4030
Sarn-y-bryn-caled	burial + Beaker and tanged copper knife	human bone	BM-3017	3900±40	2471–2208	4340
Shrewton 5k	turf under mound	twigs	I-4136	4095±95	2896–2354	4625
Silbury Hill	S ditch, secondary	antler	BM-842	3849±43		
Silbury Hill	S ditch, secondary	antler	BM-841	3752±50		
	2 sample weighted mean			3807±32	2398–2141	4270
Stenness	ditch, top of primary	bone	SRR-350	4306±65	3090–2707	4900
Stenness	central stone setting	charcoal	SRR-351	4188±70	2915–2503	4710
West Heath III	round barrow with stake ring, OLS	charcoal	HAR-647	3630±100	2287–1695	3990

Site	Description	Material	Lab no.	Date	Range	
West Kennet	long barrow, NW chamber, skull II	bone	OxA-449	4825±90	3783–3373	5580
West Kennet	long barrow, SW chamber, skeleton IV	bone	OxA-451	4780±90	3709–3363	5535
West Kennet	long barrow, NW chamber, skeleton I	bone	OxA-563	4780±90	3709–3363	5535
West Kennet	long barrow, NE chamber, skeleton II	bone	OxA-450	4700±80	3646–3345	5495
West Kennet	Avenue, Hole 1	charcoal	HAR-9694	5780±80	4830–4456	6445
West Kennet	Avenue, Pit 1	antler	HAR-10501	4280±100	3304–2582	4940
West Kennet	Avenue, Hole 4	charcoal	HAR-9695	4260±80	3081–2601	4840
West Kennet	Enclosure 2, ditch	animal bone	CAR-1295	4050±70	2874–2407	4640
West Kennet	Enclosure 2, ditch	animal bone	CAR-1294	3620±70	2196–1771	3985
West Kennet	Enclosure 2, outer radial ditch 1	animal bone	CAR-1292	3930±70		
West Kennet	Enclosure 2, outer radial ditch 1	animal bone	CAR-1298	3830±70		
West Kennet		*2 sample weighted mean*		3879±49	2470–2200	4335
West Kennet	Enclosure 1, outer ditch	animal bone	CAR-1293	3960±70	2827–2208	4520
West Kennet	Enclosure 1, outer ditch	animal bone	CAR-1290	3900±70	2573–2144	4360
West Kennet	Enclosure 1, outer ditch	animal bone	CAR-1289	3860±70	2552–2069	4310
West Kennet	Enclosure 1, outer ditch	antler	BM-2597	3810±50	2459–2046	4255
West Kennet	Enclosure 1, outer ditch	antler	BM-2602	3620±50	2137–1783	3960
West Kennet	Enclosure 1, inner ditch	animal bone	CAR-1291	3890±70	2569–2142	4355
West Kennet	Enclosure 1, bone deposit	animal bone	CAR-1296	3590±70		
West Kennet	Enclosure 1, bone deposit	animal bone	CAR-1297	3550±70		
		2 sample weighted mean		3569±49	2032–1747	3890
Whitton Hill	Site 1	charcoal	BM-2206	3740±50	2291–1980	4135
Whitton Hill	palisaded ring ditch	charcoal	BM-2265	3680±80	2291–1784	4040
Whitton Hill	cremation in pit	charcoal	BM-2266	3660±50	2197–1885	4040
Woodhenge	ditch, SE side, primary	antler	BM-677	3817±74		
Woodhenge	ditch, SE side, primary	animal bone	BM-678	3755±54		

Site	Context	Material	Lab ref	BP: radio-carbon age before 1950	cal BC: calibrated date range (95% confidence)	Years ago (cal BC mean +2000)
		2 sample weighted mean		3766±43	2394–2039	4215
Wyke Down	Pit I, primary	antler	BM-2395	4040±90	2897–2304	4590
Wyke Down	Pit I, recut	charcoal	BM-2396	4140±80	2902–2471	4685
Wyke Down	Pit K, recut	charcoal	BM-2397	4150±50	2883–2503	4690

Appendix 3: All radiocarbon dates in chronological order

Full data in Appendix 1 and 2.

Site	Context	Lab ref	cal BC: calibrated date range (95% confidence)	Years ago (cal BC mean +2000)	Stonehenge phase
Stonehenge	Car Park post pit A	HAR-455	8788–7806	10295	pre
Stonehenge	Car Park post pit 9580, secondary fill	GU-5109	8289–7602	9945	pre
Stonehenge	Car Park post pit 9580, secondary fill	OxA-4919	7706–7380	9545	pre
Stonehenge	Car Park post pit 9580, tertiary fill	OxA-4920	7597–7144	9370	pre
Stonehenge	Car Park post pit 8	HAR-456	7516–6643	9080	pre
Stonehenge	bone in Sarsen hole 27	OxA-4902	4345–3979	6160	pre
Fir Tree Field Shaft	L6b hearth (Early Neol:thic)	2 samples	3967–3798	5885	
West Kennet	long barrow, NW chamber, skull II	OxA-449	3783–3373	5580	
West Kennet	long barrow, SW chamber, skeleton IV	OxA-451	3709–3363	5535	
West Kennet	long barrow, NW chamber, skeleton I	OxA-563	3709–3363	5535	
Netheravon Bake	long barrow ditch	OxA-1407	3706–3358	5530	
West Kennet	long barrow, NE chamber, skeleton II	OxA-450	3646–3345	5495	
Avebury	old land surface under henge bank	HAR-10325	3633–3104	5370	
Lesser Cursus	Phase 2 ditch	OxA-1404	3642–3039	5340	
Meare Heath	bow	Q-646	3653–3021	5335	
Durrington Walls	old land surface under henge bank	3 samples	3489–3104	5295	

Site	Context	Lab ref	cal BC: calibrated date range (95% confidence)	Years ago (cal BC mean +2000)	Stonehenge phase
Ashcott Heath	bow	Q-598	3645–2924	5285	
Lesser Cursus	Phase 1 ditch	OxA-1405	3635–2906	5270	
Ötztal, Italy	objects found with the 'Iceman'	8 samples	3358–3122	5240	
Normanton Down	long mortuary enclosure	BM-505	3518–2903	5210	
Flagstones	burial on ditch bottom	HAR-9158	3486–2919	5205	
Llandegai A	cremation circle outside henge entrance	NPL-224	3630–2766	5200	
Stonehenge	curated bone in ditch	4 samples	3340–3030	5185	pre
Flagstones	ditch primary	OxA-2322	3486–2886	5185	
Arminghall	post pit	BM-129	3622–2679	5150	
Newgrange	turves in cairn	2 samples	3363–2928	5145	
Fir Tree Field Shaft	L5 turf (Peterborough)	2 samples	3332–2925	5130	
Knowth 1	mound	3 samples	3325–2927	5125	
Avebury	old land surface under henge bank	HAR-10063	3345–2879	5110	
Barford	henge	Birm-7	3326–2881	5105	
Newgrange	earth between passage roof slabs	2 samples	3262–2921	5090	
Coneybury	pit 1601	OxA-1409	3349–2764	5055	
Stonehenge	Bayesian estimate for start of ditch filling	(86%)	3110–2950	5030	Start 2
Dorchester, Oxon	Site XI: multiple ring ditch and pit circle	2 samples	3078–2881	4980	
Stonehenge	Bayesian estimate for excavation of ditch		3015–2935	4975	1
Avebury	henge ditch, S entrance, primary	HAR-10502	3304–2625	4965	
West Kennet	Avenue, Pit 1	HAR-10501	3304–2582	4940	
Durrington Walls	Midden	NPL-192	3254–2582	4920	

Stenness	ditch, top of primary	SRR-350	3090–2707	4900
Meldon Bridge	palisade	HAR-796	3092–2625	4860
West Kennet	Avenue, Hole 4	HAR-9695	3081–2601	4840
Flagstones	burial on ditch bottom	OxA-2321	3084–2473	4780
Dorchester, Oxon	Site 2: penannular ditch, primary	BM-4225N	2916–2639	4780
Coneybury	ditch primary	OxA-1408	3081–2471	4775
Avebury	old land surface under henge bank	HAR-10500	3007–2495	4750
Amesbury	chalk plaque pit	2 samples	2903–2581	4740
Stenness	central stone setting	SRR-351	2915–2503	4710
Avebury	henge bank, NW side	HAR-10326	2917–2471	4695
Maes Howe	ditch, N side	SRR-505	2885–2493	4690
Fir Tree Field	Pit 11a (Grooved Ware)	BM-2406	2884–2497	4690
Wyke Down	Pit K, recut	BM-2397	2883–2503	4690
Wyke Down	Pit I, recut	BM-2396	2902–2471	4685
Avebury	great stone circle, 41	HAR-10062	2906–2466	4685
North Mains	Ring A post hole primary	GU-1353	2879–2472	4675
Dorchester, Oxon	Site 3: post circle	3 samples	2879–2467	4675
Dorchester, Dorset	Greyhound Yard, post pit 1631	2 samples	2878–2473	4675
Dorchester, Dorset	Greyhound Yard, post pit 4163	HAR-6664	2877–2462	4670
Mount Pleasant	old land surface under henge bank	BM-644	2878–2462	4670
Mount Pleasant	Conquer Barrow ditch	BM-795	2867–2470	4670
Fir Tree Field	Pit 32 (Grooved Ware)	BM-2407	2866–2471	4670
Dorchester, Dorset	Greyhound Yard, post pit 1631	2 samples	2861–2467	4665
Mount Pleasant	henge ditch, N entrance, primary	2 samples	2855–2469	4660
West Kennet	Enclosure 2, ditch	CAR-1295	2874–2407	4640
Silbury Hill	turf under mound	I-4136	2896–2354	4625

Site	Context	Lab ref	cal BC: calibrated date range (95% confidence)	Years ago (cal BC mean +2000)	Stonehenge phase
Dorchester, Dorset	Church St, post pit	HAR-5508	2881–2346	4615	
North Mains	Ring A post hole primary	GU-1354	2866–2352	4610	
Irthlingborough 1	aurochs tooth above human burial	OxA-2085	2876–2346	4610	
Meldon Bridge	palisade	HAR-797	2921–2291	4605	
Wyke Down	Pit 1, primary	BM-2395	2879–2304	4590	
Dorchester, Dorset	Greyhound Yard, post pit 4885	HAR-6663	2865–2303	4585	
Flagstones	ditch primary	HAR-8578	2880–2236	4560	
Dorchester, Oxon	Site 3: post circle, cremation	BM-2163R	2915–2206	4560	
Radley	burial with Beaker	OxA-1875	2858–2236	4545	
Maes Howe	ditch, N side	Q-1482	2831–2236	4535	
Dorchester, Oxon	Site 3: post circle, pipe fill	BM-2166R	2898–2147	4525	
West Kennet	Enclosure 1, outer ditch	CAR-1293	2827–2208	4520	
Devil's Quoits	henge ditch, primary	HAR-1887	2882–2147	4515	
Radley 611	Ring ditch L14 (Grooved Ware)	BM-2713	2830–2202	4515	
Amesbury 71	grave pit in barrow with stake rings	NPL-77	2865–2141	4505	
Durrington Walls	henge ditch, S entrance, primary	3 samples	2617–2304	4460	
Grimes Graves	Greenwell C Gallery 105–106	3 samples	2548–2345	4445	
Mount Pleasant	Site IV ditch, primary	3 samples	2573–2296	4435	
Durrington Walls	N Circle post hole 42	NPL-240	2836–2038	4435	
Marden	henge ditch, N entrance, primary	BM-557	2571–2291	4430	
Radley	Pit 917 (Grooved Ware)	BM-2715	2616–2208	4410	
Stonehenge	Avenue ditch at Stonehenge	OxA-4884	2571–2239	4405	3

Site	Description	Lab code	cal range		
Radley 919	burial with Beaker and copper rings	OxA-1874	2620–2147	4385	
Grimes Graves	Greenwell Gallery 108–109	3 samples	2468–2294	4380	
West Kennet	Enclosure 1, outer ditch	CAR-1290	2573–2144	4360	
West Kennet	Enclosure 1, inner ditch	CAR-1291	2569–2142	4355	
Mount Pleasant	ditch, N entrance, top primary	BM-791	2566–2144	4355	
Sarn-y-bryn-caled	primary cremation	BM-2809	2471–2208	4340	
Shrewton 5k	burial + Beaker and tanged copper knife	BM-3017	2471–2208	4340	
Stonehenge	Bayesian estimate for end of ditch filling		2460–2210	4335	End 2
Stonehenge	Avenue ditch .9km from Avon	OxA-4905	2466–2201	4335	3
Stonehenge	large sarsen structures	3 samples	2461–2205	4335	3ii
Durrington Walls	S Circle post holes	4 samples	2471–2201	4335	
West Kennet	Enclosure 2, outer radial ditch	2 samples	2470–2200	4335	
Grimes Graves	Greenwell Gallery 104–107	BM-1049	2470–2202	4335	
Radley 4A	burial with Beaker and 2 gold ornaments	OxA-4356	2616–2042	4330	
Fordington Farm	Grave 61	UB-3306	2458–2200	4330	
West Kennet	Enclosure 1, outer ditch	CAR-1289	2552–2069	4310	
Avebury	great stone circle, 44	HAR-10327	2575–2039	4305	
Grimes Graves	Greenwell A Gallery 200–201	2 samples	2460–2153	4305	
Radley 611	Ring ditch L 13 (Grooved Ware)	BM-2712	2564–2042	4305	
Stonehenge	Human skeleton in ditch	5 samples	2398–2144	4270	3
Silbury Hill	S ditch, secondary	2 samples	2398–2141	4270	
Radley	Pit 3196 (Grooved Ware)	BM-2706	2558–1982	4270	
Corlea, Co Longford	timbers cut with metal blades	dendro	2259±9 BC	4260	
West Kennet	Enclosure 1, outer ditch	BM-2597	2459–2046	4255	
Grimes Graves	Greenwell C Gallery	BM-1046	2459–2039	4250	
Grimes Graves	Greenwell Gallery 101–102	2 samples	2462–2001	4230	

Site	Context	Lab ref	cal BC: calibrated date range (95% confidence)	Years ago (cal BC mean +2000)	Stonehenge phase
Dagenham	carved pine figure	OxA-1721	2464-1983	4225	
Gorsey Bigbury	lower ditch fill	BM-1088	2466-1982	4225	
Gorsey Bigbury	lower ditch fill	BM-1089	2458-1983	4220	
Grimes Graves	1971 shaft	BM-778	2462-1981	4220	
Woodhenge	ditch, SE side, primary	2 samples	2394-2039	4215	
Fir Tree Field Shaft	L2a chalk dump (Beaker)	OxA-7985	2395-2037	4215	
Chilbolton	round barrow, secondary burial	OxA-1073	2464-1959	4210	
Chilbolton	burial + copper knife and gold ornaments	OxA-1027	2456-1919	4190	
Chilbolton	Outer ditch	OxA-2315	2456-1919	4190	
Hemp Knoll	aurochs scapula in chalk from mound	BM-1585	2399-1980	4190	
Irthlingborough 1	cattle teeth above human burial	3 samples	2396-1986	4190	
Fordington Farm	Grave 59	UB-3305	2330-2034	4180	
Barnack	burial + Beaker, copper dagger and gold	BM-2596	2291-2041	4165	
Llandegai B	cremations outside henge entrance	NPL-2202	2569-1742	4155	
Condicote henge	inner ditch, lower secondary silts	HAR-3064	2399-1885	4140	
Whitton Hill	Site 1	BM-2206	2291-1980	4135	
Amesbury 51	burial with Beaker, bronze awl etc.	BM-287	2294-1978	4135	
Mount Pleasant	henge ditch, W entrance, primary	2 samples	2273-1984	4130	
Loftus	palisade	2 samples	2269-1980	4125	
Stonehenge	Bluestone circle and oval	2 samples	2267-1983	4125	3iv
Stonehenge	Avenue ditch 42m from Stonehenge	HAR-2013	2326-1919	4125	3
Fordington Farm	Grave 70	UB-3304	2285-1945	4120	

Site	Description	Lab code	Date range	
Durrington 7	grave pit with 2 juveniles, 1 cremated	OxA-1398	2456–1777	4115
Cambridge Fens	bow	Q-684	2456–1744	4100
Sarn-y-bryn-caled	outer timber ring	2 samples	2198–1979	4090
Sarn-y-bryn-caled	inner timber ring	2 samples	2196–1980	4090
Dorchester, Oxon	Site 4: paired ring ditches, grave pit	BM-2167R	2466–1695	4080
Gorsey Bigbury	lower ditch fill	BM-1090	2456–1696	4075
Condicote henge	inner ditch, lower secondary silts	HAR-3067	2396–1747	4070
Avebury	ditch, SE side, secondary burial	HAR-10064	2295–1830	4065
Mount Pleasant	palisade event	5 samples	2139–1979	4060
Irthlingborough 1	burial with Beaker	UB-3148	2199–1921	4060
Stonehenge	Avenue ditch at Stonehenge	BM-1164	2281–1832	4055
Holme next the Sea	timber post ring	dendro	2050–2049 BC	4050
Whitton Hill	palisaded ring ditch	BM-2265	2291–1784	4040
Whitton Hill	cremation in pit	BM-2266	2197–1885	4040
Sarn-y-bryn-caled	secondary cremation	BM-2810	2140–1917	4030
Maumbury Rings	top of Shaft 3	BM-2281	2265–1780	4020
Gorsey Bigbury	lower ditch fill	BM-1086	2201–1832	4015
Ratfyn	Grooved Ware pit	OxA-3318	2287–1747	4015
Radley 4460	burial + Beaker and tanged copper knife	BM-2704	2194–1834	4015
Mount Pleasant	palisade trench, construction	2 samples	2136–1888	4010
Amesbury 39	cremation with amber and jet beads	HAR-1237	2272–1741	4005
Maumbury Rings	bottom of Shaft 1	BM-2282	2200–1777	3990
West Heath III	round barrow with stake ring, OLS	HAR-647	2287–1695	3990
Barnack	coffin round burial with Beaker	2 samples	2138–1830	3985
West Kennet	Enclosure 2, ditch	CAR-1294	2196–1771	3985
Mount Pleasant	Site IV ditch, secondary (sarsen flakes)	BM-668	2194–1780	3985

3

Site	Context	Lab ref	cal BC: calibrated date range (95% confidence)	Years ago (cal BC mean +2000)	Stonehenge phase
Gorsey Bigbury	lower ditch fill	BM-1087	2191–1744	3970	
West Kennet	Enclosure 1, outer ditch	BM-2602	2137–1783	3960	
Durrington Walls	henge ditch, N side, secondary	2 samples	2196–1697	3945	
Buckskin II	barrow with stake rings, central post	HAR-8370	2201–1687	3945	
Gorsey Bigbury	lower ditch fill	BM-1091	2140–1748	3945	
Devil's Quoits	henge ditch, top of primary	HAR-1888	2139–1742	3940	
Gallibury	round barrow with stake ring	BM-2232R	2271–1605	3940	
Hemp Knoll	round barrow, coffin in pit	2 samples	2134–1744	3940	
Flagstones	central burial	HAR-9159	2132–1692	3910	
Dorchester, Oxon	Site 3: post circle, cremation	BM-2165R	2277–1525	3900	
West Kennet	Enclosure 1, bone deposit	2 samples	2032–1747	3890	
Stonehenge	Z hole 29	OxA-4836	2013–1742	3880	3vi
Amesbury 61	round barrow with stake ring	HAR-6227	2137–1605	3870	
Mount Pleasant	henge ditch, N entrance, secondary	3 samples	1939–1744	3840	
Edmondsham	'Wessex' barrow	BM-709	1934–1642	3790	
Stonehenge	Y hole 30	UB-3824	1876–1687	3780	3vi
Mount Pleasant	henge ditch, W entrance, secondary	BM-664	2108–1413	3760	
Caldicot Castle	plank sewn boat	UB-3472	1859–1664	3760	
Norton Bavant	barrow burial with 2 bronze daggers	BM-2909	1862–1621	3740	
Llandysilio	round barrow with 6 stake rings, pit	CAR-666	1883–1525	3705	
Hungerford	pit circle with Aldbourne cups	BM-2737	1741–1523	3630	
Stonehenge	Y hole 30	UB-3822	1687–1525	3605	3vi

3vi

Stonehenge	Y hole 30	UB-3823	1680–1520	3600
Edington Burtle	bow	Q-669	1872–1316	3595
Llandysilio	round barrow with 6 stake rings, OLS	CAR-667	1743–1431	3585
Mount Pleasant	Site IV ditch, tertiary	BM-669	1685–1432	3560
Denny, Falkirk	bow	Q-1196	1737–1320	3530
Hove	'Wessex' barrow	BM-682	1594–1322	3460
Earl's Barton	'Wessex' barrow	2 samples	1521–1324	3420
Ferriby	Boat 2	Q-3123	1496–1263	3380
Ferriby	Boat 2	Q-3044	1434–1224	3330
Edmondsham	'Wessex' barrow	BM-708	1430–1133	3280
Ferriby	Boat 1	Q-3124	1394–1129	3260
Ferriby	Boat 1	Q-3043	1389–1010	3200
Ferriby	Boat 3	Q-3045	1373–1023	3200
Ferriby	Boat 3	Q-3047	1293–1006	3150
Stonehenge	Sarsen hole 8, upper fill	OxA-4885	1210–834	3020
Goldcliff	timber structure including boat planks	CAR-1434	1005–794	2900
Stonehenge	Palisade, human burial	UB-3820	774–409	2590

Notes

1   Atkinson 1979. Described by the publisher as 'reprinted with revisions', this is substantially the original 1956 text, with appendices added at first and second paperback prints. The influence of this book has been quite remarkable. 'Virtually all modern guidebooks and displays which describe the sequence of construction [at Stonehenge] reiterate or plagiarise' it (Lawson 1992, 934). I like to think that somewhere out there in cyberspace there is informed stuff about Stonehenge archaeology not produced by specialist archaeologists. I have yet to find it.

2   Reviewing *Stonehenge in its Landscape*, Roger Mercer wrote: 'Atkinson worked in the days when an excavator was expected to produce unassisted, in his own time, the results of his work. The very size and complexity of the volume illustrates how impossible was that demand' (*Antiquaries Journal* 77, 1997, 407–12).

3   In 1923 by Hawley, and in 1979 by me.

4   Cleal et al. 1995.

5   Reviewing *Stonehenge in its Landscape*, one archaeologist noted that the book's authors were 'careful not to be judgmental'. 'We, on the other hand', he continued, 'are perhaps entitled to make judgements . . . ; in addition to "scandalous", the adjectives "incompetent" and even "immoral" come to mind' (Anthony Harding in *The Archaeological Journal* 153, 1966, 359–63). Both Richard Atkinson and his colleague Stuart Piggott, in different ways, tried to interfere with its successful completion. Piggott died in September 1996.

6   Bowman 1995.

7   According to OxCal version 2.18 and Calib 4.

8   Also breaking convention, for the purposes of the 'single date' I have taken the present to be AD 2000, not 1950 (see Appendix 1, etc). If you try to use these single dates with those taken from other published sources, you will get in a real muddle.

9   The Stanton Drew story is based on conversations with Andrew

David and Paul Linford (January 1998).

[10] In 1961 'Professor L. S. Palmer started an extensive electrical resistivity survey of the Great Circle but ill health prevented the completion of the work and, after his death, the records were examined in the Physics Department of the University [of Bristol] and pronounced to be essentially negative in that they provided little evidence of any value in assessing the site' (Tratman 1966).

[11] This story of archaeological geophysics draws on an excellent book by Clark (1996).

[12] A summary of the results, with pictures of the geophysics plots, is at www.english-heritage.org.uk/knowledge/archaeology/ stantondrew.asp.

[13] Fassbinder et al. 1990.

[14] Media quotations from: 'Prehistoric English ceremonial site uncovered'. BBC Online 10 November 1997; 'Woodhenge find rivals stone circles'. *Times* 11 November 1997 (N. Hawkes); 'Hi-tech uncovers ancient temple'. *Guardian* 11 November 1997 (O. Bowcott).

[15] Bradley 1998, 20–35.

[16] McNairn 1980, 91–8.

[17] This European story is particularly well told by Whittle 1996.

[18] Hodder 1990.

[19] Bradley 1998, 33.

[20] Bradley 1998, 34. See also Hodder 1990, Thomas 1996 and 1999, Tilley 1996, Whittle 1996.

[21] Annable and Simpson 1964.

[22] Atkinson 1979, 91–3.

[23] Kendrick and Hawkes 1932.

[24] Clark 1936.

[25] Atkinson et al. 1951.

[26] Clare 1986 and Harding and Lee 1987. For a full review of henge and similar sites, see also Piggott and Piggott 1939, Wainwright 1969, Burl 1970, Catherall 1971, Burl 1976a, Clare 1987, Gibson 1994.

[27] Kendrick and Hawkes 1932, 83.

[28] 'Group Captain Gilbert Stuart Martin Insall, VC, MC'. *Times* 21 February 1972.

[29] e.g. Bowyer 1992, 49–56.

[30] *Wiltshire Archaeological and Natural History Magazine* 67 (1972), 195.

[31] 'Ancient earthworks "target" for First World War Air VC'.

Nottingham Evening News 5 August 1952.

[32] Capper 1907. The Rev. John Bacon had attempted this feat in 1900, but his balloon was too high for his camera to register the stones: Chippindale 1994, 175.

[33] That the Royal Flying Corps wished to remove Stonehenge as a danger to aircraft taking off and landing is thought to be gossip (Chippindale 1994, 175). That the army recently ploughed within 1m of a well-preserved Neolithic enclosure north of Stonehenge at Robin Hood's Ball to grow cover for the officers' pheasant shoot is a fact. Roy Canham, the County Archaeologist, reported visiting the site soon after the ploughing, and walking on a carpet of prehistoric pottery (interview with Julian Richards April 1999).

[34] Ralegh Radford in Hudson 1981, 130.

[35] 'You know,' said Crawford to Wheeler, 'I am a journalist.' *Antiquity* 32, 1958, 4.

[36] Insall 1927.

[37] Cunnington, M. E. 1927.

[38] Deuel 1969; Crawford and Keiller 1928, 3–7.

[39] 'Stonehenge from the air'. *Observer* 22 July 1923 (O. G. S. Crawford); Crawford 1924.

[40] A few of which were beautifully published by Keiller in what is now a collector's book: Crawford and Keiller 1928.

[41] Piggott in Daniel and Chippindale 1991, 26.

[42] Insall 'bought centuries old Monks Mill Screwby Notts . . . from the mill he organises field surveys in Britain. Last year he surveyed more than 200 sites in Notts for MOW.' Undated press release put out by 2nd Tactical Air Force HQ for the Air Ministry, RAF Museum Hendon file ref. DC76/74/504.

[43] Though a popular craft, only two survive, one in the National Air and Space Museum in Washington DC, and a fuselage in the Canadian War Museum, Ottawa (the Champlin Fighter Museum, Mesa, Arizona, has a replica). There is a replica Vickers FB5 in the RAF Museum, Hendon.

[44] Insall 1927.

[45] Cunnington, M. E. 1929.

[46] Using the formula in Wainwright and Longworth 1971, 220, which converts to 1.07 tons/cubic m of green oak.

[47] At least, that is how the archaeologists reported it. It sounds like a strange exclamation.

[48] e.g. Clark 1936, 49: 'a dedicatory or sacrificial rite'; Burl 1987, 125: '. . . one of the clearest examples of sacrifice in prehistoric Britain';

Castleden 1993, 85: 'She had been brutally killed with a blow on the head . . . It is the clearest evidence of child sacrifice . . . the little girl may have been killed as a foundation offering'. Despite this, it is not the clearest evidence of anything. The bones were poorly preserved, and Arthur Keith, who examined them, suggested the child was three and a half years old, and possibly female – though this was 'not an inference which should be too much depended on' (in Cunnington 1929, 52). He was quite right to be cautious about the sex of the child. He made no reference at all in his report to wounds or cut marks. The pit is now marked by a low flint cairn.

[49] Cunnington, M. E. 1929, 18.

[50] A rather more memorable name than 'The Dough Cover', as Woodhenge was known before Insall's discovery, because of the similarity the low bank and slightly domed interior gave to the wooden lid of a bread dough dish (Cunnington, M. E. 1929, 8–9).

[51] Chippindale 1994, 20.

[52] Cunnington, M. E. 1929, 19.

[53] 'This desecration of the site,' the excavator wrote of the pylons, 'made after its significance had been made public . . . regrettable though it must be considered on general grounds, yet provided us with an admirable vantage point for photography. In this last connection we must be grateful to the Central Electricity Board . . .' (Clark 1936, 2).

[54] O. G. S. Crawford, *Antiquity* 3, 1929, 257–8.

[55] Clark 1936.

[56] This is how Cunnington told the story (1931, 301–2), and is doubtless what happened. I can't help wondering, though, if asking local people might have been easier. The site was known a hundred years before. About 1826, Henry Browne was shown the location by a ninety-two-year-old man (Isaac Hart of West Overton) who could remember the stone circles (presumably the site rather than the stones themselves, as Stukeley records them moved about a decade before Hart's birth). Cunnington almost certainly did not know of Browne's note (written on a drawing of Avebury in a Hampshire museum: Piggott 1946a). But Wiltshire's own Colt Hoare placed the Sanctuary quite precisely enough on a map published around the same time (Hoare 1821, plate X). He dug into a round barrow (still easily identified) 'on the south side of the great road to Marlborough, and adjoining the head of the Hakpen temple', a reference to Stukeley's identification of the Sanctuary as the head of a serpent (Hoare 1821, 90). And

Cunnington herself recognised that when Hoare wrote that he could see no ditch surrounding the stones, the implication was that 'where the circles had stood must still have been known in Hoare's time' (Cunnington, M. E. 1931, 311).

[57] The story of the Sanctuary dig is taken from the published report (Cunnington, M. E. 1931), reminiscences by Robert Cunnington, who was present at part of the dig (Cunnington, R. H. 1954), correspondence in the Museum of the Wiltshire Archaeological Society (Devizes) and the Alexander Keiller Museum (Avebury), and Young's diaries, now in Devizes Museum library (Young 1930–35, 1930–40).

[58] Young 1930–40 (1931, 15–16 June).

[59] Cunnington, R. H. 1975.

[60] It is now owned by English Heritage.

[61] Murray 1999.

[62] Cunnington, R. H. 1954, 229.

[63] Cunnington, R. H. 1954, 229.

[64] Cunnington, R. H. 1954, 229–31.

[65] Three years later, Keiller was surveyor at the excavation of Thickthorn Down long barrow in Dorset (Piggott 1983), and after was employed by Wheeler as surveyor at Maiden Castle (Murray 1999, 66–7).

[66] Keiller, much enamoured of things new, shiny and scientific, was not impressed by the homespun technology employed by the less wealthy Cunningtons. Their equipment, he wrote to Wiltshire amateur archaeologist A. D. Passmore, was 'not very satisfactory, consisting as it does of: one 30 foot tape – much stretched, and never hitherto corrected since purchased a good many years ago – a broomstick "notched to feet"; and two slips of wood nailed to the top of the aforementioned broomstick to form some sort of sight vane. To this, of course, must be added Mrs Cunnington's umbrella.' Keiller to Passmore, 21 October 1936 (Alexander Keiller Museum ref. 78510174).

[67] For example, if the Curwens, father and son doctors in East Sussex, had dug the Sanctuary, we would likely have better records all round. The Curwens inspired many other amateurs in Sussex to excellent work. There were also battles as vituperative as that between the Cunningtons and Keiller.

[68] Cunnington, M. E. 1931, 309.

[69] 'The Avebury "serpent": Another "Woodhenge" in Wiltshire'. *Times* 1 August 1930.

[70] e.g. Castleden 1993; *Stonehenge and Neighbouring Monuments* (English Heritage official guidebook to Stonehenge) 1995; *Ancient Voices: Stonehenge*, BBC Manchester/The Learning Channel/Time Life, broadcast BBC2 May 1998.

[71] Cunnington, R. H. 1931.

[72] Piggott 1940.

[73] Piggott 1940, 210.

[74] Geoffrey Wainwright, lecture to the Prehistoric Society 27 October 1999.

[75] Burl 1987, 215.

[76] By the evidence of *The Prehistoric Temples of Stonehenge and Avebury* (Pitkin Guides, 1994), maidens in those days came pretty well endowed.

[77] Information from Geoff Hallchurch, Planning and Highways, Wiltshire County Council.

[78] *Wiltshire Times and News* 7 June 1968.

[79] Wiltshire County Record Office, Durrington PC File F4/300/92.

[80] *Antiquity* 41 (1967), 255.

[81] *Western Gazette* 19 July 1968.

[82] *Bath and Wiltshire Evening Chronicle* 27 May 1968.

[83] *Wiltshire Times and News* 7 June 1968.

[84] Undated letter from King to Daniel, Library of the Wiltshire Archaeological Society (Devizes).

[85] Daniel to Grant King, 9 June 1970, Library of the Wiltshire Archaeological Society. Not for the first time, King so upset the Society by his over-enthusiastic protestations that they threatened to expel him. By King's account in his letter to Daniel, they sent a 'secret' statement to the parties lambasted by King, explaining that he was merely a 'militant and irresponsible' character who did not represent the Society's views (which presumably held that protest about destruction of the ancient heritage was all right, so long as it was polite). King regularly returned the favour by resigning from the Society, then rejoining – or at least threatening to resign until persuaded against it.

[86] Interview with Wainwright January 1998.

[87] 'Setting things straight with the Chief'. *British Archaeological News* 19, December 1994, 12 (S. Denison).

[88] Hoare 1812, quoted in Wainwright and Longworth 1971, 7.

[89] Lubbock 1865, 53.

[90] Farrer 1918.

[91] See chapter 9.

92   Crawford 1929.

93   Stone et al. 1954.

94   Which is why most of the reports – and they're not all done yet – have been written recently by others.

95   Green and Rollo-Smith 1984, 258.

96   Gingell 1988, Table 1.

97   'Normally a barrow should be excavated in its entirety . . . but the Ancient Monuments Inspectorate insisted on partial excavation': Ashbee 1985, 40.

98   Interview with Wainwright January 1998. Getting English Heritage funding and approval to dig a scheduled monument is now just a little more complex, not least because of regulations introduced by Wainwright.

99   Cunnington, M. E. 1929, 2.

100 The description of the dig is based largely on interviews with Peter Drewett, Nick Griffiths (December 1998) and Geoffrey Wainwright, on papers in the Ministry of Works Ancient Monuments Laboratory file at English Heritage (file 422) and published reports, especially Wainwright and Longworth 1971.

101 George McDonic, County Planning Officer at the time, remembers that improved public car access to Woodhenge was seen as one of the benefits of the road project (interview March 1999).

102 Wainwright and Longworth 1971, xii.

103 Piggott to Faith Vatcher, 25 September 1966 (Alexander Keiller Museum, Avebury).

104 Robert Newall, a wealthy amateur archaeologist who, as we will see, played an important role in early excavations at Stonehenge, 'thought it was wonderful' (interview with Wainwright January 1998).

105 Machines and labour were provided by what some of the archaeologists might now have ruefully felt to be the aptly named Butchers of Warminster.

106 Wainwright and Longworth 1971.

107 The style was first defined by Stuart Piggott, and named Grooved Ware, in 1936. He later changed the name to Rinyo-Clacton (Piggott 1954, 321–46), to reflect the wide geographical occurrence of the style, after places in Orkney and Essex, respectively, where such pottery had been found. Wainwright and Longworth (1971, 236) reverted to the term Grooved Ware. In Russell Hoban's novel, *Mr Rinyo-Clacton's Offer* (1998, London: Cape), the

eponymous narrator tenders a man £1m for a year in return for his life. Some archaeologists might feel they have made the exchange for rather less.

[108] Ideally, field archaeologists work as part of a team of scientists, each contributing a skill towards the understanding of a site. In the Fifties and Sixties, excavators often used the late arrival of their specialists' reports as excuse for not publishing. But when the specialists concerned knew nothing about the dig, and would find their reports ignored by the archaeologists, you can hardly blame them for a lack of enthusiasm. Wainwright did not spare his scientists, issuing strict memos as to when he needed their work. Ralph Harcourt, who studied the animal bone, was delighted: 'What is gratifying in [the published report] is that some notice has clearly been taken [of my work] . . . rather than just stuffed at the end as an appendix simply because that is the fashionable thing to do with a bone report. Such an excavator is a pleasure to work with.'

[109] Wainwright 1969.

[110] In the same year, Atkinson was digging a tunnel into Silbury Hill with BBC sponsorship. Wainwright has recently written that he 'would gaze at the busy scene around the shored mouth of the tunnel . . . and speculate what might lie at journey's end.' Atkinson speculated, too: 'If I am right it is the largest [burial mound] in the world and could contain a royal tomb of quite exceptional richness', he told expectant journalists. 'If I am not right, I don't know what it is' (*Wiltshire Times and News* 22 September 1967). 'Not for us 30 years ago was there agonising over the ethics of allowing a unique monument to be penetrated in this way . . .', continues Wainwright, 'in an unrepeatable experiment and under the supervision of one who already had a number of unpublished excavations on his record' (in Whittle 1997a, v). Atkinson's deputy was a Ministry digger with a string of unpublished digs himself. This was bad archaeology, and bad television; fortunately for Silbury, the BBC pulled the plug halfway through the project (Atkinson 1978, 167–8).

[111] Cunnington, R. H. 1955; 1975, 122–8.

[112] Wainwright et al. 1971.

[113] Piggott and Piggott 1939, 157–8.

[114] Clark A. J., 'The geophysical surveys', in Wainwright 1979, 256.

[115] In one tent was a schoolboy named Mike Pitts.

[116] Wainwright 1979.

[117] Interview with Wainwright January 1998.

[118] Appendix 2: BM-792, 793, 645, 646. Primary silts are those thought to have accumulated in a ditch immediately after it was dug, taken to be approximately contemporary with its excavation.

[119] Wainwright 1979, xiii.

[120] The archaeologists in the employ of the Ministry of Works became, in 1984, the staff of English Heritage.

[121] Mercer 1981a; Mercer et al. 1988. Most archaeologists describe this site as having six post circles. Only the large ring described in the text emerged clearly from the excavation. Others are hypothetical arrangements selected from a confusing mass of small pits. In a statistical analysis, Brock and Williams (in Mercer 1981a, 144) concluded that 'there are no independent grounds for identifying any circles concentric with the tested centre points aside from circle A', i.e. the large ring.

[122] Barclay 1983.

[123] Gibson 1994.

[124] Gibson 1994.

[125] I have long familiarity with this area and its archaeology; it is for others with more knowledge than me to explore the discoveries emerging from a much better preserved landscape that is Scotland's heritage.

[126] Whittle 1997a.

[127] Richards 1990, 123–58.

[128] Piggott 1954, 224.

[129] Atkinson 1979, 165 (written in 1955). His emphases.

[130] The story of this dig is related as described to me by Margaret Ehrenburg (November 1998) and John Evans (December 1998), and in the published report (Evans et al. 1984).

[131] Durrington: Wainwright and Longworth 1971, 329–37; Marden: Wainwright 1971, 228–33; Mount Pleasant: Wainwright 1979, 190–213; Avebury: Evans 1972, Evans et al. 1985.

[132] Wainwright 1971, 208–13.

[133] 'It is fitting', he wrote in the Mount Pleasant report, 'to acknowledge with gratitude the debt which we owe to Dr G. J. Wainwright . . . His hospitality on site, his willingness to explain the archaeological context of the various horizons, and his silent endurance of the devastation we have wreaked on his beautiful sections can go unrecorded no longer' (Wainwright 1971, 190).

[134] Chippindale 1978, 118–19.

[135] Not to say that they are not an intimate part of that particular

confrontation: Chippindale et al 1990; McKay 1996; Bender 1998.

[136] The word was used by Keiller to describe Avebury before the war: 'the tangle of rusty pig-wire, the accumulations . . . of old tins and bottles . . . [and] the refuse-heaps . . . contributed ungenerously towards rendering the once majestic site . . . the outstanding archaeological disgrace of Britain' (1939, 223).

[137] Lord Cavendish of Furness at the House of Lords, 30 June 1997 (*Hansard*); *Daily Graphic* 22 August 1899 (Chippindale 1978, 113).

[138] The definitive history of Stonehenge is Chippindale 1994. See also Andrew Lawson in Cleal et al. 1995, 345–7.

[139] Most of their remarkable finds and much of their records are now in Devizes Museum. See Cunnington, R. H. 1975.

[140] Cunnington, R. H. 1975, 10, 39 and 151.

[141] Chippindale 1994, 157 and 176.

[142] Chippindale 1994, 161.

[143] Petrie found local landowners less bothersome in Egypt.

[144] Chippindale 1994, 136. Atkinson turned to the topic of worms and soil movement, with particular reference to Stonehenge, in an influential paper (1957); he thought the stones Darwin examined were probably nos 12 and 127.

[145] Chippindale 1978, 111 and note 34.

[146] Stone 22, lintel 122.

[147] 18 February 1901 (W. M. F. Petrie).

[148] Chippindale 1994, 167. But he had studied megaliths, 'during a long residence' in Japan (Gowland 1897, 440). He was head of the Japanese Mint (*Antiquaries Journal* 3, 1922, 391).

[149] Gowland 1902. The paper that preceded his in the volume of *Archaeologia* makes instructive comparison. In less than a quarter of the pages in which Gowland considered the results of his small excavations, W. H. St John Hope presented the full report on the 1901 season (the 12th year) of six months' work at the Roman town of Silchester. 'The area examined was between 5 and 6 acres' (*Archaeologia* 58, 1902, 17–36).

[150] The actual straightening of the stone took place over eight days with the aid of two winches (Gowland 1902, 43–4).

[151] Atkinson (1979, 193) noted that these were the first archaeological sections ever to be drawn from nature rather than reconstructed at a desk.

[152] Judd 1902.

[153] Gowland 1902, 47–8.

[154] Gowland 1902, 49.

155 Gowland 1902, 67–70.

156 Gowland 1902, 56.

157 Judd 1902, 115–16.

158 Gowland 1902, 87–9. Over previous decades, estimates of Stonehenge's age had varied from before the Flood to AD 730, and the builders from Belgic tribes and Phoenicians to Appalachian Indians and King Efroc. Gowland's conclusions may now seem uncontroversial, but in 1902 for many people they must have been as mysterious as anyone else's.

159 Gowland 1902, 84.

160 Wainwright 1979, 73; Appendix 2: BM-677.

161 Clarke 1970. Lest you imagine archaeologists scouring the British Isles like latterday grave-robbers, it should be said that these days almost all such burials are excavated to save them from complete destruction by roadworks, farming or other development.

162 Atkinson and Evans 1978.

163 'The lighter side of archaeology'. *Antiquity* 11, 1937, 86 (E. C. Curwen). 'Tuppenny' is two (old) pence.

164 Cleal et al. 1995, 18–19 and passim.

165 Atkinson 1979, 194.

166 Letter to *The Times* 18 February 1901.

167 Chippindale 1994, 179.

168 Table 2 in Cleal et al. 1995 lists 504 cuttings at Stonehenge and along the Avenue between 1901 (Gowland's) and 1994. More recent reasons given for excavation include 'floodlight cable trench', 'sewage pipe', 'temporary toilets' and 'footpath through monument'.

169 The principal sources for this story are Hawley's diary transcripts, typed out for and annotated by Robert Newall (Hawley 1920–26); Hawley's seasonal reports and the summaries of discussions held after each of his talks (Hawley 1921/2/3/4/5/6/8); Chippindale 1994; Karen Walker in Cleal et al. 1995, 12–15 (the best published description of his work). I have also benefited from conversations with Mike Allen and Julie Gardiner, who recently discussed Hawley with some of his descendants; and with Margaret Ehrenburg.

170 Sir Hercules Read in Hawley 1921, 41.

171 Pronounced 'Filedean'.

172 Hawley 1920–6, 13 March 1920 (Saturday): '. . . Mrs Smith at the Cottages is leaving until [Tuesday] and I can have no meals there until she comes back.'

[173] Hawley 1920–26, 9 September 1920.

[174] Cleal et al. 1995, fig. 7.

[175] Hawley 1920–6, 23 March 1920.

[176] Hawley 1920–6, 30 April 1920.

[177] Letter in Wessex Archaeology archive, Hawley to Gowland, 15 June 1921.

[178] Hawley 1920–6, 23 April 1921.

[179] Hawley 1920–6, 25 June 1921.

[180] Hawley 1920–6, 7 November 1921.

[181] Hawley 1920–6, 28 April 1920: 'A better day with snow squalls and thunder.'

[182] Hawley 1920–6, 7 April 1923.

[183] Hawley 1920–6, 1 July 1926.

[184] Atkinson 1979, 196–7; the angry archaeologists are not named.

[185] Obituary in *Antiquaries Journal* 21, 1941, 241. I experienced vehemence when preparing the publication on my own excavations at Stonehenge (chapters 17 and 19). Extensive negative comments from an anonymous referee amounted to a recommendation not to publish. Young as I was, I typed twelve single-spaced pages dealing intemperately with the objections, almost all of which I felt contrived or based on a misreading of my text. The critic seemed to have privileged access to the results of Atkinson's work (then unpublished) and the typewriter font was unmistakable. My report was printed almost as written.

[186] A view further argued by Chippindale (1994, 180–3), and questioned only by Walker in Cleal et al. 1995.

[187] Hawley opened his sixth report 'On behalf of Mr Newall and myself . . .' (Hawley 1926, 1). In his first, he referred to 'my friend and colleague Mr R. S. Newall' (Hawley 1921, 36).

[188] Hawley 1920–6, 8 December 1919: 'Tried several places with my steel rod I have brought . . .' He was famous for his bar, one of several gadgets he introduced as digging aids. It was said that with it he could tell whether a buried coin was silver or bronze (*Antiquaries Journal* 21, 1941, 241).

[189] Hawley 1920–6, 19 February 1920: 'Since these holes were discovered it has been decided by Mr Newall and myself to call them "Aubrey's" Holes; he having first observed them in 1666.' But see chapter 17.

[190] Petrie 1880. The survey was completed over three years between 1874 and 1880, ending on midsummer day. After sunrise, 'Whitcombe the photographer rigged up a table and coffee and

did a good trade, and the place was rather a bear garden' (Drower 1985, 22–4).

[191] Hawley to Gowland, 15 June 1921 (punctuation adjusted). See also Hawley 1922, 50.

[192] Hawley 1924, 36.

[193] Hawley 1928, 174–5. Encouraged by Maud Cunnington and her interpretation of Woodhenge (excavated 1926–7) as a series of post holes, he later decided the Aubrey Holes too held posts, not stones.

[194] Hawley 1924, 36.

[195] Engleheart in Hawley 1924, 38.

[196] Atkinson 1979, ch 3. Curiously, the complex phasing described by Atkinson appeared at the same time under Stuart Piggott's name alone, with acknowledgement to Hawley (Piggott 1956).

[197] O'Connor in Evans et al. 1984, 13–17.

[198] McKinley in Cleal et al. 1995, 451–61.

[199] I have also referred to Mays 1998.

[200] *Ancient Voices: Stonehenge*, BBC Manchester/The Learning Channel/Time Life, broadcast BBC2 May 1998.

[201] Appendix 1: 5 sample weighted mean 2398–2144 cal BC.

[202] Young 1930–5 (1935, 22, 28, 29 January); Walker in Cleal et al. 1995, 18–19. Serjeantson (Cleal et al. 1995, 438) says the four sandbags of animal bones returned after analysis by Jackson to Salisbury Museum (which Chippindale [1994, 193–4] thought were the bones buried by Newall) seem still to be there. Strictly, only re-re-excavation will prove this (but see Preface).

[203] Allen and Bayliss in Cleal et al. 1995, 511–35; Bayliss et al. 1997; Bronk Ramsey and Bayliss 2000.

[204] Interview with Bronk Ramsey February 1999.

[205] Cleal et al. 1995, chapter 5.

[206] Atkinson 1979, 215.

[207] Appendix 1.

[208] Interview with Bayliss January 1998.

[209] Cleal et al. 1995, fig. 98.

[210] Heaps of antlers were found on the bottom of the ditches around Avebury (Gray 1935), Durrington Walls and Woodhenge, and in post holes at Durrington Walls: chapters 6 and 21.

[211] Serjeantson in Cleal et al. 1995, 442.

[212] Smith et al. 1997, 27–41; Cleal et al. 1995, 113–14; Appendix 2: OxA-2322, HAR-8578, HAR-9158.

[213] Houlder 1968; Appendix 2: NPL-224.

[214] Tratman 1967.

[215] Walker in Cleal et al. 1995, 94–107; 112–13.

[216] Appendix 1: C-602.

[217] Piggott 1946b.

[218] It was said that the excavation of 'ritual pits' that had apparently never held posts, by Atkinson at Dorchester (Oxford) and by Piggott at Cairnpapple (West Lothian), influenced the interpretation of the Aubrey Holes when Atkinson, Piggott and Stone came to dig two out in 1950 (Atkinson et al. 1952, 15). In fact, Piggott originally described the Cairnpapple pits as the remains of a ring of seven standing stones. The Dorchester dig made him change his mind on this, too (Piggott 1951, 279). The latest interpretation sees posts at Cairnpapple (Barclay 1999).

[219] Hawkins and White 1966; Krupp 1980.

[220] Renfrew 1979, chapter V. Brogar is technically a 'true' henge, with its ditch inside the bank.

[221] Cleal et al. 1995, 477; Richards 1990, 93–6, 266; Burl 1987, 43–7.

[222] O'Connor in Evans et al. 1984, 13. The following section is based on this report and an interview with O'Connor June 1999.

[223] Appendix 1: BM-1582, OxA-4886, 5044 to 5046.

[224] Appendix 2: Ashcott Heath, Q-598; Cambridge Fens, Q-684; Denny, Q-1196; Edington Burtle, Q-669; Meare Heath, Q-646.

[225] Clark 1963; Switsur 1974. The discovery by peat cutters of the two Somerset bows was announced in the *Illustrated London News* (February 1962, 219–21) under the heading 'Prehistoric ancestors of the weapons which brought England victory at Crécy, Poitiers and Agincourt'.

[226] Bergman et al. 1988, 663–4. I'm not aware that anyone has examined the bow fragments with this suggestion in mind. Use of natural wood variation in this way is tantamount to the construction of a 'composite bow', in which different materials (e.g. wood, horn and sinew) are fixed together for their different properties.

[227] Coles 1973, 125.

[228] A. Saville in Mercer 1981b, 122–6.

[229] Dixon 1988.

[230] Green 1980, 178–9.

[231] *London Archaeologist* 5, 1988, 412.

[232] Gibson (1994, 155, 187) says the relatively unburnt state of some barbed and tanged arrowheads found with cremated human bone suggests they were embedded in flesh.

[233] Green 1980, Table VI.17.

[234] Copies of correspondence in Salisbury and South Wiltshire Museum; Cave 1936.

[235] Kennard et al. 1935. That the bones Stevens sent to London are those identified by Kennard seems unlikely. If there was the communication between Newall and Stevens that this would imply, one would have to wonder why some bones were sent for safekeeping to London (Stevens'), while others (Newall's) were buried at Stonehenge. The animal bones are still in Manchester. Even my own excavation, some distance from the stones, turned up a human bone (from the Heelstone ditch). I was unaware of it until Tony King, examining what I imagined was all animal bone, found a human toe bone (Pitts 1982, 90).

[236] Ditch cuttings 18–25: 1.25 human remains finds per segment; other ditch dug by Hawley: .55 finds per segment. Data from Cleal et al. 1995, ch 6.

[237] McKinley 1997, 130–1.

[238] Site 2, in silts of ditch dug *c*. 4780 years ago (Appendix 2: BM-2440, BM-2442). Mary Harman thought ten of the twenty-five deposits examined probably contained more than one person, three had three or more, and one had at least five adults. Two contained bone pins similar to those from Stonehenge. Whittle et al. 1992, 153–8.

[239] McKinley knows what she is talking about. 'Observations at modern crematoria and a number of experimental pyre cremations have greatly assisted the understanding of the process of cremation . . .' (1997, 129).

[240] Piggott 1958.

[241] Atkinson called Piggott 'leader', himself 'follower'. After delivering a BBC radio talk in 1953, Atkinson was approached by Hamish Hamilton to write the book that became the Stonehenge classic (Atkinson lecture transcript 14 December 1978, Devizes Museum). Until then, Piggott had been main publicist. Stone, a scientist at Porton Down research laboratories (at a time of controversial experiments in chemical warfare, a story only now emerging), was 'the most outstanding "amateur" of his generation' (Piggott 1958).

[242] It was one of these ditch sections that John Evans re-excavated in 1978 (chapter 8). Principal source for the 1954 excavations is Cleal et al. 1995.

[243] All modern descriptions of Stonehenge human remains are taken

from McKinley in Cleal et al. 1995, 451–61.

244 Context 3893: McKinley in Cleal et al. 1995, 457, Table 58.

245 Interview with Ehrenburg November 1998.

246 Atkinson (1979, figure 1) maps one in Aubrey Hole 31 and none in 1, 22 and 23. The archive suggests there was none in 31, burials in 22 and 23 and a single bone fragment in 1 (Walker in Cleal et al. 1995, 152).

247 Atkinson (1979, fig. 1) placed them between Aubrey Holes 11 and 16, and the bank.

248 Hoare and Cunnington may have found a cremation burial in an Aubrey Hole on the west side (46) when they dug into the North Barrow (Newall 1929, 82).

249 Cleal et al. 1995, 409, 394, 360–1.

250 Cleal et al. 1995, 459.

251 Cleal et al. 1995, 154, 163.

252 Cleal et al. 1995, 161–5.

253 Bronk Ramsey and Bayliss 2000; Appendix 1.

254 Atkinson et al. 1951; Whittle et al. 1992; see also Appendix 2.

255 More likely than the Aubrey Holes, as suggested by Hawley (chapter 11).

256 Richards studied a quarter of the interior area at Coneybury. In the excavated segment where preservation was good, was a line of seven small pits following the curve of the ditch. If this was representative of the entire circuit, there would have been fifty-six: the same number as Aubrey Holes at Stonehenge (Richards 1990, 137).

257 Appendix 3.

258 e.g. Newham 1972, 15–16; Burl 1987, 67–8; Castleden 1993, 54–7 (he calls these entrance pits 'stake holes', an inappropriate term for holes that can be over 0.5m across).

259 Newall 1959 (first edition 1953). Hawley's remark about pits between the stones and the bank to the south is a little disconcerting: 'Some of these holes were evidently of late date, only those that could undoubtedly be called post-holes of early date were taken into consideration' in a 'surface . . . pitted with holes of various sorts and sizes' (Hawley 1928, 172).

260 Piggott 1951, 290.

261 Atkinson 1979, 72. Piggott also cautioned against over-imaginative interpretation of a badly disturbed area (1951, 290).

262 Burl 1987, 51–6.

263 Castleden 1993, 67–71.

264 North 1996, 325–8.
265 Although the timber henge still lives on in imaginations: Gibson 1998a, 113; Castleden 1999, 13.
266 Piggott 1956, 237.
267 Cleal et al. 1995, 140–52, 164–5.
268 Palisades are something altogether different.
269 As indirectly proposed by Hawley (1928, 172): 'I would hazard the suggestion that the post-holes on the south might have something to do with a wooden passage grave', which might be 'some sort of long roofed construction', many holes being too shallow for uprights not held in place by rafters or 'imposts' (i.e. lintels).
270 Cleal et al. 1995, 127, 454 (context 1398, incorrectly printed as 1399).
271 Cleal et al. 1995, 267, 454 (context 1676, incorrectly printed as 1678).
272 Cleal et al. 1995, 265, 454 (context 2724).
273 Smith 1965, 177–79; Ucko et al. 1991, 178–80.
274 'We may rightly look upon the British people', he wrote, 'as the least mongrel, the most uniform, to be found in any country of Europe' (*Daily Mail* 26 February 1931).
275 Keith 1929, 24.
276 Pitts and Roberts 1997.
277 Keith in Cunnington 1931, 330.
278 Burl 1979a, 198. 'It was a Beaker custom in Wessex to bury women with their heads to the south, men with their heads to the north.' There is a tendency for bodies to be laid out this way, but it is not universal.
279 Stukeley's view of the Sanctuary (plate 13), drawn in 1723, shows most of the stones of the outer circle still in place (they were removed the following year), but the inner circle stones had already gone.
280 Young 1930–40 (1930, 4 June).
281 Cunnington 1929, 41–5; Pollard 1995a, 125.
282 Cunnington 1929, 82.
283 Smith 1965, 177.
284 Cave 1938.
285 Keiller to Cave, 4 July 1938.
286 I recently met a former student of Cave's, who described him as a man of abundant and outspoken energy.
287 Cave to Keiller, 16 August 1938.
288 A word so apt it is easy to forget it was coined by William Stukeley

around 1740. The use of the word 'avenue' to describe linear arrangements of chalk (Stonehenge) and megaliths (Avebury and other sites) radiating from henges and stone circles is also Stukeley's (Piggott 1985, 92).

[289] Put simply, igneous rocks are cooled material formed from the molten core of the earth, while sedimentary rocks are made from fossil creatures and/or eroded grains of other rocks.

[290] Stone weights are approximate, and mostly borrowed from writers no better equipped than me to estimate mass. The heights are from a combination of a 1919 Office of Works survey and records left by Atkinson (not always consistent). Astonishingly, Stonehenge awaits a full three-dimensional survey. The bluestone/sarsen distinction at Stonehenge was made long ago, and much discussion was resolved in 1923 when geologist Herbert Thomas identified the Preseli Hills, Pembrokeshire, as the source of the igneous stones (Thomas 1923). The most detailed study of bluestone geology is Thorpe et al. 1991. See also Green 1997 for a useful review of both bluestone and sarsen.

[291] The Slaughter Stone was probably standing in the mid-seventeenth century: Burl 1994.

[292] Piggott 1956; Atkinson 1979.

[293] Cleal et al. 1995, chapter 7 (at 164 pages and 116 illustrations, this chapter outbulks Atkinson's entire book).

[294] Despite Castleden 1999, 12.

[295] Hawley 1926, 8.

[296] A point Castleden (1999) seems not to understand. His suggestion that Mesolithic post pits found in the old Stonehenge car park be known as the first phase of Stonehenge is also missing the mark. They are dated to 9000–10,000 years ago (Appendix 1: HAR-455 to 456, OxA-4919 to 4920, GU-5109), when no one had thought of Stonehenge. A similar post-hole has recently been found the other side of the River Avon (information Mike Allen). At the time of the earliest indications we have for Neolithic activity at the Stonehenge site, the Mesolithic posts would long since have vanished. It occurred to me that these posts could have been fossil trees preserved in Mesolithic peats in East Anglia that were 'quarried' and brought to Stonehenge in the Neolithic (much as some of the stones were brought from Wales). I put this to Allen, who was clearly being polite when he said this required special pleading. There is independent evidence for the age of these pits in the mollusc fauna, which is early post-glacial.

297 There are doubts as to which of all these pits really are part of the same structure, but that need not concern us here. See Cleal in Cleal et al. 1995, 169–88.

298 Two Beaker sherds (of later date than Phases 1 and 2) were found in the fill of Q hole 5 (Cleal et al. 1995, 177), but as Cleal says, these could have entered the pit at the time the stone was removed (Cleal et al. 1995, 469).

299 Chippindale 1994, 34–6.

300 Bronk Ramsey and Allen in Cleal et al. 1995, 532–3; Bronk Ramsey and Bayliss 2000.

301 Atkinson 1979, 77–8.

302 Cleal in Cleal et al. 1995, 486.

303 Case 1997.

304 Cleal et al. 1995, 285–6.

305 Appendix 3.

306 The next morning you will send them a copy of the book.

307 Dialling code currently 01980.

308 I found out later that the men had been laying the exchange cable in the area for eight weeks before Prince Charles' visit. To this day, I don't know whether he realises the impact his tour had on our knowledge of Stonehenge.

309 Two months after the dig was over, I was reimbursed £499.37½p by the Wessex Archaeology Committee. The team boasted a high number of professional or would-be professional archaeologists, including: Arthur ApSimon (now retired Lecturer in Archaeology, University of Southampton); Mark Brisbane (now Bournemouth University); Sarah Colley (now Lecturer, University of Sydney); Sue Davies (now Deputy Director, Wessex Archaeology); David Hinton (now Professor, Southampton University); Hilary Howard (at the time working on a PhD and responsible for the study of our rock fragments); Linda Hurcombe (now Dept. of Archaeology, Exeter University); Elaine Morris (now Research Fellow, Southampton University); Mike Parker Pearson (now Reader in Archaeology, Sheffield University); Phil Planel; Paul Stamper (now English Heritage); Simyu Wandibba; and Todd Whitelaw (now Reader in Archaeology, UC London). Only seven of us were there for more than five days.

310 Nearly twenty years later I discovered that Newall had recorded a section along this area when the water pipe we found was laid in 1919 (Cleal et al. 1995, 301).

311 Stone (1924) and Newall (1929).

[312] Cleal et al. 1995, 283–7.

[313] Cleal et al. 1995, 287–8.

[314] Whatever Aubrey saw on his visit to Stonehenge, it almost certainly wasn't the holes that now bear his name. He described but five 'cavities' (and two Station Stones). Why would 4000-year-old pits – and only five of fifty-six – have been visible at Aubrey's visit, yet invisible to other perceptive antiquarians less than sixty years later (a puzzle noted when they were discovered, e.g. Newall 1929, 82)? It makes more sense if disturbance had occurred not long before Aubrey's visit – megaliths or bushes removed? Pitts 1981a and b.

[315] 'There were two long holes about two and a half inches in diameter and about 3 ft long which may have been caused by sticks which rotted away and left casts or they may have been handles of picks discarded as digging sticks with points' (Diary 2 June 1920, quoted by Cleal et al. 1995, 284).

[316] It was near the southern edge of the trench, approximately parallel to the grooves on the bottom but slightly higher, partly over the stone impression and partly to the east (cf. Pitts 1982, fig. 7).

[317] The Ancient Monuments Laboratory also took a latex mould of the pit bottom.

[318] Atkinson 1979, 30.

[319] Atkinson and I thought a feature he had excavated close to the Heelstone (the other side of the fence) in 1956, originally interpreted as the Heelstone's erection ramp, was probably also part of pit 97. This would make the pit a minimum of nearly 2.5m long, which even for Stonehenge stone pits is a very large hole. If this is a single pit, the stone must have been of a size comparable to those in the sarsen circle.

[320] 'Dead Man Talking'. First Take for Channel 4, broadcast March 1999.

[321] Prag and Neave 1997, chapter 2.

[322] Drewery 1999.

[323] Cleal et al. 1995, 190.

[324] Howard 1982. In this report, sample 121a on p. 116 should read 1212a; and 105 on pp. 122–3 109 throughout.

[325] Montague in Cleal et al. 1995, 291–327.

[326] Appendix 1: OxA-4884 and BM-1164.

[327] Cleal et al. 1995, 311.

[328] Cleal et al. 1995, 307.

[329] Appendix 1: OxA-4878. Letters were added to the numeric

sequence of stones known above ground for buried stumps identified by excavation. They imply nothing about the status of the stones in the past.

330 Atkinson 1979, 49–50.

331 Appendix 1: OxA-4877.

332 Cleal et al. 1995, 212–31.

333 Cleal et al. 1995, 207.

334 Cleal et al. 1995, 211.

335 Stone 1947.

336 Atkinson 1979, 127.

337 Pitts 1982.

338 HAR-4878: 3400±150 BP, 2131–1324 cal BC.

339 Bayliss, Housley and McCormac in Cleal et al. 1995, 519.

340 Pitts 1982, 125.

341 Atkinson first argued that 'apathy' had led Bronze Age excavators to give up at this point, failing to empty Z8 (1979, 82). Later probing convinced him the pit is there (Cleal et al. 1995, 205). His concern was to argue that the layout of the Z holes could not support the early felling of sarsen 8.

342 Hawley 1925, 27.

343 Appendix 1: UB-3822 to 3823; OxA-4836 and UB-3824.

344 Knight and Lomas 1999.

345 Dames 1977, 67.

346 Devereux 1992.

347 Meaden 1999, 22–24.

348 Devereux 1992, 152.

349 Devereux 1992, 162.

350 Restall Orr 1998.

351 Bewley et al. 1996.

352 Gray 1935, 145–6.

353 Ucko et al. 1991, 254 note 2.

354 Appendix 2: henge ditch around 4965 years ago (HAR-10502); burial around 4065 years ago (HAR-10064). Pitts and Whittle 1992.

355 There seems to be a millennial attack of seeing faces. Edward Peterson (*Stone Age Alpha*, 1999) believes the Avebury stones are sculpted seal heads, while the name of Robert Lamont's little *Guide to the Avebury Sphinx* (1999), available in the village pub, speaks for itself. In his book confidently titled THE secrets of Avebury, Meaden (1999) finds on almost every megalith human faces, mostly female.

[356] Knight and Lomas 1999, 303. The concept of a nationwide 'Grooved Ware People' is anachronistic and unsupported by any evidence. Ruggles and Barclay 2000, 65.

[357] Dames 1976, 77. He obviously never worked in an espresso bar.

[358] Burl 1979a, 202.

[359] Hence the worst part of Bernard Cornwell's *Stonehenge: a Novel of 2000 BC* (1999) is the 'Historical Note' at the end. Although he lists Cleal et al. 1995 in his reading, his archaeology derives from Atkinson's 1956 text (1979) – and, he claims, the overwrought astronomical theories of North (1996). Thus the story mixes things we now know to be of widely different dates (such as Stonehenge and gold lozenges). Just enjoy the novel.

[360] A post then held jointly with Clare Conybeare.

[361] Young 1930–40 (1940, February 7).

[362] Maud Cunnington felt the same. Robert Newall's copy of the journal in which her report appeared is in Avebury Museum. He wrote in the margin, quoting a letter Maud sent in 1931. Someone had suggested that each oval pit held two posts supporting lintels, like Stonehenge trilithons. 'It seems quite a good idea', she wrote. 'I can't think why none of us hit on it before?'

[363] Cunnington, R. H. 1931; Piggott 1940; Musson in Wainwright and Longworth 1971, 363–77; Burl 1976a, 318–20, which is quite different from Burl 1979a, 124–5 and 193–6; Pollard 1992; Lees 1999.

[364] Pollard 1992.

[365] Barrett 1994, chapter 1. It's not just archaeologists who have this problem. Dames' goddess vision at Silbury (1976) derives from indoor study of archaeological surveys and air photos; familiarity on the ground engenders a very different relationship with this enigmatic monument. Ley lines, by definition, can only be seen on maps or from the air (which is why we all have to buy the books to learn about them).

[366] Tilley 1993; 1994.

[367] Interview with Gillings, Pollard and Wheatley September 1999.

[368] Avebury Museum recently acquired some fine drawings by Doris Chapman, of megaliths fully exposed by Keiller's excavations.

[369] Pollard and Gillings 1998.

[370] Gray's Avebury story is taken from his published report (1935) and notes at the Alexander Keiller Museum. 'I have spent a full year of my life at Avebury', he wrote, 'and my wife 6 months . . . [these were] some of my happiest days.'

[371] The original contoured plan at 40 feet to the inch (with 1700 levelling points) and a model of Avebury (650 hours of work) were given to the British Museum. The model was bombed in the war (or so Gray records), but the plan survived, and is perhaps still in London. Finds were given to various museums (there was none at Avebury at the time), where many still exist. What makes his photos so interesting, apart from the expression of a romantic creativity we see less in his writing, is the comprehensiveness: glass negatives in their wooden boxes, mounted and marked up prints, and notebook entries detailing light conditions, camera settings etc. This is not common for photography before the First World War. And the photos are superb.

[372] A local word for the earthwork that may derive from Saxon settlers 1400 years ago.

[373] Gray 1911–22, 22–23 April 1911. Parsons must have had his reasons: less than four months later, the Cunningtons were digging in his pasture on the West Kennet Avenue (Cunnington M. E. 1913a, 8).

[374] Gray 1908–9, 1 June 1908.

[375] Appendix 2: HAR–10502.

[376] Jewell 1963.

[377] Serjeantson and Gardiner in Cleal et al. 1995, 428. They may have been used in some flint mines, where the extreme confinement would have demanded unusual tools (Curwen and Curwen 1926), although there is no evidence for their use at Grimes Graves.

[378] Startin 1982, 153.

[379] Clutton-Brock 1984; Legge 1981.

[380] Gray 1935, 148–55.

[381] Pitts and Roberts 1997.

[382] e.g. in the excavation of ditches at the Hazleton North long barrow: Levitan 1990, 205–9.

[383] It is sometimes said that antlers have to be collected at shedding time in February or March, else the deer eat them. This only seems to happen, however, when the deer's diet is impoverished, an unlikely situation in the Neolithic.

[384] Pitts and Whittle 1992.

[385] Appendix 2: HAR–10325, 10063 and 10500.

[386] Whittle 1993, Table 1.

[387] Appendix 2: HAR–10502.

[388] Johnstone 1957, chapter VIII. 'The operation had much in common with the pleasant pastime of punting agreeable

companions . . . upon the quiet waters of the Cherwell or the Cam' (Atkinson 1979, 113–5).

389 Startin 1976, 1978, 1982; Startin and Bradley 1981.

390 Cleal et al. 1995, 415: in the half-circuit excavated by Hawley, Atkinson reported eighty picks, Newall said over 100.

391 Wainwright and Longworth 1971, 22. To reinforce a point, they did not find one scapula in the primary ditch fill.

392 Inside the bank on the south-west side of the henge: Pitts and Whittle 1992, 210.

393 19 May–5 June 1908: Gray 1908–9.

394 Gray (1935, 104–5) noted that the top of the chalk fill had consolidated to the hardness of concrete, so this may be a not unreasonable thing to do.

395 37 x 18 days x 4 sectors = 380 weeks.

396 Startin (1982, Table 42) gives a figure of 500,000 hours with an estimated labour force of 250–500. His calculations assumed that the earthwork was dug in one go.

397 Atkinson 1979, 166–7.

398 Renfrew 1973.

399 Barrett 1994; Whittle 1997a, Part 3.

400 Lehner 1997, 227.

401 Whittle 1997a.

402 Robinson in Whittle 1997a, 43–4.

403 'Aquatic insects are entirely absent from Silbury' (Robinson in Whittle 1997a, 44); Evans et al. 1993.

404 Whittle 1997a, 140.

405 Smith 1965, 194 and Plate XXXII.

406 Appendix 2: I-4136, BM-841 to 842.

407 Whittle 1997a, 12.

408 Startin 1982, Table 42. Labour estimates for ancient constructions decrease with understanding. Startin's figure of 1.75 million hours for the late Stonehenge compares with Atkinson's 30 million (Renfrew 1973; Startin 1982), while nothing short of Merlin's magic was required in medieval versions of what happened. Egypt's greatest pyramid, Giza, was said by Herodotus to have taken the labour of 100,000 men; Wier (1996) suggested a workforce of 10,000.

409 '. . . it is unlikely from the stratigraphic evidence . . . that the span [of construction] lasted more than one or two generations' (Whittle 1997a, 145).

410 Startin 1982, Table 42.

[411] Felder 1981; Longworth and Varndell 1996.

[412] A comprehensive description of these is in Pitts 1996; see also Barber et al. 1999.

[413] Following photography in 1995 by Roger Featherstone of a new cropmark that may be a flattened prehistoric burial mound, the whole north-west quadrant was subjected to a resistivity survey by David and Payne (Bewley et al. 1996).

[414] The earlier geophysics work at Avebury is reported in Ucko et al. 1991. An index might help the interested reader. Plate numbers are followed by the page reference in brackets. Avebury general: 158–60; Pl. 45 (159), 73 (261). NE quadrant: 167, 224–7; Pl. 53 (169), 67 (223), 69 (228). Cove: Pl. 68 (225). E quadrant: 167, 212, 220; Pl. 54 (169), 66 (219). E entrance 184–5; Pl. 58 (185). West Kennet Avenue: 189–94; Pl. 59 (188), 62 (192). Beckhampton Avenue: 196–9; Pl. 63 (197).

[415] Interview with Andy Payne and Louise Martin, September 1999.

[416] David 1999; www.eng-h.gov.uk/reports/beckhampton/.

[417] Morgan 1887.

[418] Lambrick 1988, 27–8.

[419] Burl 1999. Nonetheless, Burl did dispute Thorpe and Williams-Thorpe's claim that the Devil's Arrows, four or five large standing stones in Yorkshire, were brought to the site by another glacier rather than moved the 14km necessary in the Neolithic (Burl 1991).

[420] Kellaway 1971, 34.

[421] Thorpe et al. 1991.

[422] Judd 1902.

[423] Thorpe and Williams-Thorpe 1991.

[424] Pronounced 'Hatesb'ry'.

[425] Burl 1999, chapter 7.

[426] Cunnington B. H. 1924; Cunnington R. H. 1975, 15–16.

[427] Green 1997, 265–7.

[428] Confirmed by Thorpe et al. 1991, 113, 134.

[429] Cunnington R. H. 1975, 11.

[430] Burl 1999, 118.

[431] Lord Antrobus was told in 1871, before the completion of Petrie's survey, by a 'distinguished archaeologist' that he had obtained for himself a piece of megalith from Stonehenge (Chippindale 1994, 159). The narrow end of the Slaughter Stone has a row of holes across it, like a perforation ready to tear, where a mason has begun the task of cutting off a chunk that would do any country

garden proud.

[432] Cleal et al. 1995, 338.

[433] Pitts 1996.

[434] Whittle 1997a, 21.

[435] Cunnington may have found more than one bluestone. A note in Robert Newall's handwriting at the end of Ben Cunnington's article (1924) in Avebury Museum's copy of the journal reads: 'In a copy of a letter signed "W.C. 1801" in possession of Mr Priestly of Batheaston Cunnington says – "I have brought away ten of them to my house" and adds "since writing the above I find some of these stones are blue and grey like the upright stones of the inner Circle at Stonehenge"' (Newall's underlining).

[436] Cunnington W. 1889; Cunnington B. H. 1924.

[437] Thorpe et al. 1991, 107–8.

[438] Green 1973. The Anglian glaciation is the only one remotely in the running for having reached Stonehenge. Geologist J. D. Scourse (1997) provides an excellent wide-ranging review of the glacial hypothesis, and like Green, comes down firmly and convincingly against it; geologist Bill Cummins also agrees (1992, 59–64).

[439] Patton (1992), with reference to evidence from Jersey, makes the important point that even when megaliths have been moved only a few kilometres from their source, it still doesn't follow that the close proximity of that source was the only consideration in the minds of the people who selected the stone.

[440] Piggott 1985; Ucko et al. 1991.

[441] Keiller's Avebury work is described by Isobel Smith (1965). His interim reports are useful for illustrating the way in which ideas developed as he and Stuart Piggott worked, although they should only be used with modern commentaries (Keiller and Piggott 1936; Keiller 1939).

[442] Ucko et al. 1991, Pl. 8, 33. Stukeley copied Aubrey's plan into his notebook.

[443] Burl 1979a, 191.

[444] Ucko et al. 1991, Pl. 60, 190; see Preface.

[445] Burl 1979a, fig. 25, 50.

[446] Ucko et al. 1991, 87–9.

[447] King 1879; Smith 1965, 216–17; Burl 1979a, 191.

[448] A recent book I would strongly recommend has a map of Avebury in which the Beckhampton Avenue is not marked, even as a hypothesis (Thomas 1999, fig. 9.4).

[449] Gowland 1901, 43–4. See chapter 9.

450 Cunnington M. E. 1913; Gray 1935, Pl. XXXIII.1.

451 Stone no. 34a. Keiller to Crawford, 27 June 1934. Avebury Museum reference 78510456.

452 Story from Andrew Lawson.

453 Atkinson 1979, 105–7.

454 Switsur 1991. Ferriby boats around 3150–3350 years ago. Appendix 2: Q-3043 to 3045, 3047, 3123, 3124. NB: See Preface.

455 Caldicot around 3750 years ago; Goldcliff 2900. Appendix 2: UB-3472, CAR-1434.

456 Radiocarbon dates averaging around 1550 cal BC (3550 years ago): information from Peter Clark, Canterbury Archaeological Trust.

457 See articles in Coles et al. 1993.

458 Switsur 1991, 749.

459 Muckleroy 1980.

460 Needham 1996.

461 Appendix 2: Radley 919 (OxA-1874), Shrewton 5k (BM-3017) and Radley 4A (OxA-4356).

462 Appendix 2: Corlea, Co Longford; O'Sullivan 1996.

463 Letter to *British Archaeology* 47, 1999, 14. See also Castleden 1993, 112–14.

464 Letter to *British Archaeology* 49, 1999, 14.

465 In February 1999 a Welsh group named Menter Preseli received a £100,000 Lottery Millennium Festival grant to take a bluestone from the Preselis to Stonehenge. 'We will be using only information available at the time Stonehenge was built', said a representative. *Daily Telegraph* 23 February 1999 (Sean O'Neill). See Preface.

466 The Hampshire Avon is sometimes described as a prehistoric route, because of a concentration of Cornish stone axe blades in the valley (e.g. Castleden 1993, fig. 48). This is a myth. We do not know where the stone axes in question came from, and the 'concentration' is a figment of unsound analysis (Pitts 1996). Another much quoted 'ancient road' is the Oxford/Wiltshire Ridgeway. Again, there is no evidence that this was a track in the Neolithic or Bronze Age. It certainly was not around 2500 years ago, when cropmarks show ditches and banks of small fields cutting across the route with complete abandon. The Ridgeway happens not to have been tarmacked: that doesn't necessarily make it any older a route than the A4 road.

467 Coles and Coles 1986.

[468] Whiteman 1995. See also Hornsey 1987; Lambrick 1988, 48–51.

[469] *Secrets of Lost Empires*, BBC/WGBH Boston, broadcast BBC2 July 1996; Richards and Whitby 1997.

[470] Pavel 1992.

[471] e.g. Meaden 1999.

[472] Atkinson 1979, 122–9.

[473] Pitts 1980.

[474] Lord 1993.

[475] Stone 1924.

[476] Stone 1921.

[477] Pitts 1996.

[478] Beside Nash Road, as it happens, an old Avebury name. Nash's work has references that might be noticed only by an archaeologist. In *Landscape of the Megaliths* (1934), of two hills rendered schematically in the background, one looks remarkably like a Neolithic or Bronze Age stone 'macehead'. See Reid 1975.

[479] Gillings, Pollard and Wheatley 2000.

[480] Smith 1965, 180–1.

[481] Smith 1965, 216–7. Encouraged by this discovery, some of us feel that geophysical suggestions of paired pits outside the *east* entrance of Avebury (Ucko et al. 1991, Plate 58) now need to be investigated. There could be a third avenue.

[482] 'Megabytes of megaliths'. *The Guardian* 23 September 1999 (M. Pitts).

[483] Highly recommended: http://www.arch.soton.ac.uk/Research/Avebury/Longstones99/.

[484] http://www.earthview.com/ages/stonehenge.htm. The search that found this site also sent me to another whose summary read: 'Stonehenge is Earth's Great Broadcasting Station (among other things) Glastonbury Tor is the Heart Chakra of the Planet Join us in a World Love & Peace Meditation & Solar Eclipse Activation', but its URL was down. The web, so suited to – indeed, promoted for – the publication of up-to-the-minute research and ideas, is, as far as stone circles are concerned, overwhelmingly dominated by extremely out-of-date and ill-informed documents. If you are researching a story (for a school essay, for example) please do not use the web for archaeological information unless you can document clear archaeological credentials!

[485] 'The Earth's first early warning system'. *Sunday Telegraph* 22 November 1998 (Robert Matthews); Steel, D. 1999 'Stonehenge and the terror in the sky'. *British Archaeology* 45, 8–9 (long

barrows were air raid shelters against the cometary storm). Science historian John North's 600-page *Stonehenge: Neolithic Man and the Cosmos* (North 1996), which 'has finally solved the riddle of Stonehenge', gives short shrift to eclipses and does not mention meteors or comets, preferring stars.

[486] 'Prehistoric moon map unearthed'. BBC Online News 22 April 1999 (D. Whitehouse).

[487] Ruggles 1999: now the essential starting point for anyone with more than a passing interest in ancient astronomy in Britain.

[488] 'Ray of darkness'. *Guardian Online* 10 September 1998 (M. Pitts).

[489] Appendix 2: GrN-5462C, GrN-5463, UB-361, GrN-9057.

[490] Ruggles 1999, 12–19.

[491] While improbable, the odds against this being chance are by no means impossible: Heggie 1981, 213.

[492] Appendix 2: Q-1482, SRR-505.

[493] Ruggles 1999, 91–9; Barclay 1999, 21–2.

[494] http://www.iol.ie/~geniet/maeshowe/. Highly recommended.

[495] Knight and Lomas (1999, 278–9), worried by Heggie and others saying the Newgrange light-box does not provide a precise alignment, wonder then why the builders 'had made such a complicated construction'. This narrow (and circular) view – only accurate astronomy can explain anything – is extremely ethnocentric. Human talent, energy, skill and vision, around the world, are typically directed at communication, not investigation.

[496] Thorpe 1981.

[497] Not least the oft-quoted but ill-informed and outdated MacKie 1977. For a recent perceptive and damning critique of MacKie's ideas, see Ruggles and Barclay 2000.

[498] Charles Newham first published his ideas on how Stonehenge might have been used as a calendar, by observing the sun and moon from the centre, in the *Yorkshire Post* in 1963.

[499] Hawkins' *Stonehenge Decoded* (Hawkins and White 1966), whatever its faults, was largely responsible for modern interest in ancient astronomy and Stonehenge. It excited me as a schoolboy, not long after I'd read Atkinson's *Stonehenge*, and eventually took me to Washington DC as a thrilled guest of Hawkins.

[500] Astronomer Hoyle was brought in by the editor of *Antiquity* to mediate between the unfettered imagination of Hawkins and barely controlled bile of Atkinson, and came up with his own (to almost all archaeologists) unintelligible astronomical theories.

[501] Ruggles 1997, 203.

[502] Heggie 1981, 202.

[503] Ruggles 1999, 79.

[504] Kendall 1974; Freeman 1976; Angell 1977 and 1979; Burl & Freeman 1977; Heggie 1981; Barnatt & Moir 1984; Barnatt & Herring 1986; Ruggles 1999, 83. See also Hicks 1977; Burl 1979a, 125–6, 150–2; Ruggles & Barclay 2000, 64. Some of these articles refer to further studies that found the case for the megalithic yard wanting.

[505] Ruggles 1999, 82–3.

[506] Quoted by Ruggles 1999, 79.

[507] Parker Pearson 1993, 40–48; Cleal et al. 1995, 57–60; Thomas 1999, 167–72.

[508] Ashbee 1970; Kinnes 1992.

[509] Ruggles 1997, 218, 225.

[510] But see Pollard and Ruggles 2001.

[511] Ruggles 1997, 218–19, 220–3.

[512] Musson in Wainwright and Longworth 1971, 374.

[513] Cunnington, M. E. 1929, 17–18.

[514] Burl 1976b. He says his figures are accurate to ±2 stones.

[515] Wainwright 1979, Table I.

[516] *The Locust Farm*, Headline 1998.

[517] Scott 1977,

[518] Bourguignon 1974, Bradley 1989, Sherratt 1991, Lewis-Williams and Dowson 1993.

[519] Devereux 1997, Hoggard 1998.

[520] Eliade 1964, 161–2.

[521] Dronfield 1996a.

[522] These famous Neolithic tombs are poorly dated. Appendix 2: GrN-5462C, GrN-5463, UB-361, GrN-9057 (Newgrange); GrN-12357 and 12358, GrN-12827 (Knowth 1).

[523] Dronfield 1995.

[524] Rudgley 1993.

[525] Appendix 3.

[526] Dronfield 1995, 265; Long et al. 2000.

[527] Avebury Museum ref. 20000590.

[528] Garofalini's model can be viewed at:
http://www.arch.soton.ac.uk/research/sanctuary

[529] Whittle 1997a.

[530] Wainwright and Longworth 1971, 223–4.

[531] Wainwright 1979, 237.

[532] Wainwright and Longworth 1971, 223.

[533] Gibson 1998b, 68–72.

[534] Evans 1972; Evans et al. 1985 and 1993; Cornwall, Dimbleby, Evans, Robinson and Williams in Whittle 1997a, 26–47.

[535] Ucko et al. 1991, Plates 67 and 69.

[536] By reducing the effects of surface stress, and thus susceptibility to fracture: Pitts 1996, 315.

[537] Coles 1973, 19–21.

[538] 'Mother's got that in her garage'. Interview with Harding May 1999.

[539] Becker 1962.

[540] Cleal et al. 1995, 410.

[541] Coles 1973, 121–2.

[542] Coles 1973, 122.

[543] E4 in Cunnington, M. E. 1931; Pitts 2001.

[544] Pitts 2000.

[545] Kahn 1990.

[546] Gillings and Pollard 1999.

[547] e.g. see discussion by Garwood 1999.

[548] This site is traditionally divided into two phases, a slighter complex of post rings preceding a more massive one (chapter 6), but there are problems with this (existing radiocarbon dates are no help, as the single, bulked date from 'Phase 1', which includes samples from 'façade' post holes as well as the rings, is statistically indistinguishable from the 'Phase 2' date: Appendix 2). The orientation of some post hole ramps, and the way they intersect, suggest some of the earlier posts may have formed a non-circular arrangement close to the 'façade' pits (Barrett 1994, 20-4). There is a relationship between the posts of each 'phase' (the smaller pits almost without exception lying in pairs astride the larger) that makes it difficult to believe they were not in some way contemporary, perhaps in a pattern of uprooting and replacement that I have proposed for the Sanctuary.

[549] Termed 'lithicisation' by Wainwright: 1979, 231–2.

[550] Appendix 2: BM-663, 666, 667.

[551] Appendix 2: BM-668.

[552] This same interpretation was arrived at by Pollard: 1992, 218–19.

[553] *Ancient Voices: Stonehenge*, BBC Manchester/The Learning Channel/Time Life, broadcast BBC2 May 1998.

[554] Parker Pearson and Ramilisonina 1998. See also discussion in *Antiquity* 72 (1998), 847–56.

[555] Lehmann and Myers 1993; Steadman et al. 1996.

[556] Hodder 1982; Parker Pearson 1999a, chapter 2.

[557] Burl 1979b; Whittle 1997b, 152.

[558] Bloch 1971; Mack 1986.

[559] Pollard 1995b, 155.

[560] Appendix 2: NPL-192 (bulked charcoal).

[561] All Durrington Walls data from Wainwright and Longworth 1971; for Stonehenge see Harding in Cleal et al. 1995, 368–75.

[562] Harcourt in Wainwright and Longworth 1971, 338–9; Richards and Thomas 1984.

[563] Serjeantson in Cleal et al. 1995, 450.

[564] Unpublished work by Andrew David and Dale Serjeantson.

[565] Richards and Thomas 1984, 206.

[566] Serjeantson in Cleal et al. 1995, bones from Phase 1 and 'Phase 2 or earlier'.

[567] Appendix 1: OxA-4902.

[568] Jackson in Cunnington M. E. 1929, 62.

[569] Davis and Payne 1993.

[570] Appendix 2: UB-3148, OxA-2084 to 2087, and Appendix 3.

[571] Kinnes et al. 1983. Tusks grow continuously, worn down by opposing teeth in the other jaw. If these teeth are knocked out (as is still occasionally deliberately done in parts of the Pacific), huge curved tusks grow (at the expense of the boar, whose cheeks are perforated by the sharp fangs). One of the tusks from this Duggleby burial (no. 37) raises the possibility that this happened in Hengeworld.

[572] Radley Site 611: Barclay et al. 1999. East Lavant: Magilton 1998. Appendix 2 and 3: BM-2706, 2712, 2713, 2715.

[573] Serjeantson in Cleal et al. 1995, 442.

[574] Pollard 1995b; Richards and Thomas 1984.

[575] Cleal et al. 1995, 67.

[576] But see Pollard and Ruggles forthcoming.

[577] Cleal et al. 1995, 147.

[578] Whittle 1997b, 150.

[579] Appendix 3. Needham's 'metalwork assemblages' V and VI (1996; interview November 1999). The presence of side bumps needs testing through detailed study of the carvings.

[580] Meaden 1999, chapter 16.

[581] Petrie 1880, 14.

[582] The phallus was spotted by my friend Amanda Twohey, as we watched Meaden address a television camera, oblivious to the lusty groove above his head.

583 'A carefully worked phallus 11 cm long', found with a chalk ball 7cm across: Wainwright 1979, 167. Stonehenge: Montague in Cleal et al. 1995, fig. 224.

584 This is a truth that many writers fail to appreciate. We cannot blithely assume that people in Hengeworld would have reacted to death in the same way that we might (which in itself, if you think about it, leaves a pretty wide range of possibilities). See, for example, Huntington and Metcalf 1979; Parker Pearson 1999a.

585 Appendix 2: OxA-449 to 451, 563; Thomas and Whittle 1986.

586 Barrett 1994.

587 Appendix 2: BM-1086 to 1091; ApSimon et al. 1976.

588 Appendix 2: HAR-9159; Healy in Smith et al. 1997, 37–8.

589 Appendix 2: BM-2395 to 2397; Barrett et al. 1991.

590 Bradley 1993; Cleal et al. 1995, 473–6; Whittle 1997a, 141–2, 165 and 1997c; Thomas 1999.

591 Pollard 1995b, 153–4.

592 Loveday 1998.

593 Bloch and Parry 1982.

594 Needham 1967; Huntington and Metcalf 1979.

595 cf. Darvill 1997, 189–93.

596 Richards 1996.

597 Parker Pearson and Ramilisonina 1998.

598 Whittle 1997b, 155–61.

599 We could even extend this argument to the bluestones with mortises and tenons: perhaps they were not 're-used', but carved in symbolic representation of people in transition between life and death.

600 Cleal et al. 1995, 210–11, 231.

601 Chapter 17.

602 Ruggles and Barclay 2000, 68.

603 Dronfield 1996b.

604 Appendix 2: HAR-10502.

605 Appendix 2: HAR-10327, HAR-10062.

606 Field et al. 2001; Best in Whittle 1997a, 169–70. The chance that this may be another Silbury means that all building works etc. in Marlborough should be very carefully watched: you don't get mounds like that by themselves.

607 Wainwright 1979, 65–8. Appendix 2: BM-795.

608 Appendix 2: BM-645 and 646.

609 Bournemouth University has a small-scale project at Knowlton: http://csweb.bournemouth.ac.uk/consci/text_kn/knhome.htm.

[610] *Past* 33, December 1999 (Conor Newman).

[611] Several writers confuse the stones on the outside with those inside. Merewether 1851; Petrie 1923; Whittle 1997a, 10, 18.

[612] One is reminded of the sarsens in the ring ditch at Flagstones in Dorset, where the excavators thought they might be the remnants of a stone circle (Healy in Smith et al. 1997, 30–9); if correct, this circle would be older than Silbury (Appendix 3).

[613] Thomas 1999, 203–8.

[614] Robertson-Mackay 1980. Appendix 2: BM-1585, HAR-2998, NPL 139.

[615] Chapter 26, Radley and East Lavant.

[616] Chapter 21.

[617] Passmore (1935) says there were twenty antler picks, worn down 'old tools'. Thomas Leslie, who supervised the dig, says only 'several' antlers, and that they were 'impossible to secure . . . in a complete state, as they were damp and decayed'. He does not identify them as picks, although he does this of other antlers found in the dig (Leslie 1894). Passmore may have confused these with antlers from Gray's excavations.

[618] Pollard 1992.

[619] Parker Pearson and Ramilisonina 1998, 319.

[620] Fordington Farm Appendix 2: UB-3304 to 3306; Bellamy 1991.

[621] 'Wooden door to past'. *Guardian* 29 July 1999 (M. Pitts).

[622] Bayliss et al. 1999.

[623] *The Mystery of Seahenge*. Picture House Television, broadcast on C4 29 December 1999.

[624] Compare Garwood 1991.

[625] Appendix 2: BM-645, 646, 662, 665, 668.

[626] Davies et al. 1985.

[627] Bradley 1998, chapter 10; Thomas 1996, 232; Thomas 1999, 165–7. But contrast Allen 1997.

[628] Brodie 1994.

[629] Piggott 1938; Fleming 1973.

[630] Needham 1996.

[631] Appendix 1: OXA–4836, UB–3822 to 3824.

[632] Lawson and Walker in Cleal et al. 1995, 30–2.

[633] Barfield and Chippindale 1997, 116–20.

[634] Pit WA 1399: Cleal et al. 1995, 354.

[635] Parker Pearson 1999b.

[636] Woodward and Woodward 1996.

[637] Chapter 15.

638 Keith to Newall 14 March 1927. 'Will I send the skeleton back?' asked Keith, suggesting it was not accessioned into the college's museum.

639 My sources include papers, diaries and published Annual Reports of the Museum at the Royal College of Surgeons, and Cope 1959.

640 Paintings of Cherokee Indians, a house sparrow with enlarged testes and a turkey leg with gangrene from frostbite are amongst treasures that survived the war. In 2000, the Museums and Galleries Commission designated the collection as being of outstanding national importance.

641 In 1924, a Miss Tildesley was 'fully engaged cataloguing the collection, tracking down records and information'. At that time, however, none of Hawley's Stonehenge remains seems to appear in any catalogue.

642 Davies, 431-2, and Seager-Smith, 435, in Cleal et al. 1995.

643 There are eight Roman sherds for every late Bronze and Iron Age sherd from Stonehenge: Morris ibid. 434-5.

644 Burl 1976a, 316; Walker in Cleal et al. 1995, 338. The idea seems to have originated with Atkinson (1979, 85-6, 99-100).

645 Gardiner in Cleal et al. 1995, 343.

646 Diverres 1979.

647 Chippindale 1994, 22-4.

648 A delightful version by retired geologist Bill Cummins proposes that Stonehenge was actually built by Arthur – Arthur being a Neolithic king: Cummins 1992.

649 Liddell & Tildesley 1933; Stone & Tildesley 1932.

650 Semple 1998.

651 McKinley 1993.

652 Philpott 1991; Harman et al 1981.

653 Webster 1999.

654 Parker Pearson 1986.

655 Webster 1999.

656 'Murder at Stonehenge'. YAP for Channel 4, first broadcast 17 July 2000.

657 Atkinson 1979, 86, 98.

658 The risk assessment for the dramatic reconstructions at Stonehenge pinpointed sixteen hazards, including Compressed Gas, Animals, Night Operations, Pyrotechnics, Weapons and, a memorable addition to Stonehenge definitions, Scenery Hazards ('large heavy stones'). Beheading was easier in the past.

[659] OxA-9361: 1359±38 (621-764 cal AD); OxA-9921: 1490±60 (428-660 cal AD); average 1396±32 (603-683 cal AD).

[660] For what it's worth, when calibrated, it is around two centuries older than the new dates: HAR-???, 663-1017 cal AD. But it has a very wide range, and there are no lab data to enable assessment of its reliability.

[661] Peach 1961.

[662] Tooth analysis: http://www.archaeotrace.co.uk/ stonehenge.html. Stable isotope analysis is explained by Mays (1998, 182-90): 13C values –19.7 parts per thousand (OxA-9361) and –19.5 ppm (OxA-9921).

[663] Reynolds 1999.

[664] Yorke 1995.

Bibliography

Allen, M. 1997. Environment and land-use: the economic development of the communities who built Stonehenge. In Cunliffe, B. and Renfrew, C. (eds) *Science and Stonehenge* (London: British Academy/Oxford University Press), 115–44.

Angell, I. 1977. Are stone circles circles? *Science & Archaeology* 19, 16–19.

Angell, I. 1979. Arguments against the existence of the 'megalithic yard'. *Computer Applications in Archaeology* 1979, 13–19.

Annable, K. and Simpson, D. 1964. *Guide Catalogue of the Neolithic and Bronze Age Collections in Devizes Museum.* Devizes: Wiltshire Archaeological Society.

ApSimon, A., Musgrave, J., Sheldon, J., Tratman, E. and Van Wijngaarden-Bakker, L. 1976. Gorsey Bigbury, Cheddar. Somerset: radiocarbon dating, human and animal bones, charcoals, archaeological reassessment, *Proceedings of the University of Bristol Spelaeological Society* 14, 155–83.

Ashbee, P. 1970. *The Earthen Long Barrow in Britain.* London: Dent.

Ashbee, P. 1985. The excavation of Amesbury barrows 58, 61a, 61, 72. *Wiltshire Archaeological and Natural History Magazine* 79, 39–91.

Atkinson, R. 1978. Silbury Hill. In Sutcliffe, R. (ed.) *Chronicle* (London: BBC), 159–73.

Atkinson, R. 1979. *Stonehenge* (3rd edn.). Harmondsworth: Penguin.

Atkinson, R. and Evans, J. 1978. Recent excavations at Stonehenge. *Antiquity* 52, 235–6.

Atkinson, R., Piggott, C. M. and Sandars, N. 1951. *Excavations at Dorchester, Oxon.* Oxford: Dept of Antiquities, Ashmolean Museum.

Atkinson, R., Piggott, S. and Stone, J. 1952. The excavation of two additional holes at Stonehenge, and new evidence for the date of the monument. *Antiquaries Journal* 32, 14–20.

Barber, M., Field, D. and Topping, P. 1999. *The Neolithic Flint Mines of England.* Swindon: RCHME.

Bibliography

Barclay, G. 1983. Sites of the third millennium BC to the first millennium AD at North Mains, Strathallan, Perthshire. *Proceedings of the Society of Antiquaries of Scotland* 113, 122–81.

Barclay, G. 1999. Cairnpapple revisited: 1948–1998. *Proceedings of the Prehistoric Society* 65, 17–46.

Barclay, G. and Halpin, C. 1999. *Excavations at Barrow Hills, Radley, Oxfordshire Volume I*. Oxford: Oxford Archaeological Unit.

Barfield, L. and Chippindale, C. 1997. Meaning in the later prehistoric rock-engravings of Mont Bégo, Alpes-Maritimes, France. *Proceedings of the Prehistoric Society* 63, 103–28.

Barnatt, J. and Herring, P. 1986. Stone circles and megalithic geometry: an experiment to test alternative design practices. *Journal of Archaeological Science* 13, 431–49.

Barnatt, J. and Moir, G. 1984. Stone circles and megalithic mathematics. *Proceedings of the Prehistoric Society* 50, 197–216.

Barrett, J. 1994. *Fragments from Antiquity: An Archaeology of Social Life in Britain, 2900–1200 BC*. Oxford: Blackwell.

Barrett, J., Bradley, R. and Green, M. 1991. *Landscapes, Monuments and Society: the Prehistory of Cranbourne Chase*. Cambridge: University Press.

Bayliss, A., Bronk Ramsey, C. and McCormac, G. 1997. Dating Stonehenge. In Cunliffe, B. and Renfrew, C. (eds) *Science and Stonehenge* (London: British Academy/Oxford University Press), 39–59.

Bayliss, A., Groves, C., McCormac, G., Baillie, M., Brown, D. and Brennand, M. 1999. Precise dating of the Norfolk timber circle. *Nature* 402, 479.

Becker, C. 1962. A Danish hoard containing neolithic chisels. *Acta Archaeologica* 33, 79–92.

Bellamy, P. 1991. The excavation of Fordington Farm round barrow. *Proceedings of the Dorset Natural History and Archaeological Society* 113, 107–32.

Bender, B. 1998. *Stonehenge: Making Space*. Oxford: Berg.

Bergman, C., McEwen, E. and Miller, R. 1988. Experimental archery: projectile velocities and comparison of bow performances. *Antiquity* 62, 658–70.

Bewley, R., Cole, M., David, A., Featherstone, R., Payne, A. and Small, F. 1996. New features within the henge at Avebury, Wiltshire: aerial and geophysical evidence. *Antiquity* 70, 639–46.

Bloch, M. 1971. *Placing the Dead: Tombs, Ancestral Villages, and Kinship Organisation in Madagascar*. London: Seminar Press.

Bloch, M. and Parry, J. (eds) 1982. *Death and the Regeneration of Life*. Cambridge: University Press.

Bourguignon, E. 1974. Cross-cultural perspective on the religious uses of altered states of consciousness. In Zaretsky, I. and Leone, M. P. (eds) *Religious Movements in Contemporary America* (Princeton: Princeton University Press), 228–43.

Bowman, S. 1995. *Radiocarbon Dating*. London: British Museum Press.

Bowyer, C. 1992. *For Valour: The Air VCs*. London: Grub Street.

Bradley, R. 1976. Maumbury Rings, Dorchester: the excavations of 1908–1913. *Archaeologia* 105, 1–97.

Bradley, R. and Thomas, J. 1985. Some new information on the henge monument at Maumbury Rings, Dorchester. *Proceedings of the Dorset Natural History and Archaeological Society* 106, 132–4.

Bradley, R. 1993. *Altering the Earth: the Origins of Monuments in Britain and Continental Europe*. Edinburgh: Society of Antiquaries of Scotland.

Bradley, R. 1998. *The Significance of Monuments: On the Shaping of Human Experience in Neolithic and Bronze Age Europe*. London: Routledge.

Bradley, R. 1989. Deaths and entrances: a contextual analysis of megalithic art. *Current Anthropology* 30, 68–75.

Brennan, M. 1983. *The Stars and the Stones: Ancient Art and Astronomy in Ireland*. London: Thames & Hudson.

Brodie, N. 1994. *The Neolithic–Bronze Age Transition in Britain*. Oxford: British Archaeological Reports 238.

Bronk Ramsey, C. and Bayliss, A. 2000. Dating Stonehenge. In Lockyear, K. and Mihailescu-Bîrliba, V. (eds) *Computer Applications and Quantitative Methods in Archaeology* (Oxford: British Archaeological Reports 845), 29–39.

Burl, A. 1970. Henges: internal features and regional groups. *Archaeological Journal* 126, 1–28.

Burl, A. 1976a. *The Stone Circles of the British Isles*. London: Yale University Press.

Burl, A. 1976b. Intimations of numeracy in the Neolithic and Bronze Age societies of the British Isles. *Archaeological Journal* 133, 9–32.

Burl, A. 1979a. *Prehistoric Avebury*. London: Yale University Press.

Burl, A. 1979b. *Rings of Stone*. London: Weidenfeld.

Burl, A. 1987. *The Stonehenge People. Life and Death at the World's Greatest Stone Circle*. London: Dent.

Burl, A. 1991. Megalithic myth or man the mover? *Antiquity* 65, 297–8.

Burl, A. 1994. Stonehenge: slaughter, sacrifice and sunshine. *Wiltshire*

Archaeological and Natural History Magazine 87, 85–95.

Burl, A. 1999. *Great Stone Circles*. London: Yale University Press.

Burl, A. and Freeman, P. 1977. Local units of measurement in prehistoric Britain. *Antiquity* 51, 152–4.

Capper, J. 1907. Photographs of Stonehenge, as seen from a War Balloon. *Archaeologia* 60, 571.

Case, H. 1997. Stonehenge revisited. *Wiltshire Archaeological and Natural History Magazine* 90, 161–8.

Castleden, R. 1993. *The Making of Stonehenge*. London: Routledge.

Castleden, R. 1999. Reassessing Stonehenge (1). *3rd Stone* 35, 12–18.

Catherall, P. 1971. Henges in perspective. *Archaeological Journal* 127, 147–53.

Cave, A. 1936. Report on the human remains from Stonehenge for the South Wilts Museum. Unpublished typescript, Salisbury and South Wiltshire Museum.

Cave, A. 1938. Report on a XIV century skeleton from Avebury. Unpublished typescript, Alexander Keiller Museum, Avebury, and Royal College of Surgeons, London.

Chippindale, C. 1978. The enclosure of Stonehenge. *Wiltshire Archaeological Magazine* 70/71, 109–23.

Chippindale, C. 1994. *Stonehenge Complete* (2nd edn.). London: Thames & Hudson.

Chippindale, C., Devereux, P., Fowler, P., Jones, R. and Sebastian, T. 1990. *Who Owns Stonehenge?* London: Batsford.

Clare, T. 1986. Towards a re-appraisal of henge monuments. *Proceedings of the Prehistoric Society* 52, 281–316.

Clare, T. 1987. Towards a reappraisal of henge monuments: origins, evolutions and hierarchies. *Proceedings of the Prehistoric Society* 53, 457–77.

Clark, A. 1996. *Seeing Beneath the Soil: Prospecting Methods in Archaeology* (2nd edn.). London: Batsford.

Clark, G. 1936. The timber monument at Arminghall and its affinities. *Proceedings of the Prehistoric Society* 2, 1–51.

Clark, G. 1963. Neolithic bows from Somerset, England, and the prehistory of archery in north-western Europe. *Proceedings of the Prehistoric Society* 29, 50–98.

Clarke, D. 1970. *Beaker Pottery of Great Britain and Ireland*. Cambridge University Press.

Cleal R., Walker, K. and Montague, R. 1995. *Stonehenge in its Landscape: Twentieth Century Excavations*. London: English Heritage Archaeological Report 10.

Clutton-Brock, J. 1984. *Excavations at Grime's Graves Norfolk 1972–76. 1: Neolithic Antler Picks*. London: British Museum Publications.

Coles, B. and Coles, C. 1986. *Sweet Track to Glastonbury: the Somerset Levels in Prehistory*. London: Thames and Hudson.

Coles, J. 1973. *Archaeology by Experiment*. London: Hutchinson.

Coles, J., Fenwick, V. and Hutchinson, G. (eds) 1993. *A Spirit of Enquiry: Essays for Ted Wright*. Exeter: Wetland Archaeology Research Project Occasional Paper 7.

Cope, Z. 1959. *The Royal College of Surgeons of England. A History*. London: Blond.

Cornwell, B. 1999. *Stonehenge: a Novel of 2000 BC*. London: HarperCollins.

Crawford, O. 1924. The Stonehenge Avenue. *Antiquaries Journal* 4, 57–9.

Crawford, O. 1929. Durrington Walls. *Antiquity* 3, 49–59.

Crawford, O. and Keiller, A. 1928. *Wessex from the Air*. Oxford: Clarendon Press.

Cummins, W. 1992. *King Arthur's Place in Prehistory*. Godalming: Bramley Books.

Cunliffe, B. and Renfrew, C. (eds) 1997. *Science and Stonehenge*. Oxford: Proceedings of the British Academy 92.

Cunnington, B. H. 1924. The 'blue stone' from Boles Barrow. *Wiltshire Archaeological and Natural History Magazine* 42, 431–7.

Cunnington, M. E. 1913. The re-erection of two fallen stones, and discovery of an interment with drinking cup, at Avebury. *Wiltshire Archaeological and Natural History Magazine* 38, 1–11.

Cunnington, M. E. 1927. Prehistoric timber circles. *Antiquity* 1, 92–5.

Cunnington, M. E. 1929. *Woodhenge*. Devizes: George Simpson.

Cunnington, M. E. 1931. The 'Sanctuary' on Overton Hill, near Avebury. *Wiltshire Archaeological and Natural History Magazine* 45, 300–35.

Cunnington, R. H. 1931. The 'Sanctuary' on Overton Hill. Was it roofed? *Wiltshire Archaeological and Natural History Magazine* 45, 486–8.

Cunnington, R. H. 1954. The Cunningtons of Wiltshire. *Wiltshire Archaeological and Natural History Magazine* 55, 211–36.

Cunnington, R. H. 1955. Marden and the Cunnington manuscripts. *Wiltshire Archaeological and Natural History Magazine* 56, 4–11.

Cunnington, R. H. 1975. *From Antiquary to Archaeologist: a Biography of William Cunnington 1754–1810*. Aylesbury: Shire.

Cunnington, W. 1889. Notes on Bowl's Barrow. *Wiltshire Archaeological Magazine* 24, 104–17.

Curwen, E. and E. C. 1926. On the use of scapulae as shovels. *Sussex Archaeological Collections* 67, 193–45.

Dames, M. 1976. *The Silbury Treasure*. London: Thames & Hudson.

Dames, M. 1977. *The Avebury Cycle*. London: Thames & Hudson.

Daniel, G. 1975. *150 Years of Archaeology*. London: Duckworth.

Daniel, G. and Chippindale, C. 1991. *The Pastmasters*. London: Thames & Hudson.

Darvill, T. 1997. Ever increasing circles: the sacred geographies of Stonehenge and its landscape. In Cunliffe, B. and Renfrew, C. (eds) *Science and Stonehenge* (London: British Academy/Oxford University Press), 167–202.

David, A. 1999. *Beckhampton, near Avebury, Wilts. Report on Geophysical Survey, May 1999*. Ancient Monuments Laboratory Draft Report.

Davies, S., Stacey, L. and Woodward, O. 1985. Excavations at Alington Avenue, Fordington, Dorchester, 1984/85: interim report. *Proceedings of the Dorset Natural History and Archaeological Society* 107, 101–110.

Davis, S. and Payne, S. 1993. A barrow full of cattle skulls. *Antiquity* 67, 12–22.

Deuel, L. 1969. *Flights into Yesterday*. Harmondsworth: Pelican Books.

Devereux, P. 1992. *Symbolic Landscapes: the Dreamtime Earth and Avebury's Open Secrets*. Glastonbury: Gothic Image Publications.

Devereux, P. 1997. *The Long Trip. A Prehistory of Psychedelia*. New York: Penguin/Arkana.

Diverres, A. H. 1979. Saint Melor: what is the truth behind the legend? In Chandler, J. (ed.) *The Amesbury Millennium Lectures* (Amesbury: Amesbury Society), 9–19.

Dixon, P. 1988. The Neolithic settlements on Crickley Hill. In Burgess, C., Topping, P., Mordant, C. and Maddison, M. (eds) *Enclosures and Defences in the Neolithic of Western Europe* (Oxford: British Archaeological Reports International Series 403), 75–87.

Drewery, B. 1999. Identity crisis. *New Scientist* 27 Feb. 1999, 40–3.

Dronfield, J. 1995. Migraine, light and hallucinogens: the neurocognitive basis of Irish megalithic art. *Oxford Journal of Archaeology* 14, 261–75.

Dronfield, J. 1996a. The vision thing: diagnosis of endogenous derivation in abstract arts. *Current Anthropology* 37, 373–91.

Dronfield, J. 1996b. Entering alternative realities: cognition, art and architecture in Irish passage-tombs. *Cambridge Archaeological Journal* 6, 37–72.

Drower, M. 1985. *Flinders Petrie: A Life in Archaeology.* London: Gollancz.

Eliade, M. 1964. *Shamanism: Archaic Techniques of Ecstasy.* Princeton: Princeton University Press (1972).

Evans, J. 1972. *Land Snails in Archaeology.* London: Seminar Press.

Evans, J. Atkinson, R., O'Connor, T. and Green, S. 1984. Stonehenge – the environment in the Late Neolithic and Early Bronze Age *and* a Beaker-age burial. *Wiltshire Archaeological and Natural History Magazine* 78, 7–30.

Evans, J., Limbrey, S., Máté, I. and Mount, R. 1993. An environmental history of the upper Kennet valley, Wiltshire, for the last 10,000 years. *Proceedings of the Prehistoric Society* 59, 139–95.

Evans, J., Pitts, M. and Williams, D. 1985. An excavation at Avebury, Wiltshire, 1982. *Proceedings of the Prehistoric Society* 51, 305–10.

Farrer, P. 1918. Durrington Walls, or Long Walls. *Wiltshire Archaeological and Natural History Magazine* 40, 95–103.

Fassbinder, J., Stanjek, H. and Vali, H. 1990. Occurrence of magnetic bacteria in soil. *Nature* 343, 161–3.

Felder, P. 1981. Prehistoric flint mining at Ryckholt-St Geertruid (Netherlands) and Grimes Graves (England). In Engelen, F. (ed.) *Third International Symposium on Flint* (Amsterdam: Staringia), 57–62.

Field, D., Brown, G. and Crockett, A. 2001. The Marlborough Mount revisited. *Wiltshire Archaeological and Natural History Magazine* 94, 195-204.

Fleming, A. 1973. Models for the development of the Wessex culture. In Renfrew, C. (ed.) *The Explanation of Culture Change* (London: Duckworth), 571–85.

Freeman, P. 1976. A Bayesian analysis of the megalithic yard. *Journal of the Royal Statistical Society* A139, 20–55.

Garwood, P. 1991. Ritual tradition and the reconstitution of society. In Garwood, P. et al. (eds) *Sacred and Profane* (Oxford: Oxford Committee for Archaeology), 10–32.

Garwood, P. 1999. Grooved Ware in southern Britain. Chronology and interpretation. In Cleal, R. and MacSween, A. (eds) *Grooved Ware in Britain and Ireland* (Oxford: Oxbow), 145–76.

Gibson, A. 1994. Excavations at the Sarn-y-bryn-caled cursus complex, Welshpool, Powys, and the timber circles of Great Britain and Ireland. *Proceedings of the Prehistoric Society* 60, 143–223.

Gibson, A. 1998a. *Stonehenge and Timber Circles.* Stroud: Tempus.

Gibson, A. 1998b. Hindwell and the Neolithic palisaded sites of

Britain and Ireland. In Gibson, A. and Simpson, D. (eds) *Prehistoric Ritual and Religion* (Stroud: Sutton), 68–79.

Gibson, A. and Kinnes, I. 1997. On the urns of a dilemma: radiocarbon and the Peterborough problem. *Oxford Journal of Archaeology* 16, 65–72.

Gillings, M. and Pollard, J. 1999. Non-portable stone artefacts and contexts of meaning: the tale of Grey Wether (www.museum.ncl.ac.uk/Avebury/stone4.htm). *World Archaeology* 31, 179–93.

Gillings, M., Pollard, J. and Wheatley, D. 2000. The Beckhampton Avenue and a 'new' Neolithic enclosure near Avebury: an interim report on the 1999 excavations. *Wiltshire Archaeological Magazine* 93, 1–8.

Gingell, C. 1988. Twelve Wiltshire round barrows. Excavations in 1959 and 1961 by F. de M. and H. L. Vatcher. *Wiltshire Archaeological and Natural History Society* 82, 19–76.

Gowland, W. 1897. The dolmens and burial mounds in Japan. *Archaeologia* 55, 439–524.

Gowland, W. 1902. Recent excavations at Stonehenge. *Archaeologia* 58, 37–105.

Gray, H. St G. 1908–9. *Avebury. 1908–1909.* Manuscript Diary, Alexander Keiller Museum (Avebury) accession 78510459.

Gray, H. St G. 1911–22. *Avebury. 1911–1922.* Manuscript Diary, Alexander Keiller Museum (Avebury) accession 78510459.

Gray, H. St G. 1935. The Avebury excavations, 1908–1922. *Archaeologia* 84, 99–162.

Green, C. and Rollo-Smith, S. 1984. The excavation of eighteen round barrows near Shrewton, Wiltshire. *Proceedings of the Prehistoric Society* 50, 255–318.

Green, C. P. 1973. Pleistocene river gravels and the Stonehenge problem. *Nature* 243, 214–6.

Green, C. P. 1997. The provenance of rocks used in the construction of Stonehenge. In Cunliffe, B. and Renfrew, C. (eds) *Science and Stonehenge* (London: British Academy/Oxford University Press), 257–70.

Green, S. 1980. *The Flint Arrowheads of the British Isles.* Oxford: British Archaeological Reports 75.

Harding, A. and Lee, G. 1987. *Henge Monuments and Related sites of Great Britain: Air Photographic Evidence and Catalogue.* Oxford: British Archaeological Reports 175.

Harman, M., Molleson, T. and Price, J. 1981. Burials, bodies and beheadings in Romano-British and Anglo-Saxon cemeteries. *Bulletin of the British Museum Natural History (Geology)* 35, 145–88.

Hawkins, G. and White, J. 1966. *Stonehenge Decoded*. London: Souvenir Press.

Hawley, W. 1920–6. *Excavations at Stonehenge*. Typed transcripts of manuscript diaries, Archives of Wessex Archaeology and Salisbury and South Wiltshire Museum.

Hawley, W. 1921. Stonehenge: interim report on the exploration. *Antiquaries Journal* 1, 19–41.

Hawley, W. 1922. Second report on the excavations at Stonehenge. *Antiquaries Journal* 2, 36–52.

Hawley, W. 1923. Third report on the excavations at Stonehenge. *Antiquaries Journal* 3, 13–20.

Hawley, W. 1924. Fourth report on the excavations at Stonehenge (June to November 1922). *Antiquaries Journal* 4, 30–9.

Hawley, W. 1925. Report on the excavations at Stonehenge during the season of 1923. *Antiquaries Journal* 5, 21–50.

Hawley, W. 1926. Report on the excavations at Stonehenge during the season of 1924. *Antiquaries Journal* 6, 1–25.

Hawley, W. 1928. Report on the excavations at Stonehenge during 1925 and 1926. *Antiquaries Journal* 8, 149–76.

Heggie, D. 1981. *Megalithic Science*. London: Thames & Hudson.

Hicks, R. 1977. Thom's megalithic yard and traditional measurements. *Irish Archaeological Forum* 4, 1–7.

Hoare, R. 1821. *The Ancient History of Wiltshire II*. Republished Wakefield 1975: E P Publishing.

Hodder, I. 1982. *The Present Past: an Introduction to Anthropology for Archaeologists*. London: Batsford.

Hodder, I. 1990. *The Domestication of Europe: Structure and Contingency in Neolithic Societies*. Oxford: Blackwell.

Hoggard, B. 1998. Spirit flight – an inquiry. *The Ley Hunter* 129, 11–13.

Hornsey, R. 1987. The Grand Menhir Brisé: megalithic success or failure? *Oxford Journal of Archaeology* 6, 185–217.

Houlder, C. 1968. The henge monuments at Llandegai. *Antiquity* 42, 216–21.

Howard, H. 1982. A petrological study of the rock specimens from excavations at Stonehenge, 1979–1980. *Proceedings of the Prehistoric Society* 48, 104–24.

Hudson, K. 1981. *A Social History of Archaeology: The British Experience*. London: Macmillan.

Huntington, R. and Metcalf, P. 1979. *Celebrations of Death: the Anthropology of Mortuary Ritual*. Cambridge: University Press.

Jewell, P. (ed.) 1963. *The Experimental Earthwork on Overton Down, Wiltshire 1960*. London: British Association for the Advancement of Science.

Johnstone, P. 1957. *Buried Treasure*. London: Phoenix House.

Judd, J. 1902. Note on the nature and origin of the rock-fragments found in the excavations made at Stonehenge by Mr Gowland in 1901. *Archaeologia* 58, 106–18.

Kahn, M. 1990. Stone-faced ancestors: the spatial anchoring of myth in Wamira, Papua New Guinea. *Ethnology* 29, 51–66.

Keiller, A. 1939. Avebury: summary of excavations, 1937 and 1938. *Antiquity* 13, 223–33.

Keiller, A. and Piggott, S. 1936. The recent excavations at Avebury. *Antiquity* 10, 417–27.

Keith, A. (ed.) 1929. *Annual Report of the Museum by the Conservator, Royal College of Surgeons of England*. London: Royal College of Surgeons.

Kellaway, G. 1971. Glaciation and the stones of Stonehenge. *Nature* 232, 30–5.

Kendall, D. 1974. Hunting quanta. In Hodson, R. (ed.) *The Place of Astronomy in the Ancient World* (London: Royal Society), 231–66.

Kendrick, T. and Hawkes, C. 1932. *Archaeology in England and Wales 1914–1931*. London: Methuen.

Kennard, A., Jackson, J. and Newall, R. 1935. Reports on 1. The non-marine mollusca, and 2. The animal remains from the Stonehenge excavations of 1920–6. *Antiquaries Journal* 15, 432–40.

King, B. 1879. Avebury – the Beckhampton Avenue. *Wiltshire Archaeological Magazine* 18, 377–83.

Kinnes, I. 1992. *Non-Megalithic Long Barrows and Allied Structures in the British Neolithic*. London: British Museum Occasional Paper 52.

Kinnes, I. and Gibson, A. 1991. Radiocarbon dating and British Beakers: the British Museum programme. *Scottish Archaeological Review* 8, 35–68.

Kinnes, I., Schadla-Hall, T., Chadwick, P. and Dean, P. 1983. Duggleby Howe reconsidered. *Archaeological Journal* 140, 83–108.

Knight, C. and Lomas, R. 1999. *Uriel's Machine*. London: Century.

Krupp, E. 1980. The Stonehenge chronicles. In Krupp, E. (ed.) *In Search of Ancient Astronomies* (Harmondsworth: Penguin Books), 77–126.

Lambrick, G. 1988. *The Rollright Stones*. London: English Heritage Archaeological Report 6.

Lawson, A. 1992. Stonehenge: creating a definitive account. *Antiquity* 66, 934–41.

Lees, D. 1999. The 'Sanctuary', Avebury. An architectural re-assessment. *Wiltshire Archaeological and Natural History Magazine* 92, 1–6.

Legge, A. 1981. The agricultural economy. In Mercer, R. *Grime's Graves Norfolk Excavations 1971–72: Volume 1* (London: Department of the Environment Archaeological Reports 11), 169–81.

Lehmann, A. and Myers, J. 1993. Ghosts, souls, and ancestors: power of the dead. In Lehmann, A. and Myers, J. (eds) *Magic, Witchcraft and Religion: an Anthropological Study of the Supernatural* (Mountain View: Mayfield), 283–6.

Lehner, M. 1997. *The Complete Pyramids*. London: Thames & Hudson.

Leslie, T. 1894. *Excavations at Avebury*. Letter and typed diary transcript in Library of the Wiltshire Archaeological Society (Devizes).

Levitan, B. 1990. The non-human vertebrate remains. In Saville, A. *Hazleton North* (London: English Heritage Archaeological Report 13), 199–213.

Lewis-Williams, J. and Dowson, T. 1993. On vision and power in the Neolithic: evidence from the decorated monuments. *Current Anthropology* 34, 55–65.

Liddell, D. and Tildesley, M. 1933. Excavations at Meon Hill. *Proceedings of the Hampshire Field Club and Archaeological Society* 12, 127.

Long, D., Tipping, R., Holden, T., Bunting, M. and Milburn, P. 2000. The use of henbane (*Hyoscyamus niger* L.) as a hallucinogen at Neolithic 'ritual' sites: a re-evaluation. *Antiquity* 74, 49–53.

Longworth, I. and Varndell, G. 1996. *Excavations at Grime's Graves, Norfolk 1972–1976. Fascicule 5: Mining in the Deep Mines*. London: British Museum Press.

Lord, J. 1993. *The Basics of Lithic Technology*. Norfolk: John Lord.

Loveday, R. 1998. Double entrance henges – routes to the past? In Gibson, A. and Simpson, D. (eds) *Prehistoric Ritual and Religion* (Stroud: Sutton), 14–31.

Lubbock, J. 1865. *Pre-Historic Times*. London.

Mack, J. 1986. *Madagascar. Island of the Ancestors*. London: British Museum.

McKay, G. 1996. *Senseless Acts of Beauty: Cultures of Resistance since the Sixties*. London: Verso.

MacKie, E. 1977. *Science and Society in Prehistoric Britain*. London: Paul Elek.

McKinley, J. 1993. A decapitation from the Romano-British cemetery at Baldock, Hertfordshire. *International Journal of Osteoarchaeology* 3, 41–44.

McKinley, J. 1997. Bronze age 'barrows' and funerary rites and rituals of cremation. *Proceedings of the Prehistoric Society* 63, 129–45.

McNairn, B. 1980. *The Method and Theory of V. Gordon Childe*. Edinburgh: University Press.

Magilton, J. 1998. Sussex's first henge? *Sussex Past and Present* April 1998, 4–5.

Mays, S. 1998. *The Archaeology of Human Bones*. London: Routledge.

Meaden, T. 1999. *The Secrets of the Avebury Stones*. London: Souvenir Press.

Mercer, R. 1981a. The excavation of a Late Neolithic henge-type enclosure at Balfarg, Markinch, Fife, Scotland, 1977–8. *Proceedings of the Society of Antiquaries of Scotland* 111, 63–171.

Mercer, R. 1981b. Excavations at Carn Brea, Illogan, Cornwall, 1970–73. *Cornish Archaeology* 20, 1–204.

Mercer, R., Barclay, G., Jordan D. and Russell-White, C. 1988. The Neolithic henge-type enclosure at Balfarg – a re-assessment of the evidence for an incomplete ditch circuit. *Proceedings of the Society of Antiquaries of Scotland* 118, 61–8.

Merewether, J. 1851. The examination of Silbury Hill. *Proceedings of the Archaeological Institute (Salisbury)*, 73–81.

Morgan, C. 1887. The stones of Stanton Drew: their source and origin. *Somerset Archaeological and Natural History Society Proceedings* 33, 37–50.

Muckleroy, K. 1980. Two Bronze Age cargoes in British waters. *Antiquity* 54, 100–9.

Murray, L. 1999. *A Zest for Life: the Story of Alexander Keiller*. Swindon: Morven Books.

Needham, R. 1967. Percussion and transition. *Man* 2, 606–14.

Needham, S. 1996. Chronology and periodisation in the British Bronze Age. *Acta Archaeologica* 67, 121–40.

Newall, R. 1929. Stonehenge. *Antiquity* 3, 75–88.

Newall, R. 1959. *Stonehenge, Wiltshire* (3rd ed.). London: Her Majesty's Stationery Office.

Newham, C. 1972. *The Astronomical Significance of Stonehenge*. Shirenewton: Moon Publications.

North, J. 1996. *Stonehenge: Neolithic Man and the Cosmos*. London: HarperCollins.

O'Sullivan, A. 1996. Neolithic, Bronze Age and Iron Age woodworking techniques. In Raftery, B. *Trackway Excavations in the Mountdillon Bogs, Co Longford, 1985–1991* (Dublin: Irish Archaeological Wetland Unit Transactions 3), 291–342.

Parker Pearson, M. 1986. Lindow man and the Danish connection. *Anthropology Today* 2, 15–18.

Parker Pearson, M. 1993. *Bronze Age Britain*. London: English Heritage.

Parker Pearson, M. 1999a. *The Archaeology of Death and Burial*. Stroud: Sutton.

Parker Pearson, M. 1999b. From ancestor cult to divine religion. *British Archaeology* 45, 10–11.

Parker Pearson, M. and Ramilisonina, 1998. Stonehenge for the ancestors: the stones pass on the message. *Antiquity* 72, 308–26.

Passmore, A. 1935. The Meux excavation at Avebury. *Wiltshire Archaeological Magazine* 47, 288–9.

Patton, M. 1992. Megalithic transport and territorial markers: evidence from the Channel Islands. *Antiquity* 66, 392–5.

Pavel, P. 1992. Raising the Stonehenge lintels in Czechoslovakia. *Antiquity* 66, 389–91.

Peach, W. 1961. *Stonehenge: A New Theory*. Cardiff: the author.

Petrie, W. 1880. *Stonehenge: Plans, Description, and Theories*. London: Stanford.

Petrie, W. 1923. Report of diggings in Silbury Hill, August 1922. *Wiltshire Archaeological Magazine* 42, 215–18.

Philpott, R. 1991. *Burial Practices in Roman Britain*. Oxford: British Archaeological Report 219.

Piggott, S. 1938. The Early Bronze Age in Wessex. *Proceedings of the Prehistoric Society* 4, 52–106.

Piggott, S. 1940. Timber circles: a re-examination. *Archaeological Journal* 96, 193–222.

Piggott, S. 1946a. The destruction of 'The Sanctuary' on Overton Hill. *Wiltshire Archaeological and Natural History Magazine* 51, 470–1.

Piggott, S. 1946b. Who built Stonehenge? *The Listener* 21 November 1946, 709–10.

Piggott, S. 1951. Stonehenge reviewed. In Grimes, W. F. (ed.) *Aspects of Archaeology in Britain and Beyond* (London: Edwards), 274–92.

Piggott, S. 1954. Recent work at Stonehenge. *Antiquity* 28, 221–4.

Piggott, S. 1956. Stonehenge. *Wiltshire Archaeological and Natural*

History Magazine 56, 232–7.

Piggott, S. 1958. Obituary Dr J. F. S. Stone. *Wiltshire Archaeological and Natural History Magazine* 57, 89–91.

Piggott, S. 1983. Archaeological retrospect. *Antiquity* 57, 28–37.

Piggott, S. 1985. *William Stukeley: An Eighteenth-Century Antiquary* (2nd ed.). London: Thames & Hudson.

Piggott, S. and Piggott, C. M. 1939. Stone and earth circles in Dorset. *Antiquity* 13, 138–58.

Pitts, M. 1980. *Later Stone Implements*. Aylesbury: Shire.

Pitts, M. 1981a. Stones, pits and Stonehenge. *Nature* 290, 46–7.

Pitts, M. 1981b. The discovery of a new stone at Stonehenge. *Archaeoastronomy* 4.2, 16–21.

Pitts, M. 1982. On the road to Stonehenge: report on the investigations beside the A344 in 1968, 1979 and 1980. *Proceedings of the Prehistoric Society* 48, 75–132.

Pitts, M. 1996. The stone axe in neolithic Britain. *Proceedings of the Prehistoric Society* 62, 311–71.

Pitts, M. 2000. Return to the Sanctuary. *British Archaeology* 51, 15–19.

Pitts, M. 2001. Excavating the Sanctuary: new investigations on Overton Hill, Avebury. *Wiltshire Archaeological and Natural History Magazine* 94, 1-23.

Pitts, M. and Roberts, M. 1997. *Fairweather Eden*. London: Arrow.

Pitts, M. and Whittle, A. 1992. The development and date of Avebury. *Proceedings of the Prehistoric Society* 58, 203–12.

Pollard, J. 1992. The Sanctuary, Overton Hill, Wiltshire: a re-examination. *Proceedings of the Prehistoric Society* 58, 213–26.

Pollard, J. 1995a. The Durrington 68 timber circle: a forgotten Late Neolithic monument. *Wiltshire Archaeological and Natural History Magazine* 88, 122–5.

Pollard, J. 1995b. Inscribing space: formal deposition at the Later Neolithic monument of Woodhenge, Wiltshire. *Proceedings of the Prehistoric Society* 61, 137–56.

Pollard, J. and Gillings, M. 1998. Romancing the stones: towards a virtual and elemental Avebury. *Archaeological Dialogues* 5, 143–64.

Pollard, J. and Ruggles, C. 2001. Shifting perceptions: spatial order, cosmology, and patterns of deposition at Stonehenge. *Cambridge Archaeological Journal* 11.

Prag, J. and Neave, R. 1997. *Making Faces: Using Forensic and Archaeological Evidence*. London: British Museum Press.

Reid, N. (ed.) 1975. *Paul Nash: Paintings and Watercolours*. London: Tate Gallery.

Renfrew, C. 1973. Monuments, mobilisation and social organisation in Neolithic Wessex. In Renfrew (ed.), *The Explanation of Culture Change* (London: Duckworth), 539–58.

Renfrew, C. 1979. *Investigations in Orkney*. London: Society of Antiquaries/Thames & Hudson.

Restall Orr, E. 1998. *Spirits of the Sacred Grove: The World of a Druid Priestess*. London: Thorsons.

Reynolds, A. 1999. *Later Anglo-Saxon England: Life and Landscape*. Stroud: Sutton.

Richards, C. 1996. Henges and water: towards an elemental understanding of monumentality and landscape in late neolithic Britain. *Journal of Material Culture* 1, 313–35.

Richards, C. and Thomas, J. 1984. Ritual activity and structured deposition in Later Neolithic Wessex. In Bradley, R. and Gardiner, J. (eds) *Neolithic Studies* (Oxford: British Archaeological Report 133), 189–218.

Richards, J. 1990. *The Stonehenge Environs Project*. London: English Heritage.

Richards, J. 1991. *English Heritage Book of Stonehenge*. London: Batsford.

Richards, J. and Whitby, M. 1997. The engineering of Stonehenge. In Cunliffe, B. and Renfrew, C. (eds) *Science and Stonehenge* (London: British Academy/Oxford University Press), 231–56.

Robertson-Mackay, M. E. 1980. A 'head and hooves' burial beneath a round barrow with other Neolithic and Bronze Age sites, on Hemp Knoll, near Avebury, Wiltshire. *Proceedings of the Prehistoric Society* 46, 123–76.

Rudgley, R. 1993. *The Alchemy of Culture: Intoxicants in Society*. London: British Museum Press.

Ruggles, C. 1997. Astronomy and Stonehenge. In Cunliffe, B. and Renfrew, C. (eds) *Science and Stonehenge* (London: British Academy/Oxford University Press), 203–29.

Ruggles, C. 1999. *Astronomy in Prehistoric Britain and Ireland*. Yale: University Press.

Ruggles, C. and Barclay, G. 2000. Cosmology, calendars and society in Neolithic Orkney: a rejoinder to Euan MacKie. *Antiquity* 74, 62–74.

Scott, B. 1977. Dancing, drink or drugs? Comments on the 'Beaker cult-package' hypothesis. *Irish Archaeological Forum*, 4, 29–34.

Scourse, J. 1997. Transport of the Stonehenge bluestones: testing the glacial hypothesis. In Cunliffe, B. and Renfrew, C. (eds) *Science and*

Stonehenge (London: British Academy/Oxford University Press), 271–314.

Semple, S. 1998. A fear of the past: the place of the prehistoric burial mound in the ideology of middle and later Anglo-Saxon England. *World Archaeology* 30, 109–26.

Sherratt, A. 1991. Sacred and profane substances: the ritual of narcotics in Later Neolithic Europe. In Garwood, P. et al. (eds) *Sacred and Profane* (Oxford: Oxford Committee for Archaeology), 50–64.

Smith, I. 1965. *Windmill Hill and Avebury: Excavations by Alexander Keiller, 1925–1939.* Oxford: Clarendon Press.

Smith, R., Healy, F., Allen, M., Morris, E., Barnes, I. and Woodward, P. 1997. *Excavations along the Route of the Dorchester By-pass, Dorset, 1986–8.* Salisbury: Wessex Archaeology Report 11.

Startin, W. 1976. *Mathematics and Manpower in Archaeological Explanation.* B Phil, Balfour Library, Oxford.

Startin, W. 1978. Linear pottery culture houses: reconstruction and manpower. *Proceedings of the Prehistoric Society* 44, 143–59.

Startin, W. 1982. Prehistoric earthmoving. In Case, H. and Whittle, A. (eds) *Settlement Patterns in the Oxford Region: Excavations at the Abingdon Causewayed Enclosure and Other Sites* (London: Council for British Archaeology), 153–6.

Startin, W. and Bradley, R. 1981. Some notes on work organisation and society in prehistoric Wessex. In Ruggles, C. and Whittle, A. (eds) *Astronomy and Society in Britain during the Period 4000–1500 BC* (Oxford: British Archaeological Reports 88), 289–96.

Steadman, L., Palmer, C. and Tilley, C. 1996. The universality of ancestor worship. *Ethnology* 35, 63–76.

Stone, E. 1921. Quarrying and Shaping the Stones. Typescript (7pp.) Library of the Wiltshire Archaeological Society (Devizes).

Stone, E. 1924. *The Stones of Stonehenge.* London: Robert Scott.

Stone, J. 1947. The Stonehenge Cursus and its affinities. *Archaeological Journal* 104, 7–19.

Stone, J., Piggott, S. and Booth, A. St J. 1954. Durrington Walls, Wiltshire: recent excavations at a ceremonial site of the early second millennium BC. *Antiquaries Journal* 34, 155–77.

Stone, J. and Tildesley, M. 1932. Saxon interments on Roche Court Down, Winterslow. *Wiltshire Archaeological Magazine* 45, 568–99.

Switsur, R. 1974. The prehistoric longbow from Denny, Scotland. *Antiquity* 48, 56–8.

Switsur, R. 1991. Review of *The Ferriby Boats* by Edward Wright. *Antiquity* 65, 749–51.

Thomas, H. 1923. The source of the stones of Stonehenge. *Antiquaries Journal* 3, 239–60.

Thomas, J. 1996. *Time, Culture and Identity: an Interpretive Archaeology*. London: Routledge.

Thomas, J. 1999. *Understanding the Neolithic*. London: Routledge.

Thomas, J. and Whittle, A. 1986. Anatomy of a tomb – West Kennet revisited. *Oxford Journal of Archaeology* 5, 129–156.

Thorpe, I. 1981. Ethnoastronomy: its patterns and archaeological implications. In Ruggles, C. and Whittle, A. (eds) *Astronomy and Society in Britain During the Period 4000–1500 BC* (Oxford: British Archaeological Reports 88), 275–88.

Thorpe, R. S. and Williams-Thorpe O. 1991. The myth of long-distance megalith transport. *Antiquity* 65, 64–73.

Thorpe, R. S., Williams-Thorpe, O., Jenkins, D. and Watson, J. 1991. The geological sources and transport of the bluestones of Stonehenge, Wiltshire, UK. *Proceedings of the Prehistoric Society* 57.2, 103–57.

Tilley, C. 1993. Art, architecture, landscape [in Neolithic Sweden]. In Bender, B. (ed.) *Landscape: Politics and Perspectives* (Oxford: Berg), 49–84.

Tilley, C. 1994. *A Phenomenology of Landscape*. Oxford: Berg.

Tilley, C. 1996. *An Ethnography of the Neolithic*. Cambridge: University Press.

Tratman, E. 1966. Investigations at Stanton Drew stone circles, Somerset. *Proceedings of the University of Bristol Spelaeological Society* 11, 40–2.

Tratman, E. 1967. The Priddy circles, Mendip, Somerset, henge monuments. *Proceedings of the University of Bristol Spelaeological Society* 11, 97–125.

Ucko, P., Hunter, M., Clark, A. and David, A. 1991. *Avebury Reconsidered; from the 1660s to the 1990s*. London: Unwin Hyman.

Wainwright, G. 1969. A review of henge monuments in the light of recent research. *Proceedings of the Prehistoric Society* 35, 112–33.

Wainwright, G. 1971. The excavation of a Late Neolithic enclosure at Marden, Wiltshire. *Antiquaries Journal* 51, 177–239.

Wainwright, G. 1979. *Mount Pleasant, Dorset: Excavations 1970–71*. London: Society of Antiquaries.

Wainwright, G. and Longworth, I. 1971. *Durrington Walls: Excavations 1966–1968*. London: Society of Antiquaries.

Webster, J. 1999. At the end of the world: Druidic and other revitalisation movements in post-conquest Gaul and Britain.

Britannia 30, 1–20.

Whiteman, A. 1995. The labour involved in constructing the monument. In Barclay, A., Gray, M. and Lambrick, G. *Excavations at the Devil's Quoits, Stanton Harcourt, Oxfordshire, 1972–3 and 1988* (Oxford: Oxford Archaeological Unit), 117–22.

Whittle, A. 1993. The Neolithic of the Avebury area: sequence, environment, settlement and monuments. *Oxford Journal of Archaeology* 12, 29–50.

Whittle, A. 1996. *Europe in the Neolithic: the Creation of New Worlds.* Cambridge: University Press.

Whittle, A. 1997a. *Sacred Mound, Holy Rings. Silbury Hill and the West Kennet Palisade Enclosures: a Later Neolithic Complex in North Wiltshire.* Oxford: Oxbow Monograph 74.

Whittle, A. 1997b. Remembered and imagined belongings: Stonehenge in its traditions and structures of meaning. In Cunliffe, B. and Renfrew, C. (eds) *Science and Stonehenge* (London: British Academy/Oxford University Press), 145–66.

Whittle, A. 1997c. Moving on and moving around: Neolithic settlement mobility. In Topping, P. (ed.) *Neolithic Landscapes* (Oxford: Oxbow Books), 15–22.

Whittle, A., Atkinson, R., Chambers, R. and Thomas, N. 1992. Excavations in the Neolithic and Bronze Age complex at Dorchester-on-Thames, Oxfordshire, 1947–52 and 1981. *Proceedings of the Prehistoric Society* 58, 143–201.

Wier, S. 1996. Insight from geometry and physics into the construction of Egyptian Old Kingdom pyramids. *Cambridge Archaeological Journal* 6, 150–63.

Woodward, A. and Woodward, P. 1996. The topography of some barrow cemeteries in Bronze Age Wessex. *Proceedings of the Prehistoric Society* 62, 275–91.

Yorke, B. 1995. *Wessex in the Early Middle Ages.* London: Leicester University Press.

Young, W. 1930–35. Leaves from my Journal. Manuscript Diaries, Library of the Wiltshire Archaeological Society (Devizes).

Young, W. 1930–40. Diary with Archaeological Notes. Manuscript Diaries, Library of the Wiltshire Archaeological Society (Devizes).

Index

Numbers in italics are page
numbers of illustrations; in bold
are plate numbers. *fn* precedes
footnote no.

400

LOST CIVILISATIONS OF THE STONE AGE

By Richard Rudgley

The rise of civilisation 5,000 years ago has often been portrayed as a cultural 'big bang', as if it were somehow created out of nothing but the savage and backward prehistory of the human race. But was the prehistoric period really an interminably long and uneventful prelude to civilisation?

Bringing together for the first time evidence from the fields of archaeology, ancient history and anthropology, Richard Rudgley shows how distorted a picture such views give us of our own past. He argues convincingly that the achievements, inventions and discoveries of prehistoric times have been all but edited out of many popular accounts of the human story.

The author describes how the intrepid explorers of the stone age discovered all the world's major land masses long before the so-called Age of Discovery. The roots of the first written script of the ancient Sumerians are traced back via Neolithic systems of accounting to their Palaeolithic origins. The mathematical and astronomical sciences of civilised societies are shown to have drawn on a reservoir of stone age scientific knowledge. Technological and industrial activities such as tool-making, mining and pyrotechnics all date back to the stone age as do many significant medical practices, including cranial surgery.

Lost Civilisations of the Stone Age brings into question many assumptions about our own cultural superiority, and argues that without the creativity, passion and inventiveness of our remote ancestors, none of the achievements of later cultures would have been possible.

'This book will transform our view of BC'.
Doris Lessing, *Literary Review*

'Fascinating'.
Andrew Roberts, *Mail on Sunday*

THE CRYSTAL SUN

By Robert Temple

Robert Temple here reconstructs a wholly forgotten story: the story of light technology in ancient civilisation. Dating back at least to 2600BC in Old Kingdom Egypt, but unknown to modern archaeologists and historians, a science of optics and a sophisticated technology for the manufacture of lenses was widespread and fundamental in ancient times. It inspired awe in cultures who used it, so became encoded in their mythologies and religions.

This is one of the most revolutionary studies in the history of science and civilisation to be published for decades.

'the focus is as wide, and as deep, as civilisation itself . . . frighteningly clever'.
Sunday Times